I'm not trying to brag or anything, but I don't think there are many manga creators who redo their storyboards exactly as they are told by their editors as I do.

—Tsugumi Ohba

Akito Takagi. AKA Shujin. The one in charge of the pain of giving birth to manga... I really think it's a tough job.

—Takeshi Obata

Tsugumi Ohba

Born in Tokyo, Tsugumi Ohba is the author of the hit series *Death Note*. His latest series *Bakuman。* was serialized in *Weekly Shonen Jump*.

Takeshi Obata

Takeshi Obata was born in 1969 in Niigata, Japan, and is the artist of the wildly popular SHONEN JUMP title *Hikaru no Go*, which won the 2003 Tezuka Osamu Cultural Prize: Shinsei "New Hope" award and the 2000 Shogakukan Manga award. Obata is also the artist of *Arabian Majin Bokentan Lamp Lamp*, *Ayatsuri Sakon*, *Cyborg Jichan G.*, and the smash hit manga *Death Note*. His latest series *Bakuman。* was serialized in *Weekly Shonen Jump*.

Volume 17

SHONEN JUMP Manga Edition

Story by **TSUGUMI OHBA**
Art by **TAKESHI OBATA**

Translation | **Tetsuichiro Miyaki**
English Adaptation | **Julie Lutz**
Touch-up Art & Lettering | **James Gaubatz**
Design | **Fawn Lau**
Editor | **Alexis Kirsch**

BAKUMAN₀ © 2008 by Tsugumi Ohba, Takeshi Obata
All rights reserved.
First published in Japan in 2008 by SHUEISHA Inc., Tokyo.
English translation rights arranged by SHUEISHA Inc.

Printed in the U.S.A.

Published by VIZ Media, LLC
P.O. Box 77010
San Francisco, CA 94107

10 9 8 7 6 5 4 3 2 1
First printing, December 2012

BAKUMAN.

17

ONE-SHOT
and
STAND
ALONE

STORY BY

TSUGUMI OHBA

ART BY

TAKESHI OBATA

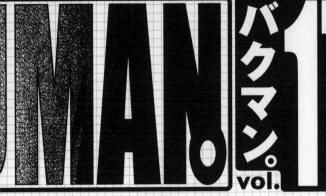

BAKUMAN。 vol. 17

バクマン。

D
C
B
A
LOVE

EIJI Nizuma

A manga prodigy and Tezuka Award winner at the age of 15. His goal is to create the world's best manga.

Age: 23

KAYA Takagi

Miho's friend and Akito's wife. A nice girl who actively works as the interceder between Moritaka and Azuki.

Age: 23

AKITO Takagi

Manga writer. An extremely smart guy who gets the best grades in his class. A cool guy who becomes very passionate when it comes to manga.

Age: 22

MIHO Azuki

A girl who dreams of becoming a voice actress. She promised to marry Moritaka under the condition that they not see each other until their dreams come true.

Age: 22

MORITAKA Mashiro

Manga artist. An extreme romantic who believes that he will marry Miho Azuki once their dreams come true.

Age: 22

*These ages are from October 2016.

STORY In order to attain the glory that only a handful of people can, two young men decide to walk the rough "path of manga" and become professional manga creators. This is the story of a great artist, Moritaka Mashiro, a talented writer, Akito Takagi, and their quest to become manga legends!

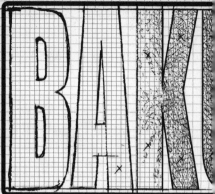

WEEKLY SHONEN JUMP
Editorial Department

1. Editor in Chief Sasaki
2. Deputy Editor in Chief Heishi
3. Soichi Aida
4. Yujiro Hattori
5. Akira Hattori
6. Koji Yoshida
7. Goro Miura
8. Masakazu Yamahisa
9. Kosugi

The MANGA ARTISTS and ASSISTANTS

A. SHINTA FUKUDA
B. KO AOKI
C. AIKO IWASE
D. KAZUYA HIRAMARU
E. RYU SHIZUKA
F. NATSUMI KATO
G. YASUOKA
H. SHOYO TAKAHAMA

I. TAKURO NAKAI
J. SHUICHI MORIYA
K. SHUN SHIRATORI
L. ICHIRIKI ORIHARA
M. TOHRU NANAMINE
N. MIKIHIKO AZUMA

BAKUMAN。

vol. 17

CONTENTS

(ONE-SHOT AND STAND ALONE)

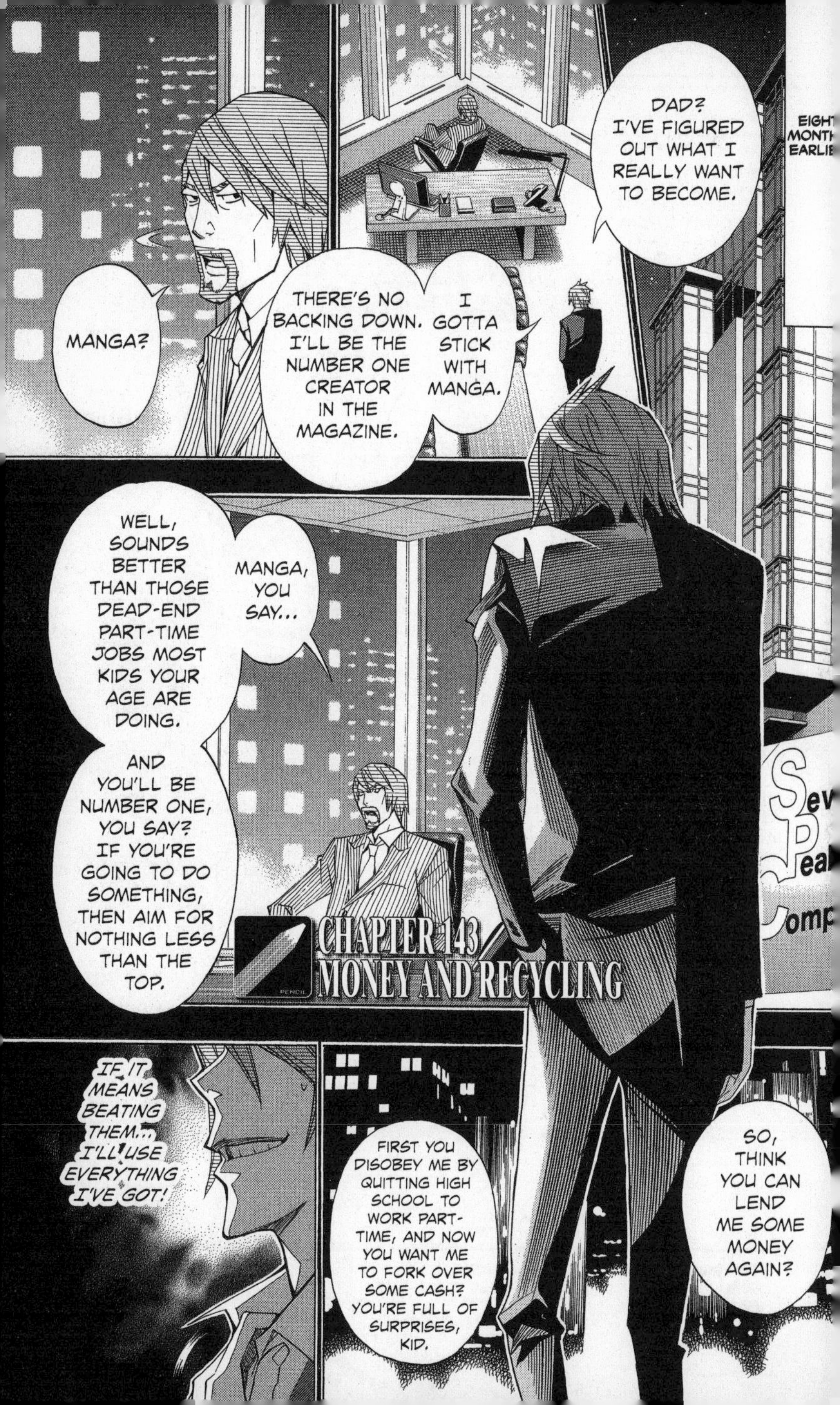
EIGHT MONTH EARLIE
DAD? I'VE FIGURED OUT WHAT I REALLY WANT TO BECOME.
I GOTTA STICK WITH MANGA.
THERE'S NO BACKING DOWN. I'LL BE THE NUMBER ONE CREATOR IN THE MAGAZINE.
MANGA?
MANGA, YOU SAY...
WELL, SOUNDS BETTER THAN THOSE DEAD-END PART-TIME JOBS MOST KIDS YOUR AGE ARE DOING.
AND YOU'LL BE NUMBER ONE, YOU SAY? IF YOU'RE GOING TO DO SOMETHING, THEN AIM FOR NOTHING LESS THAN THE TOP.
CHAPTER 143
MONEY AND RECYCLING
SO, THINK YOU CAN LEND ME SOME MONEY AGAIN?
FIRST YOU DISOBEY ME BY QUITTING HIGH SCHOOL TO WORK PART-TIME, AND NOW YOU WANT ME TO FORK OVER SOME CASH? YOU'RE FULL OF SURPRISES, KID.
IF IT MEANS BEATING THEM... I'LL USE EVERYTHING I'VE GOT!

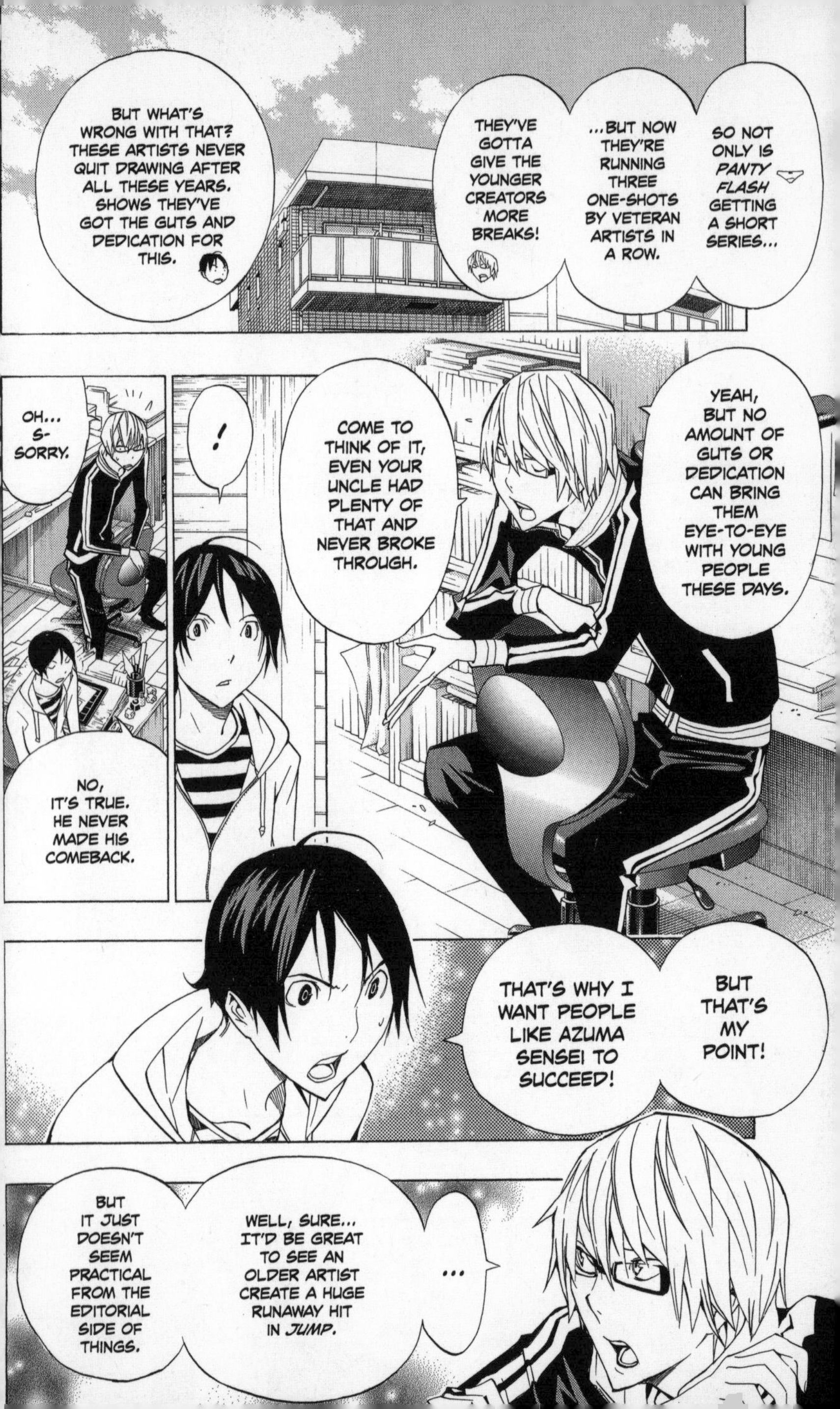
SO NOT ONLY IS *PANTY FLASH* GETTING A SHORT SERIES...
...BUT NOW THEY'RE RUNNING THREE ONE-SHOTS BY VETERAN ARTISTS IN A ROW.
THEY'VE GOTTA GIVE THE YOUNGER CREATORS MORE BREAKS!
BUT WHAT'S WRONG WITH THAT? THESE ARTISTS NEVER QUIT DRAWING AFTER ALL THESE YEARS. SHOWS THEY'VE GOT THE GUTS AND DEDICATION FOR THIS.
YEAH, BUT NO AMOUNT OF GUTS OR DEDICATION CAN BRING THEM EYE-TO-EYE WITH YOUNG PEOPLE THESE DAYS.
COME TO THINK OF IT, EVEN YOUR UNCLE HAD PLENTY OF THAT AND NEVER BROKE THROUGH.
!
OH... S-SORRY.
NO, IT'S TRUE. HE NEVER MADE HIS COMEBACK.
BUT THAT'S MY POINT!
THAT'S WHY I WANT PEOPLE LIKE AZUMA SENSEI TO SUCCEED!
...
WELL, SURE... IT'D BE GREAT TO SEE AN OLDER ARTIST CREATE A HUGE RUNAWAY HIT IN *JUMP*.
BUT IT JUST DOESN'T SEEM PRACTICAL FROM THE EDITORIAL SIDE OF THINGS.

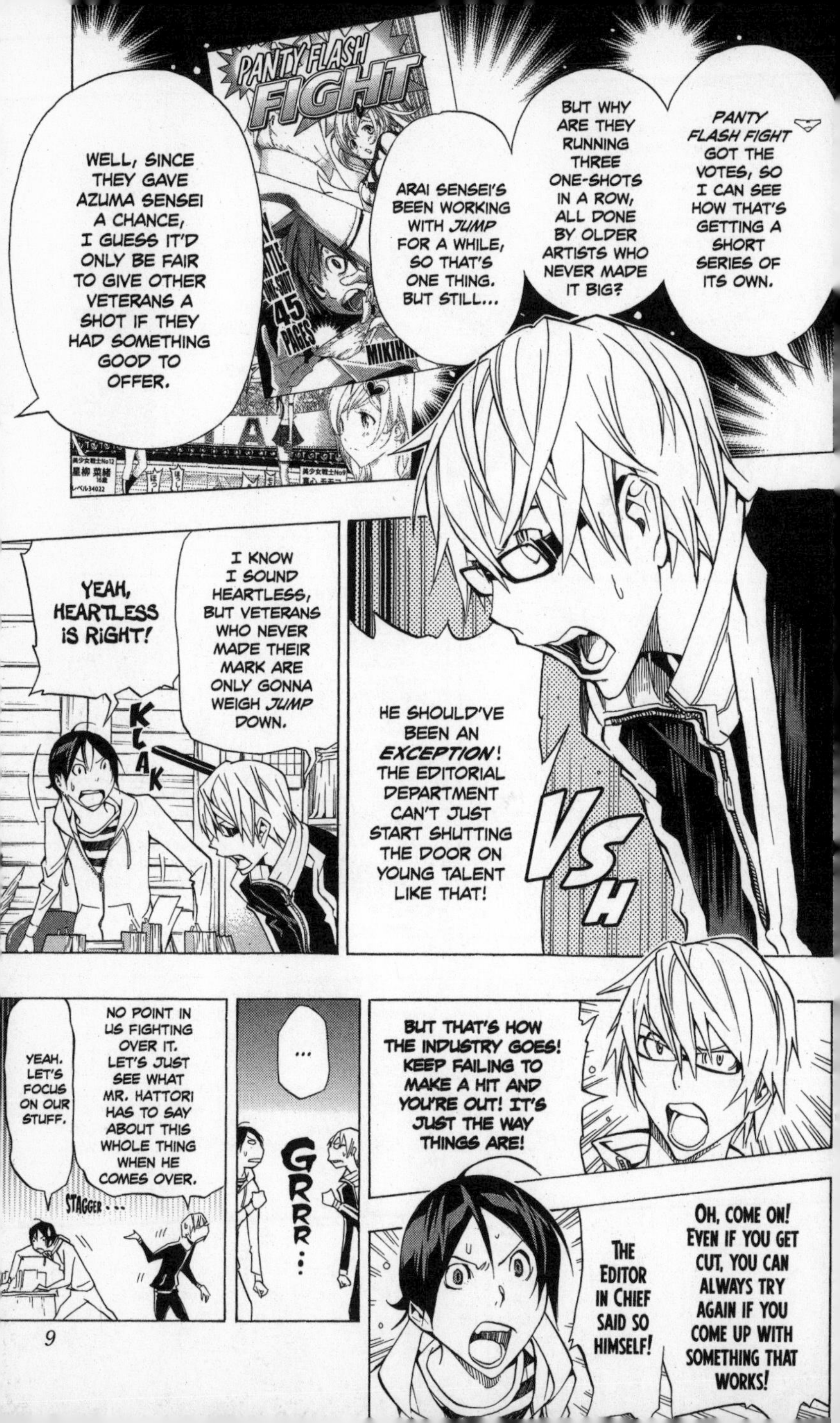
PANTY FLASH FIGHT
45 PAGES
PANTY FLASH FIGHT GOT THE VOTES, SO I CAN SEE HOW THAT'S GETTING A SHORT SERIES OF ITS OWN.
BUT WHY ARE THEY RUNNING THREE ONE-SHOTS IN A ROW, ALL DONE BY OLDER ARTISTS WHO NEVER MADE IT BIG?
ARAI SENSEI'S BEEN WORKING WITH *JUMP* FOR A WHILE, SO THAT'S ONE THING. BUT STILL...
WELL, SINCE THEY GAVE AZUMA SENSEI A CHANCE, I GUESS IT'D ONLY BE FAIR TO GIVE OTHER VETERANS A SHOT IF THEY HAD SOMETHING GOOD TO OFFER.
HE SHOULD'VE BEEN AN *EXCEPTION*! THE EDITORIAL DEPARTMENT CAN'T JUST START SHUTTING THE DOOR ON YOUNG TALENT LIKE THAT!
VSH
I KNOW I SOUND HEARTLESS, BUT VETERANS WHO NEVER MADE THEIR MARK ARE ONLY GONNA WEIGH *JUMP* DOWN.
YEAH, HEARTLESS IS RIGHT!
KLAK
BUT THAT'S HOW THE INDUSTRY GOES! KEEP FAILING TO MAKE A HIT AND YOU'RE OUT! IT'S JUST THE WAY THINGS ARE!
OH, COME ON! EVEN IF YOU GET CUT, YOU CAN ALWAYS TRY AGAIN IF YOU COME UP WITH SOMETHING THAT WORKS!
THE EDITOR IN CHIEF SAID SO HIMSELF!
...
GRRR...
NO POINT IN US FIGHTING OVER IT. LET'S JUST SEE WHAT MR. HATTORI HAS TO SAY ABOUT THIS WHOLE THING WHEN HE COMES OVER.
YEAH. LET'S FOCUS ON OUR STUFF.
STAGGER...

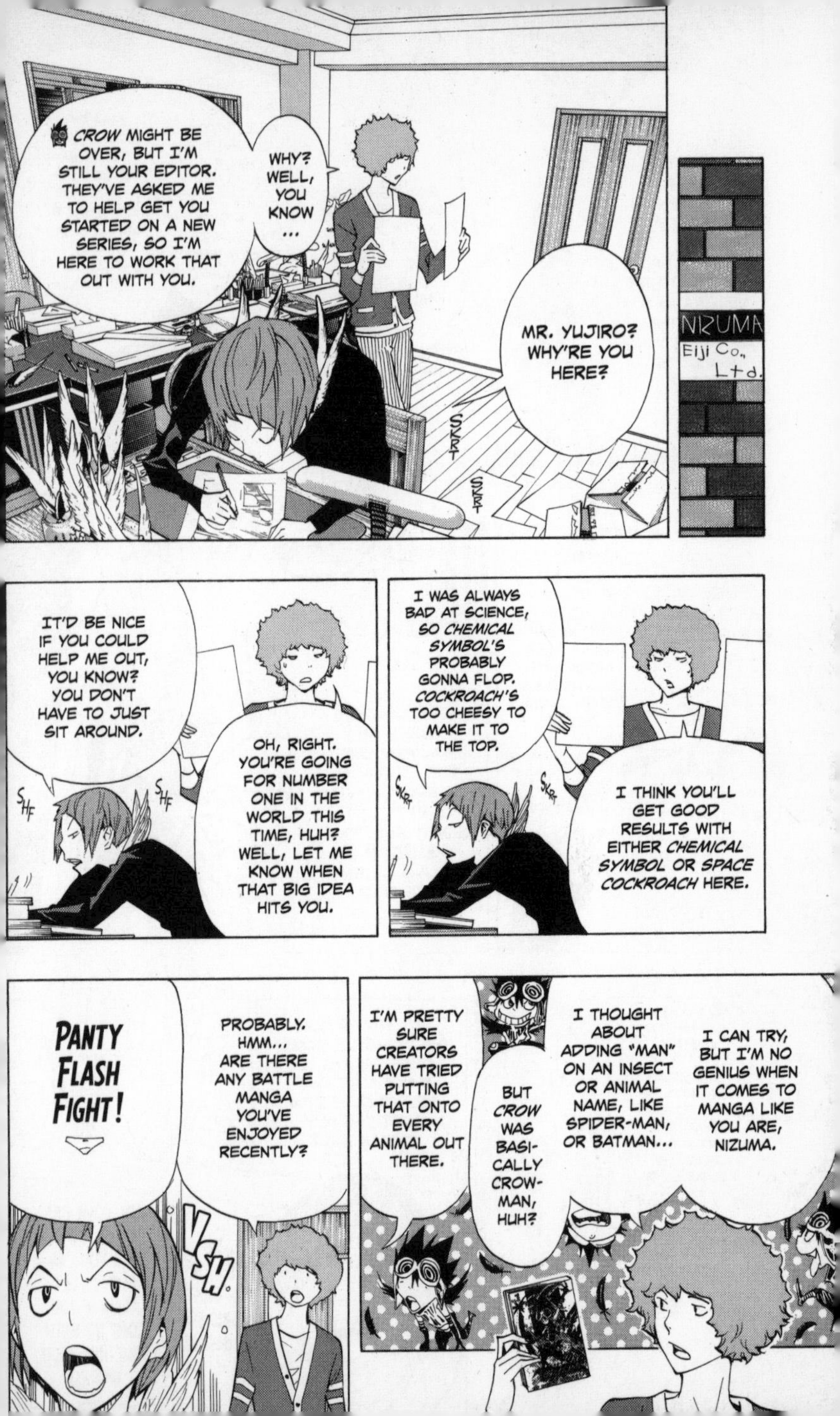
NIZUMA
Eiji Co., Ltd.
MR. YUJIRO? WHY'RE YOU HERE?
WHY? WELL, YOU KNOW ...
CROW MIGHT BE OVER, BUT I'M STILL YOUR EDITOR. THEY'VE ASKED ME TO HELP GET YOU STARTED ON A NEW SERIES, SO I'M HERE TO WORK THAT OUT WITH YOU.
SKRT
SKRT
I THINK YOU'LL GET GOOD RESULTS WITH EITHER *CHEMICAL SYMBOL* OR *SPACE COCKROACH* HERE.
I WAS ALWAYS BAD AT SCIENCE, SO *CHEMICAL SYMBOL'S* PROBABLY GONNA FLOP. *COCKROACH'S* TOO CHEESY TO MAKE IT TO THE TOP.
SKRT
SKRT
IT'D BE NICE IF YOU COULD HELP ME OUT, YOU KNOW? YOU DON'T HAVE TO JUST SIT AROUND.
OH, RIGHT. YOU'RE GOING FOR NUMBER ONE IN THE WORLD THIS TIME, HUH? WELL, LET ME KNOW WHEN THAT BIG IDEA HITS YOU.
SHF
SHF
I CAN TRY, BUT I'M NO GENIUS WHEN IT COMES TO MANGA LIKE YOU ARE, NIZUMA.
I THOUGHT ABOUT ADDING "MAN" ON AN INSECT OR ANIMAL NAME, LIKE SPIDER-MAN, OR BATMAN...
BUT *CROW* WAS BASI-CALLY CROW-MAN, HUH?
I'M PRETTY SURE CREATORS HAVE TRIED PUTTING THAT ONTO EVERY ANIMAL OUT THERE.
PROBABLY. HMM... ARE THERE ANY BATTLE MANGA YOU'VE ENJOYED RECENTLY?
PANTY FLASH FIGHT!
VSH

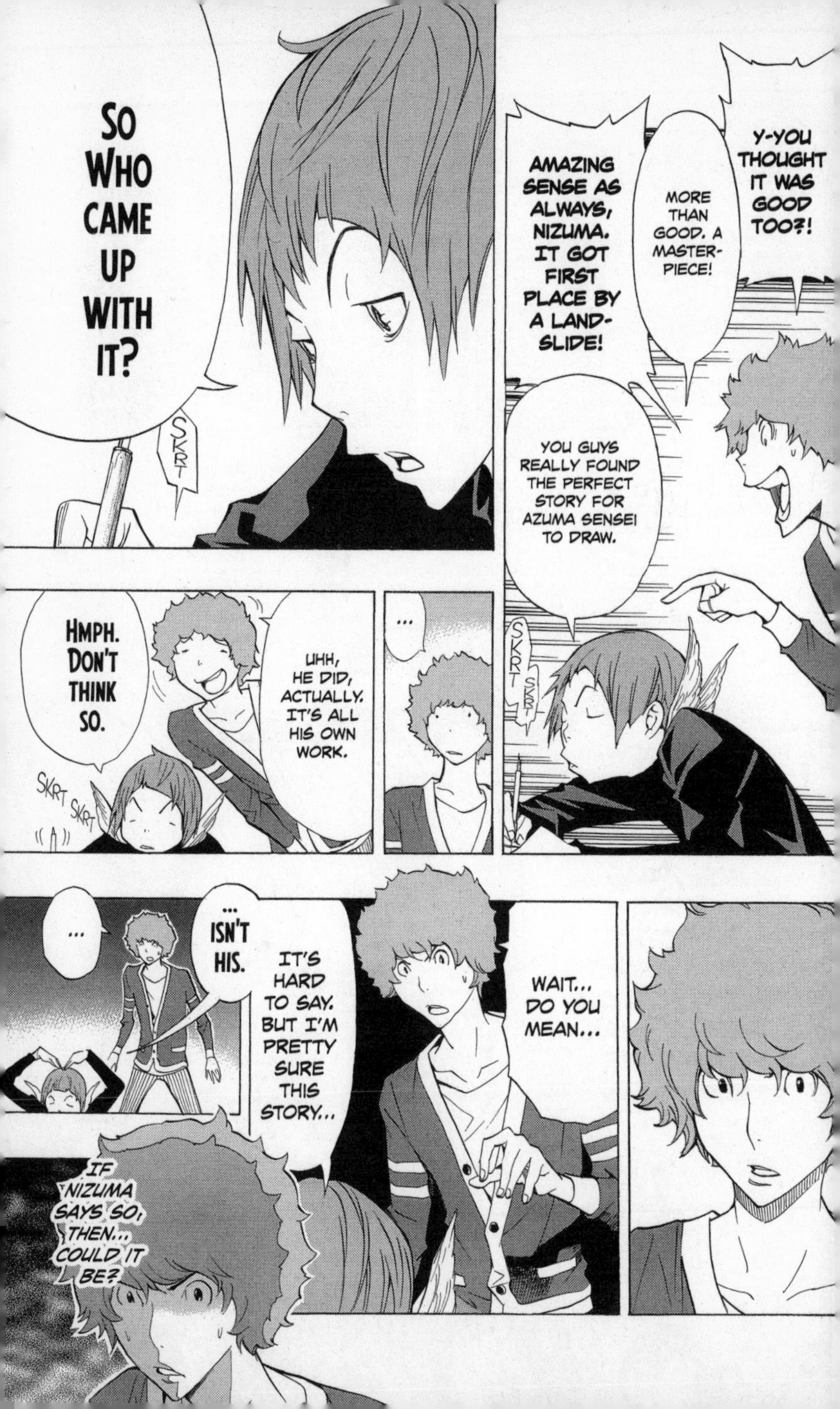
Y-YOU THOUGHT IT WAS GOOD TOO?!
MORE THAN GOOD. A MASTER-PIECE!
AMAZING SENSE AS ALWAYS, NIZUMA. IT GOT FIRST PLACE BY A LAND-SLIDE!
YOU GUYS REALLY FOUND THE PERFECT STORY FOR AZUMA SENSEI TO DRAW.
SKRT
SKRT
SO WHO CAME UP WITH IT?
SKRT
...
UHH, HE DID, ACTUALLY. IT'S ALL HIS OWN WORK.
HMPH. DON'T THINK SO.
SKRT SKRT
WAIT... DO YOU MEAN...
IT'S HARD TO SAY. BUT I'M PRETTY SURE THIS STORY...
... ISN'T HIS.
...
IF NIZUMA SAYS SO, THEN... COULD IT BE?

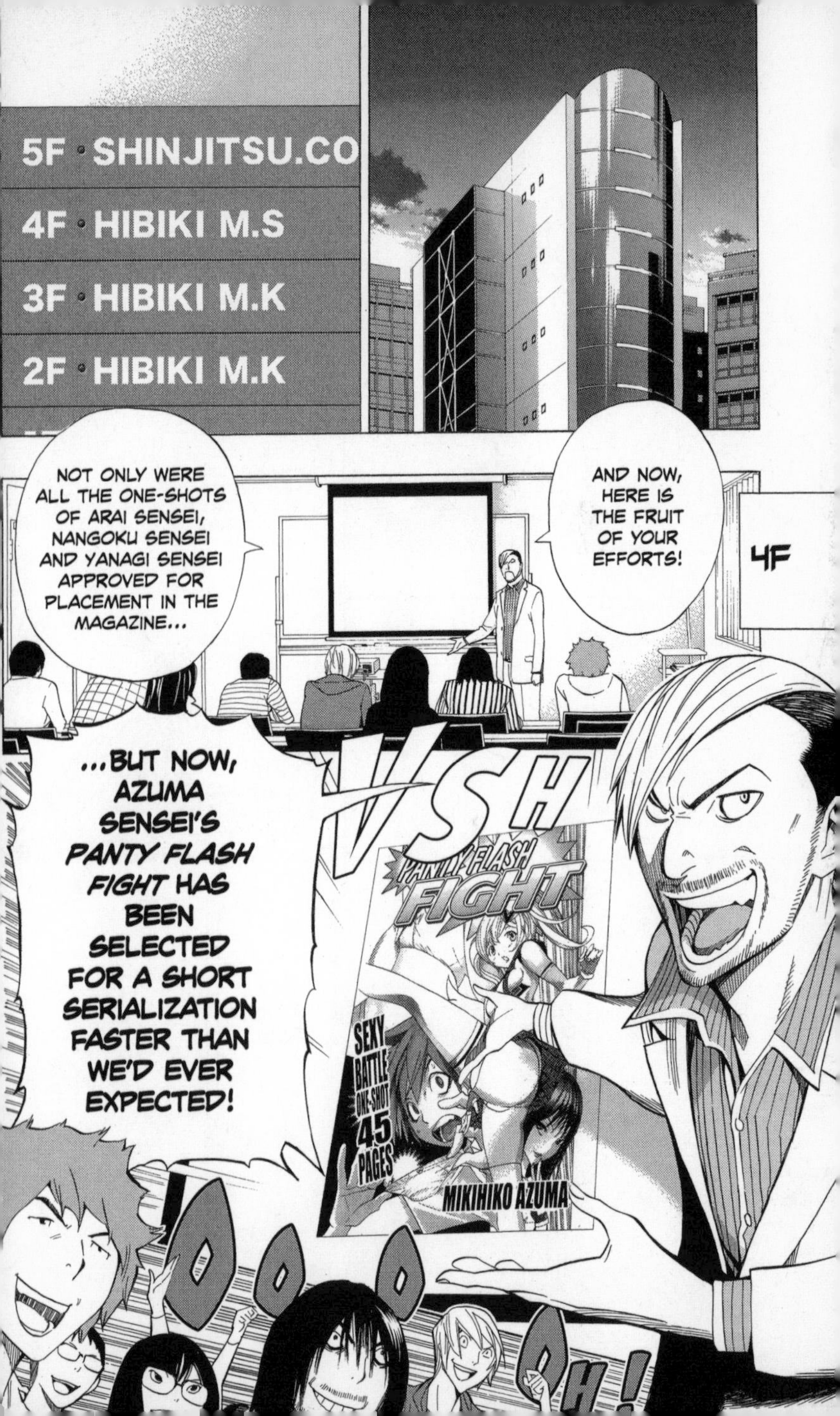
5F • SHINJITSU.CO
4F • HIBIKI M.S
3F • HIBIKI M.K
2F • HIBIKI M.K
4F
AND NOW, HERE IS THE FRUIT OF YOUR EFFORTS!
NOT ONLY WERE ALL THE ONE-SHOTS OF ARAI SENSEI, NANGOKU SENSEI AND YANAGI SENSEI APPROVED FOR PLACEMENT IN THE MAGAZINE...
VSH
...BUT NOW, AZUMA SENSEI'S *PANTY FLASH FIGHT* HAS BEEN SELECTED FOR A SHORT SERIALIZATION FASTER THAN WE'D EVER EXPECTED!
PANTY FLASH FIGHT
SEXY BATTLE ONE-SHOT 45 PAGES
MIKIHIKO AZUMA
OOOH!

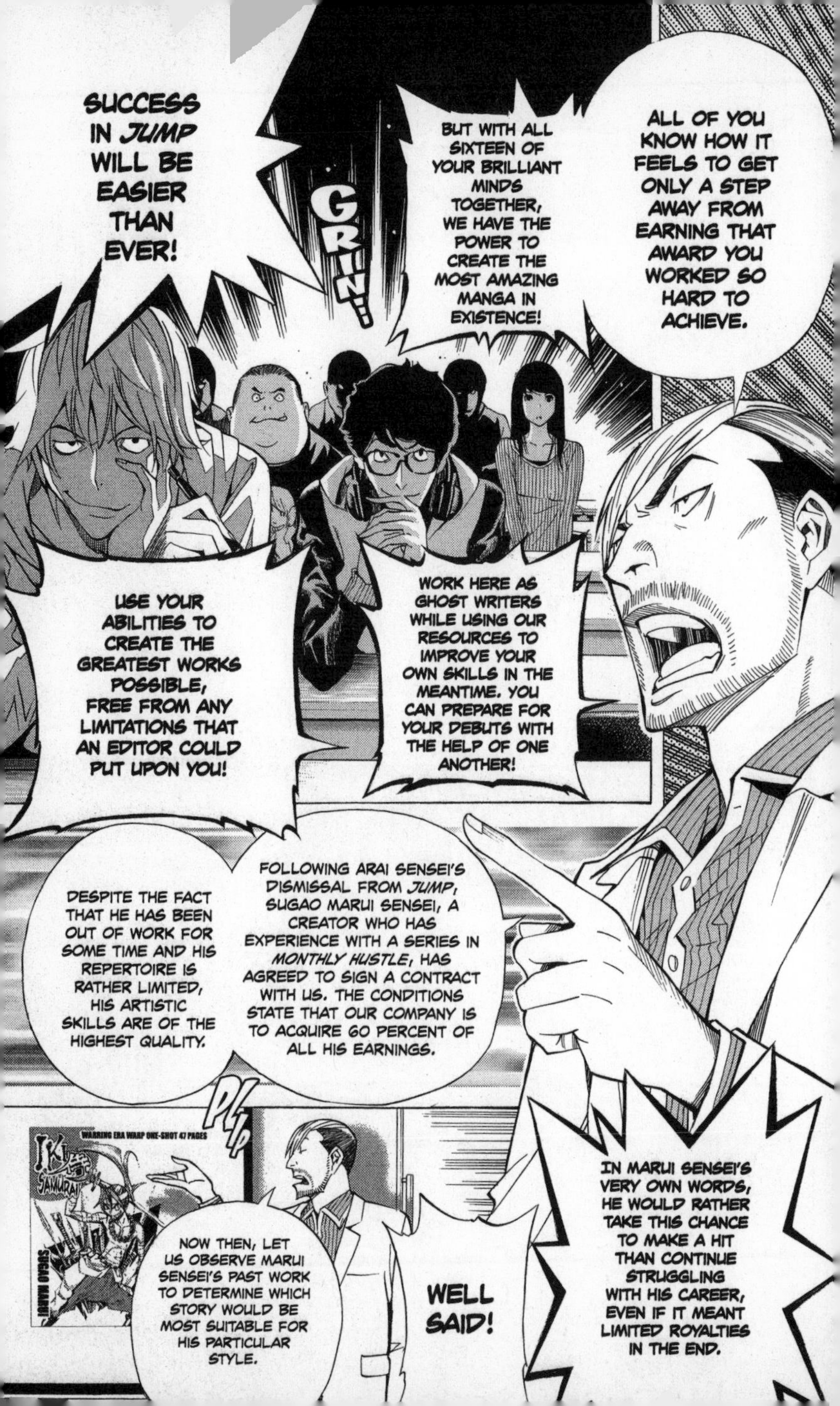
ALL OF YOU KNOW HOW IT FEELS TO GET ONLY A STEP AWAY FROM EARNING THAT AWARD YOU WORKED SO HARD TO ACHIEVE.
BUT WITH ALL SIXTEEN OF YOUR BRILLIANT MINDS TOGETHER, WE HAVE THE POWER TO CREATE THE MOST AMAZING MANGA IN EXISTENCE!
GRIN...
SUCCESS IN *JUMP* WILL BE EASIER THAN EVER!
WORK HERE AS GHOST WRITERS WHILE USING OUR RESOURCES TO IMPROVE YOUR OWN SKILLS IN THE MEANTIME. YOU CAN PREPARE FOR YOUR DEBUTS WITH THE HELP OF ONE ANOTHER!
USE YOUR ABILITIES TO CREATE THE GREATEST WORKS POSSIBLE, FREE FROM ANY LIMITATIONS THAT AN EDITOR COULD PUT UPON YOU!
FOLLOWING ARAI SENSEI'S DISMISSAL FROM *JUMP*, SUGAO MARUI SENSEI, A CREATOR WHO HAS EXPERIENCE WITH A SERIES IN *MONTHLY HUSTLE*, HAS AGREED TO SIGN A CONTRACT WITH US. THE CONDITIONS STATE THAT OUR COMPANY IS TO ACQUIRE 60 PERCENT OF ALL HIS EARNINGS.
DESPITE THE FACT THAT HE HAS BEEN OUT OF WORK FOR SOME TIME AND HIS REPERTOIRE IS RATHER LIMITED, HIS ARTISTIC SKILLS ARE OF THE HIGHEST QUALITY.
IN MARUI SENSEI'S VERY OWN WORDS, HE WOULD RATHER TAKE THIS CHANCE TO MAKE A HIT THAN CONTINUE STRUGGLING WITH HIS CAREER, EVEN IF IT MEANT LIMITED ROYALTIES IN THE END.
WELL SAID!
PLIP
NOW THEN, LET US OBSERVE MARUI SENSEI'S PAST WORK TO DETERMINE WHICH STORY WOULD BE MOST SUITABLE FOR HIS PARTICULAR STYLE.
WARRING ERA WARP ONE-SHOT 47 PAGES
SAMURAI
SUGAO MARUI

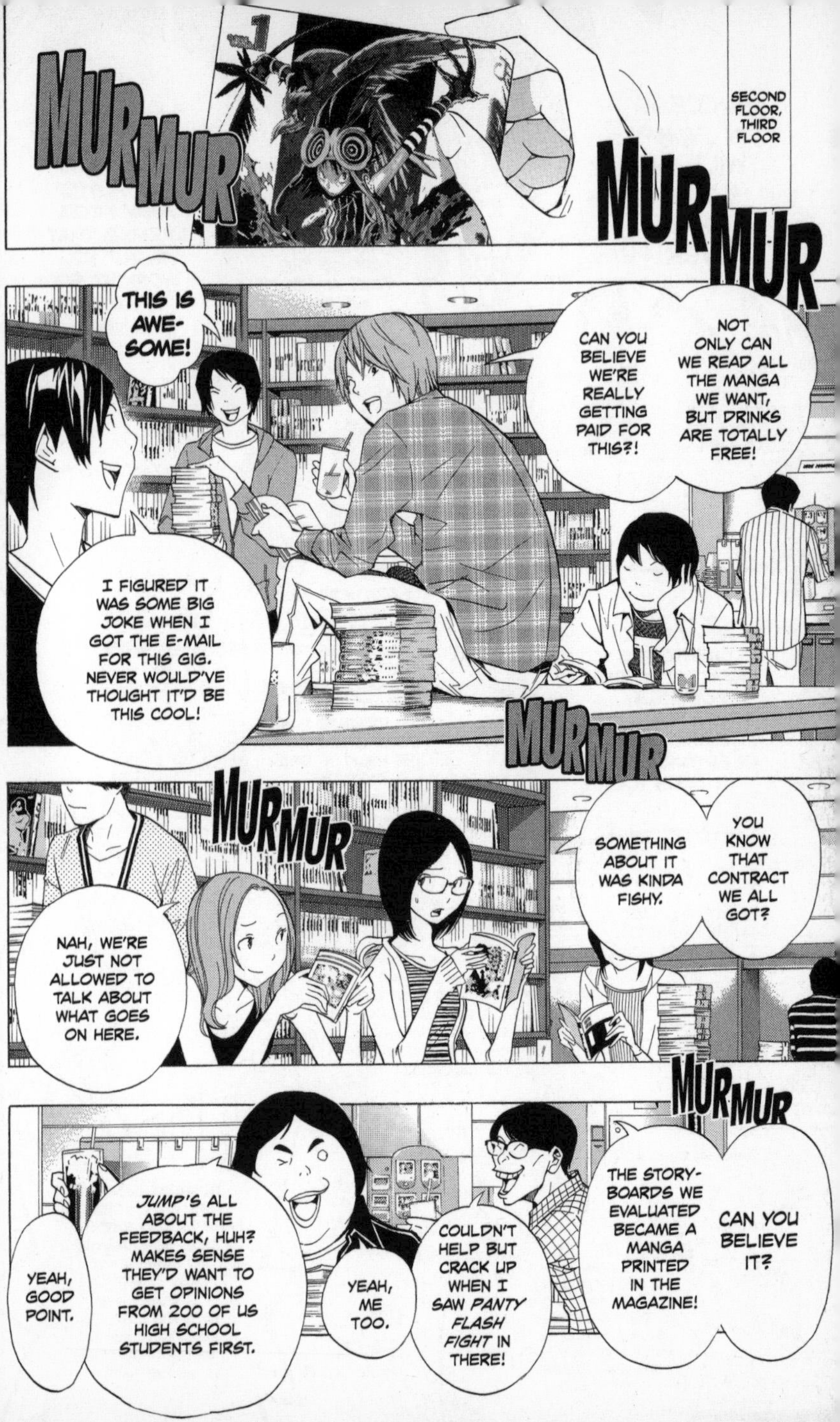
SECOND FLOOR, THIRD FLOOR
MURMUR
MURMUR
NOT ONLY CAN WE READ ALL THE MANGA WE WANT, BUT DRINKS ARE TOTALLY FREE!
CAN YOU BELIEVE WE'RE REALLY GETTING PAID FOR THIS?!
THIS IS AWESOME!
I FIGURED IT WAS SOME BIG JOKE WHEN I GOT THE E-MAIL FOR THIS GIG. NEVER WOULD'VE THOUGHT IT'D BE THIS COOL!
MURMUR
MURMUR
YOU KNOW THAT CONTRACT WE ALL GOT?
SOMETHING ABOUT IT WAS KINDA FISHY.
NAH, WE'RE JUST NOT ALLOWED TO TALK ABOUT WHAT GOES ON HERE.
MURMUR
CAN YOU BELIEVE IT?
THE STORYBOARDS WE EVALUATED BECAME A MANGA PRINTED IN THE MAGAZINE!
COULDN'T HELP BUT CRACK UP WHEN I SAW *PANTY FLASH FIGHT* IN THERE!
YEAH, ME TOO.
JUMP'S ALL ABOUT THE FEEDBACK, HUH? MAKES SENSE THEY'D WANT TO GET OPINIONS FROM 200 OF US HIGH SCHOOL STUDENTS FIRST.
YEAH, GOOD POINT.

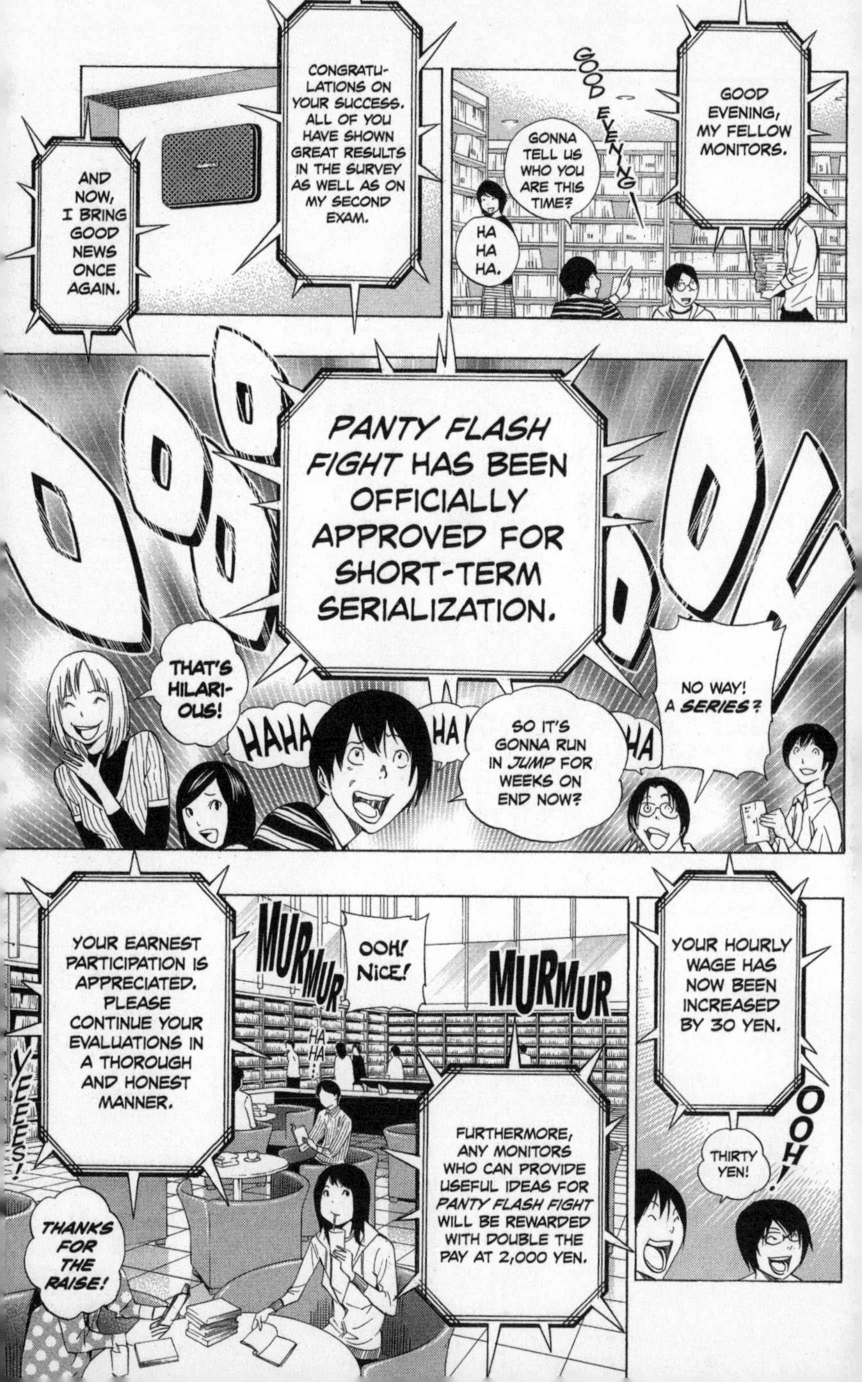
GOOD EVENING, MY FELLOW MONITORS.
GOOD EVENING
GONNA TELL US WHO YOU ARE THIS TIME?
HA HA HA.
CONGRATULATIONS ON YOUR SUCCESS. ALL OF YOU HAVE SHOWN GREAT RESULTS IN THE SURVEY AS WELL AS ON MY SECOND EXAM.
AND NOW, I BRING GOOD NEWS ONCE AGAIN.
PANTY FLASH FIGHT HAS BEEN OFFICIALLY APPROVED FOR SHORT-TERM SERIALIZATION.
NO WAY! A *SERIES*?
SO IT'S GONNA RUN IN *JUMP* FOR WEEKS ON END NOW?
HA
HA
HAHA
THAT'S HILARIOUS!
YOUR HOURLY WAGE HAS NOW BEEN INCREASED BY 30 YEN.
OOOH!
THIRTY YEN!
FURTHERMORE, ANY MONITORS WHO CAN PROVIDE USEFUL IDEAS FOR *PANTY FLASH FIGHT* WILL BE REWARDED WITH DOUBLE THE PAY AT 2,000 YEN.
MURMUR
OOH! NICE!
MURMUR
HA HA
YOUR EARNEST PARTICIPATION IS APPRECIATED. PLEASE CONTINUE YOUR EVALUATIONS IN A THOROUGH AND HONEST MANNER.
YEEEES!
THANKS FOR THE RAISE!

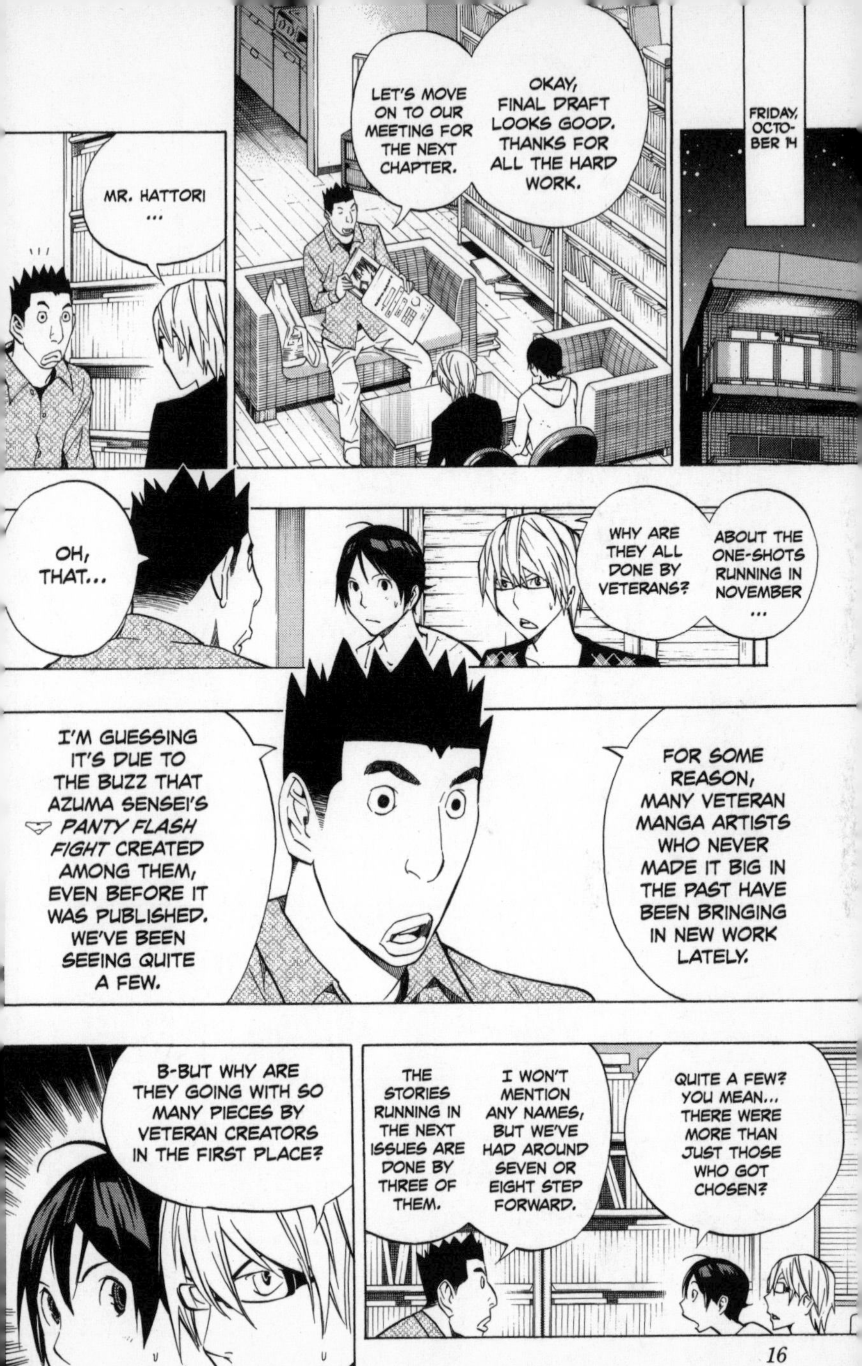

FRIDAY, OCTOBER 14
OKAY, FINAL DRAFT LOOKS GOOD. THANKS FOR ALL THE HARD WORK.
LET'S MOVE ON TO OUR MEETING FOR THE NEXT CHAPTER.
MR. HATTORI ...
ABOUT THE ONE-SHOTS RUNNING IN NOVEMBER ...
WHY ARE THEY ALL DONE BY VETERANS?
OH, THAT...
FOR SOME REASON, MANY VETERAN MANGA ARTISTS WHO NEVER MADE IT BIG IN THE PAST HAVE BEEN BRINGING IN NEW WORK LATELY.
I'M GUESSING IT'S DUE TO THE BUZZ THAT AZUMA SENSEI'S *PANTY FLASH FIGHT* CREATED AMONG THEM, EVEN BEFORE IT WAS PUBLISHED. WE'VE BEEN SEEING QUITE A FEW.
QUITE A FEW? YOU MEAN... THERE WERE MORE THAN JUST THOSE WHO GOT CHOSEN?
I WON'T MENTION ANY NAMES, BUT WE'VE HAD AROUND SEVEN OR EIGHT STEP FORWARD.
THE STORIES RUNNING IN THE NEXT ISSUES ARE DONE BY THREE OF THEM.
B-BUT WHY ARE THEY GOING WITH SO MANY PIECES BY VETERAN CREATORS IN THE FIRST PLACE?

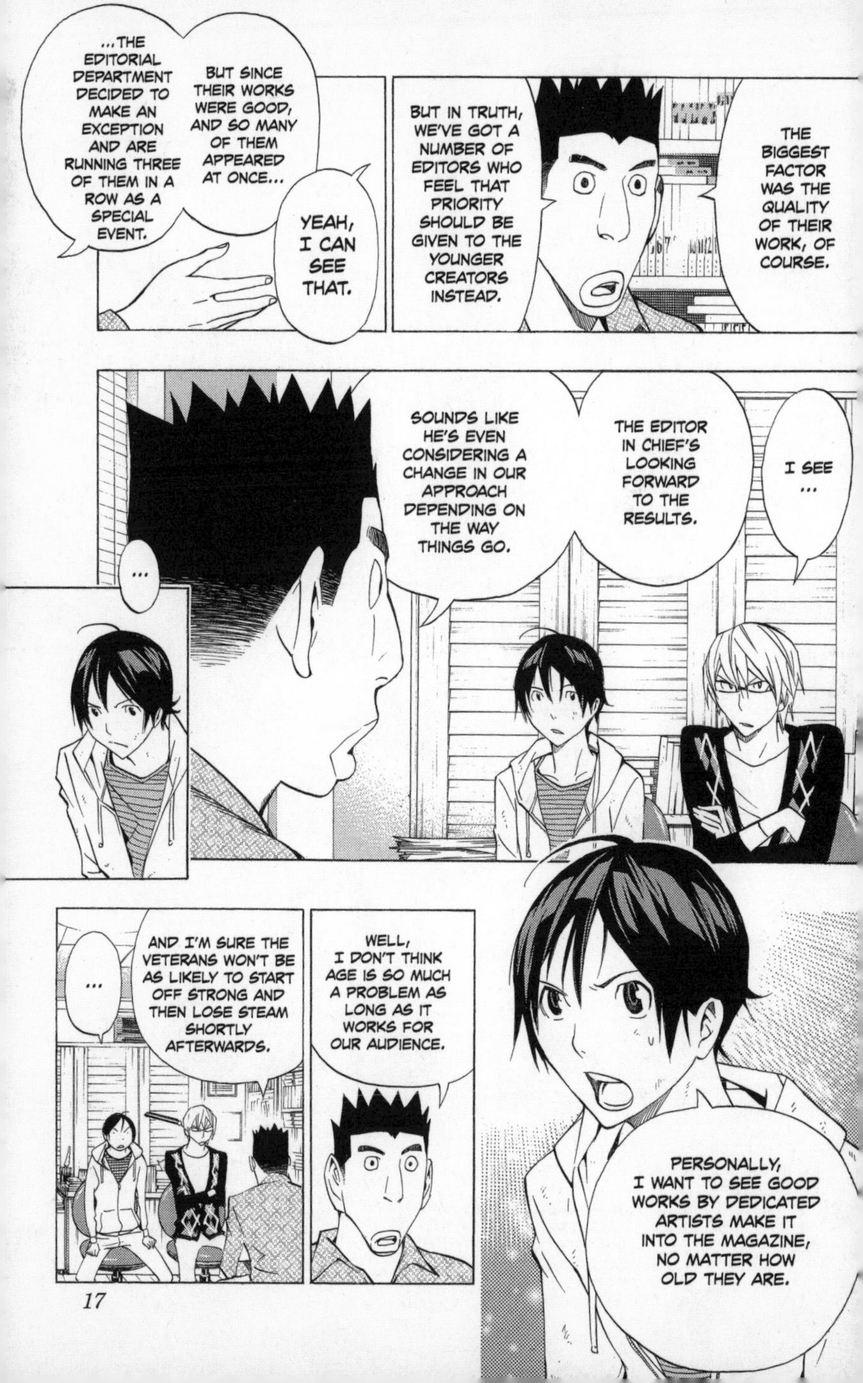
THE BIGGEST FACTOR WAS THE QUALITY OF THEIR WORK, OF COURSE.
BUT IN TRUTH, WE'VE GOT A NUMBER OF EDITORS WHO FEEL THAT PRIORITY SHOULD BE GIVEN TO THE YOUNGER CREATORS INSTEAD.
BUT SINCE THEIR WORKS WERE GOOD, AND SO MANY OF THEM APPEARED AT ONCE...
...THE EDITORIAL DEPARTMENT DECIDED TO MAKE AN EXCEPTION AND ARE RUNNING THREE OF THEM IN A ROW AS A SPECIAL EVENT.
YEAH, I CAN SEE THAT.
I SEE ...
THE EDITOR IN CHIEF'S LOOKING FORWARD TO THE RESULTS.
SOUNDS LIKE HE'S EVEN CONSIDERING A CHANGE IN OUR APPROACH DEPENDING ON THE WAY THINGS GO.
...
PERSONALLY, I WANT TO SEE GOOD WORKS BY DEDICATED ARTISTS MAKE IT INTO THE MAGAZINE, NO MATTER HOW OLD THEY ARE.
WELL, I DON'T THINK AGE IS SO MUCH A PROBLEM AS LONG AS IT WORKS FOR OUR AUDIENCE.
AND I'M SURE THE VETERANS WON'T BE AS LIKELY TO START OFF STRONG AND THEN LOSE STEAM SHORTLY AFTERWARDS.
...

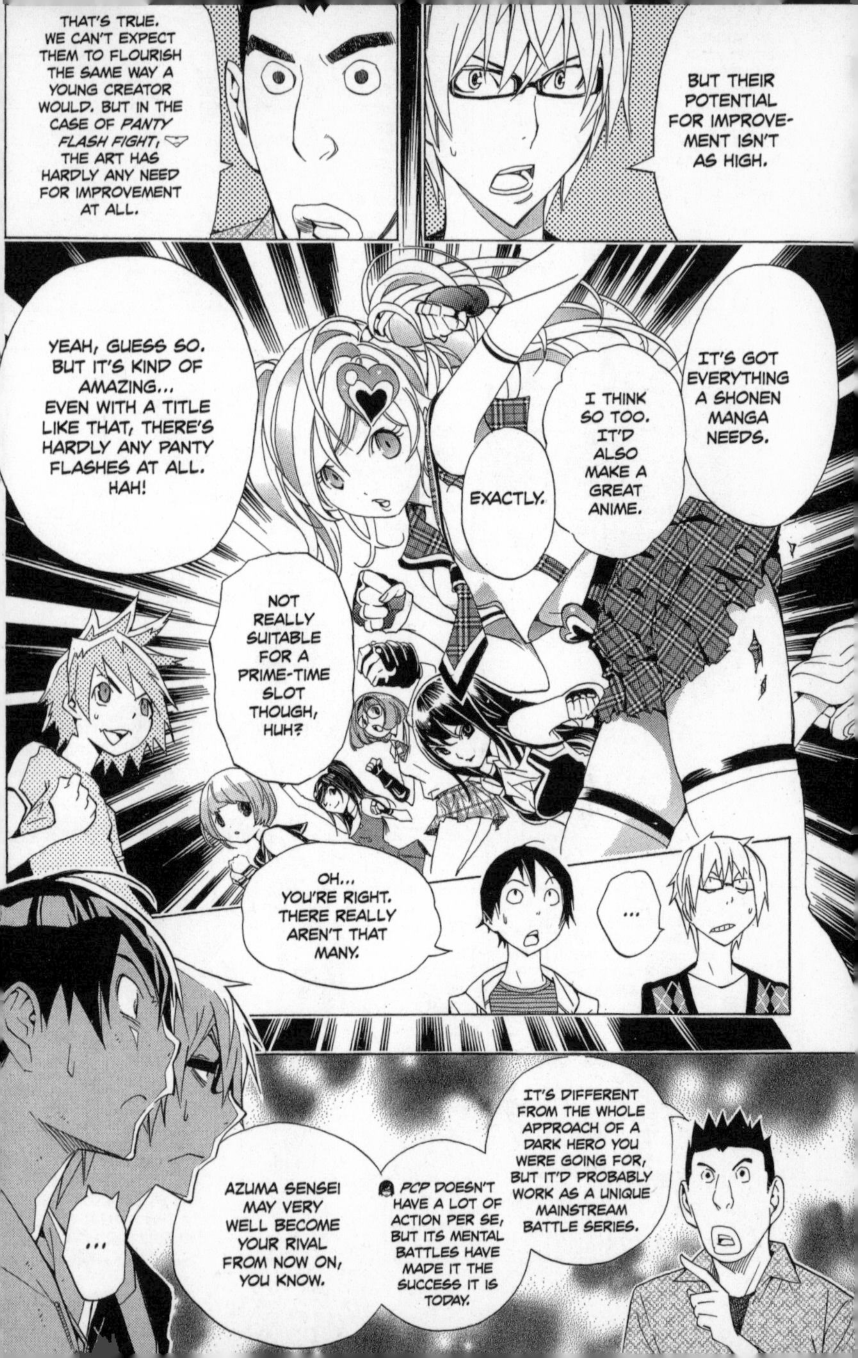
BUT THEIR POTENTIAL FOR IMPROVEMENT ISN'T AS HIGH.
THAT'S TRUE. WE CAN'T EXPECT THEM TO FLOURISH THE SAME WAY A YOUNG CREATOR WOULD. BUT IN THE CASE OF *PANTY FLASH FIGHT*, THE ART HAS HARDLY ANY NEED FOR IMPROVEMENT AT ALL.
IT'S GOT EVERYTHING A SHONEN MANGA NEEDS.
I THINK SO TOO. IT'D ALSO MAKE A GREAT ANIME.
EXACTLY.
YEAH, GUESS SO. BUT IT'S KIND OF AMAZING... EVEN WITH A TITLE LIKE THAT, THERE'S HARDLY ANY PANTY FLASHES AT ALL. HAH!
NOT REALLY SUITABLE FOR A PRIME-TIME SLOT THOUGH, HUH?
...
OH... YOU'RE RIGHT. THERE REALLY AREN'T THAT MANY.
IT'S DIFFERENT FROM THE WHOLE APPROACH OF A DARK HERO YOU WERE GOING FOR, BUT IT'D PROBABLY WORK AS A UNIQUE MAINSTREAM BATTLE SERIES.
PCP DOESN'T HAVE A LOT OF ACTION PER SE, BUT ITS MENTAL BATTLES HAVE MADE IT THE SUCCESS IT IS TODAY.
AZUMA SENSEI MAY VERY WELL BECOME YOUR RIVAL FROM NOW ON, YOU KNOW.
...

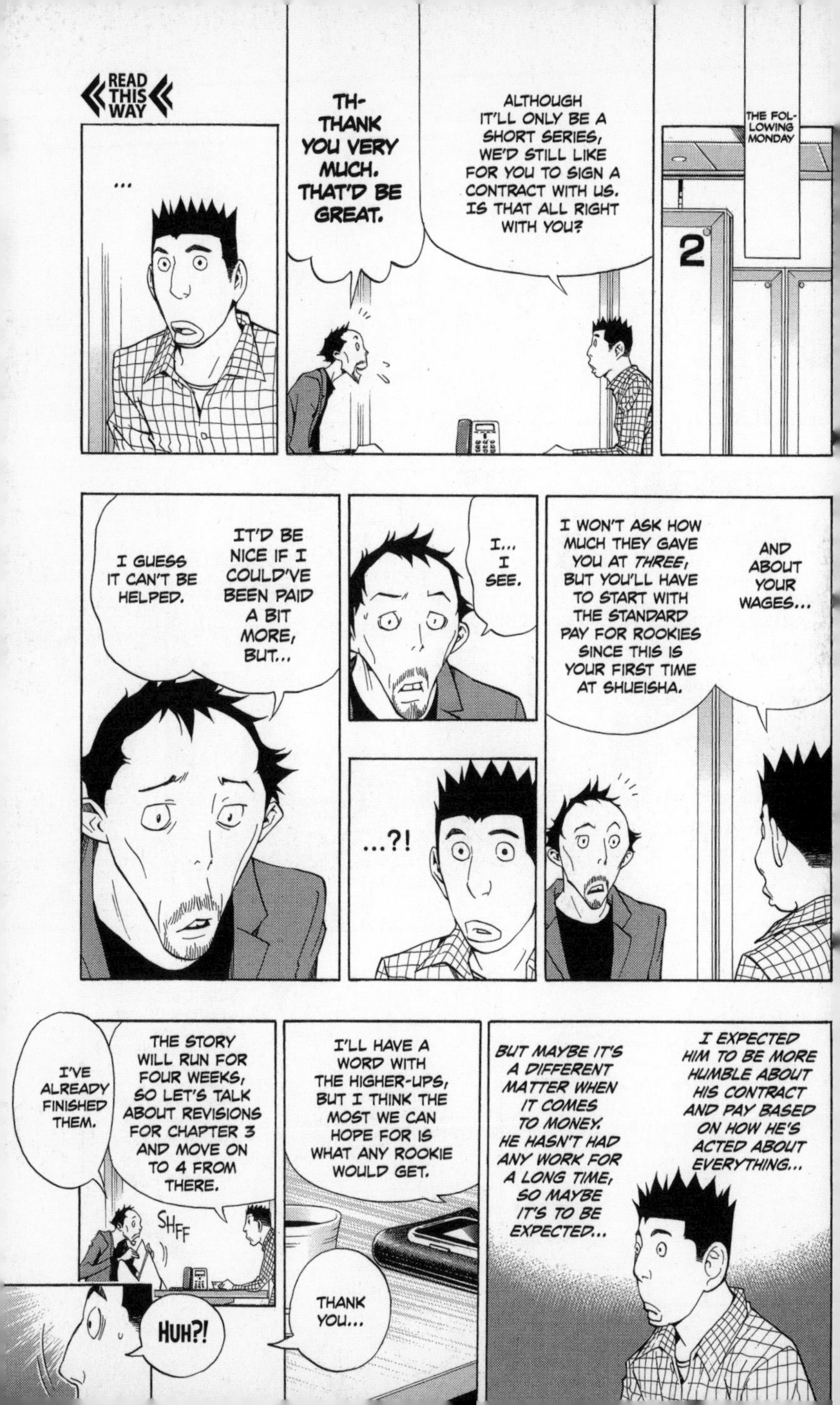
READ THIS WAY
THE FOL-LOWING MONDAY
2
ALTHOUGH IT'LL ONLY BE A SHORT SERIES, WE'D STILL LIKE FOR YOU TO SIGN A CONTRACT WITH US. IS THAT ALL RIGHT WITH YOU?
TH-THANK YOU VERY MUCH. THAT'D BE GREAT.
...
AND ABOUT YOUR WAGES...
I WON'T ASK HOW MUCH THEY GAVE YOU AT *THREE*, BUT YOU'LL HAVE TO START WITH THE STANDARD PAY FOR ROOKIES SINCE THIS IS YOUR FIRST TIME AT SHUEISHA.
I... I SEE.
...?!
IT'D BE NICE IF I COULD'VE BEEN PAID A BIT MORE, BUT...
I GUESS IT CAN'T BE HELPED.
I EXPECTED HIM TO BE MORE HUMBLE ABOUT HIS CONTRACT AND PAY BASED ON HOW HE'S ACTED ABOUT EVERYTHING...
BUT MAYBE IT'S A DIFFERENT MATTER WHEN IT COMES TO MONEY. HE HASN'T HAD ANY WORK FOR A LONG TIME, SO MAYBE IT'S TO BE EXPECTED...
I'LL HAVE A WORD WITH THE HIGHER-UPS, BUT I THINK THE MOST WE CAN HOPE FOR IS WHAT ANY ROOKIE WOULD GET.
THANK YOU...
THE STORY WILL RUN FOR FOUR WEEKS, SO LET'S TALK ABOUT REVISIONS FOR CHAPTER 3 AND MOVE ON TO 4 FROM THERE.
I'VE ALREADY FINISHED THEM.
SHFF
HUH?!

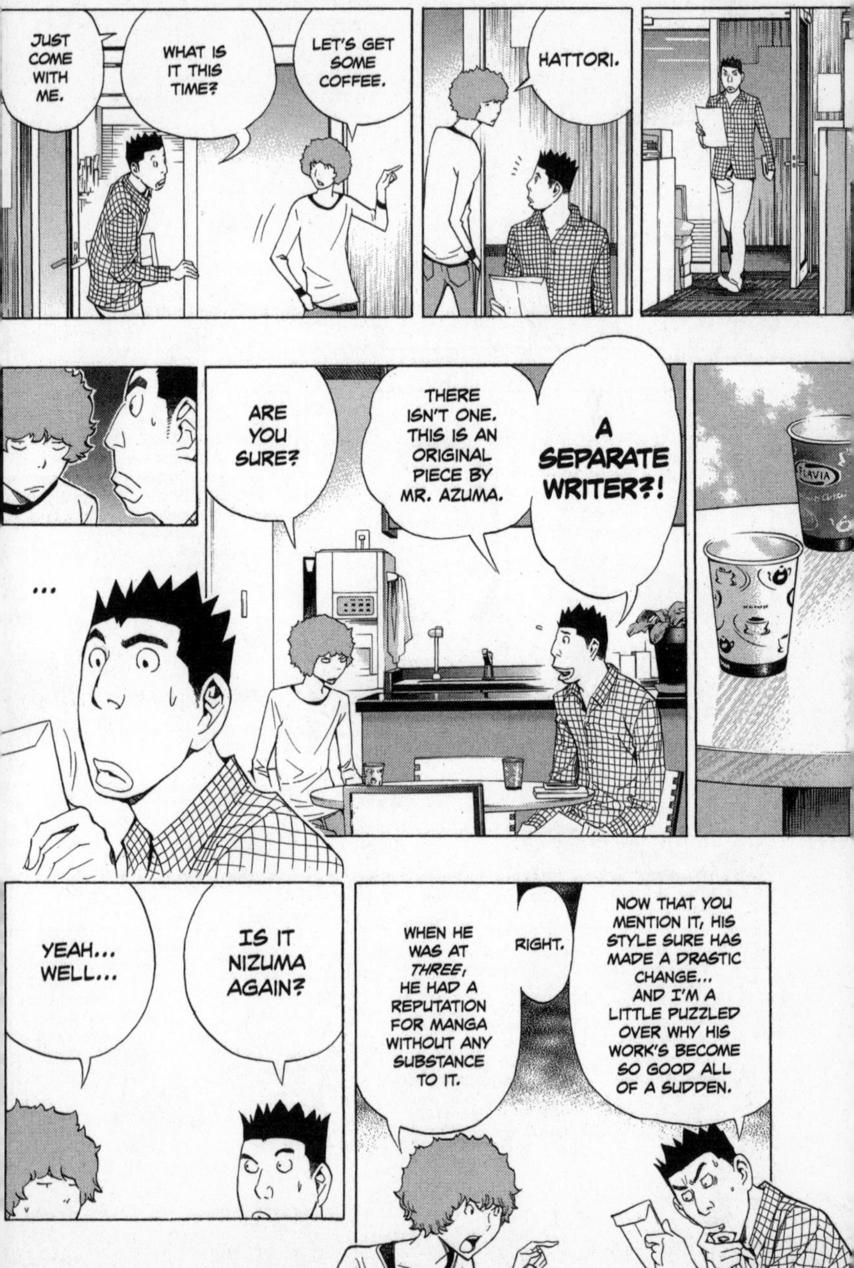
HATTORI.
LET'S GET SOME COFFEE.
WHAT IS IT THIS TIME?
JUST COME WITH ME.
A SEPARATE WRITER?!
THERE ISN'T ONE. THIS IS AN ORIGINAL PIECE BY MR. AZUMA.
ARE YOU SURE?
...
NOW THAT YOU MENTION IT, HIS STYLE SURE HAS MADE A DRASTIC CHANGE... AND I'M A LITTLE PUZZLED OVER WHY HIS WORK'S BECOME SO GOOD ALL OF A SUDDEN.
RIGHT.
WHEN HE WAS AT *THREE*, HE HAD A REPUTATION FOR MANGA WITHOUT ANY SUBSTANCE TO IT.
IS IT NIZUMA AGAIN?
YEAH... WELL...

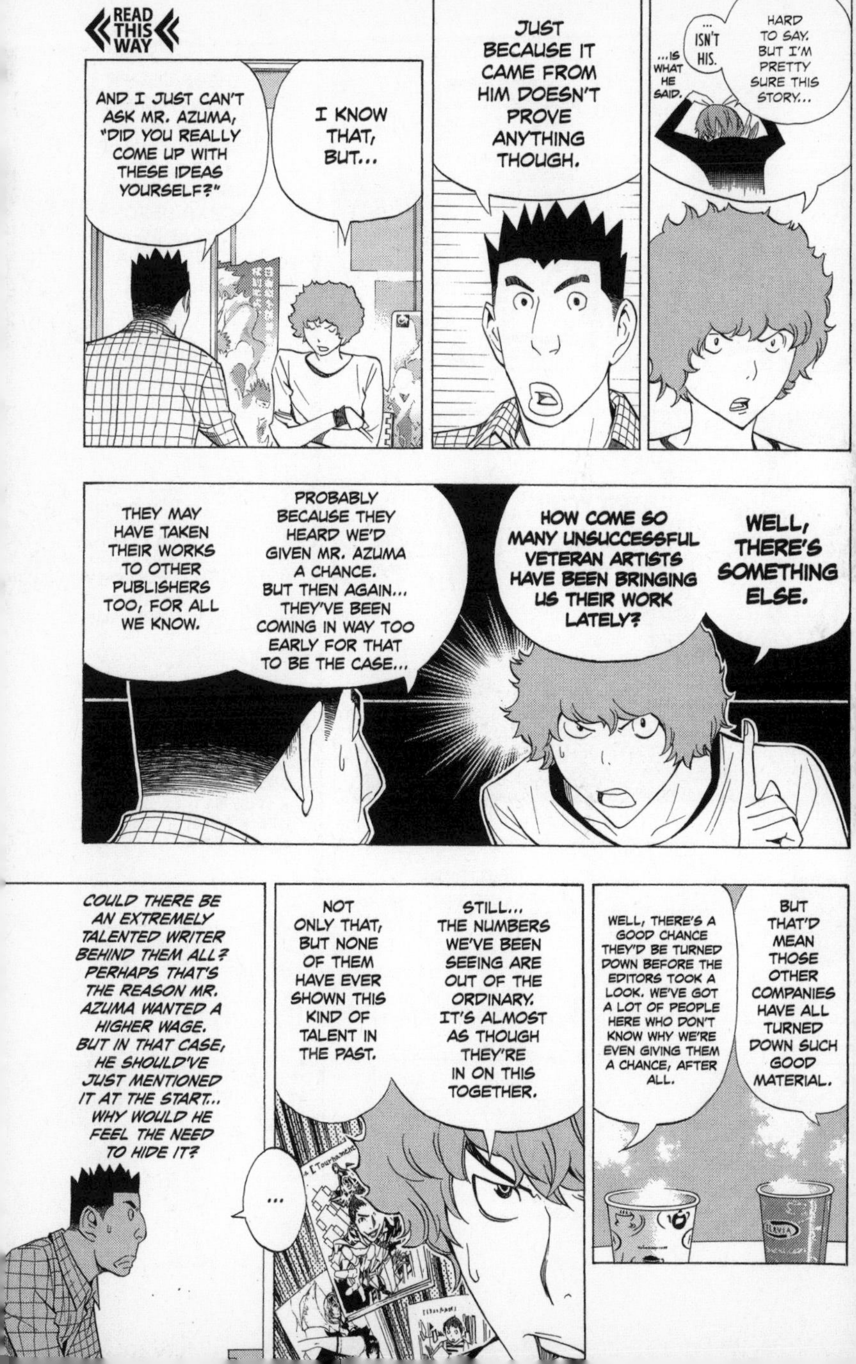
READ THIS WAY
HARD TO SAY. BUT I'M PRETTY SURE THIS STORY...
...ISN'T HIS.
...IS WHAT HE SAID.
JUST BECAUSE IT CAME FROM HIM DOESN'T PROVE ANYTHING THOUGH.
I KNOW THAT, BUT...
AND I JUST CAN'T ASK MR. AZUMA, "DID YOU REALLY COME UP WITH THESE IDEAS YOURSELF?"
WELL, THERE'S SOMETHING ELSE.
HOW COME SO MANY UNSUCCESSFUL VETERAN ARTISTS HAVE BEEN BRINGING US THEIR WORK LATELY?
PROBABLY BECAUSE THEY HEARD WE'D GIVEN MR. AZUMA A CHANCE. BUT THEN AGAIN... THEY'VE BEEN COMING IN WAY TOO EARLY FOR THAT TO BE THE CASE...
THEY MAY HAVE TAKEN THEIR WORKS TO OTHER PUBLISHERS TOO, FOR ALL WE KNOW.
BUT THAT'D MEAN THOSE OTHER COMPANIES HAVE ALL TURNED DOWN SUCH GOOD MATERIAL.
WELL, THERE'S A GOOD CHANCE THEY'D BE TURNED DOWN BEFORE THE EDITORS TOOK A LOOK. WE'VE GOT A LOT OF PEOPLE HERE WHO DON'T KNOW WHY WE'RE EVEN GIVING THEM A CHANCE, AFTER ALL.
STILL... THE NUMBERS WE'VE BEEN SEEING ARE OUT OF THE ORDINARY. IT'S ALMOST AS THOUGH THEY'RE IN ON THIS TOGETHER.
NOT ONLY THAT, BUT NONE OF THEM HAVE EVER SHOWN THIS KIND OF TALENT IN THE PAST.
...
COULD THERE BE AN EXTREMELY TALENTED WRITER BEHIND THEM ALL? PERHAPS THAT'S THE REASON MR. AZUMA WANTED A HIGHER WAGE. BUT IN THAT CASE, HE SHOULD'VE JUST MENTIONED IT AT THE START... WHY WOULD HE FEEL THE NEED TO HIDE IT?

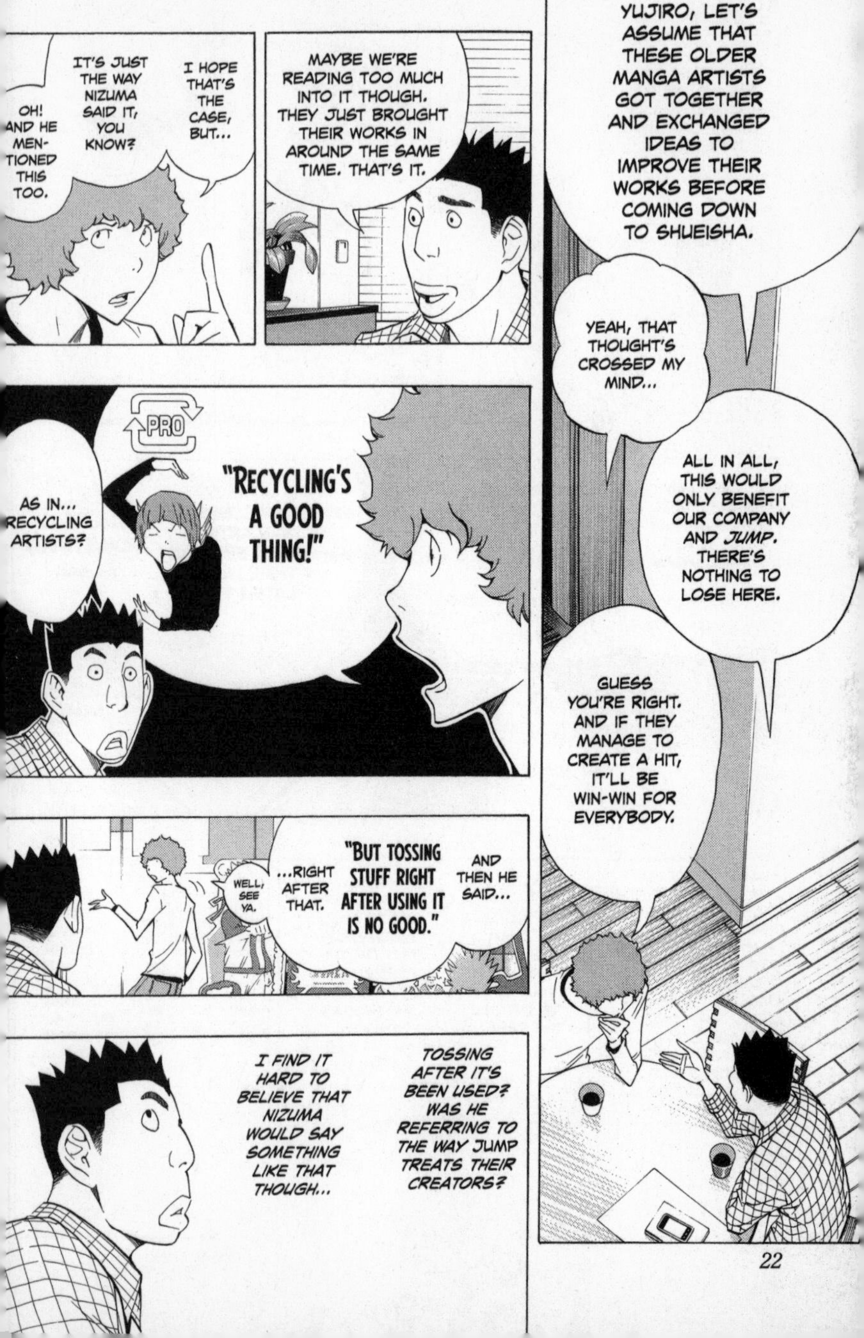

YUJIRO, LET'S ASSUME THAT THESE OLDER MANGA ARTISTS GOT TOGETHER AND EXCHANGED IDEAS TO IMPROVE THEIR WORKS BEFORE COMING DOWN TO SHUEISHA.
YEAH, THAT THOUGHT'S CROSSED MY MIND...
ALL IN ALL, THIS WOULD ONLY BENEFIT OUR COMPANY AND *JUMP*. THERE'S NOTHING TO LOSE HERE.
GUESS YOU'RE RIGHT. AND IF THEY MANAGE TO CREATE A HIT, IT'LL BE WIN-WIN FOR EVERYBODY.
MAYBE WE'RE READING TOO MUCH INTO IT THOUGH. THEY JUST BROUGHT THEIR WORKS IN AROUND THE SAME TIME. THAT'S IT.
I HOPE THAT'S THE CASE, BUT...
IT'S JUST THE WAY NIZUMA SAID IT, YOU KNOW?
OH! AND HE MEN-TIONED THIS TOO.
PRO
"RECYCLING'S A GOOD THING!"
AS IN... RECYCLING ARTISTS?
AND THEN HE SAID...
"BUT TOSSING STUFF RIGHT AFTER USING IT IS NO GOOD."
...RIGHT AFTER THAT.
WELL, SEE YA.
TOSSING AFTER IT'S BEEN USED? WAS HE REFERRING TO THE WAY JUMP TREATS THEIR CREATORS?
I FIND IT HARD TO BELIEVE THAT NIZUMA WOULD SAY SOMETHING LIKE THAT THOUGH...

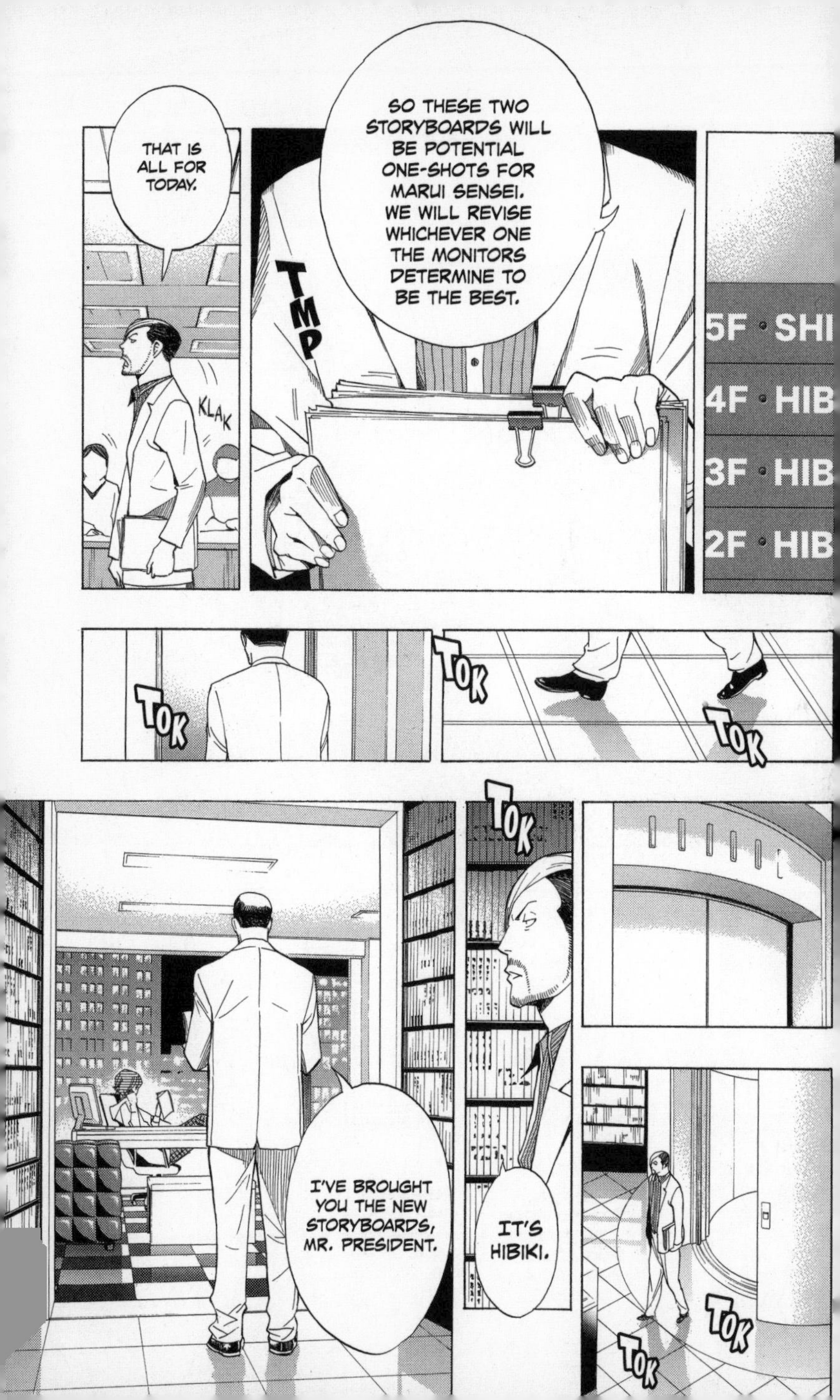
5F • SHI
4F • HIB
3F • HIB
2F • HIB
SO THESE TWO STORYBOARDS WILL BE POTENTIAL ONE-SHOTS FOR MARUI SENSEI. WE WILL REVISE WHICHEVER ONE THE MONITORS DETERMINE TO BE THE BEST.
TMP
THAT IS ALL FOR TODAY.
KLAK
TOK
TOK
TOK
TOK
TOK
TOK
IT'S HIBIKI.
I'VE BROUGHT YOU THE NEW STORYBOARDS, MR. PRESIDENT.

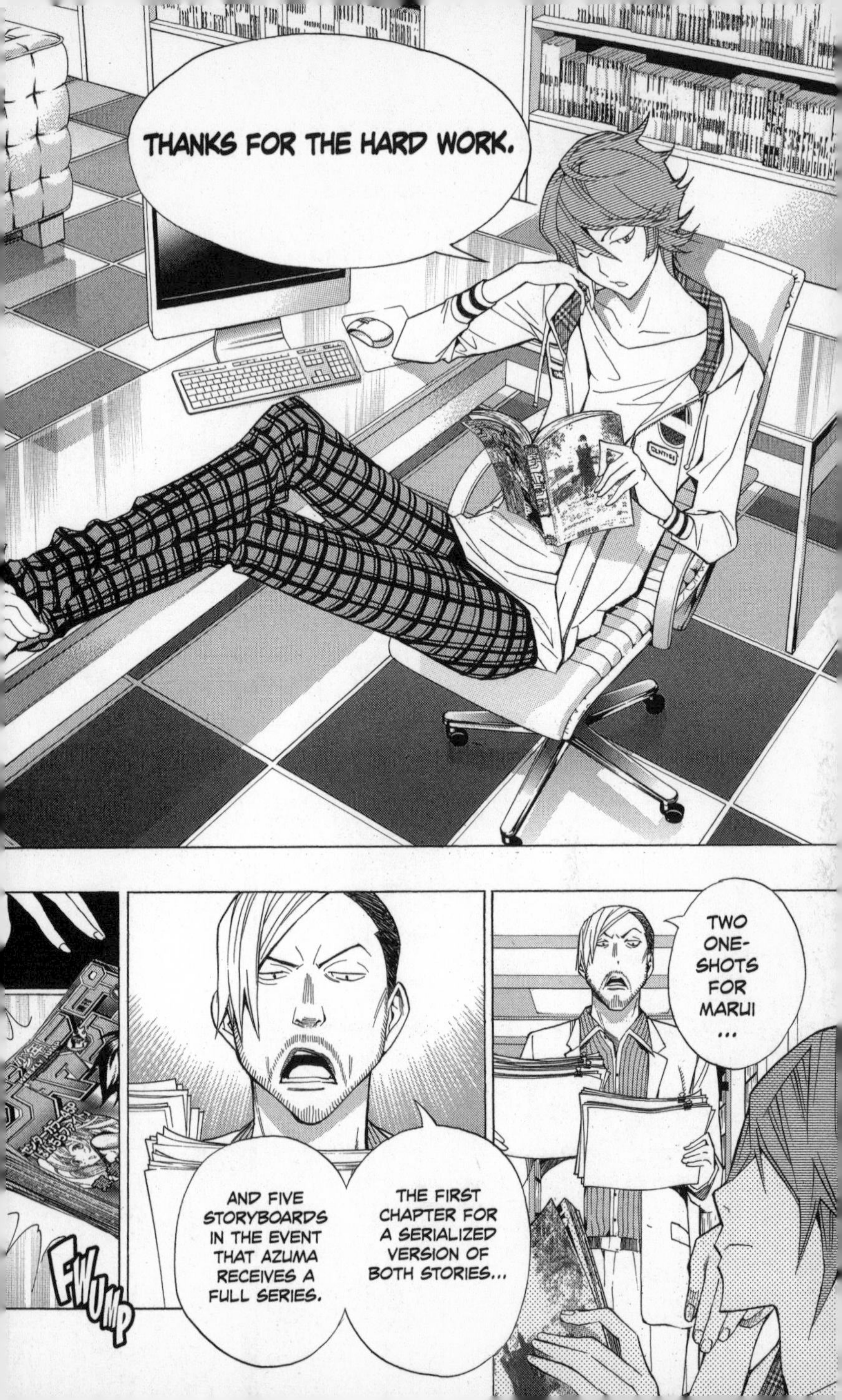
THANKS FOR THE HARD WORK.
TWO ONE-SHOTS FOR MARUI...
THE FIRST CHAPTER FOR A SERIALIZED VERSION OF BOTH STORIES...
AND FIVE STORYBOARDS IN THE EVENT THAT AZUMA RECEIVES A FULL SERIES.
FWUMP

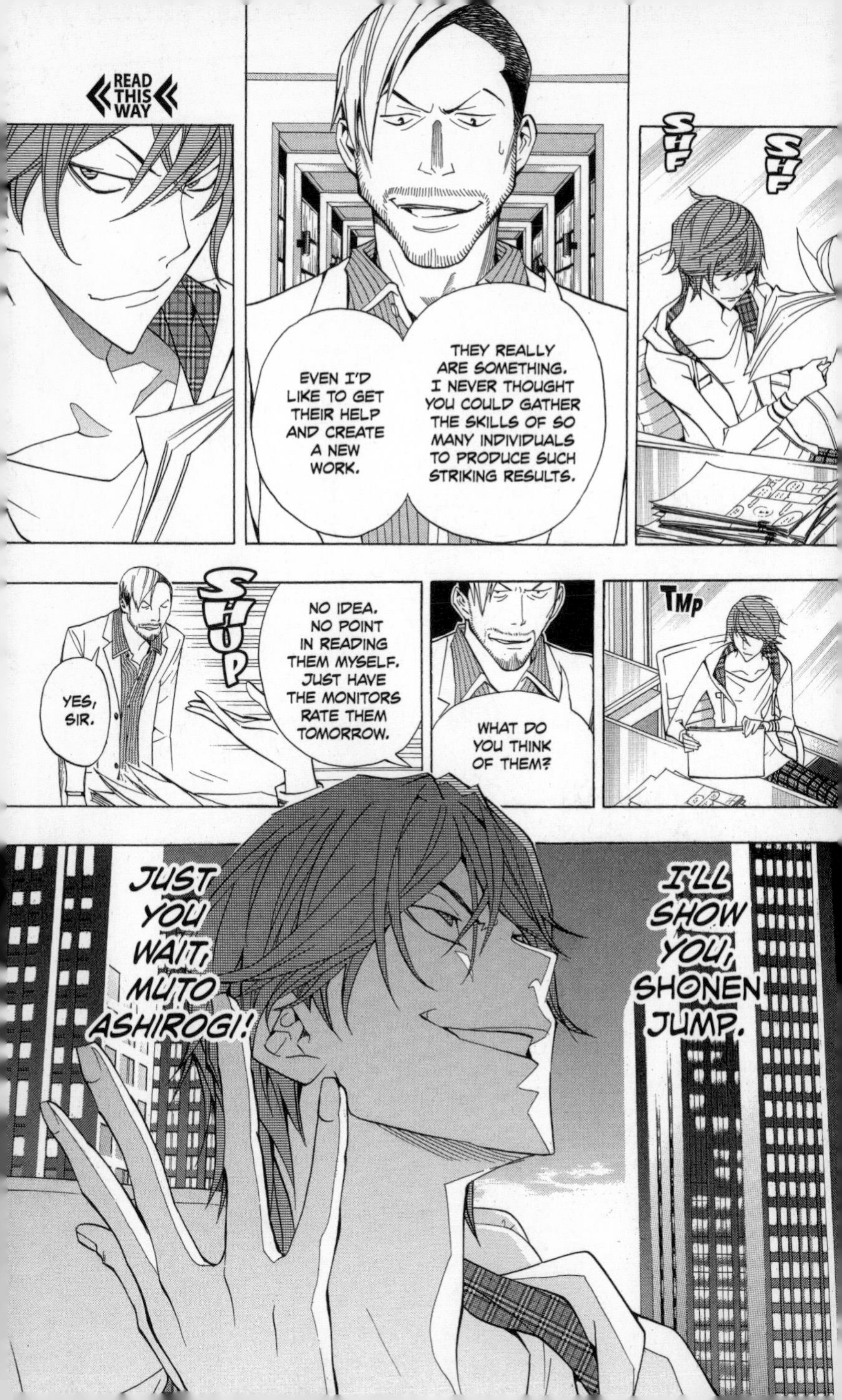
READ THIS WAY
SHF SHF
THEY REALLY ARE SOMETHING. I NEVER THOUGHT YOU COULD GATHER THE SKILLS OF SO MANY INDIVIDUALS TO PRODUCE SUCH STRIKING RESULTS.
EVEN I'D LIKE TO GET THEIR HELP AND CREATE A NEW WORK.
TMP
WHAT DO YOU THINK OF THEM?
NO IDEA. NO POINT IN READING THEM MYSELF. JUST HAVE THE MONITORS RATE THEM TOMORROW.
SHUP
YES, SIR.
I'LL SHOW YOU, SHONEN JUMP.
JUST YOU WAIT, MUTO ASHIROGI!

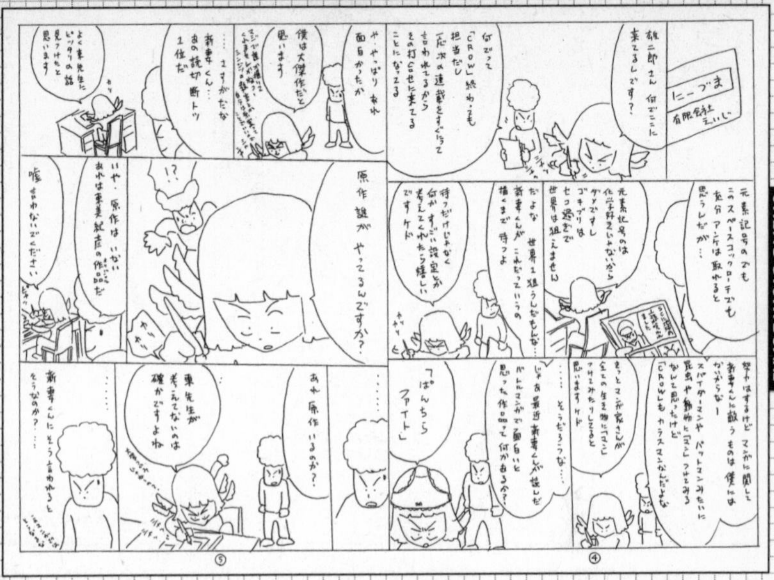
にーづま
有限会社えいじ
雄二郎さん 何でここに 来てるんです？
何でって 「CROW」終わっても 担当だし 一応次の連載をすぐにって 言われてるから その打ち合わせに来てる ことになってる
元素記号のでも このスペースコックローチでも 充分アンケは取れると 思うんだが…
元素記号のは 化学好きじゃないから ダメですし ゴキブリは セコ過ぎで 世界は狙えません
だよな 世界を狙うんだもんな… 新妻くんが これだっていうの 描くまで待つよ
待つだけじゃなく 何かすごい設定とか 考えてくれたら嬉しい ですケド
努力はするけど マンガに関して 新妻くんに敵う ものは 僕には ないからなー
スパイダーマンや バットマンみたいに 昆虫や動物に「マン」つけてみる なんて思ったけど 「CROW」も カラスマンなんだよな
きっとマンガ家さんが 全ての生き物に「マン」 つけてみたりしてると 思いますケド
……そうだろうな…
じゃあ最近新妻くんが読んだ バトルマンガで面白いと 思った作品って何かあるか？
「ぱんちらファイト」
④
や・やっぱり あれ 面白かったか
僕は大傑作だと 思います
…さすがだな 新妻くん… あの読切断トツ 1位だ
よく東先生に ピッタリの話 見つけたと 思います
原作誰が やってるんですか？
!?
いや・原作は いない あれは東美紀彦の作品だ
嘘 言わないでください
……
あれ原作いるのか？
東先生が 考えてないのは 確かですよね
……
新妻くんにそう言われると そうなのか？…
⑤

OHBA'S STORYBOARD

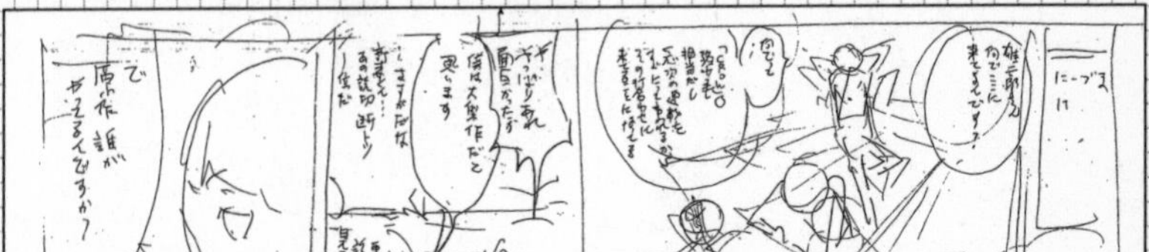

OBATA'S STORYBOARD

COMPLETE!

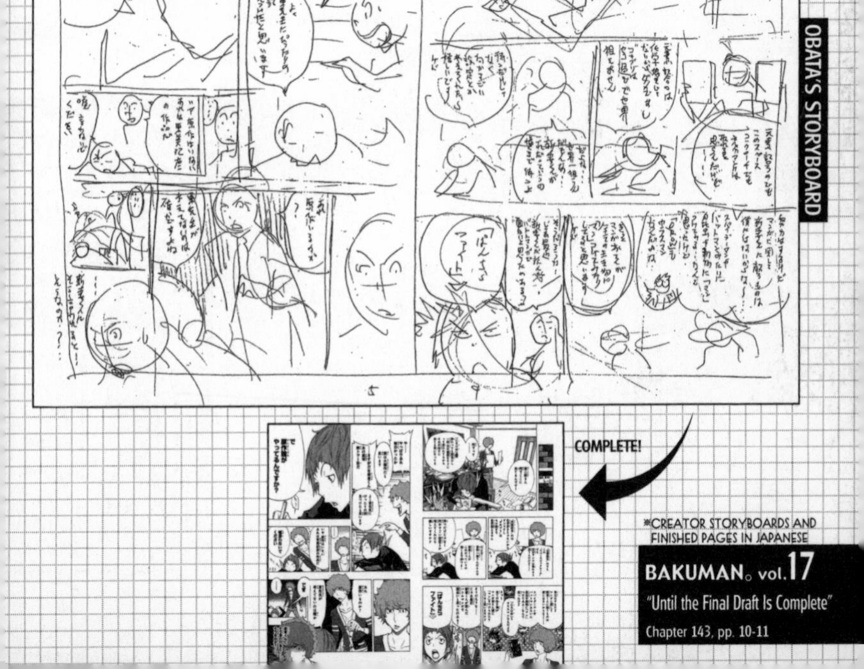

※CREATOR STORYBOARDS AND FINISHED PAGES IN JAPANESE

BAKUMAN。 vol.17

"Until the Final Draft Is Complete"

Chapter 143, pp. 10-11

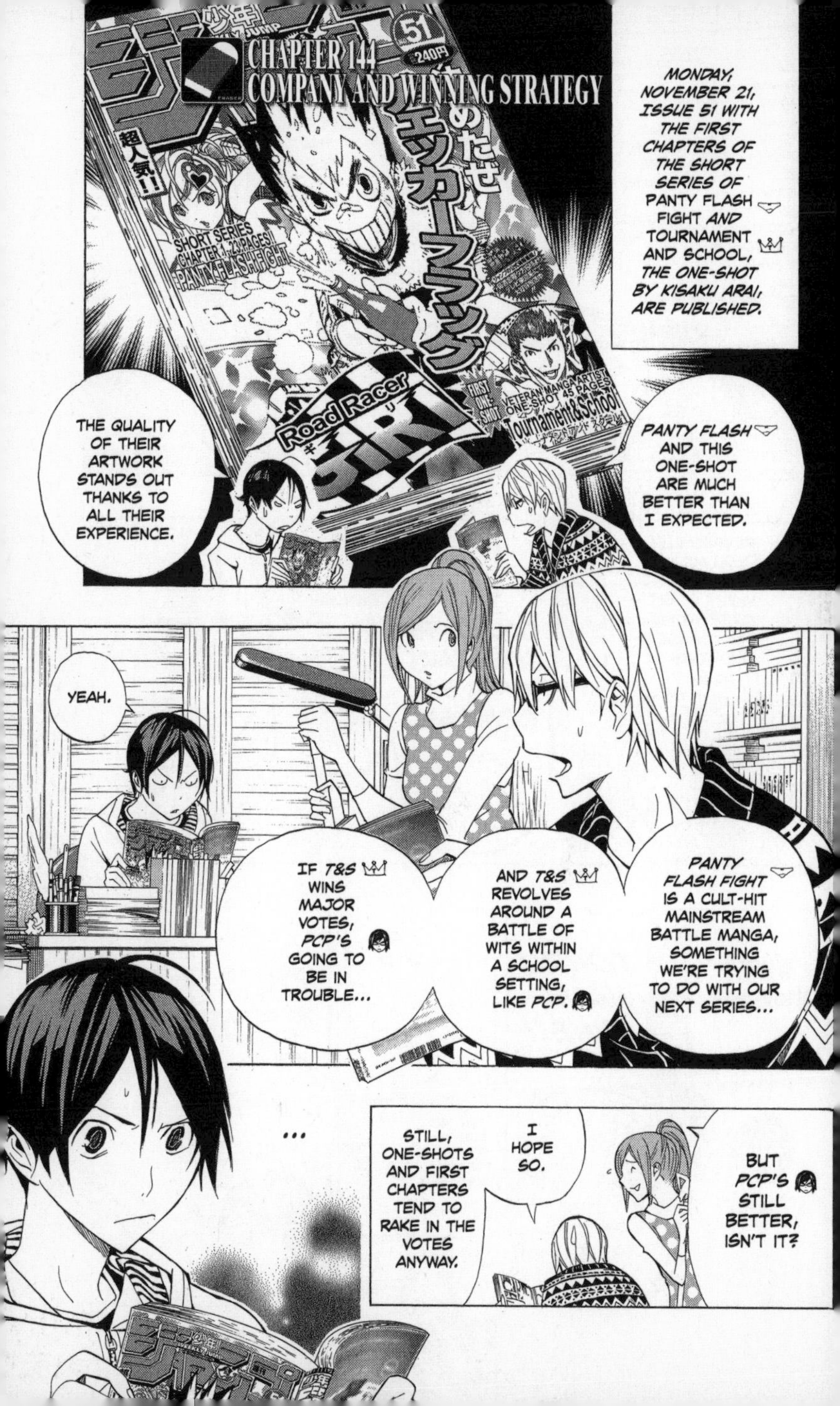
CHAPTER 144
COMPANY AND WINNING STRATEGY
51
240円
超人気!!
SHORT SERIES CHAPTER 1 22 PAGES!
VETERAN MANGA ARTIST ONE-SHOT 45 PAGES
Tournament&School
Road Racer
MONDAY, NOVEMBER 21, ISSUE 51 WITH THE FIRST CHAPTERS OF THE SHORT SERIES OF PANTY FLASH FIGHT AND TOURNAMENT AND SCHOOL, THE ONE-SHOT BY KISAKU ARAI, ARE PUBLISHED.
PANTY FLASH AND THIS ONE-SHOT ARE MUCH BETTER THAN I EXPECTED.
THE QUALITY OF THEIR ARTWORK STANDS OUT THANKS TO ALL THEIR EXPERIENCE.
YEAH.
PANTY FLASH FIGHT IS A CULT-HIT MAINSTREAM BATTLE MANGA, SOMETHING WE'RE TRYING TO DO WITH OUR NEXT SERIES...
AND T&S REVOLVES AROUND A BATTLE OF WITS WITHIN A SCHOOL SETTING, LIKE PCP.
IF T&S WINS MAJOR VOTES, PCP'S GOING TO BE IN TROUBLE...
BUT PCP'S STILL BETTER, ISN'T IT?
I HOPE SO.
STILL, ONE-SHOTS AND FIRST CHAPTERS TEND TO RAKE IN THE VOTES ANYWAY.
...

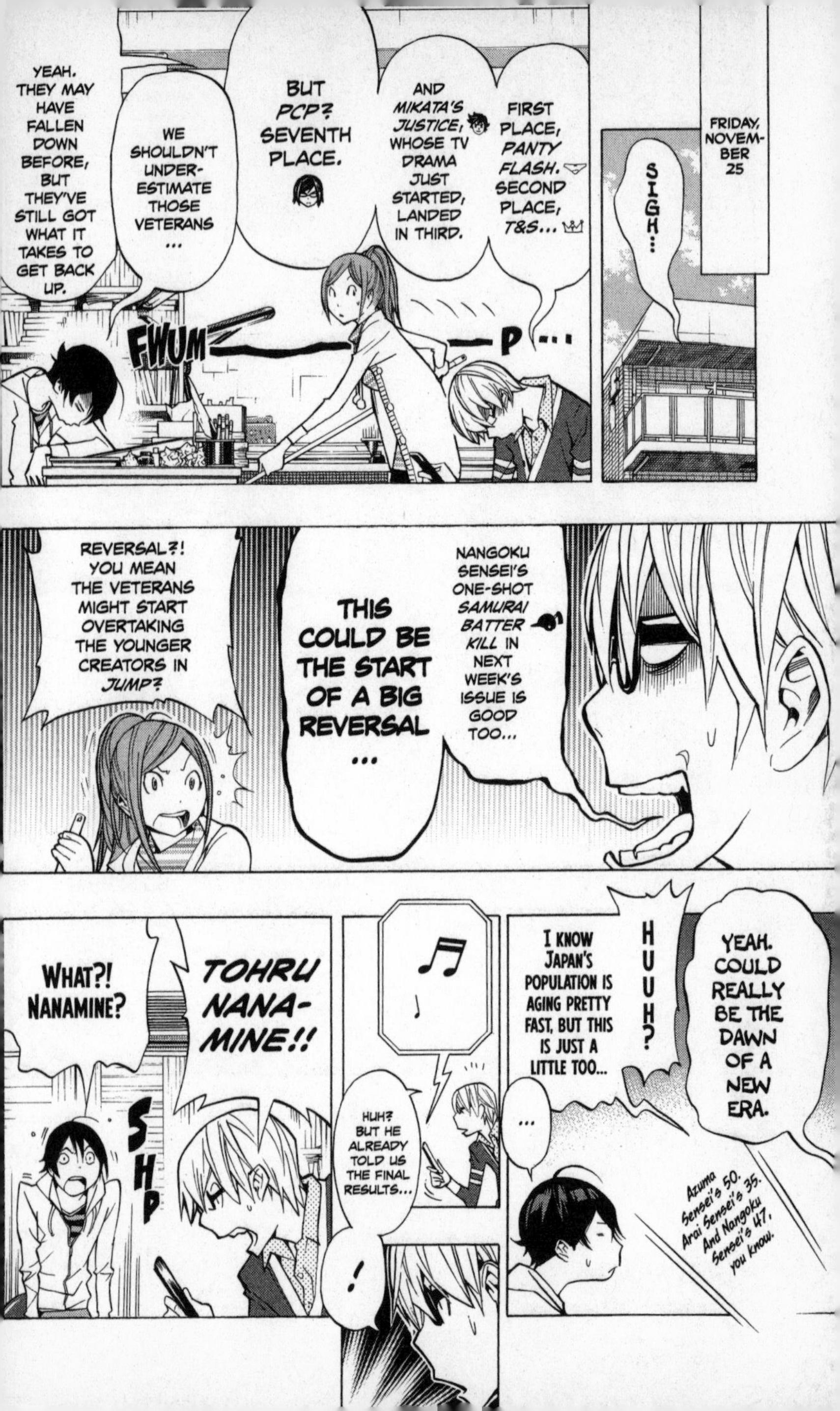

FRIDAY, NOVEMBER 25
SIGH...
FIRST PLACE, PANTY FLASH. SECOND PLACE, T&S...
AND MIKATA'S JUSTICE, WHOSE TV DRAMA JUST STARTED, LANDED IN THIRD.
BUT PCP? SEVENTH PLACE.
WE SHOULDN'T UNDERESTIMATE THOSE VETERANS...
YEAH. THEY MAY HAVE FALLEN DOWN BEFORE, BUT THEY'VE STILL GOT WHAT IT TAKES TO GET BACK UP.
FWUM—P...
NANGOKU SENSEI'S ONE-SHOT SAMURAI BATTER KILL IN NEXT WEEK'S ISSUE IS GOOD TOO...
THIS COULD BE THE START OF A BIG REVERSAL...
REVERSAL?! YOU MEAN THE VETERANS MIGHT START OVERTAKING THE YOUNGER CREATORS IN JUMP?
YEAH. COULD REALLY BE THE DAWN OF A NEW ERA.
HUUH?
I KNOW JAPAN'S POPULATION IS AGING PRETTY FAST, BUT THIS IS JUST A LITTLE TOO...
...
Azuma Sensei's 50. Arai Sensei's 35. And Nangoku Sensei's 47, you know.
♫
HUH? BUT HE ALREADY TOLD US THE FINAL RESULTS...
!
TOHRU NANAMINE!!
WHAT?! NANAMINE?
SHP

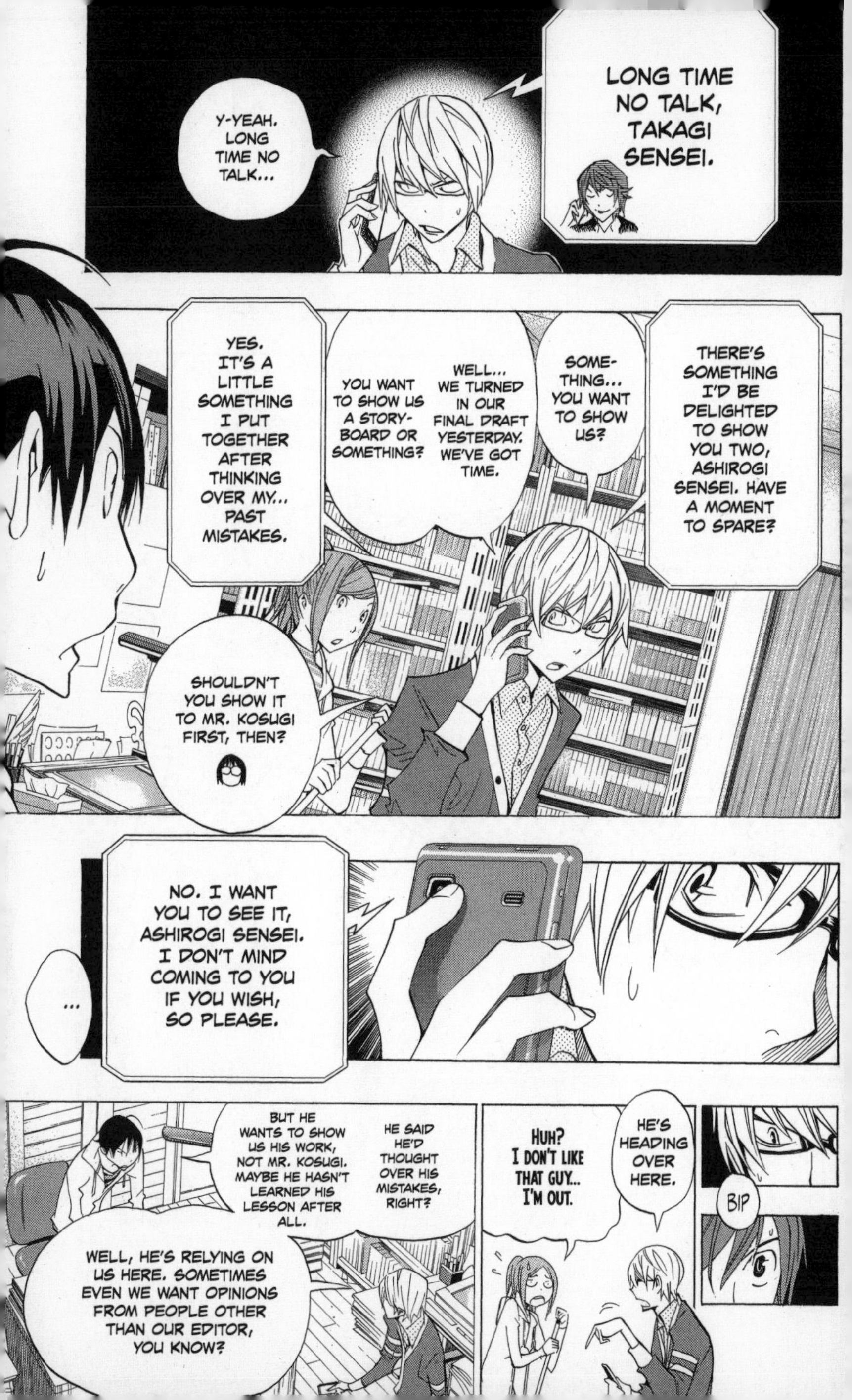
LONG TIME NO TALK, TAKAGI SENSEI.
Y-YEAH. LONG TIME NO TALK...
THERE'S SOMETHING I'D BE DELIGHTED TO SHOW YOU TWO, ASHIROGI SENSEI. HAVE A MOMENT TO SPARE?
SOME-THING... YOU WANT TO SHOW US?
WELL... WE TURNED IN OUR FINAL DRAFT YESTERDAY. WE'VE GOT TIME.
YOU WANT TO SHOW US A STORY-BOARD OR SOMETHING?
YES. IT'S A LITTLE SOMETHING I PUT TOGETHER AFTER THINKING OVER MY... PAST MISTAKES.
SHOULDN'T YOU SHOW IT TO MR. KOSUGI FIRST, THEN?
NO. I WANT YOU TO SEE IT, ASHIROGI SENSEI. I DON'T MIND COMING TO YOU IF YOU WISH, SO PLEASE.
...
BIP
HE'S HEADING OVER HERE.
HUH? I DON'T LIKE THAT GUY... I'M OUT.
HE SAID HE'D THOUGHT OVER HIS MISTAKES, RIGHT?
BUT HE WANTS TO SHOW US HIS WORK, NOT MR. KOSUGI. MAYBE HE HASN'T LEARNED HIS LESSON AFTER ALL.
WELL, HE'S RELYING ON US HERE. SOMETIMES EVEN WE WANT OPINIONS FROM PEOPLE OTHER THAN OUR EDITOR, YOU KNOW?

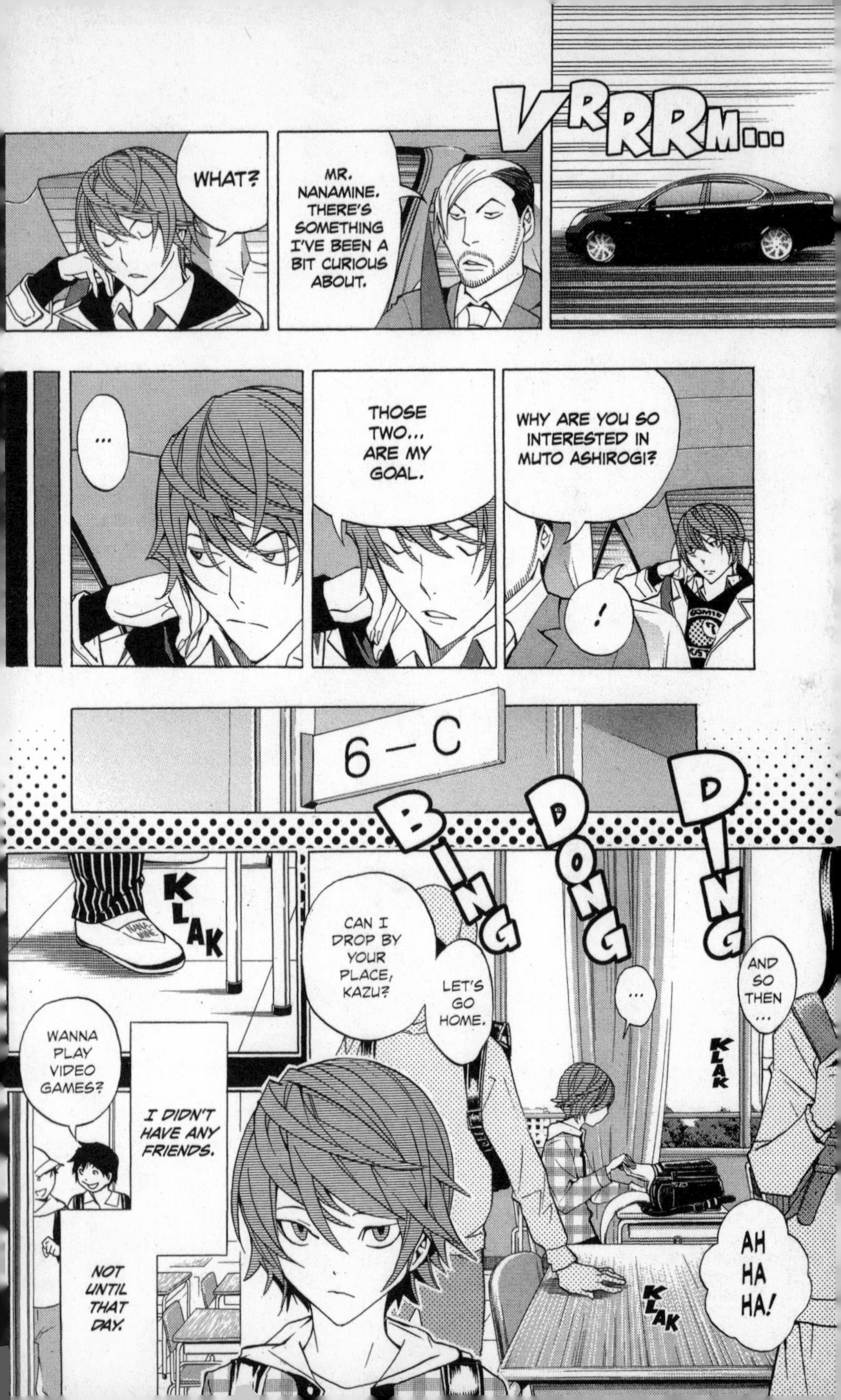
VRRRM...
MR. NANAMINE. THERE'S SOMETHING I'VE BEEN A BIT CURIOUS ABOUT.
WHAT?
WHY ARE YOU SO INTERESTED IN MUTO ASHIROGI?
!
THOSE TWO... ARE MY GOAL.
...
6-C
BING DONG DING
AND SO THEN...
KLAK
...
LET'S GO HOME.
CAN I DROP BY YOUR PLACE, KAZU?
AH HA HA!
KLAK
KLAK
NANA-MINE
WANNA PLAY VIDEO GAMES?
I DIDN'T HAVE ANY FRIENDS.
NOT UNTIL THAT DAY.

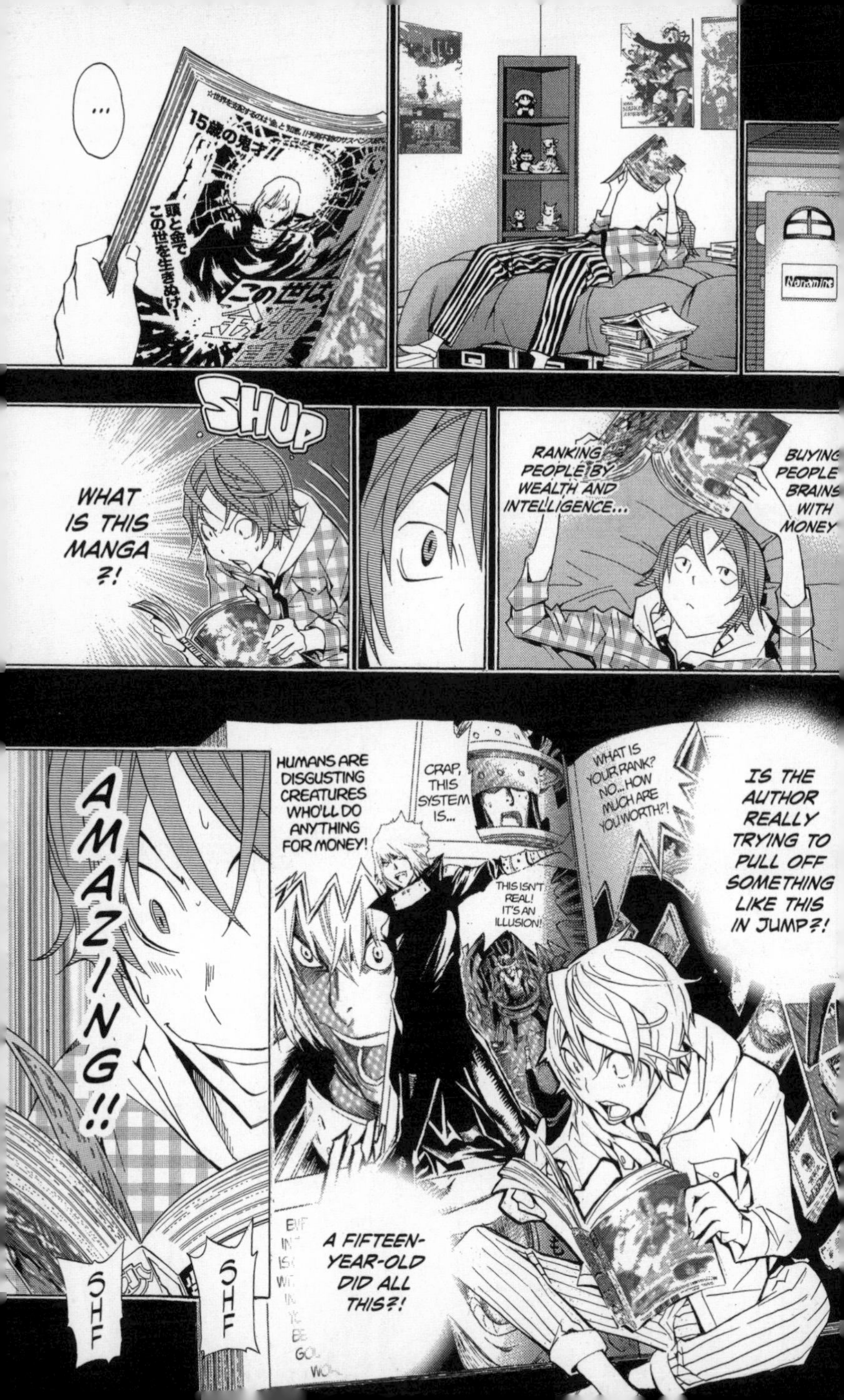

Nanamine
...
15歳の鬼才!!
頭と金でこの世を生きぬけ!
BUYING PEOPLE BRAINS WITH MONEY
RANKING PEOPLE BY WEALTH AND INTELLIGENCE...
SHUP
WHAT IS THIS MANGA ?!
IS THE AUTHOR REALLY TRYING TO PULL OFF SOMETHING LIKE THIS IN JUMP?!
WHAT IS YOUR RANK? NO...HOW MUCH ARE YOU WORTH?!
CRAP, THIS SYSTEM IS...
HUMANS ARE DISGUSTING CREATURES WHO'LL DO ANYTHING FOR MONEY!
THIS ISN'T REAL! IT'S AN ILLUSION!
A FIFTEEN-YEAR-OLD DID ALL THIS?!
AMAZING!!
SHF
SHF

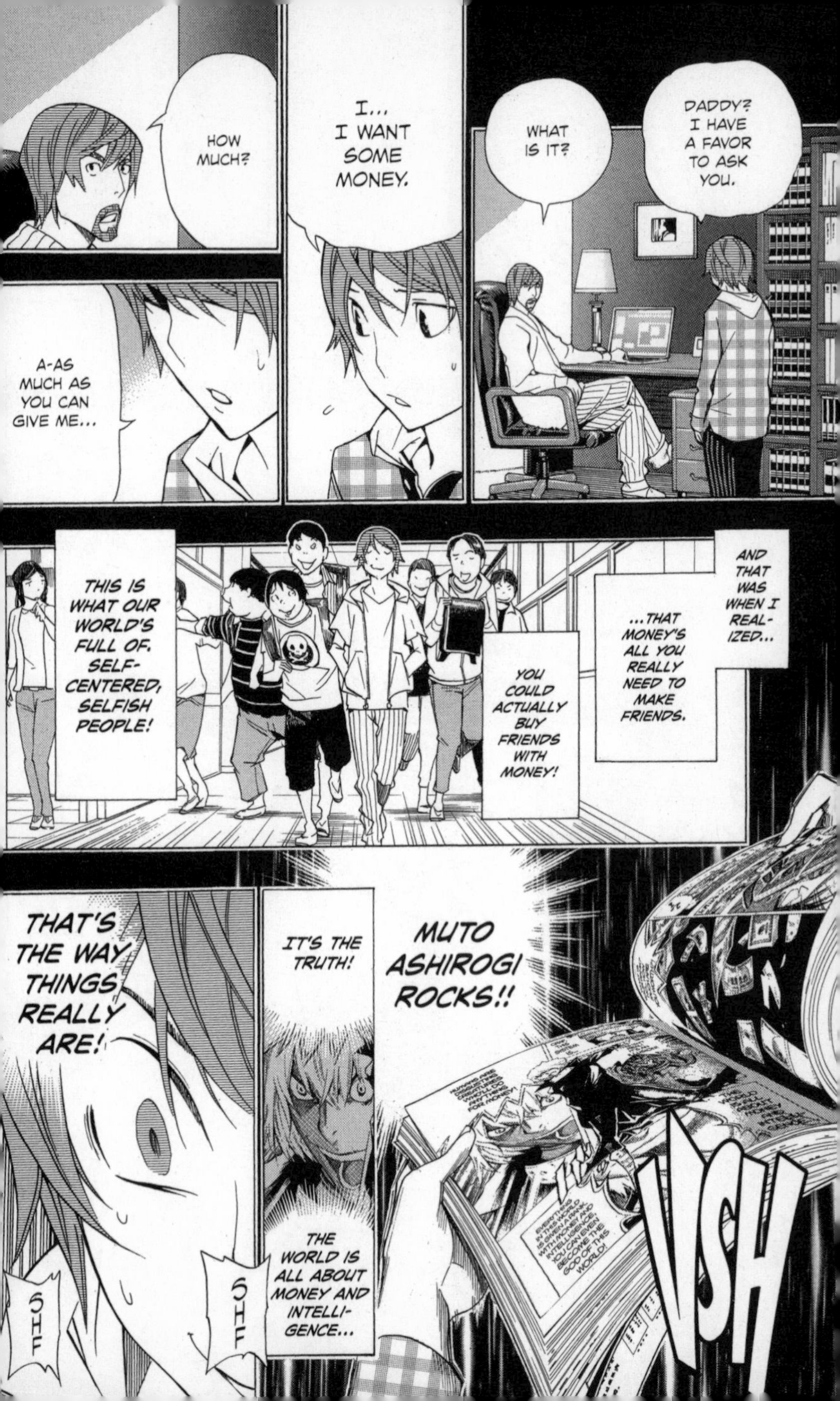
DADDY? I HAVE A FAVOR TO ASK YOU.
WHAT IS IT?
I... I WANT SOME MONEY.
HOW MUCH?
A-AS MUCH AS YOU CAN GIVE ME...
AND THAT WAS WHEN I REALIZED...
...THAT MONEY'S ALL YOU REALLY NEED TO MAKE FRIENDS.
YOU COULD ACTUALLY BUY FRIENDS WITH MONEY!
THIS IS WHAT OUR WORLD'S FULL OF. SELF-CENTERED, SELFISH PEOPLE!
EVERYTHING IN THIS WORLD IS GIVEN A RANK WITH MONEY AND INTELLIGENCE. YOU CAN EVEN BECOME THE GOD OF THIS WORLD!
VSH
MUTO ASHIROGI ROCKS!!
IT'S THE TRUTH!
THE WORLD IS ALL ABOUT MONEY AND INTELLIGENCE...
SHF
THAT'S THE WAY THINGS REALLY ARE!
SHF

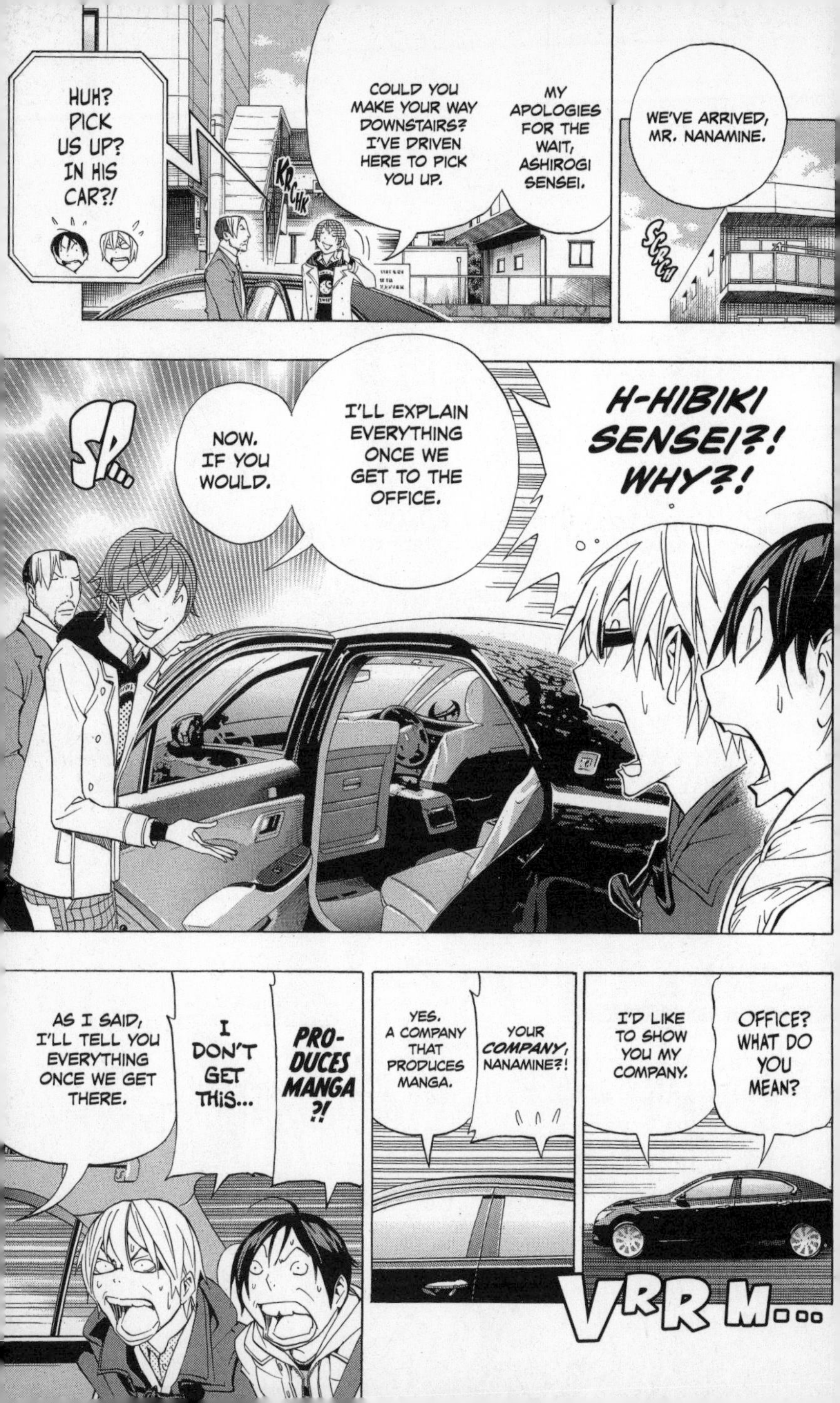
WE'VE ARRIVED, MR. NANAMINE.
SCRCH
MY APOLOGIES FOR THE WAIT, ASHIROGI SENSEI.
COULD YOU MAKE YOUR WAY DOWNSTAIRS? I'VE DRIVEN HERE TO PICK YOU UP.
KRCHK
HUH? PICK US UP? IN HIS CAR?!
H-HIBIKI SENSEI?! WHY?!
I'LL EXPLAIN EVERYTHING ONCE WE GET TO THE OFFICE.
NOW. IF YOU WOULD.
OFFICE? WHAT DO YOU MEAN?
I'D LIKE TO SHOW YOU MY COMPANY.
VRRM...
YOUR COMPANY, NANAMINE?!
YES. A COMPANY THAT PRODUCES MANGA.
PRODUCES MANGA?!
I DON'T GET THIS...
AS I SAID, I'LL TELL YOU EVERYTHING ONCE WE GET THERE.

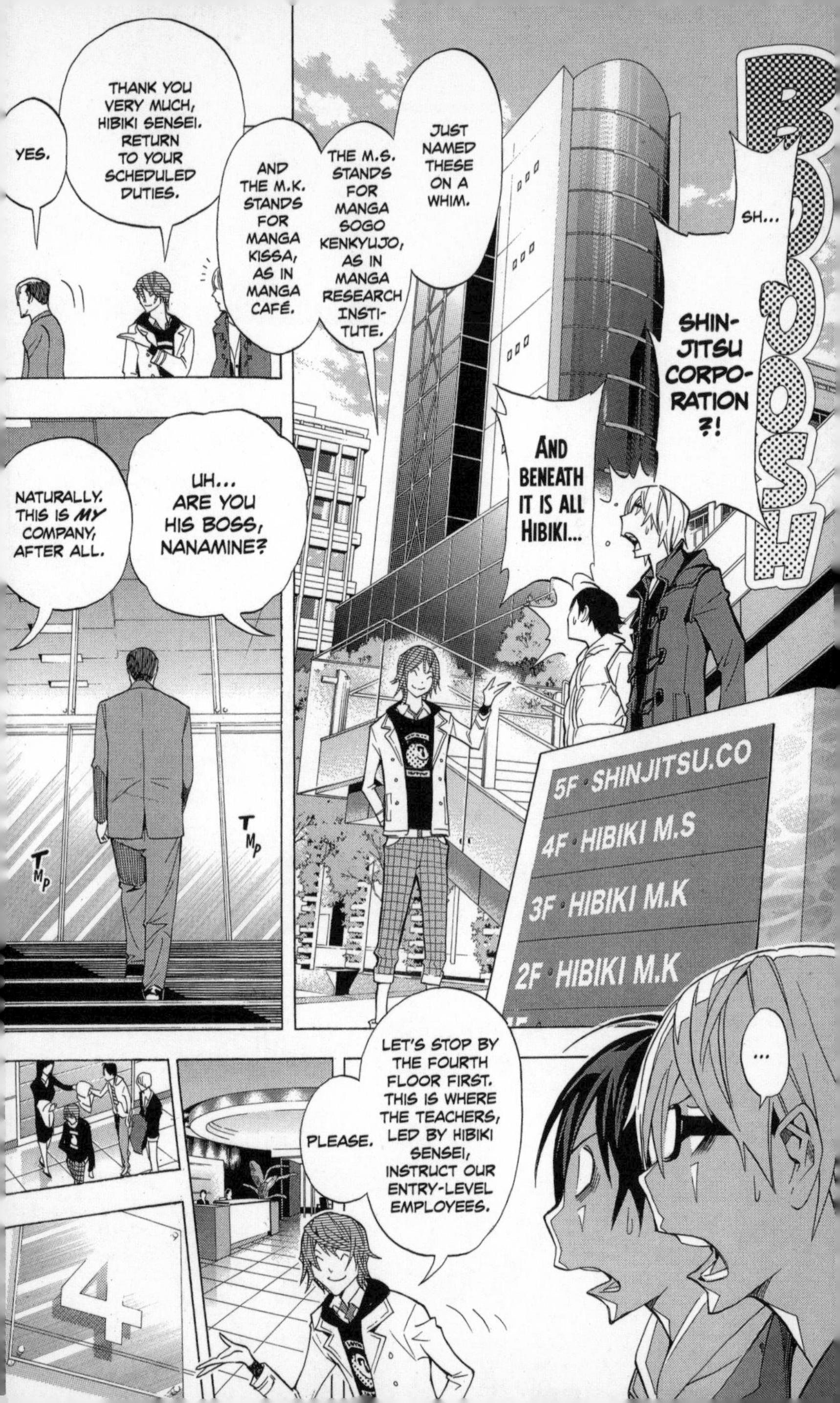
BOOSH
SH...
SHIN-JITSU CORPORATION?!
5F SHINJITSU.CO
4F HIBIKI M.S
3F HIBIKI M.K
2F HIBIKI M.K
AND BENEATH IT IS ALL HIBIKI...
JUST NAMED THESE ON A WHIM.
THE M.S. STANDS FOR MANGA SOGO KENKYUJO, AS IN MANGA RESEARCH INSTITUTE.
AND THE M.K. STANDS FOR MANGA KISSA, AS IN MANGA CAFÉ.
THANK YOU VERY MUCH, HIBIKI SENSEI. RETURN TO YOUR SCHEDULED DUTIES.
YES.
UH... ARE YOU HIS BOSS, NANAMINE?
NATURALLY. THIS IS MY COMPANY, AFTER ALL.
TMP
TMP
...
LET'S STOP BY THE FOURTH FLOOR FIRST. THIS IS WHERE THE TEACHERS, LED BY HIBIKI SENSEI, INSTRUCT OUR ENTRY-LEVEL EMPLOYEES.
PLEASE.
4

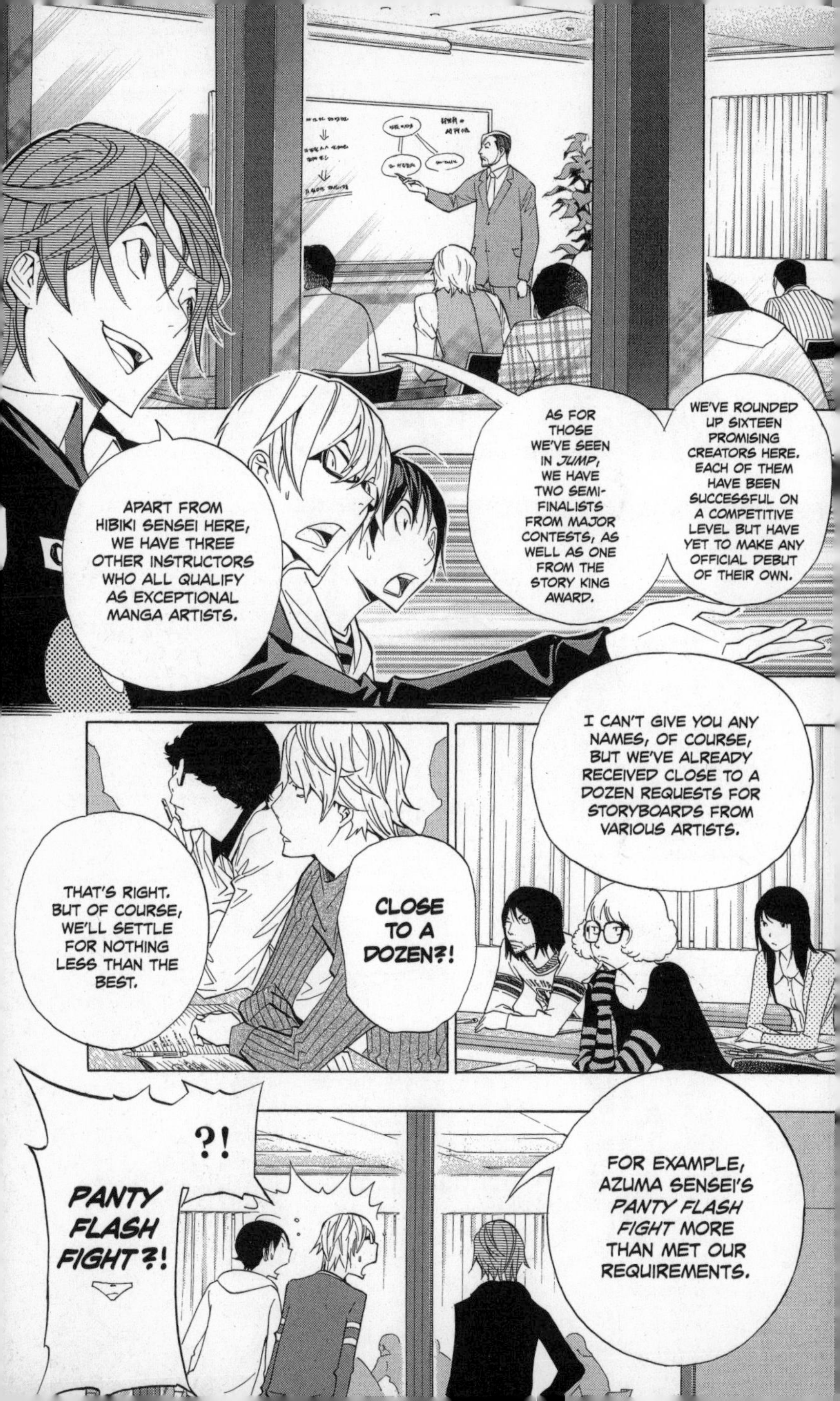
WE'VE ROUNDED UP SIXTEEN PROMISING CREATORS HERE. EACH OF THEM HAVE BEEN SUCCESSFUL ON A COMPETITIVE LEVEL BUT HAVE YET TO MAKE ANY OFFICIAL DEBUT OF THEIR OWN.
AS FOR THOSE WE'VE SEEN IN *JUMP*, WE HAVE TWO SEMI-FINALISTS FROM MAJOR CONTESTS, AS WELL AS ONE FROM THE STORY KING AWARD.
APART FROM HIBIKI SENSEI HERE, WE HAVE THREE OTHER INSTRUCTORS WHO ALL QUALIFY AS EXCEPTIONAL MANGA ARTISTS.
I CAN'T GIVE YOU ANY NAMES, OF COURSE, BUT WE'VE ALREADY RECEIVED CLOSE TO A DOZEN REQUESTS FOR STORYBOARDS FROM VARIOUS ARTISTS.
CLOSE TO A DOZEN?!
THAT'S RIGHT. BUT OF COURSE, WE'LL SETTLE FOR NOTHING LESS THAN THE BEST.
FOR EXAMPLE, AZUMA SENSEI'S *PANTY FLASH FIGHT* MORE THAN MET OUR REQUIREMENTS.
?!
PANTY FLASH FIGHT?!

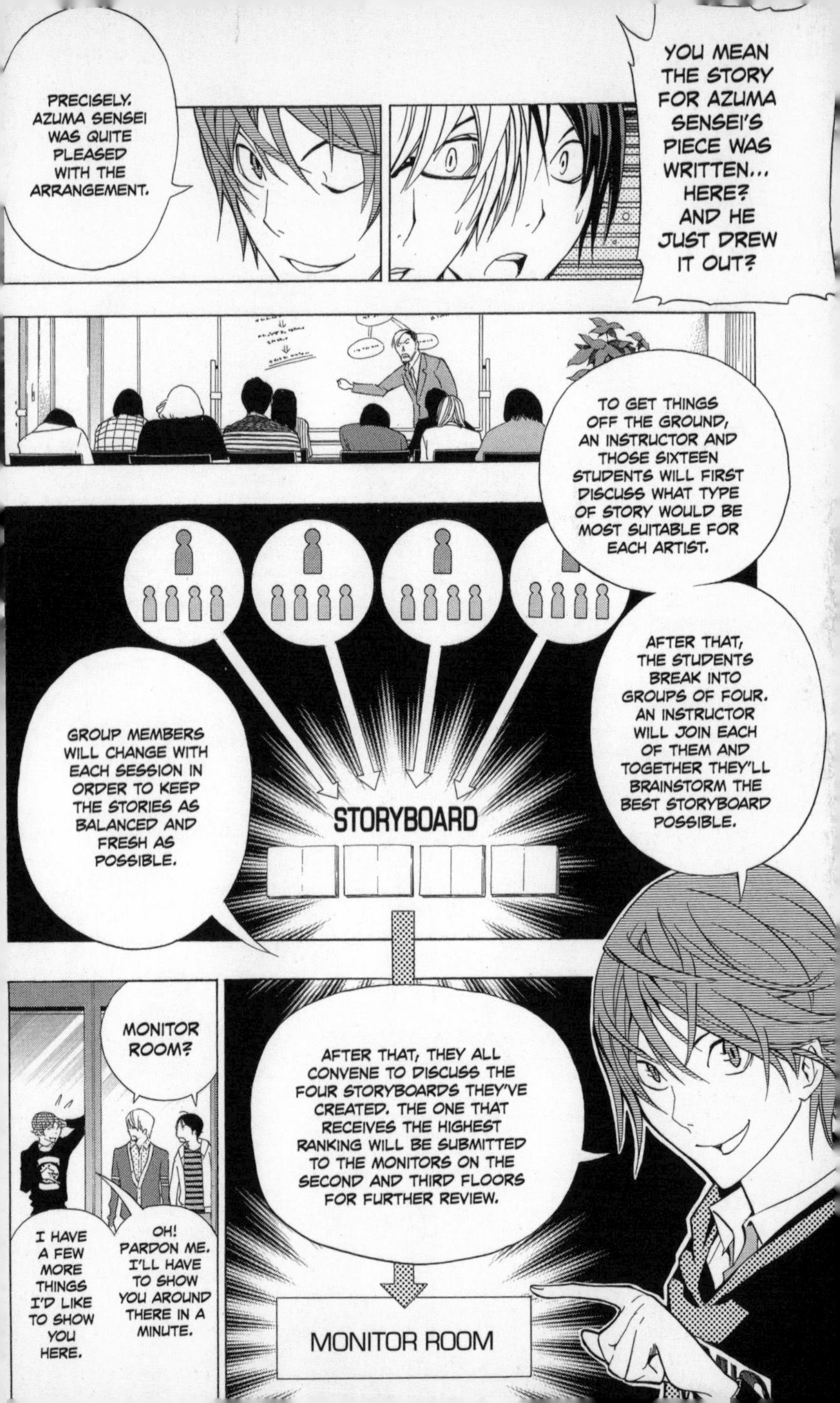

YOU MEAN THE STORY FOR AZUMA SENSEI'S PIECE WAS WRITTEN... HERE? AND HE JUST DREW IT OUT?
PRECISELY. AZUMA SENSEI WAS QUITE PLEASED WITH THE ARRANGEMENT.
TO GET THINGS OFF THE GROUND, AN INSTRUCTOR AND THOSE SIXTEEN STUDENTS WILL FIRST DISCUSS WHAT TYPE OF STORY WOULD BE MOST SUITABLE FOR EACH ARTIST.
AFTER THAT, THE STUDENTS BREAK INTO GROUPS OF FOUR. AN INSTRUCTOR WILL JOIN EACH OF THEM AND TOGETHER THEY'LL BRAINSTORM THE BEST STORYBOARD POSSIBLE.
STORYBOARD
GROUP MEMBERS WILL CHANGE WITH EACH SESSION IN ORDER TO KEEP THE STORIES AS BALANCED AND FRESH AS POSSIBLE.
AFTER THAT, THEY ALL CONVENE TO DISCUSS THE FOUR STORYBOARDS THEY'VE CREATED. THE ONE THAT RECEIVES THE HIGHEST RANKING WILL BE SUBMITTED TO THE MONITORS ON THE SECOND AND THIRD FLOORS FOR FURTHER REVIEW.
MONITOR ROOM
MONITOR ROOM?
OH! PARDON ME. I'LL HAVE TO SHOW YOU AROUND THERE IN A MINUTE.
I HAVE A FEW MORE THINGS I'D LIKE TO SHOW YOU HERE.

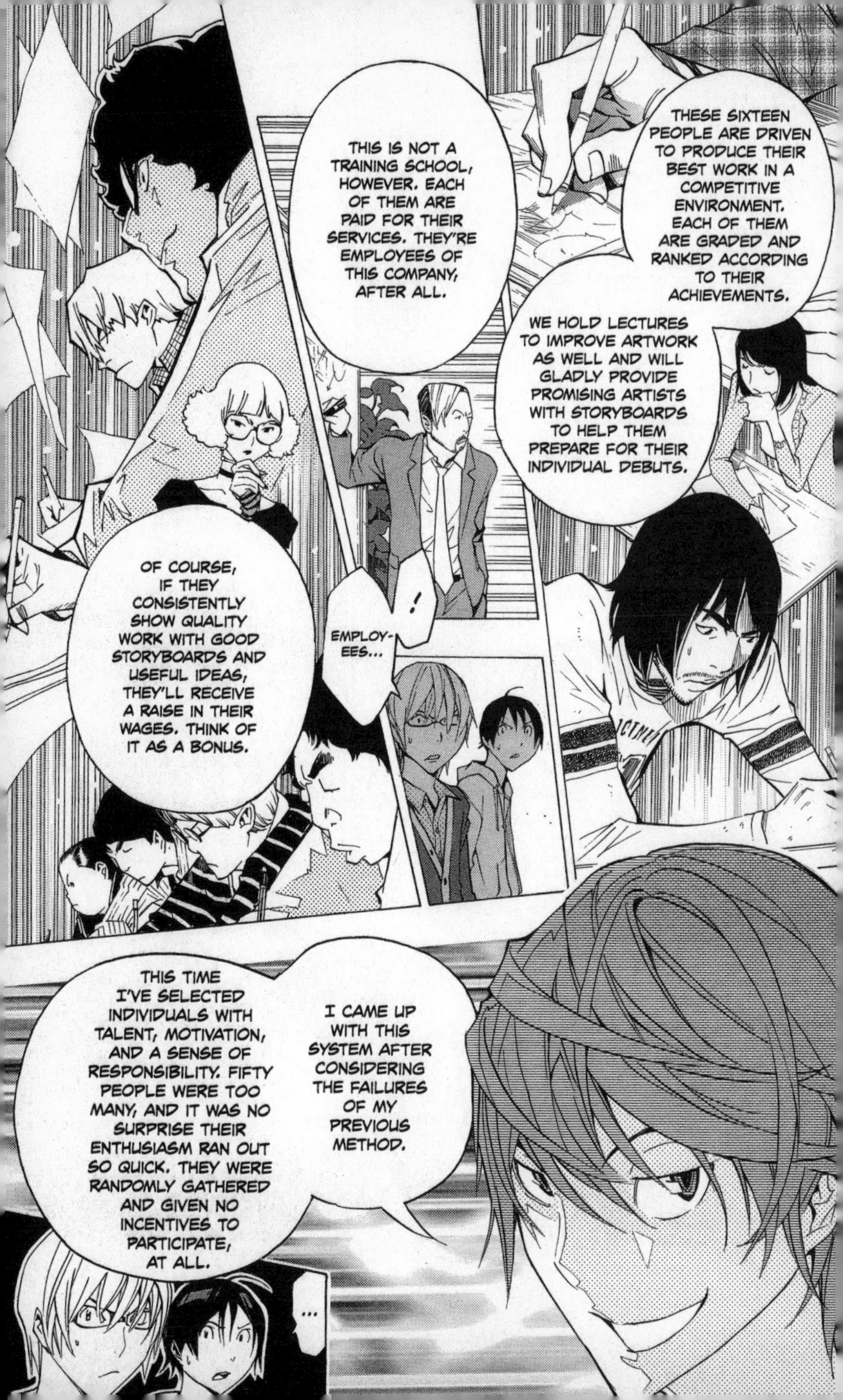
THESE SIXTEEN PEOPLE ARE DRIVEN TO PRODUCE THEIR BEST WORK IN A COMPETITIVE ENVIRONMENT. EACH OF THEM ARE GRADED AND RANKED ACCORDING TO THEIR ACHIEVEMENTS.
WE HOLD LECTURES TO IMPROVE ARTWORK AS WELL AND WILL GLADLY PROVIDE PROMISING ARTISTS WITH STORYBOARDS TO HELP THEM PREPARE FOR THEIR INDIVIDUAL DEBUTS.
THIS IS NOT A TRAINING SCHOOL, HOWEVER. EACH OF THEM ARE PAID FOR THEIR SERVICES. THEY'RE EMPLOYEES OF THIS COMPANY, AFTER ALL.
!
EMPLOY-EES...
OF COURSE, IF THEY CONSISTENTLY SHOW QUALITY WORK WITH GOOD STORYBOARDS AND USEFUL IDEAS, THEY'LL RECEIVE A RAISE IN THEIR WAGES. THINK OF IT AS A BONUS.
I CAME UP WITH THIS SYSTEM AFTER CONSIDERING THE FAILURES OF MY PREVIOUS METHOD.
THIS TIME I'VE SELECTED INDIVIDUALS WITH TALENT, MOTIVATION, AND A SENSE OF RESPONSIBILITY. FIFTY PEOPLE WERE TOO MANY, AND IT WAS NO SURPRISE THEIR ENTHUSIASM RAN OUT SO QUICK. THEY WERE RANDOMLY GATHERED AND GIVEN NO INCENTIVES TO PARTICIPATE, AT ALL.
...

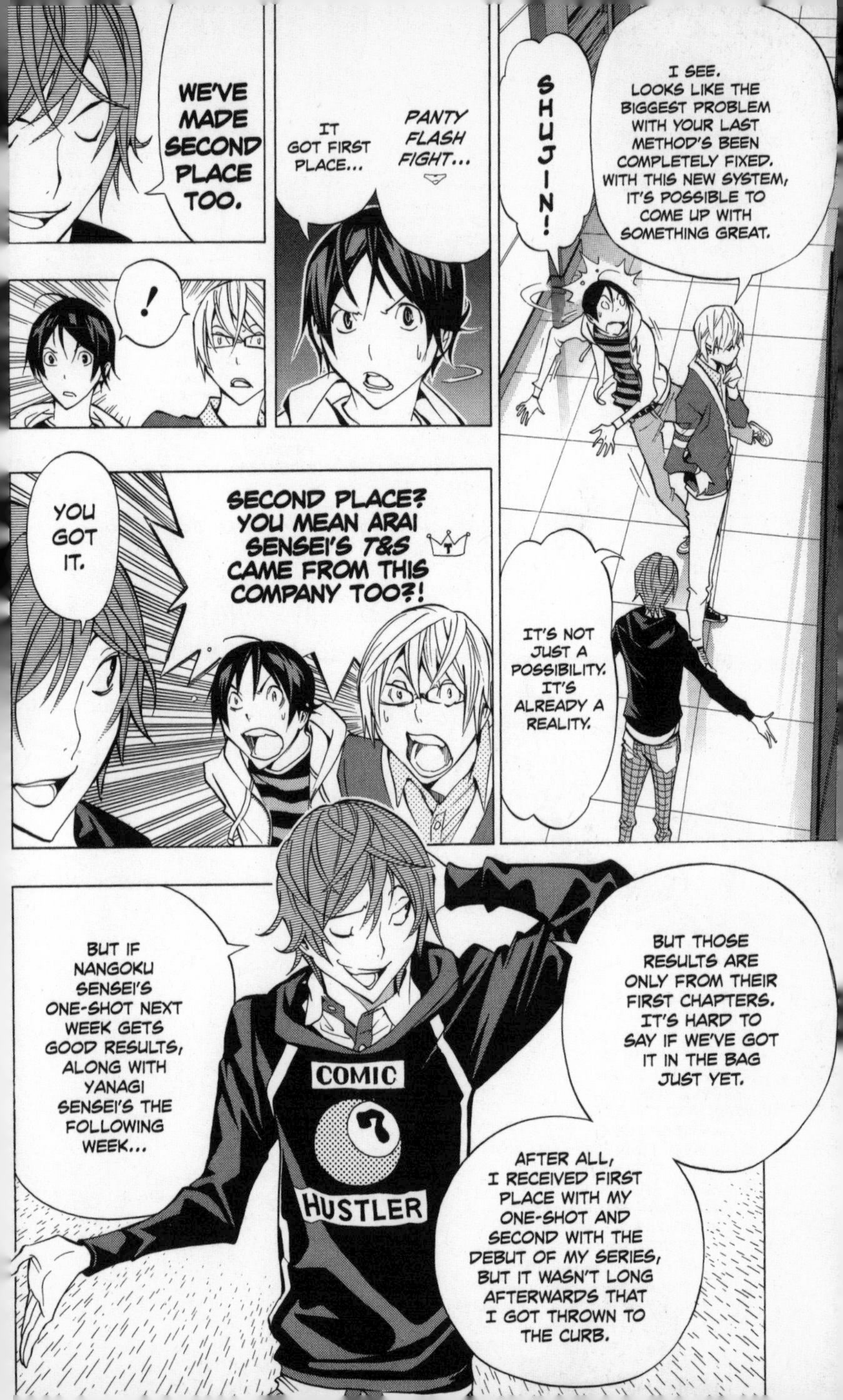
I SEE. LOOKS LIKE THE BIGGEST PROBLEM WITH YOUR LAST METHOD'S BEEN COMPLETELY FIXED. WITH THIS NEW SYSTEM, IT'S POSSIBLE TO COME UP WITH SOMETHING GREAT.
SHUJIN!
IT'S NOT JUST A POSSIBILITY. IT'S ALREADY A REALITY.
PANTY FLASH FIGHT...
IT GOT FIRST PLACE...
WE'VE MADE SECOND PLACE TOO.
!
SECOND PLACE? YOU MEAN ARAI SENSEI'S T&S CAME FROM THIS COMPANY TOO?!
YOU GOT IT.
BUT THOSE RESULTS ARE ONLY FROM THEIR FIRST CHAPTERS. IT'S HARD TO SAY IF WE'VE GOT IT IN THE BAG JUST YET.
AFTER ALL, I RECEIVED FIRST PLACE WITH MY ONE-SHOT AND SECOND WITH THE DEBUT OF MY SERIES, BUT IT WASN'T LONG AFTERWARDS THAT I GOT THROWN TO THE CURB.
BUT IF NANGOKU SENSEI'S ONE-SHOT NEXT WEEK GETS GOOD RESULTS, ALONG WITH YANAGI SENSEI'S THE FOLLOWING WEEK...
COMIC
HUSTLER

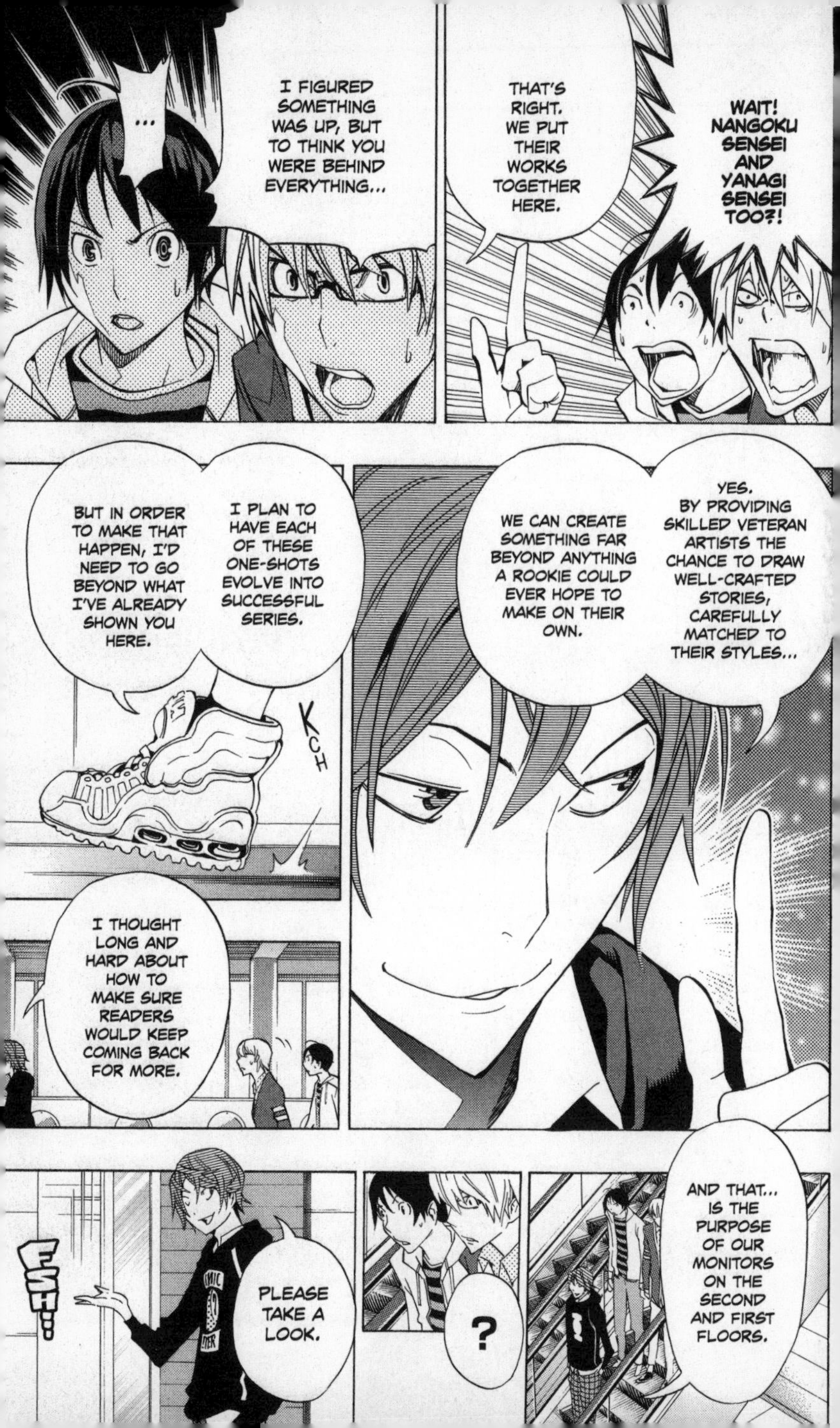
WAIT! NANGOKU SENSEI AND YANAGI SENSEI TOO?!
THAT'S RIGHT. WE PUT THEIR WORKS TOGETHER HERE.
I FIGURED SOMETHING WAS UP, BUT TO THINK YOU WERE BEHIND EVERYTHING...
...
YES. BY PROVIDING SKILLED VETERAN ARTISTS THE CHANCE TO DRAW WELL-CRAFTED STORIES, CAREFULLY MATCHED TO THEIR STYLES...
WE CAN CREATE SOMETHING FAR BEYOND ANYTHING A ROOKIE COULD EVER HOPE TO MAKE ON THEIR OWN.
I PLAN TO HAVE EACH OF THESE ONE-SHOTS EVOLVE INTO SUCCESSFUL SERIES.
BUT IN ORDER TO MAKE THAT HAPPEN, I'D NEED TO GO BEYOND WHAT I'VE ALREADY SHOWN YOU HERE.
KCH
I THOUGHT LONG AND HARD ABOUT HOW TO MAKE SURE READERS WOULD KEEP COMING BACK FOR MORE.
AND THAT... IS THE PURPOSE OF OUR MONITORS ON THE SECOND AND FIRST FLOORS.
?
PLEASE TAKE A LOOK.
FSH

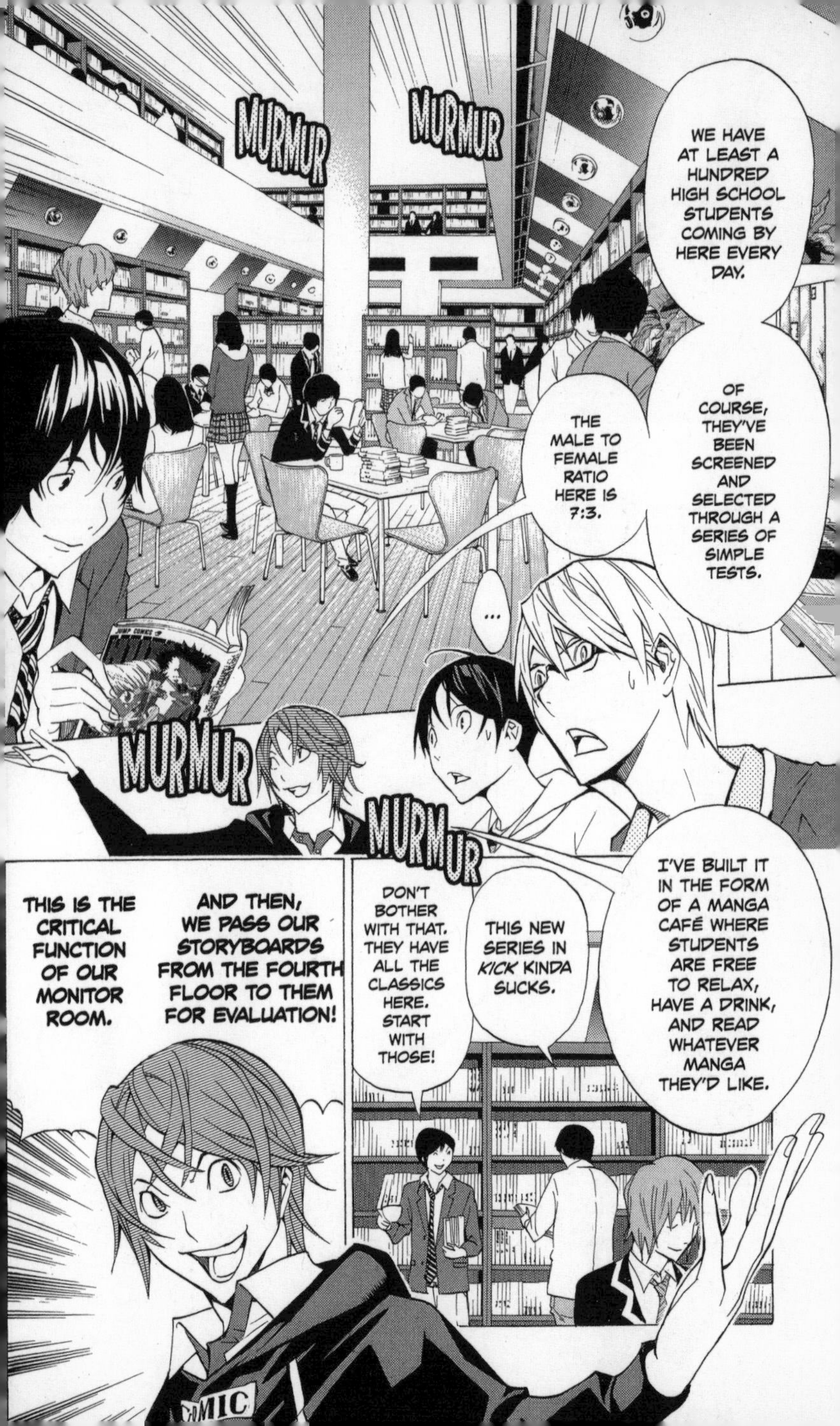
MURMUR
MURMUR
WE HAVE AT LEAST A HUNDRED HIGH SCHOOL STUDENTS COMING BY HERE EVERY DAY.
OF COURSE, THEY'VE BEEN SCREENED AND SELECTED THROUGH A SERIES OF SIMPLE TESTS.
THE MALE TO FEMALE RATIO HERE IS 7:3.
...
MURMUR
MURMUR
I'VE BUILT IT IN THE FORM OF A MANGA CAFÉ WHERE STUDENTS ARE FREE TO RELAX, HAVE A DRINK, AND READ WHATEVER MANGA THEY'D LIKE.
THIS NEW SERIES IN *KICK* KINDA SUCKS.
DON'T BOTHER WITH THAT. THEY HAVE ALL THE CLASSICS HERE. START WITH THOSE!
AND THEN, WE PASS OUR STORYBOARDS FROM THE FOURTH FLOOR TO THEM FOR EVALUATION!
THIS IS THE CRITICAL FUNCTION OF OUR MONITOR ROOM.

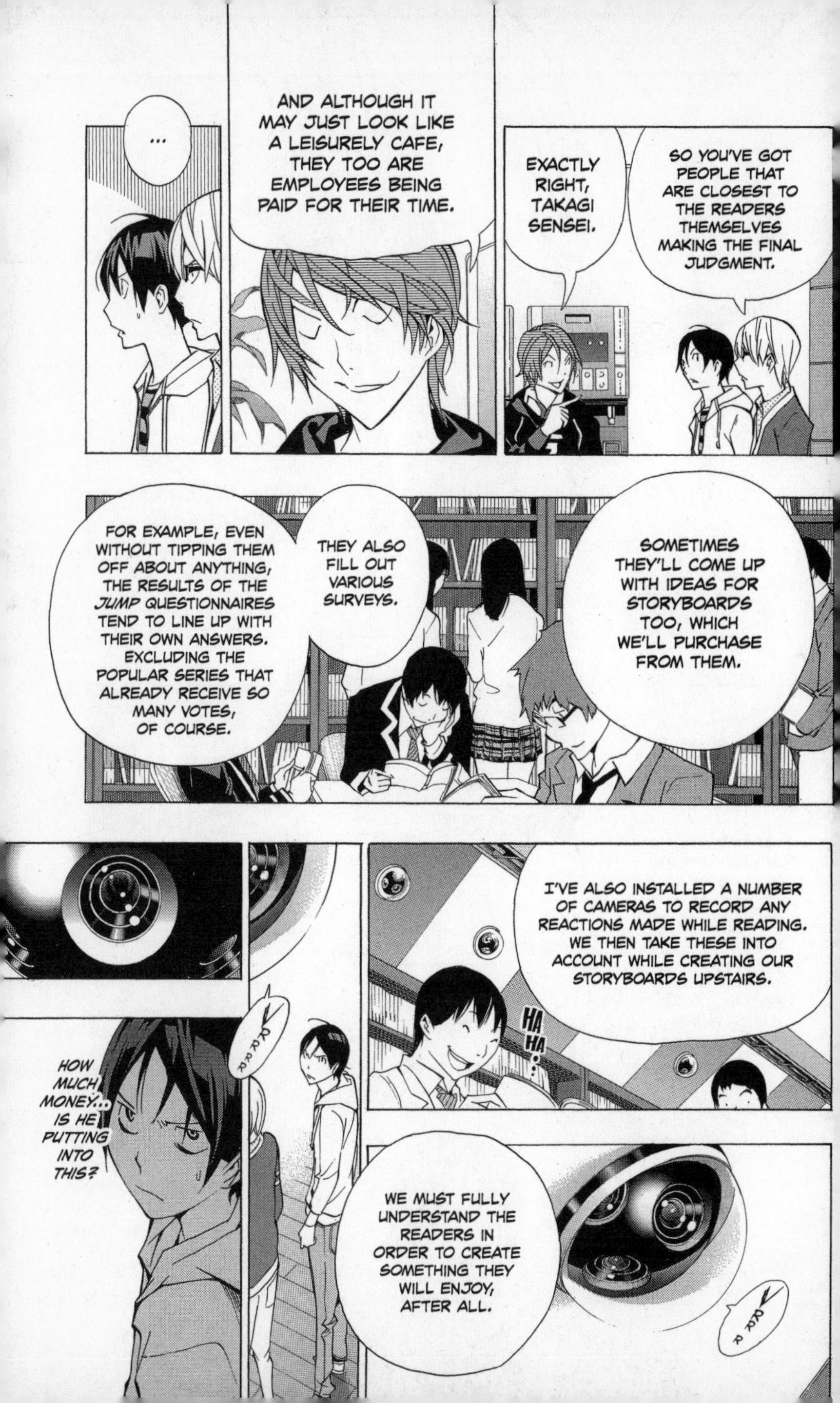
SO YOU'VE GOT PEOPLE THAT ARE CLOSEST TO THE READERS THEMSELVES MAKING THE FINAL JUDGMENT.
EXACTLY RIGHT, TAKAGI SENSEI.
AND ALTHOUGH IT MAY JUST LOOK LIKE A LEISURELY CAFE, THEY TOO ARE EMPLOYEES BEING PAID FOR THEIR TIME.
...
SOMETIMES THEY'LL COME UP WITH IDEAS FOR STORYBOARDS TOO, WHICH WE'LL PURCHASE FROM THEM.
THEY ALSO FILL OUT VARIOUS SURVEYS.
FOR EXAMPLE, EVEN WITHOUT TIPPING THEM OFF ABOUT ANYTHING, THE RESULTS OF THE *JUMP* QUESTIONNAIRES TEND TO LINE UP WITH THEIR OWN ANSWERS. EXCLUDING THE POPULAR SERIES THAT ALREADY RECEIVE SO MANY VOTES, OF COURSE.
I'VE ALSO INSTALLED A NUMBER OF CAMERAS TO RECORD ANY REACTIONS MADE WHILE READING. WE THEN TAKE THESE INTO ACCOUNT WHILE CREATING OUR STORYBOARDS UPSTAIRS.
HA HA
WE MUST FULLY UNDERSTAND THE READERS IN ORDER TO CREATE SOMETHING THEY WILL ENJOY, AFTER ALL.
VRRR
VRRR
HOW MUCH MONEY... IS HE PUTTING INTO THIS?

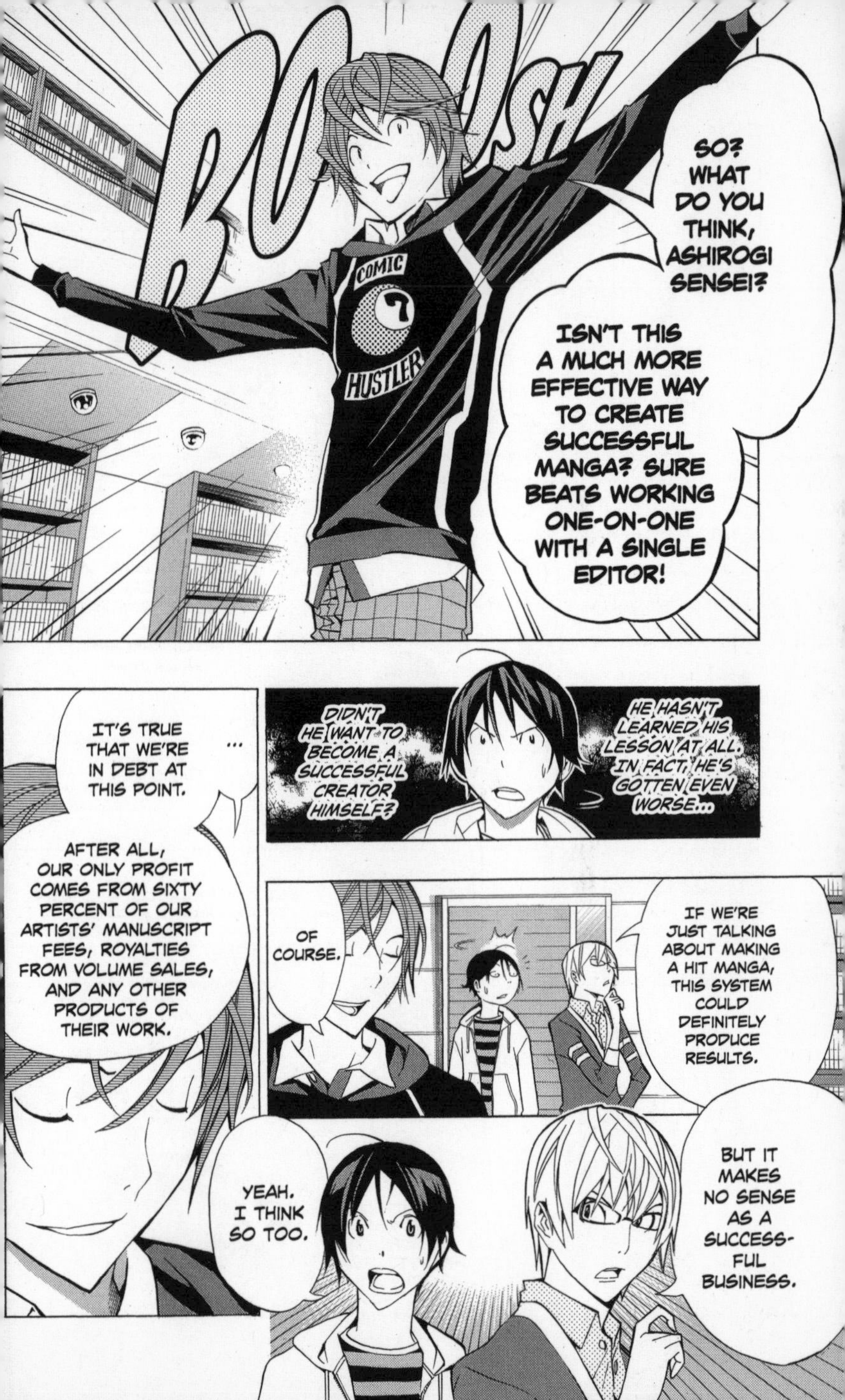
BOOSH
SO? WHAT DO YOU THINK, ASHIROGI SENSEI?
ISN'T THIS A MUCH MORE EFFECTIVE WAY TO CREATE SUCCESSFUL MANGA? SURE BEATS WORKING ONE-ON-ONE WITH A SINGLE EDITOR!
HE HASN'T LEARNED HIS LESSON AT ALL. IN FACT, HE'S GOTTEN EVEN WORSE...
DIDN'T HE WANT TO BECOME A SUCCESSFUL CREATOR HIMSELF?
IF WE'RE JUST TALKING ABOUT MAKING A HIT MANGA, THIS SYSTEM COULD DEFINITELY PRODUCE RESULTS.
OF COURSE.
BUT IT MAKES NO SENSE AS A SUCCESS-FUL BUSINESS.
YEAH. I THINK SO TOO.
...
IT'S TRUE THAT WE'RE IN DEBT AT THIS POINT.
AFTER ALL, OUR ONLY PROFIT COMES FROM SIXTY PERCENT OF OUR ARTISTS' MANUSCRIPT FEES, ROYALTIES FROM VOLUME SALES, AND ANY OTHER PRODUCTS OF THEIR WORK.
COMIC 7 HUSTLER

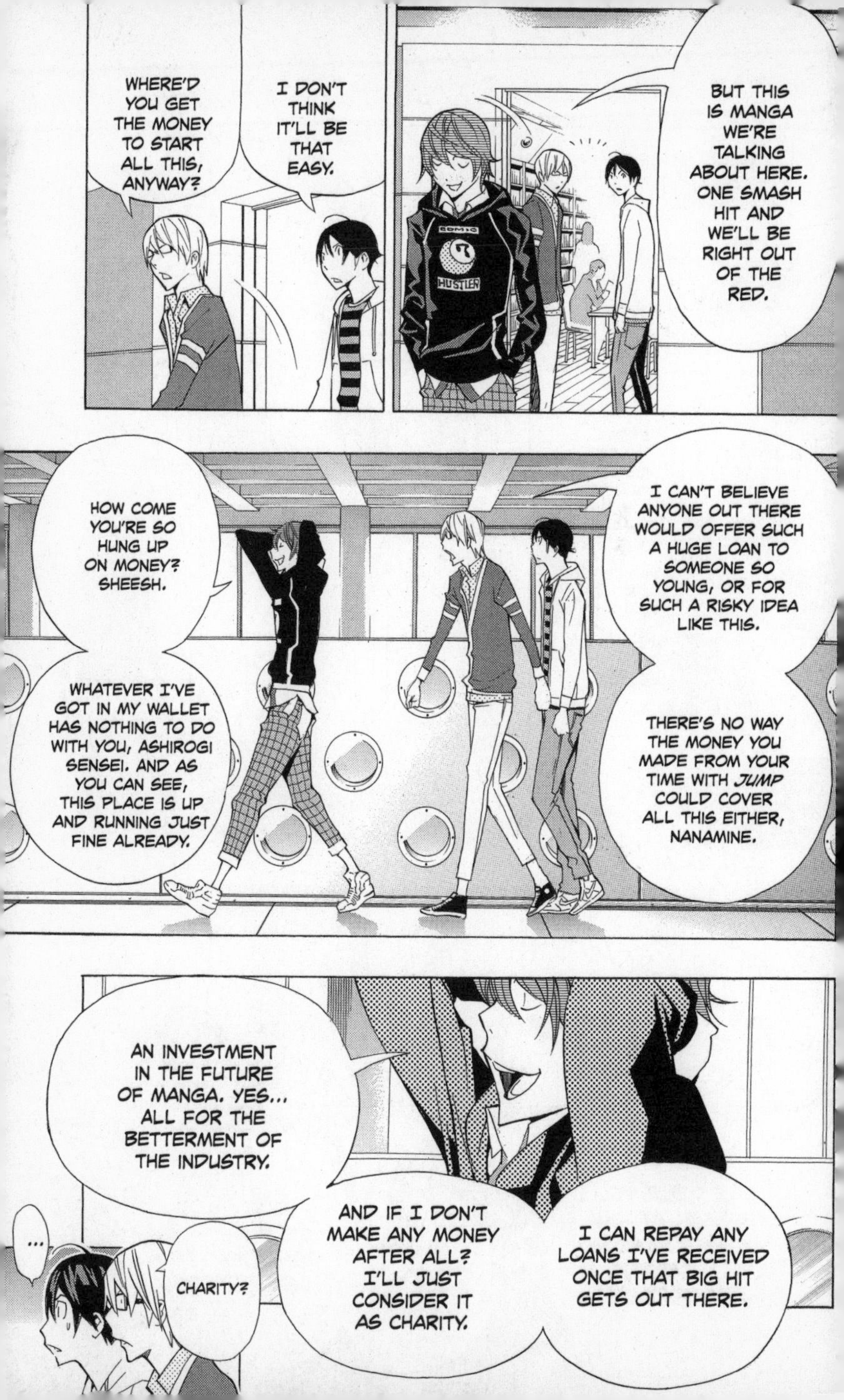
BUT THIS IS MANGA WE'RE TALKING ABOUT HERE. ONE SMASH HIT AND WE'LL BE RIGHT OUT OF THE RED.
I DON'T THINK IT'LL BE THAT EASY.
WHERE'D YOU GET THE MONEY TO START ALL THIS, ANYWAY?
I CAN'T BELIEVE ANYONE OUT THERE WOULD OFFER SUCH A HUGE LOAN TO SOMEONE SO YOUNG, OR FOR SUCH A RISKY IDEA LIKE THIS.
THERE'S NO WAY THE MONEY YOU MADE FROM YOUR TIME WITH *JUMP* COULD COVER ALL THIS EITHER, NANAMINE.
HOW COME YOU'RE SO HUNG UP ON MONEY? SHEESH.
WHATEVER I'VE GOT IN MY WALLET HAS NOTHING TO DO WITH YOU, ASHIROGI SENSEI. AND AS YOU CAN SEE, THIS PLACE IS UP AND RUNNING JUST FINE ALREADY.
AN INVESTMENT IN THE FUTURE OF MANGA. YES... ALL FOR THE BETTERMENT OF THE INDUSTRY.
I CAN REPAY ANY LOANS I'VE RECEIVED ONCE THAT BIG HIT GETS OUT THERE.
AND IF I DON'T MAKE ANY MONEY AFTER ALL? I'LL JUST CONSIDER IT AS CHARITY.
CHARITY?
...

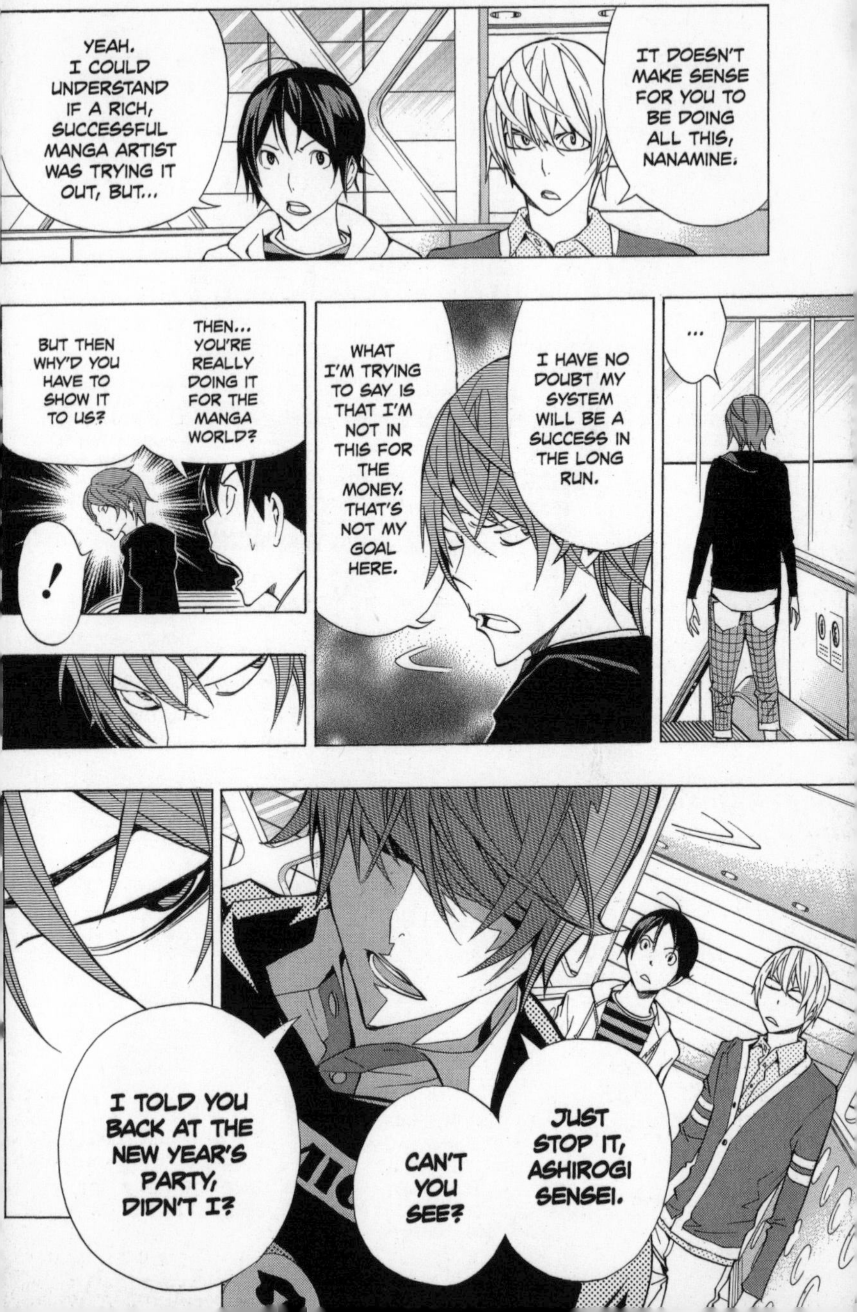
IT DOESN'T MAKE SENSE FOR YOU TO BE DOING ALL THIS, NANAMINE.
YEAH. I COULD UNDERSTAND IF A RICH, SUCCESSFUL MANGA ARTIST WAS TRYING IT OUT, BUT...
...
I HAVE NO DOUBT MY SYSTEM WILL BE A SUCCESS IN THE LONG RUN.
WHAT I'M TRYING TO SAY IS THAT I'M NOT IN THIS FOR THE MONEY. THAT'S NOT MY GOAL HERE.
THEN... YOU'RE REALLY DOING IT FOR THE MANGA WORLD?
BUT THEN WHY'D YOU HAVE TO SHOW IT TO US?
!
JUST STOP IT, ASHIROGI SENSEI.
CAN'T YOU SEE?
I TOLD YOU BACK AT THE NEW YEAR'S PARTY, DIDN'T I?

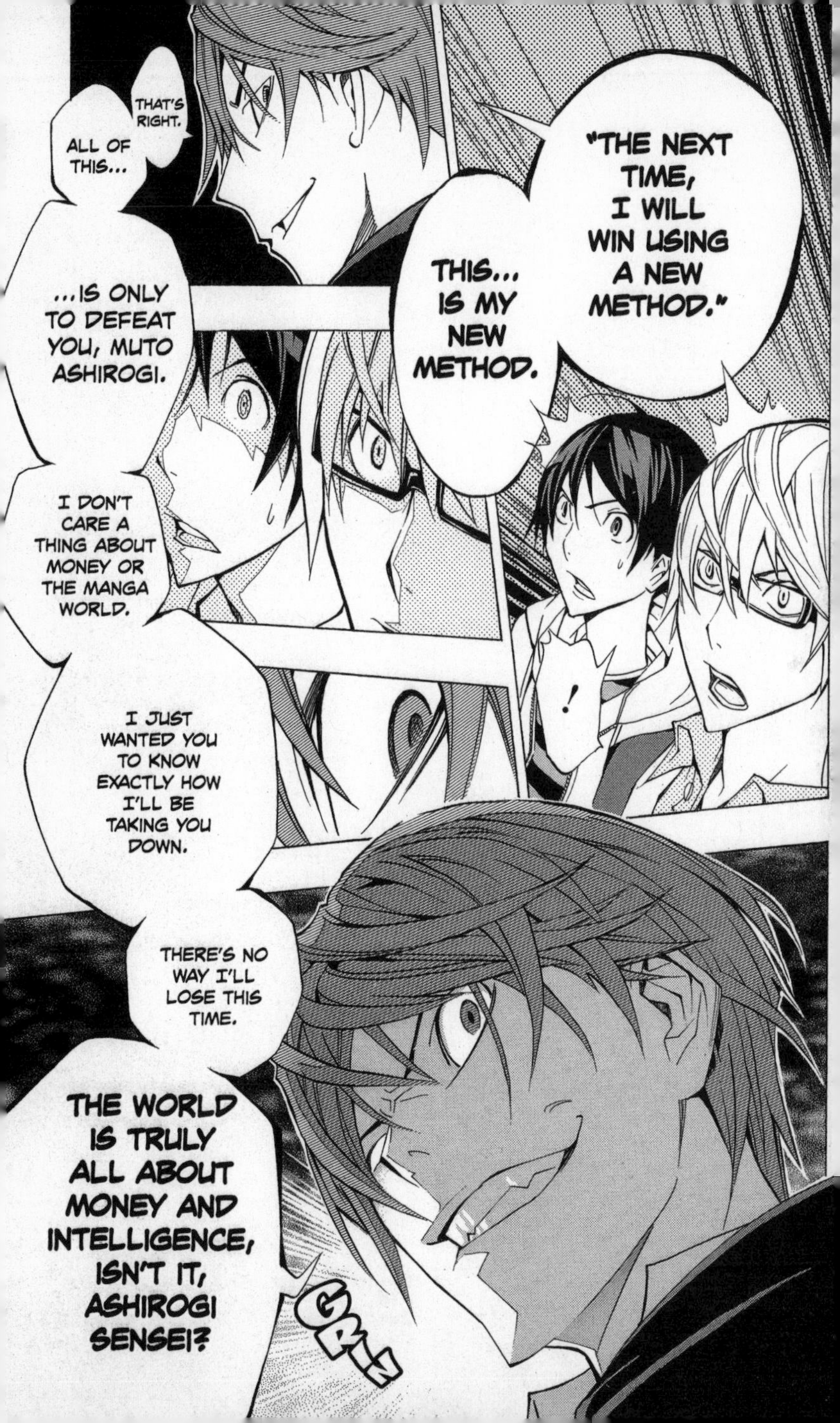
"THE NEXT TIME, I WILL WIN USING A NEW METHOD."
THIS... IS MY NEW METHOD.
THAT'S RIGHT.
ALL OF THIS...
...IS ONLY TO DEFEAT YOU, MUTO ASHIROGI.
!
I DON'T CARE A THING ABOUT MONEY OR THE MANGA WORLD.
I JUST WANTED YOU TO KNOW EXACTLY HOW I'LL BE TAKING YOU DOWN.
THERE'S NO WAY I'LL LOSE THIS TIME.
THE WORLD IS TRULY ALL ABOUT MONEY AND INTELLIGENCE, ISN'T IT, ASHIROGI SENSEI?

OHBA'S STORYBOARD

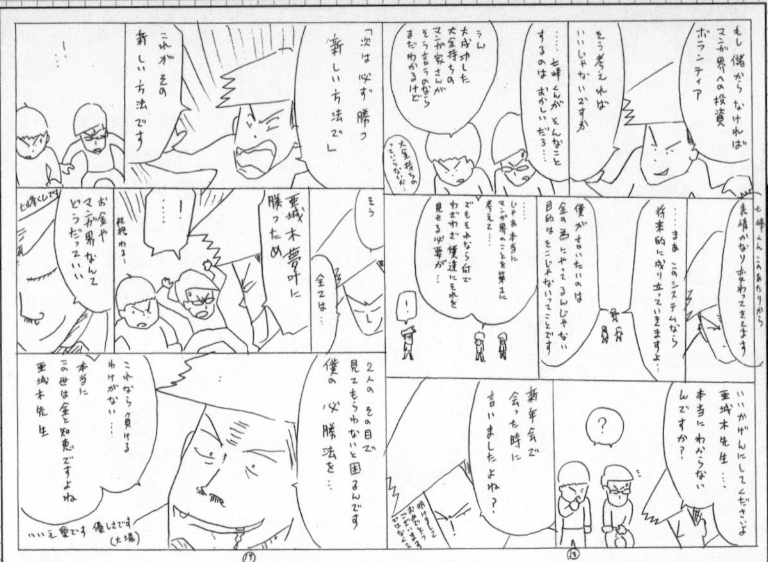
もし儲からなければマンガ界への投資ボランティア
そう考えればいいじゃないですか
……七峰くんがそんなことするのはおかしいだろ……
うん大成功した大金持ちのマンガ家さんがそう言うのならまだわかるけど
七峰くんこのあたりから表情がかなり変わってきてます
……まぁこのシステムなら将来的に成り立っていきますよ…
僕が言いたいのは金の為にやってるんじゃない目的はそこじゃないってことです
じゃあ本当にマンガ界のことを第1に考えて…
でもそれなら何でわざわざ僕達にそれを見せる必要が…
!
いいかげんにしてくださいよ亜城木先生…
本当にわからないんですか?
?
新年会で会った時に言いましたよね?
!
18
「次は必ず勝つ新しい方法で」
これがその新しい方法です
!……
そう
全ては…
亜城木夢叶に勝つため
!
……
お金やマンガ界なんてどうだっていい
2人のその目で見てもらわないと困るんです僕の必勝法を…
これなら負けるわけがない…
本当にこの世は金と知恵ですよね亜城木先生
いい表情です 優しさです (大場)
19

OBATA'S STORYBOARD

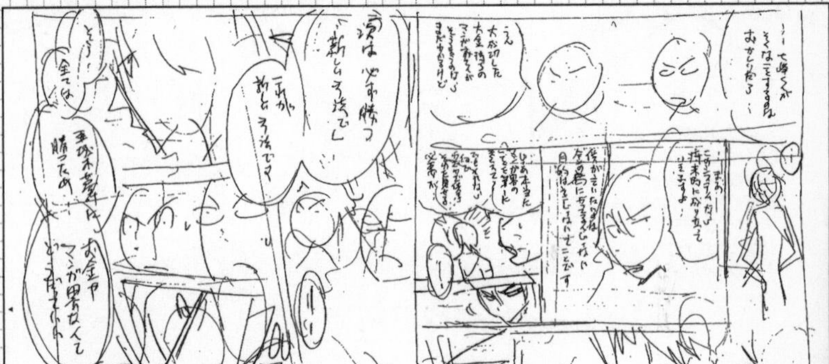

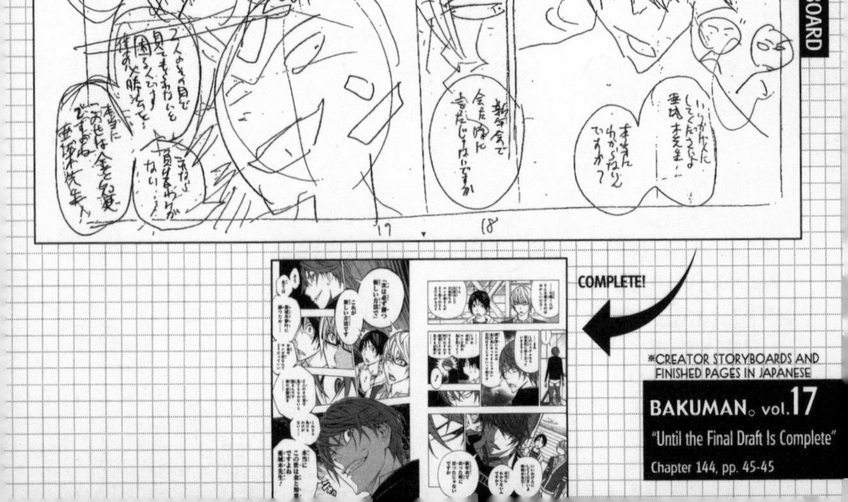

COMPLETE!

※CREATOR STORYBOARDS AND FINISHED PAGES IN JAPANESE

BAKUMAN。vol.17

"Until the Final Draft Is Complete"

Chapter 144, pp. 45-45

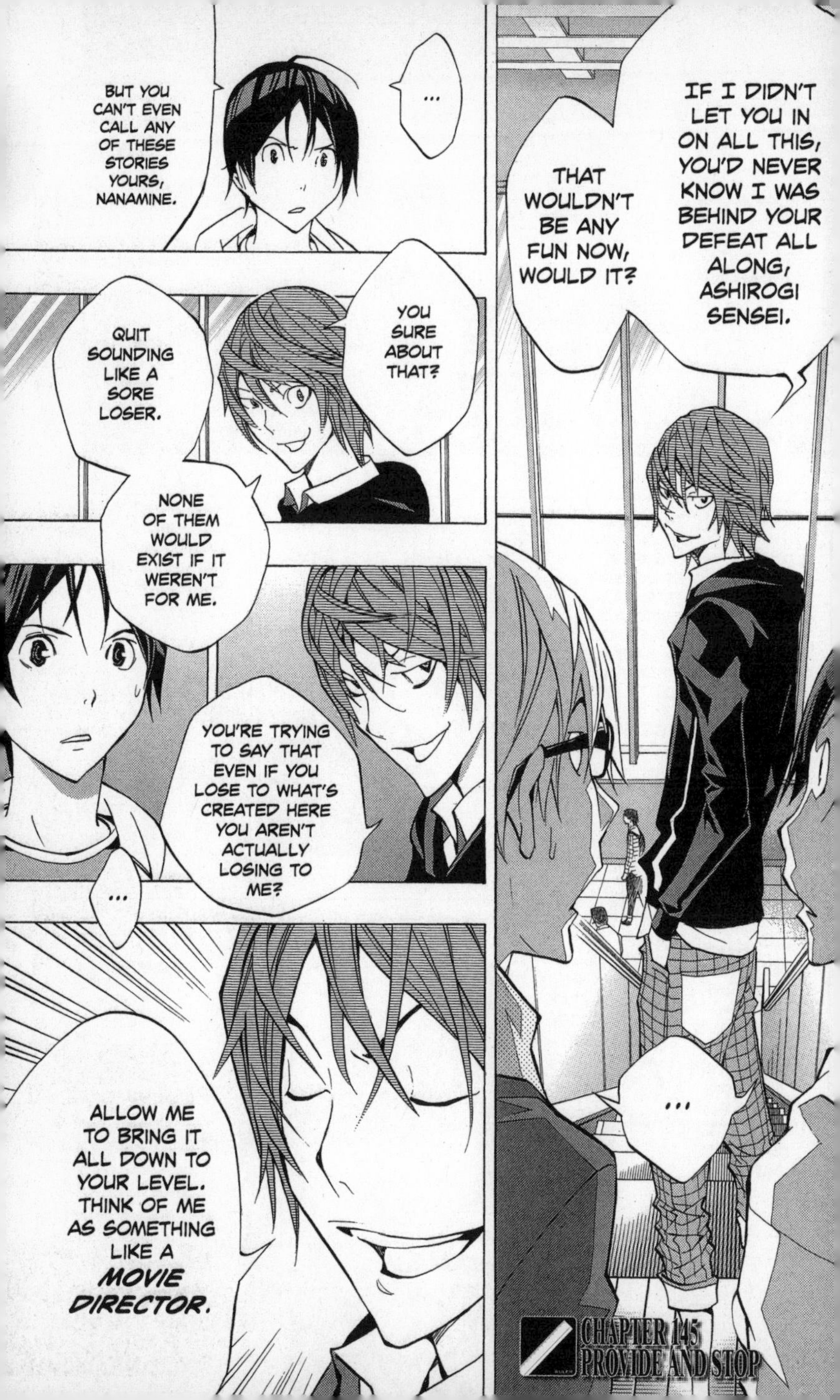
IF I DIDN'T LET YOU IN ON ALL THIS, YOU'D NEVER KNOW I WAS BEHIND YOUR DEFEAT ALL ALONG, ASHIROGI SENSEI.
THAT WOULDN'T BE ANY FUN NOW, WOULD IT?
...
CHAPTER 145 PROVIDE AND STOP
...
BUT YOU CAN'T EVEN CALL ANY OF THESE STORIES YOURS, NANAMINE.
YOU SURE ABOUT THAT?
QUIT SOUNDING LIKE A SORE LOSER.
NONE OF THEM WOULD EXIST IF IT WEREN'T FOR ME.
YOU'RE TRYING TO SAY THAT EVEN IF YOU LOSE TO WHAT'S CREATED HERE YOU AREN'T ACTUALLY LOSING TO ME?
...
ALLOW ME TO BRING IT ALL DOWN TO YOUR LEVEL. THINK OF ME AS SOMETHING LIKE A MOVIE DIRECTOR.

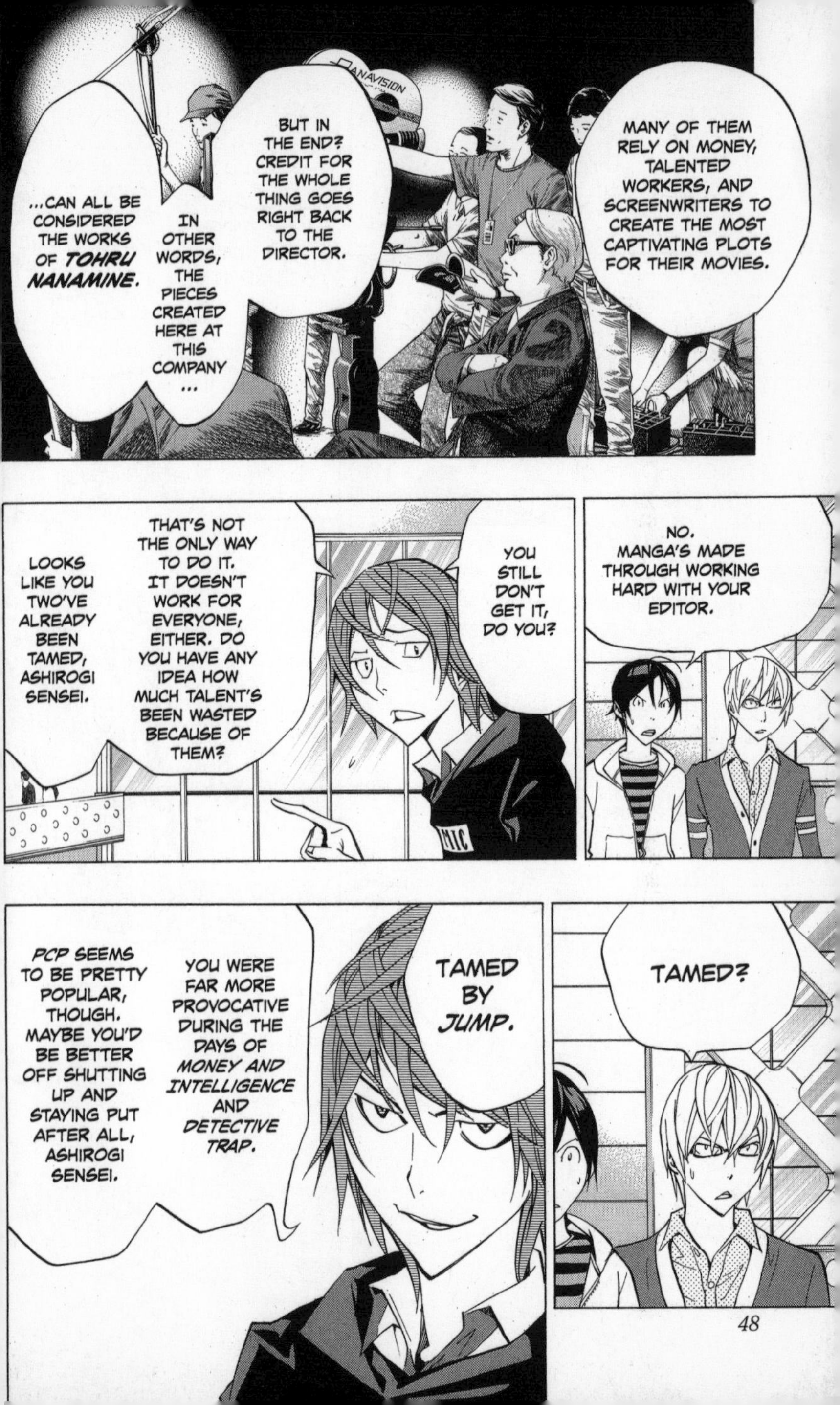
MANY OF THEM RELY ON MONEY, TALENTED WORKERS, AND SCREENWRITERS TO CREATE THE MOST CAPTIVATING PLOTS FOR THEIR MOVIES.
BUT IN THE END? CREDIT FOR THE WHOLE THING GOES RIGHT BACK TO THE DIRECTOR.
IN OTHER WORDS, THE PIECES CREATED HERE AT THIS COMPANY...
...CAN ALL BE CONSIDERED THE WORKS OF *TOHRU NANAMINE*.
NO. MANGA'S MADE THROUGH WORKING HARD WITH YOUR EDITOR.
YOU STILL DON'T GET IT, DO YOU?
THAT'S NOT THE ONLY WAY TO DO IT. IT DOESN'T WORK FOR EVERYONE, EITHER. DO YOU HAVE ANY IDEA HOW MUCH TALENT'S BEEN WASTED BECAUSE OF THEM?
LOOKS LIKE YOU TWO'VE ALREADY BEEN TAMED, ASHIROGI SENSEI.
TAMED?
TAMED BY *JUMP*.
YOU WERE FAR MORE PROVOCATIVE DURING THE DAYS OF *MONEY AND INTELLIGENCE* AND *DETECTIVE TRAP*.
PCP SEEMS TO BE PRETTY POPULAR, THOUGH. MAYBE YOU'D BE BETTER OFF SHUTTING UP AND STAYING PUT AFTER ALL, ASHIROGI SENSEI.

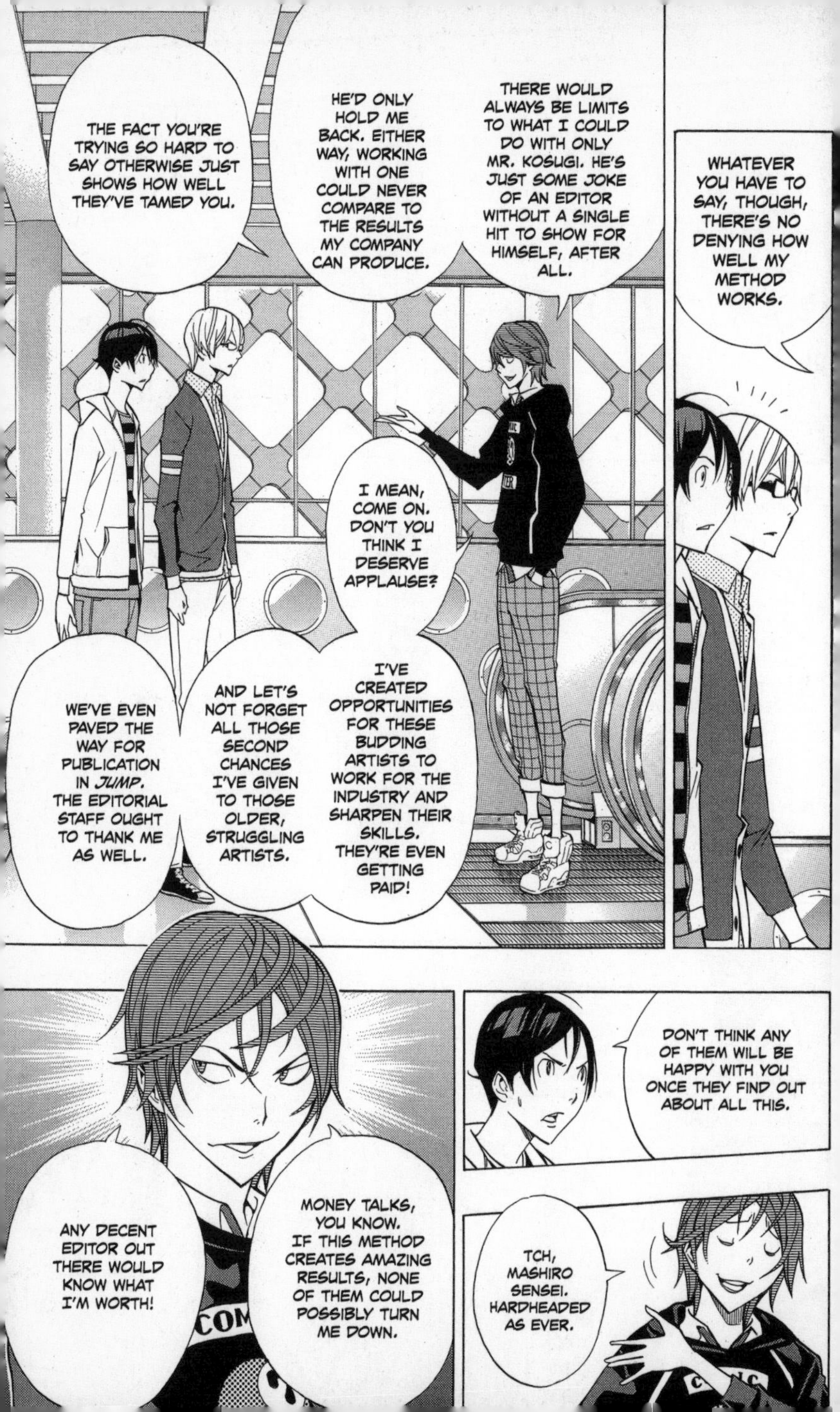
WHATEVER YOU HAVE TO SAY, THOUGH, THERE'S NO DENYING HOW WELL MY METHOD WORKS.
THERE WOULD ALWAYS BE LIMITS TO WHAT I COULD DO WITH ONLY MR. KOSUGI. HE'S JUST SOME JOKE OF AN EDITOR WITHOUT A SINGLE HIT TO SHOW FOR HIMSELF, AFTER ALL.
HE'D ONLY HOLD ME BACK. EITHER WAY, WORKING WITH ONE COULD NEVER COMPARE TO THE RESULTS MY COMPANY CAN PRODUCE.
THE FACT YOU'RE TRYING SO HARD TO SAY OTHERWISE JUST SHOWS HOW WELL THEY'VE TAMED YOU.
I MEAN, COME ON. DON'T YOU THINK I DESERVE APPLAUSE?
I'VE CREATED OPPORTUNITIES FOR THESE BUDDING ARTISTS TO WORK FOR THE INDUSTRY AND SHARPEN THEIR SKILLS. THEY'RE EVEN GETTING PAID!
AND LET'S NOT FORGET ALL THOSE SECOND CHANCES I'VE GIVEN TO THOSE OLDER, STRUGGLING ARTISTS.
WE'VE EVEN PAVED THE WAY FOR PUBLICATION IN *JUMP*. THE EDITORIAL STAFF OUGHT TO THANK ME AS WELL.
DON'T THINK ANY OF THEM WILL BE HAPPY WITH YOU ONCE THEY FIND OUT ABOUT ALL THIS.
TCH, MASHIRO SENSEI. HARDHEADED AS EVER.
MONEY TALKS, YOU KNOW. IF THIS METHOD CREATES AMAZING RESULTS, NONE OF THEM COULD POSSIBLY TURN ME DOWN.
ANY DECENT EDITOR OUT THERE WOULD KNOW WHAT I'M WORTH!

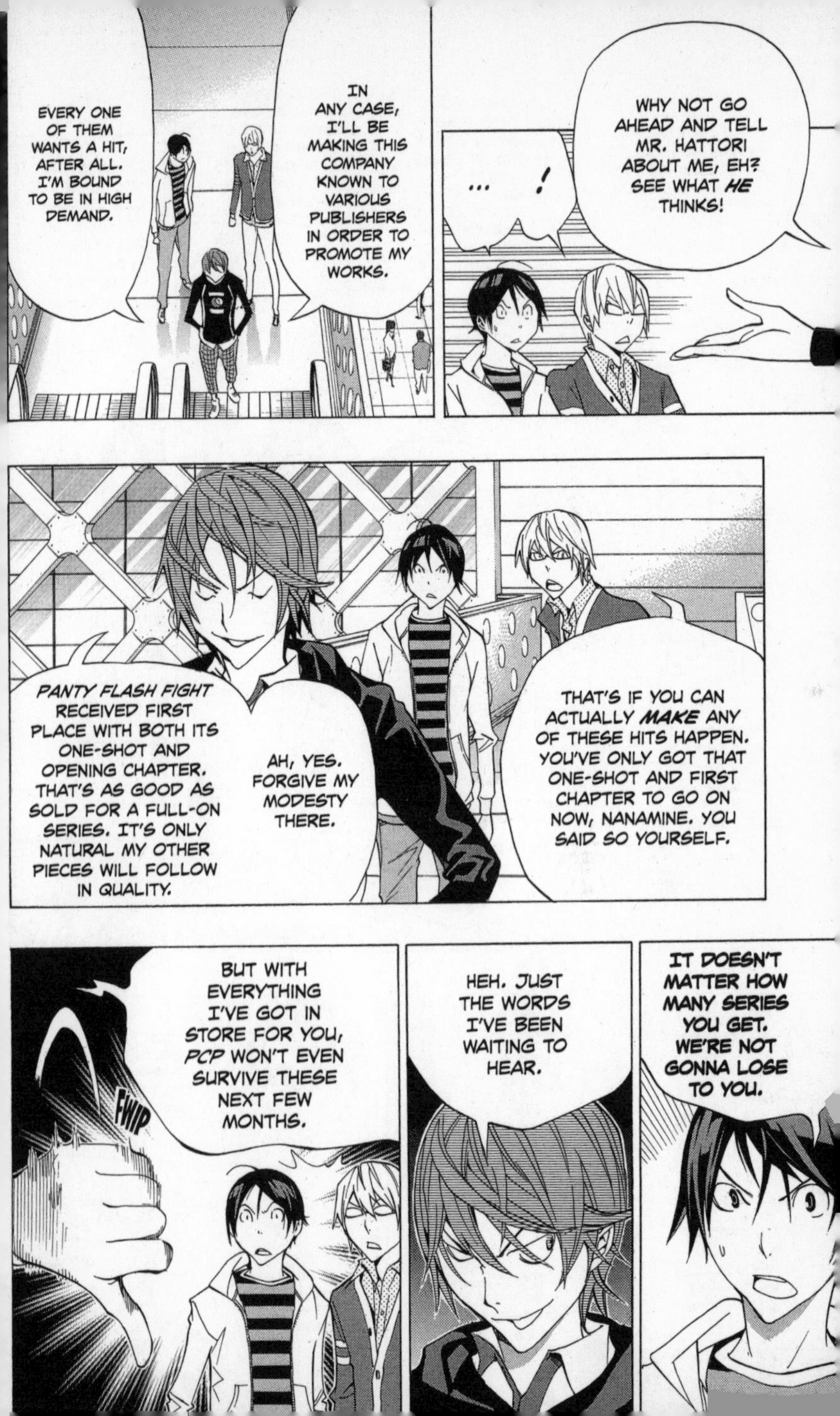
WHY NOT GO AHEAD AND TELL MR. HATTORI ABOUT ME, EH? SEE WHAT *HE* THINKS!
... !
IN ANY CASE, I'LL BE MAKING THIS COMPANY KNOWN TO VARIOUS PUBLISHERS IN ORDER TO PROMOTE MY WORKS.
EVERY ONE OF THEM WANTS A HIT, AFTER ALL. I'M BOUND TO BE IN HIGH DEMAND.
THAT'S IF YOU CAN ACTUALLY *MAKE* ANY OF THESE HITS HAPPEN. YOU'VE ONLY GOT THAT ONE-SHOT AND FIRST CHAPTER TO GO ON NOW, NANAMINE. YOU SAID SO YOURSELF.
AH, YES. FORGIVE MY MODESTY THERE.
PANTY FLASH FIGHT RECEIVED FIRST PLACE WITH BOTH ITS ONE-SHOT AND OPENING CHAPTER. THAT'S AS GOOD AS SOLD FOR A FULL-ON SERIES. IT'S ONLY NATURAL MY OTHER PIECES WILL FOLLOW IN QUALITY.
IT DOESN'T MATTER HOW MANY SERIES YOU GET. WE'RE NOT GONNA LOSE TO YOU.
HEH. JUST THE WORDS I'VE BEEN WAITING TO HEAR.
BUT WITH EVERYTHING I'VE GOT IN STORE FOR YOU, *PCP* WON'T EVEN SURVIVE THESE NEXT FEW MONTHS.
FWIP

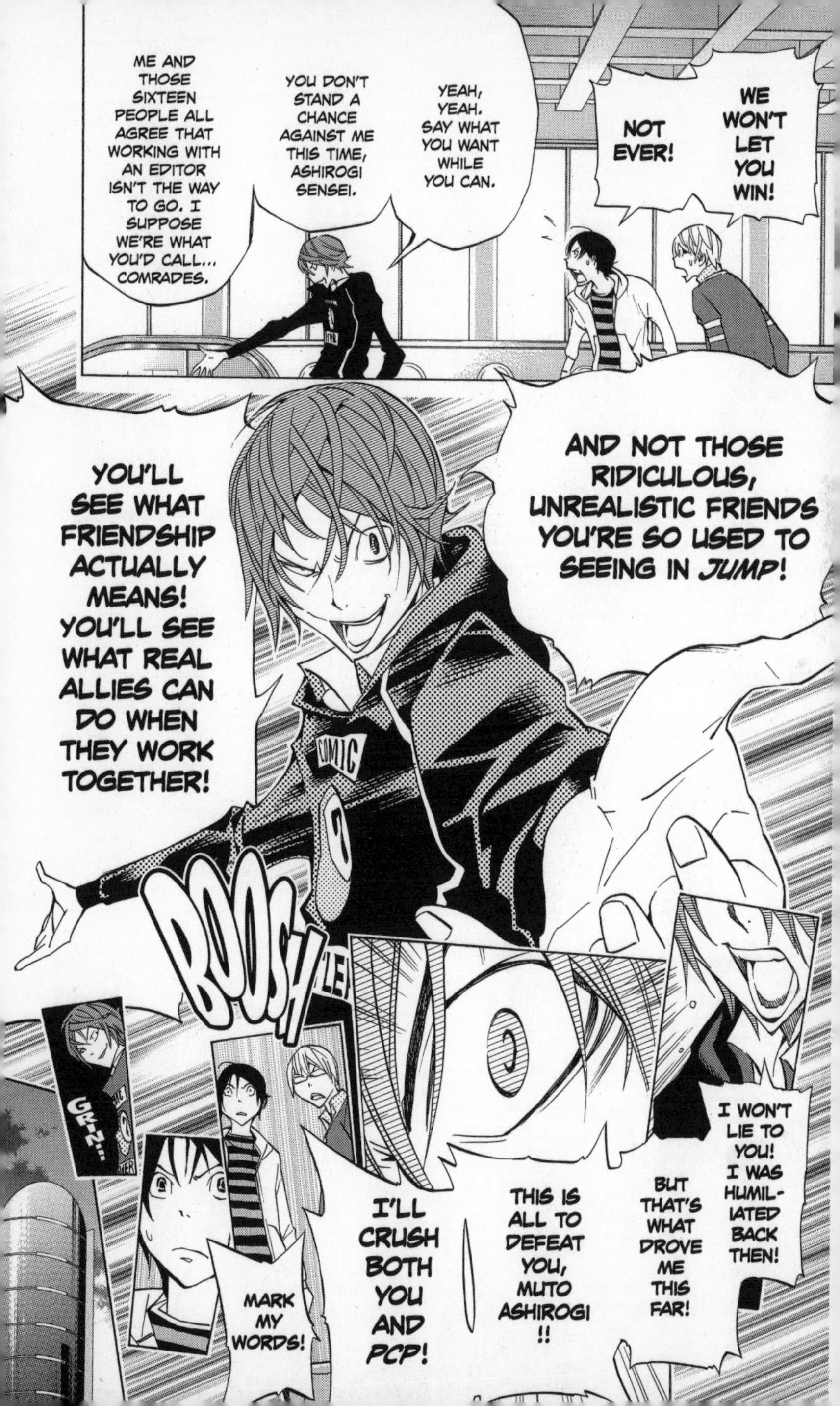
WE WON'T LET YOU WIN!
NOT EVER!
YEAH, YEAH. SAY WHAT YOU WANT WHILE YOU CAN.
YOU DON'T STAND A CHANCE AGAINST ME THIS TIME, ASHIROGI SENSEI.
ME AND THOSE SIXTEEN PEOPLE ALL AGREE THAT WORKING WITH AN EDITOR ISN'T THE WAY TO GO. I SUPPOSE WE'RE WHAT YOU'D CALL... COMRADES.
AND NOT THOSE RIDICULOUS, UNREALISTIC FRIENDS YOU'RE SO USED TO SEEING IN *JUMP*!
YOU'LL SEE WHAT FRIENDSHIP ACTUALLY MEANS! YOU'LL SEE WHAT REAL ALLIES CAN DO WHEN THEY WORK TOGETHER!
BOOSH
I WON'T LIE TO YOU! I WAS HUMIL-IATED BACK THEN!
BUT THAT'S WHAT DROVE ME THIS FAR!
THIS IS ALL TO DEFEAT YOU, MUTO ASHIROGI !!
I'LL CRUSH BOTH YOU AND *PCP*!
MARK MY WORDS!
GRIN...

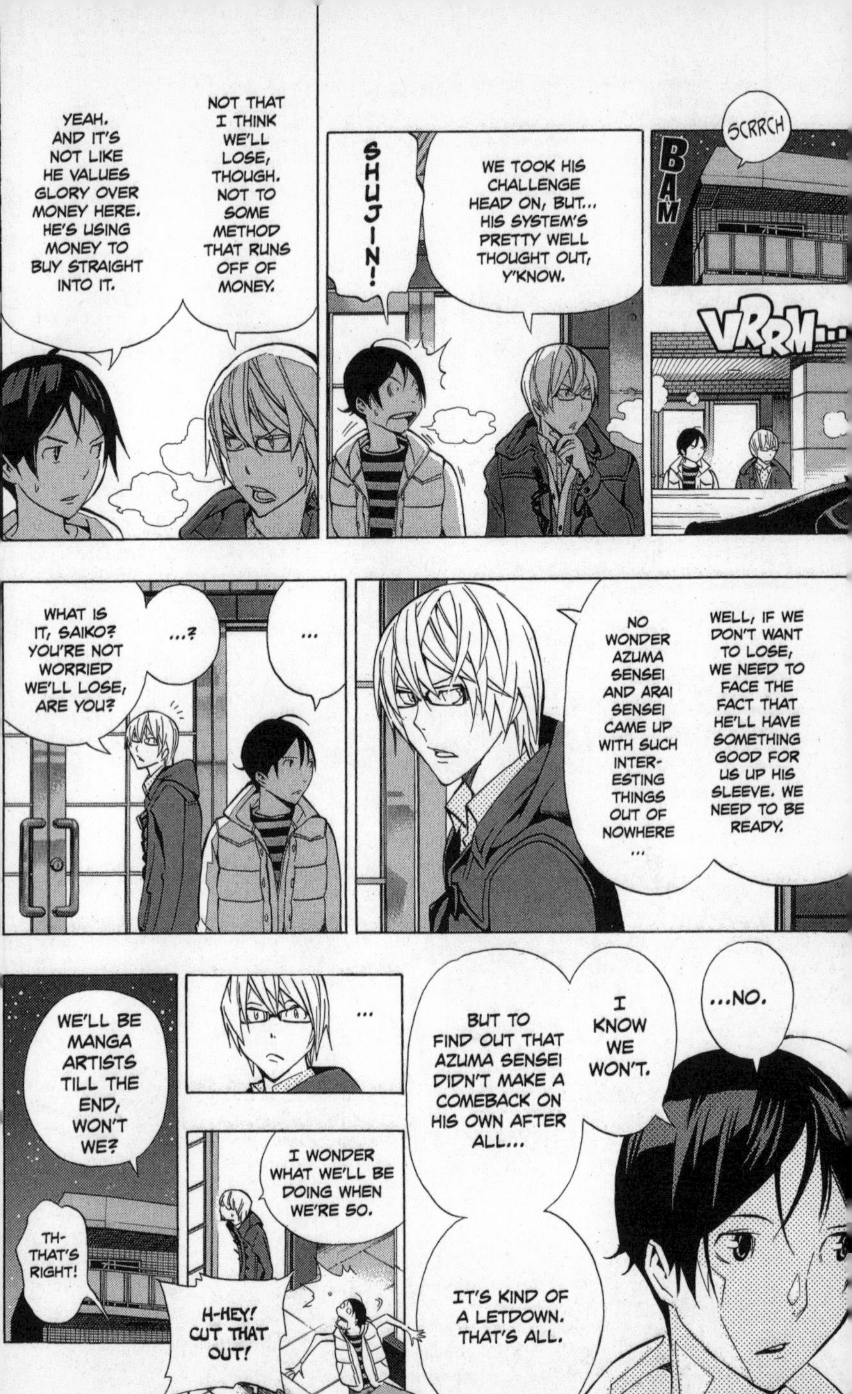
SCRRCH
BAM
VRRM...
WE TOOK HIS CHALLENGE HEAD ON, BUT... HIS SYSTEM'S PRETTY WELL THOUGHT OUT, Y'KNOW.
SHUJIN!
NOT THAT I THINK WE'LL LOSE, THOUGH. NOT TO SOME METHOD THAT RUNS OFF OF MONEY.
YEAH. AND IT'S NOT LIKE HE VALUES GLORY OVER MONEY HERE. HE'S USING MONEY TO BUY STRAIGHT INTO IT.
WELL, IF WE DON'T WANT TO LOSE, WE NEED TO FACE THE FACT THAT HE'LL HAVE SOMETHING GOOD FOR US UP HIS SLEEVE. WE NEED TO BE READY.
NO WONDER AZUMA SENSEI AND ARAI SENSEI CAME UP WITH SUCH INTER-ESTING THINGS OUT OF NOWHERE ...
...
...?
WHAT IS IT, SAIKO? YOU'RE NOT WORRIED WE'LL LOSE, ARE YOU?
...NO.
I KNOW WE WON'T.
BUT TO FIND OUT THAT AZUMA SENSEI DIDN'T MAKE A COMEBACK ON HIS OWN AFTER ALL...
IT'S KIND OF A LETDOWN. THAT'S ALL.
...
I WONDER WHAT WE'LL BE DOING WHEN WE'RE 50.
H-HEY! CUT THAT OUT!
WE'LL BE MANGA ARTISTS TILL THE END, WON'T WE?
TH- THAT'S RIGHT!

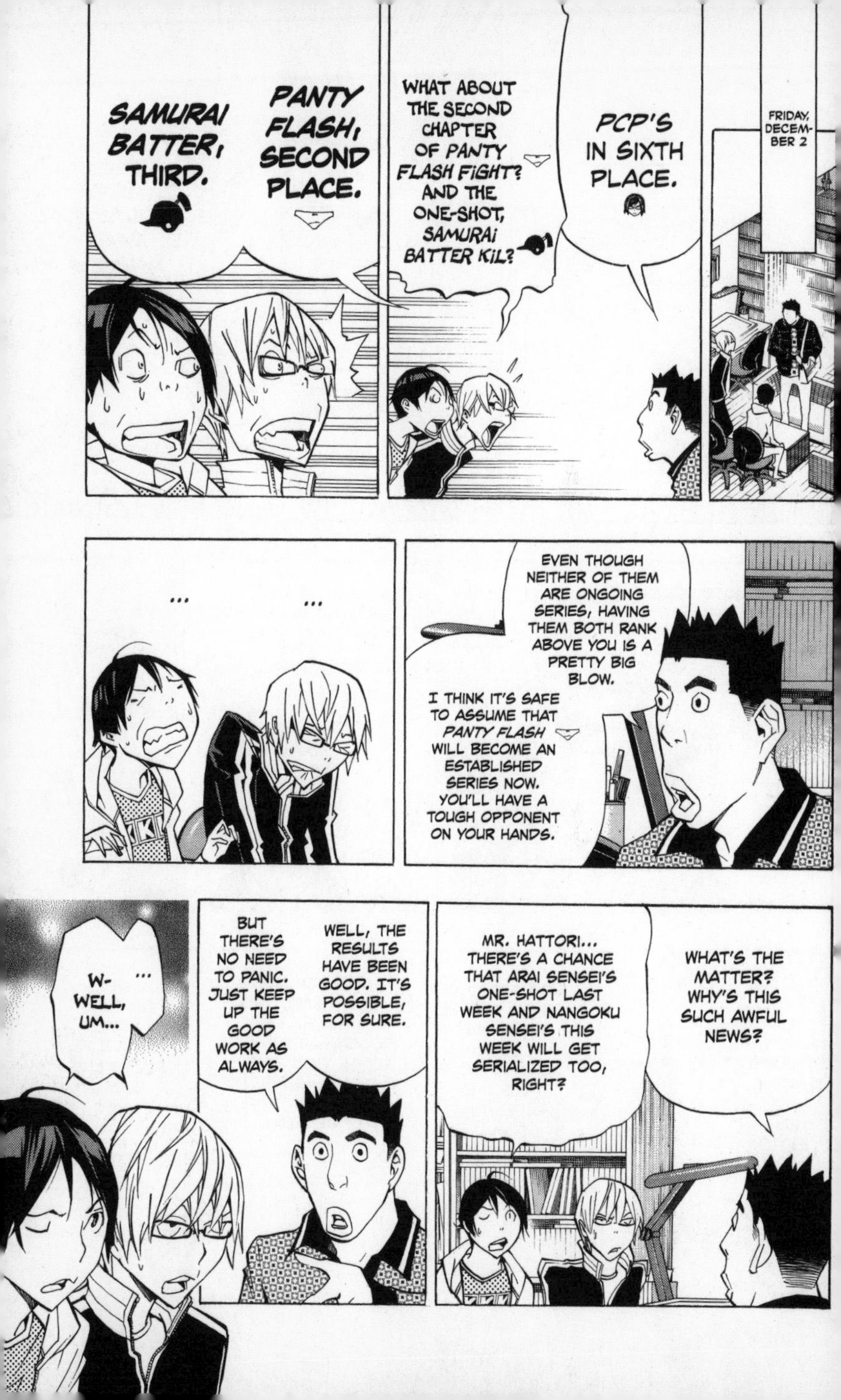
FRIDAY, DECEMBER 2
PCP'S IN SIXTH PLACE.
WHAT ABOUT THE SECOND CHAPTER OF *PANTY FLASH FIGHT*? AND THE ONE-SHOT, *SAMURAI BATTER KIL*?
PANTY FLASH, SECOND PLACE.
SAMURAI BATTER, THIRD.
EVEN THOUGH NEITHER OF THEM ARE ONGOING SERIES, HAVING THEM BOTH RANK ABOVE YOU IS A PRETTY BIG BLOW.
I THINK IT'S SAFE TO ASSUME THAT *PANTY FLASH* WILL BECOME AN ESTABLISHED SERIES NOW. YOU'LL HAVE A TOUGH OPPONENT ON YOUR HANDS.
...
...
WHAT'S THE MATTER? WHY'S THIS SUCH AWFUL NEWS?
MR. HATTORI... THERE'S A CHANCE THAT ARAI SENSEI'S ONE-SHOT LAST WEEK AND NANGOKU SENSEI'S THIS WEEK WILL GET SERIALIZED TOO, RIGHT?
WELL, THE RESULTS HAVE BEEN GOOD. IT'S POSSIBLE, FOR SURE.
BUT THERE'S NO NEED TO PANIC. JUST KEEP UP THE GOOD WORK AS ALWAYS.
...
W-WELL, UM...

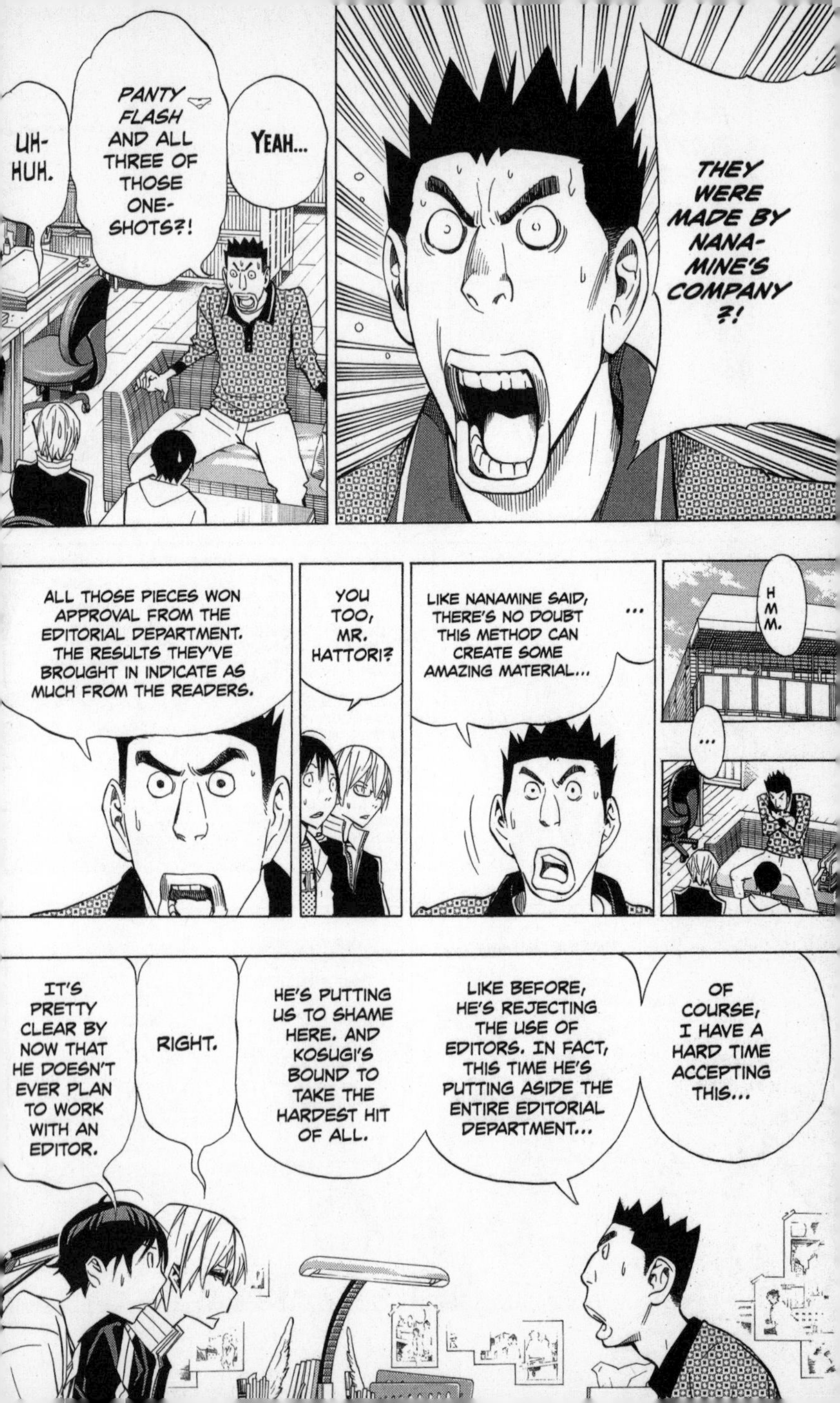
THEY WERE MADE BY NANAMINE'S COMPANY?!
YEAH...
PANTY FLASH AND ALL THREE OF THOSE ONE-SHOTS?!
UH-HUH.
HMM.
...
...
LIKE NANAMINE SAID, THERE'S NO DOUBT THIS METHOD CAN CREATE SOME AMAZING MATERIAL...
YOU TOO, MR. HATTORI?
ALL THOSE PIECES WON APPROVAL FROM THE EDITORIAL DEPARTMENT. THE RESULTS THEY'VE BROUGHT IN INDICATE AS MUCH FROM THE READERS.
OF COURSE, I HAVE A HARD TIME ACCEPTING THIS...
LIKE BEFORE, HE'S REJECTING THE USE OF EDITORS. IN FACT, THIS TIME HE'S PUTTING ASIDE THE ENTIRE EDITORIAL DEPARTMENT...
HE'S PUTTING US TO SHAME HERE. AND KOSUGI'S BOUND TO TAKE THE HARDEST HIT OF ALL.
RIGHT.
IT'S PRETTY CLEAR BY NOW THAT HE DOESN'T EVER PLAN TO WORK WITH AN EDITOR.

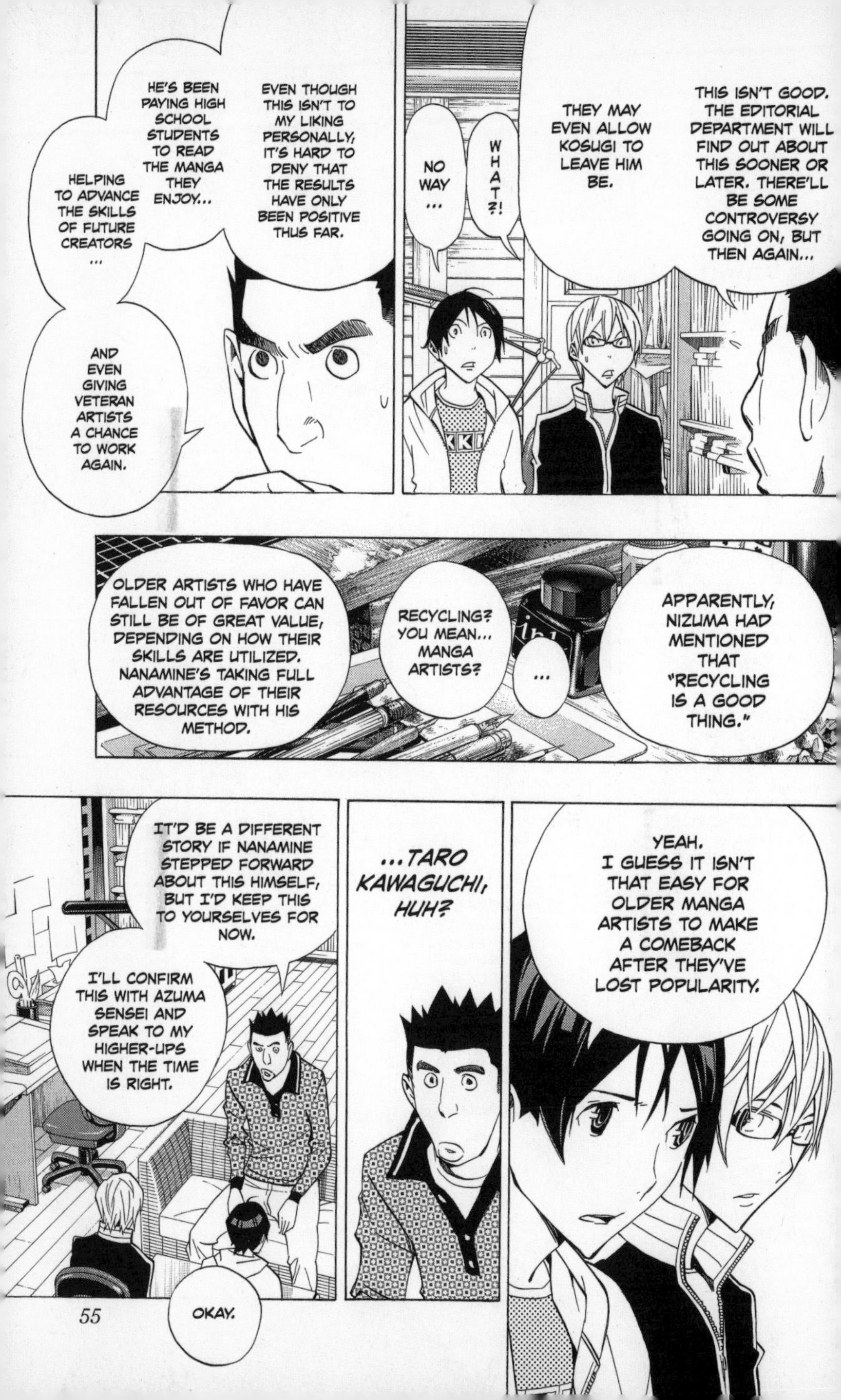
THIS ISN'T GOOD. THE EDITORIAL DEPARTMENT WILL FIND OUT ABOUT THIS SOONER OR LATER. THERE'LL BE SOME CONTROVERSY GOING ON, BUT THEN AGAIN...
THEY MAY EVEN ALLOW KOSUGI TO LEAVE HIM BE.
WHAT?!
NO WAY...
EVEN THOUGH THIS ISN'T TO MY LIKING PERSONALLY, IT'S HARD TO DENY THAT THE RESULTS HAVE ONLY BEEN POSITIVE THUS FAR.
HE'S BEEN PAYING HIGH SCHOOL STUDENTS TO READ THE MANGA THEY ENJOY...
HELPING TO ADVANCE THE SKILLS OF FUTURE CREATORS...
AND EVEN GIVING VETERAN ARTISTS A CHANCE TO WORK AGAIN.
APPARENTLY, NIZUMA HAD MENTIONED THAT "RECYCLING IS A GOOD THING."
...
RECYCLING? YOU MEAN... MANGA ARTISTS?
OLDER ARTISTS WHO HAVE FALLEN OUT OF FAVOR CAN STILL BE OF GREAT VALUE, DEPENDING ON HOW THEIR SKILLS ARE UTILIZED. NANAMINE'S TAKING FULL ADVANTAGE OF THEIR RESOURCES WITH HIS METHOD.
YEAH. I GUESS IT ISN'T THAT EASY FOR OLDER MANGA ARTISTS TO MAKE A COMEBACK AFTER THEY'VE LOST POPULARITY.
...TARO KAWAGUCHI, HUH?
IT'D BE A DIFFERENT STORY IF NANAMINE STEPPED FORWARD ABOUT THIS HIMSELF, BUT I'D KEEP THIS TO YOURSELVES FOR NOW.
I'LL CONFIRM THIS WITH AZUMA SENSEI AND SPEAK TO MY HIGHER-UPS WHEN THE TIME IS RIGHT.
OKAY.

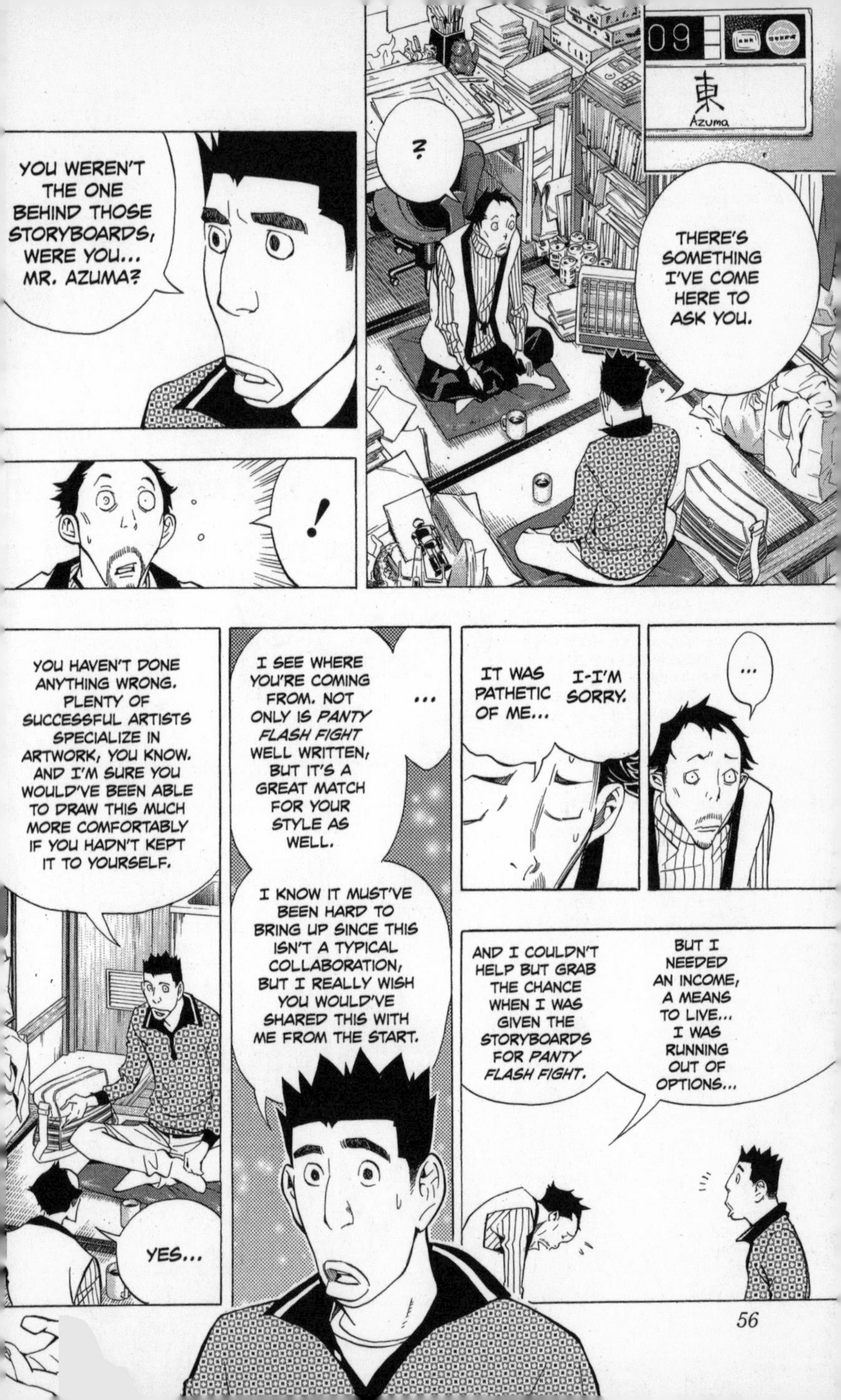
09
東
Azuma
?
THERE'S SOMETHING I'VE COME HERE TO ASK YOU.
YOU WEREN'T THE ONE BEHIND THOSE STORYBOARDS, WERE YOU... MR. AZUMA?
!
...
I-I'M SORRY.
IT WAS PATHETIC OF ME...
BUT I NEEDED AN INCOME, A MEANS TO LIVE... I WAS RUNNING OUT OF OPTIONS...
AND I COULDN'T HELP BUT GRAB THE CHANCE WHEN I WAS GIVEN THE STORYBOARDS FOR *PANTY FLASH FIGHT*.
...
I SEE WHERE YOU'RE COMING FROM. NOT ONLY IS *PANTY FLASH FIGHT* WELL WRITTEN, BUT IT'S A GREAT MATCH FOR YOUR STYLE AS WELL.
I KNOW IT MUST'VE BEEN HARD TO BRING UP SINCE THIS ISN'T A TYPICAL COLLABORATION, BUT I REALLY WISH YOU WOULD'VE SHARED THIS WITH ME FROM THE START.
YOU HAVEN'T DONE ANYTHING WRONG. PLENTY OF SUCCESSFUL ARTISTS SPECIALIZE IN ARTWORK, YOU KNOW. AND I'M SURE YOU WOULD'VE BEEN ABLE TO DRAW THIS MUCH MORE COMFORTABLY IF YOU HADN'T KEPT IT TO YOURSELF.
YES...

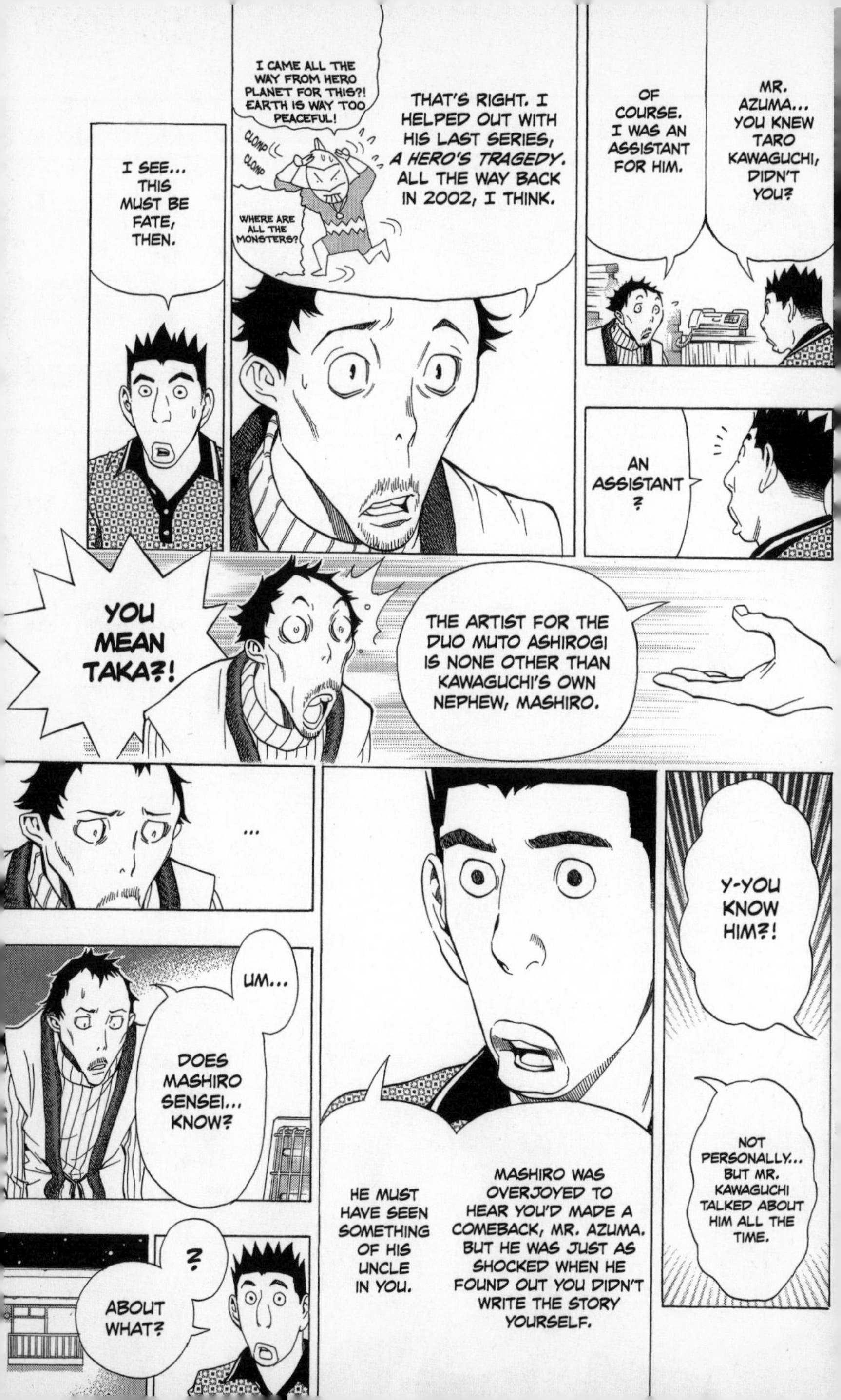
MR. AZUMA... YOU KNEW TARO KAWAGUCHI, DIDN'T YOU?
OF COURSE. I WAS AN ASSISTANT FOR HIM.
AN ASSISTANT?
THAT'S RIGHT. I HELPED OUT WITH HIS LAST SERIES, *A HERO'S TRAGEDY*. ALL THE WAY BACK IN 2002, I THINK.
I CAME ALL THE WAY FROM HERO PLANET FOR THIS?! EARTH IS WAY TOO PEACEFUL!
CLOMP
CLOMP
WHERE ARE ALL THE MONSTERS?
I SEE... THIS MUST BE FATE, THEN.
THE ARTIST FOR THE DUO MUTO ASHIROGI IS NONE OTHER THAN KAWAGUCHI'S OWN NEPHEW, MASHIRO.
YOU MEAN TAKA?!
Y-YOU KNOW HIM?!
NOT PERSONALLY... BUT MR. KAWAGUCHI TALKED ABOUT HIM ALL THE TIME.
MASHIRO WAS OVERJOYED TO HEAR YOU'D MADE A COMEBACK, MR. AZUMA. BUT HE WAS JUST AS SHOCKED WHEN HE FOUND OUT YOU DIDN'T WRITE THE STORY YOURSELF.
HE MUST HAVE SEEN SOMETHING OF HIS UNCLE IN YOU.
...
UM...
DOES MASHIRO SENSEI... KNOW?
?
ABOUT WHAT?

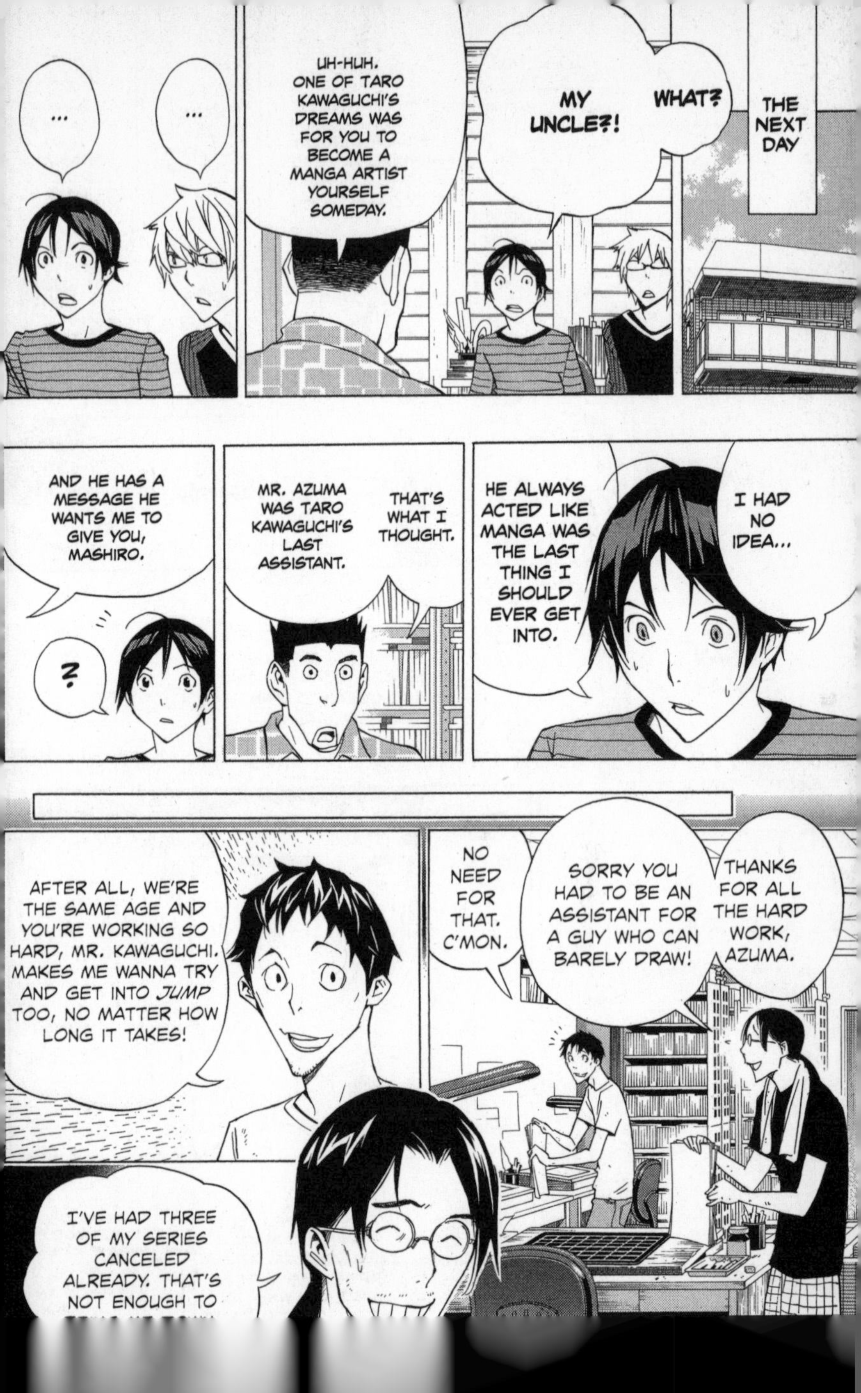

THE NEXT DAY
WHAT?
MY UNCLE?!
UH-HUH. ONE OF TARO KAWAGUCHI'S DREAMS WAS FOR YOU TO BECOME A MANGA ARTIST YOURSELF SOMEDAY.
...
...
I HAD NO IDEA...
HE ALWAYS ACTED LIKE MANGA WAS THE LAST THING I SHOULD EVER GET INTO.
THAT'S WHAT I THOUGHT.
MR. AZUMA WAS TARO KAWAGUCHI'S LAST ASSISTANT.
AND HE HAS A MESSAGE HE WANTS ME TO GIVE YOU, MASHIRO.
?
THANKS FOR ALL THE HARD WORK, AZUMA.
SORRY YOU HAD TO BE AN ASSISTANT FOR A GUY WHO CAN BARELY DRAW!
NO NEED FOR THAT. C'MON.
AFTER ALL, WE'RE THE SAME AGE AND YOU'RE WORKING SO HARD, MR. KAWAGUCHI. MAKES ME WANNA TRY AND GET INTO *JUMP* TOO, NO MATTER HOW LONG IT TAKES!
I'VE HAD THREE OF MY SERIES CANCELED ALREADY. THAT'S NOT ENOUGH TO

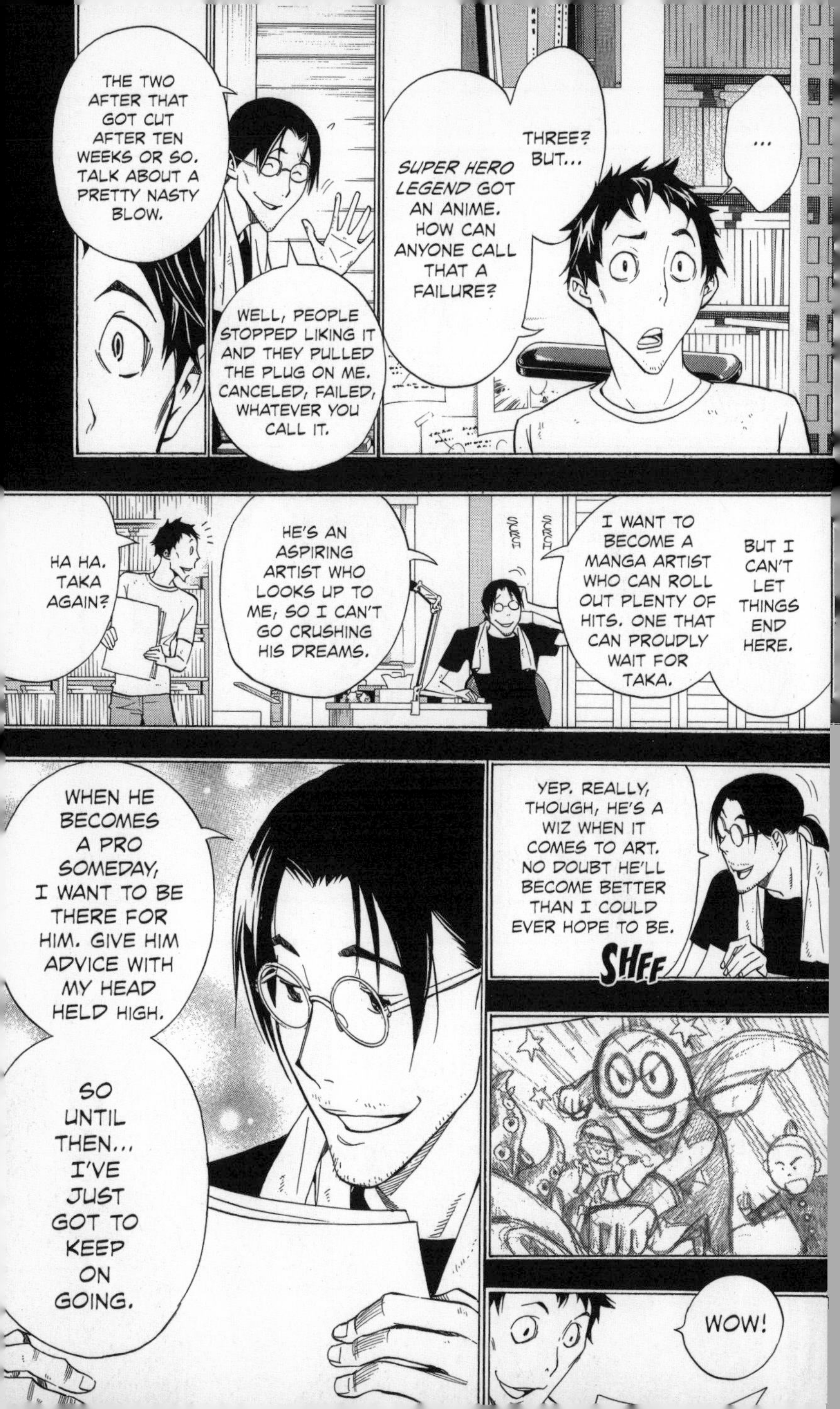
...
THREE? BUT...
SUPER HERO LEGEND GOT AN ANIME. HOW CAN ANYONE CALL THAT A FAILURE?
THE TWO AFTER THAT GOT CUT AFTER TEN WEEKS OR SO. TALK ABOUT A PRETTY NASTY BLOW.
WELL, PEOPLE STOPPED LIKING IT AND THEY PULLED THE PLUG ON ME. CANCELED, FAILED, WHATEVER YOU CALL IT.
BUT I CAN'T LET THINGS END HERE.
I WANT TO BECOME A MANGA ARTIST WHO CAN ROLL OUT PLENTY OF HITS. ONE THAT CAN PROUDLY WAIT FOR TAKA.
SCRCH
SCRCH
HE'S AN ASPIRING ARTIST WHO LOOKS UP TO ME, SO I CAN'T GO CRUSHING HIS DREAMS.
HA HA. TAKA AGAIN?
YEP. REALLY, THOUGH, HE'S A WIZ WHEN IT COMES TO ART. NO DOUBT HE'LL BECOME BETTER THAN I COULD EVER HOPE TO BE.
SHFF
WOW!
WHEN HE BECOMES A PRO SOMEDAY, I WANT TO BE THERE FOR HIM. GIVE HIM ADVICE WITH MY HEAD HELD HIGH.
SO UNTIL THEN... I'VE JUST GOT TO KEEP ON GOING.

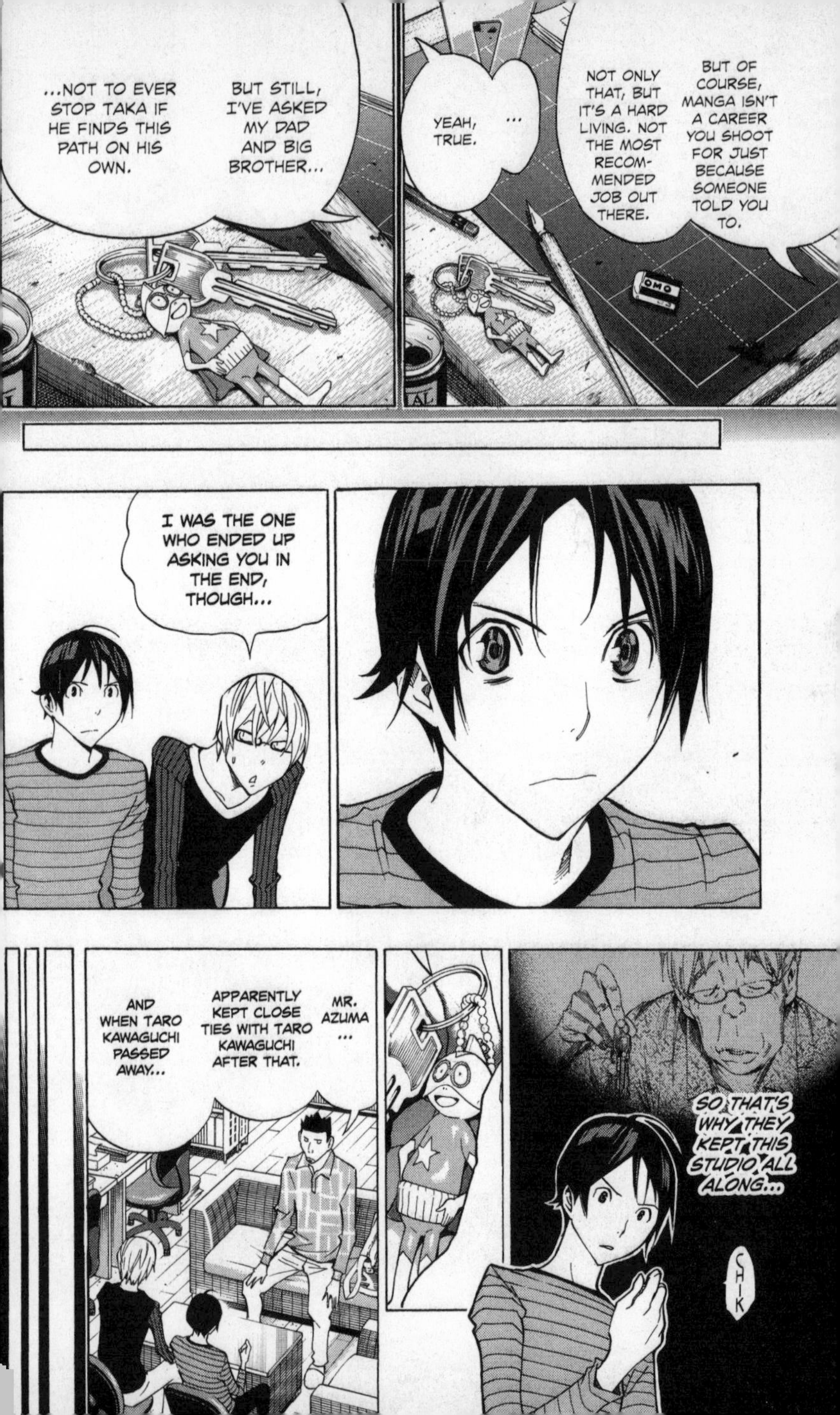
BUT OF COURSE, MANGA ISN'T A CAREER YOU SHOOT FOR JUST BECAUSE SOMEONE TOLD YOU TO.
NOT ONLY THAT, BUT IT'S A HARD LIVING. NOT THE MOST RECOMMENDED JOB OUT THERE.
...
YEAH, TRUE.
BUT STILL, I'VE ASKED MY DAD AND BIG BROTHER...
...NOT TO EVER STOP TAKA IF HE FINDS THIS PATH ON HIS OWN.
I WAS THE ONE WHO ENDED UP ASKING YOU IN THE END, THOUGH...
SO THAT'S WHY THEY KEPT THIS STUDIO ALL ALONG...
CHIK
MR. AZUMA...
APPARENTLY KEPT CLOSE TIES WITH TARO KAWAGUCHI AFTER THAT.
AND WHEN TARO KAWAGUCHI PASSED AWAY...

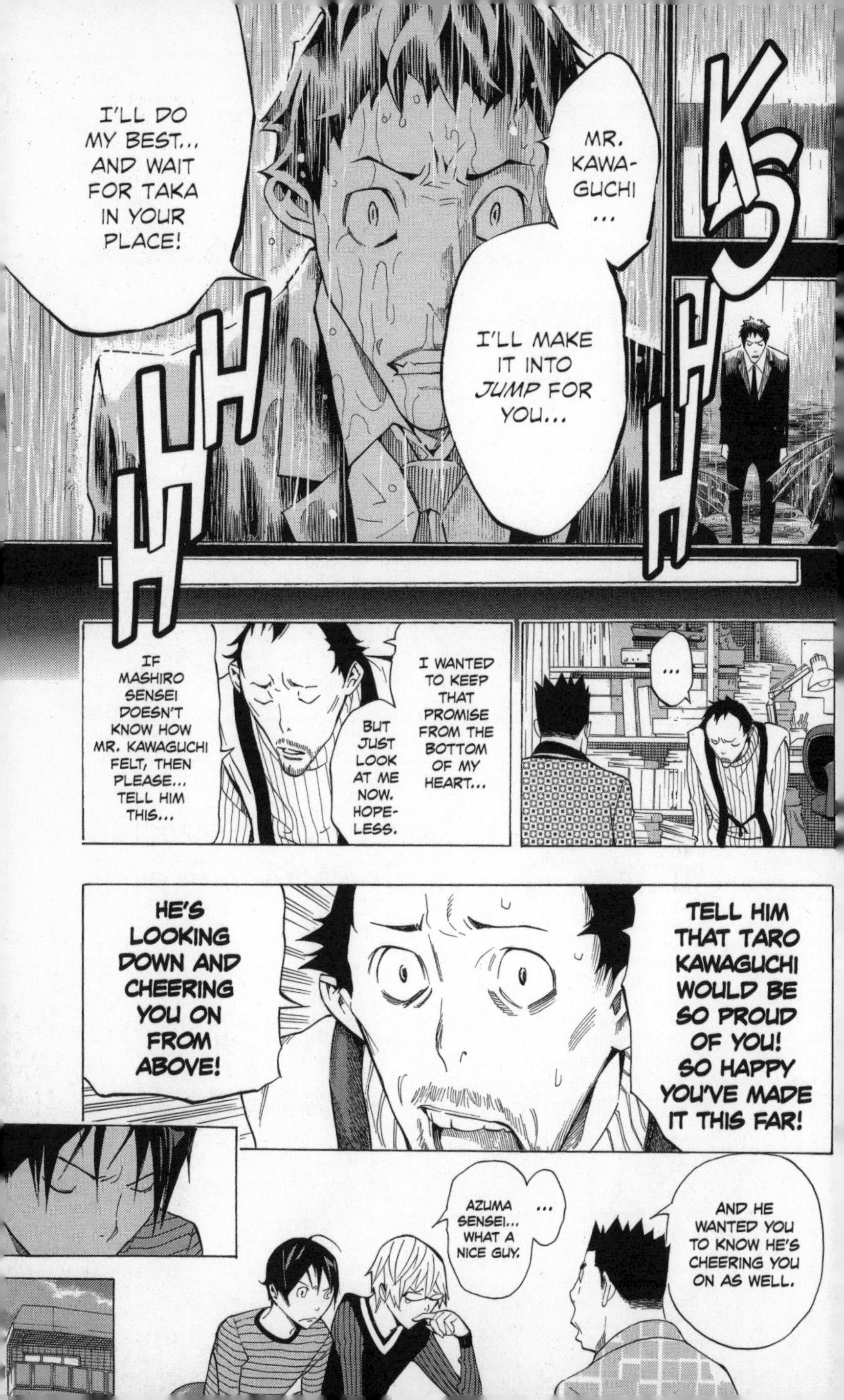
KSHHH
MR. KAWAGUCHI...
I'LL MAKE IT INTO *JUMP* FOR YOU...
I'LL DO MY BEST... AND WAIT FOR TAKA IN YOUR PLACE!
HHHH
...
I WANTED TO KEEP THAT PROMISE FROM THE BOTTOM OF MY HEART...
BUT JUST LOOK AT ME NOW. HOPELESS.
IF MASHIRO SENSEI DOESN'T KNOW HOW MR. KAWAGUCHI FELT, THEN PLEASE... TELL HIM THIS...
TELL HIM THAT TARO KAWAGUCHI WOULD BE SO PROUD OF YOU! SO HAPPY YOU'VE MADE IT THIS FAR!
HE'S LOOKING DOWN AND CHEERING YOU ON FROM ABOVE!
AND HE WANTED YOU TO KNOW HE'S CHEERING YOU ON AS WELL.
...
AZUMA SENSEI... WHAT A NICE GUY.

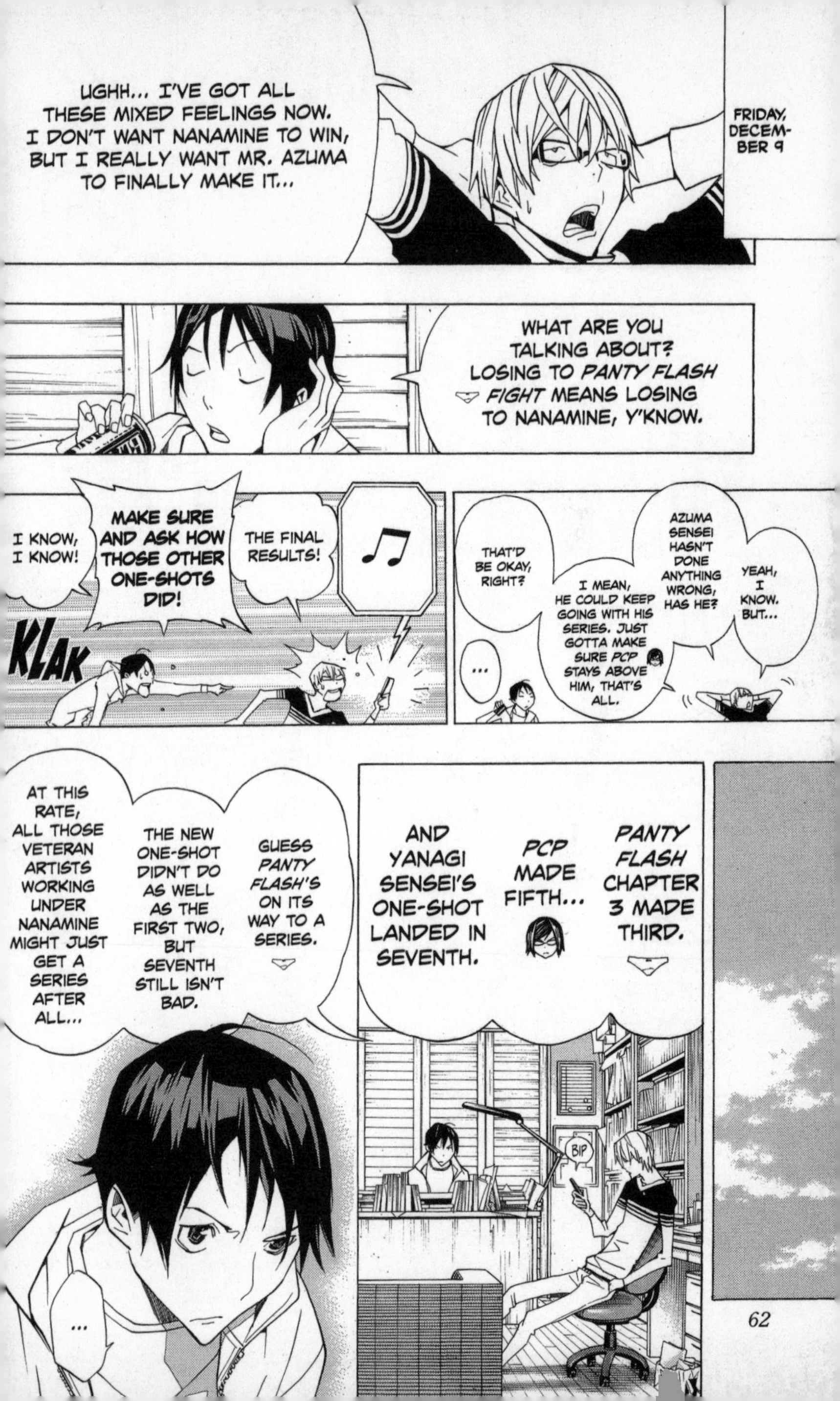
FRIDAY, DECEMBER 9
UGHH... I'VE GOT ALL THESE MIXED FEELINGS NOW. I DON'T WANT NANAMINE TO WIN, BUT I REALLY WANT MR. AZUMA TO FINALLY MAKE IT...
WHAT ARE YOU TALKING ABOUT? LOSING TO *PANTY FLASH FIGHT* MEANS LOSING TO NANAMINE, Y'KNOW.
YEAH, I KNOW. BUT...
AZUMA SENSEI HASN'T DONE ANYTHING WRONG, HAS HE?
I MEAN, HE COULD KEEP GOING WITH HIS SERIES. JUST GOTTA MAKE SURE *PCP* STAYS ABOVE HIM, THAT'S ALL.
THAT'D BE OKAY, RIGHT?
...
♫
THE FINAL RESULTS!
MAKE SURE AND ASK HOW THOSE OTHER ONE-SHOTS DID!
I KNOW, I KNOW!
KLAK
PANTY FLASH CHAPTER 3 MADE THIRD.
PCP MADE FIFTH...
AND YANAGI SENSEI'S ONE-SHOT LANDED IN SEVENTH.
BIP
GUESS *PANTY FLASH'S* ON ITS WAY TO A SERIES.
THE NEW ONE-SHOT DIDN'T DO AS WELL AS THE FIRST TWO, BUT SEVENTH STILL ISN'T BAD.
AT THIS RATE, ALL THOSE VETERAN ARTISTS WORKING UNDER NANAMINE MIGHT JUST GET A SERIES AFTER ALL...
...

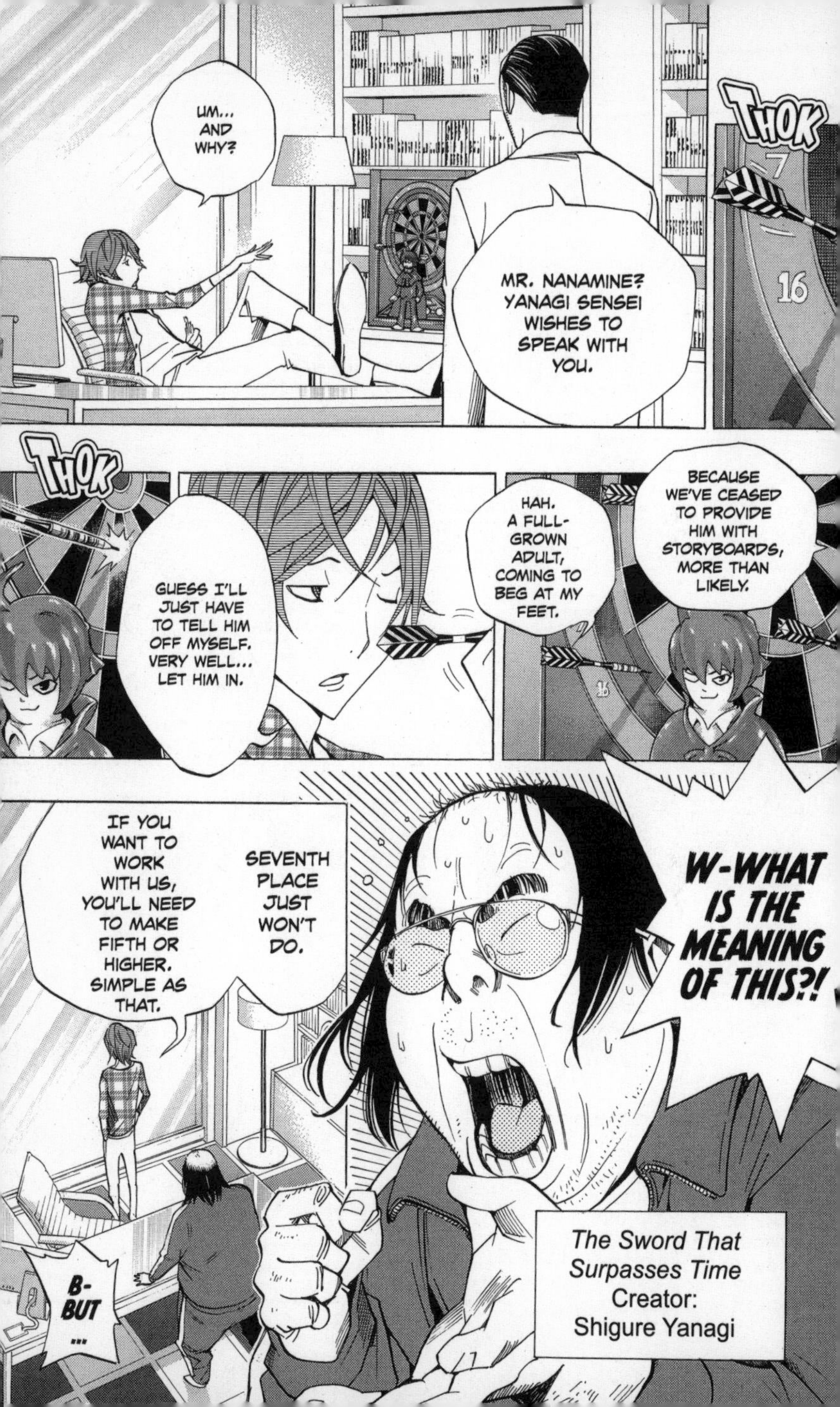
THOK
MR. NANAMINE? YANAGI SENSEI WISHES TO SPEAK WITH YOU.
UM... AND WHY?
BECAUSE WE'VE CEASED TO PROVIDE HIM WITH STORYBOARDS, MORE THAN LIKELY.
HAH. A FULL-GROWN ADULT, COMING TO BEG AT MY FEET.
GUESS I'LL JUST HAVE TO TELL HIM OFF MYSELF. VERY WELL... LET HIM IN.
THOK
W-WHAT IS THE MEANING OF THIS?!
The Sword That Surpasses Time Creator: Shigure Yanagi
SEVENTH PLACE JUST WON'T DO.
IF YOU WANT TO WORK WITH US, YOU'LL NEED TO MAKE FIFTH OR HIGHER. SIMPLE AS THAT.
B-BUT...

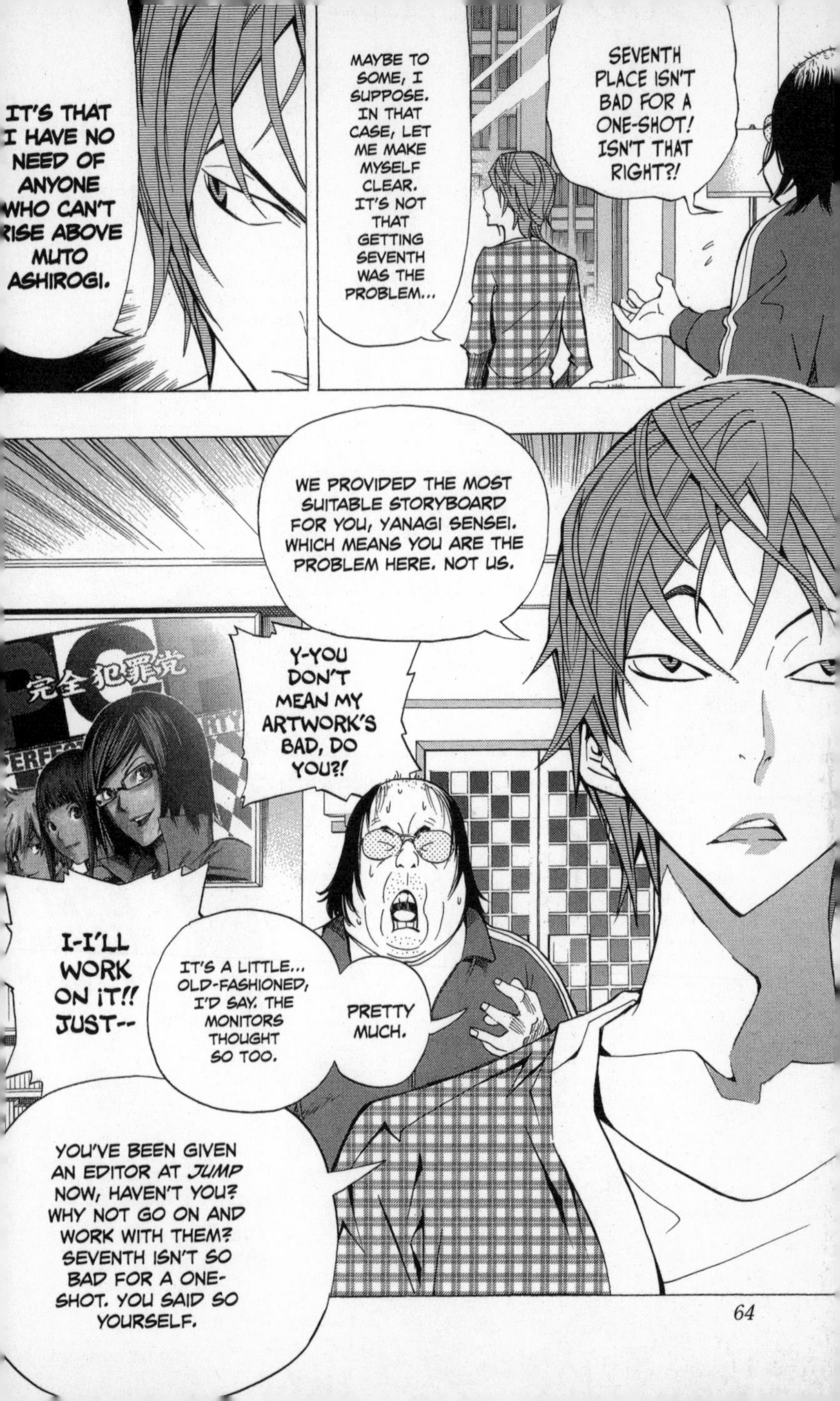
SEVENTH PLACE ISN'T BAD FOR A ONE-SHOT! ISN'T THAT RIGHT?!
MAYBE TO SOME, I SUPPOSE. IN THAT CASE, LET ME MAKE MYSELF CLEAR. IT'S NOT THAT GETTING SEVENTH WAS THE PROBLEM...
IT'S THAT I HAVE NO NEED OF ANYONE WHO CAN'T RISE ABOVE MUTO ASHIROGI.
WE PROVIDED THE MOST SUITABLE STORYBOARD FOR YOU, YANAGI SENSEI. WHICH MEANS YOU ARE THE PROBLEM HERE. NOT US.
Y-YOU DON'T MEAN MY ARTWORK'S BAD, DO YOU?!
完全犯罪党
PRETTY MUCH.
IT'S A LITTLE... OLD-FASHIONED, I'D SAY. THE MONITORS THOUGHT SO TOO.
I-I'LL WORK ON IT!! JUST--
YOU'VE BEEN GIVEN AN EDITOR AT *JUMP* NOW, HAVEN'T YOU? WHY NOT GO ON AND WORK WITH THEM? SEVENTH ISN'T SO BAD FOR A ONE-SHOT. YOU SAID SO YOURSELF.

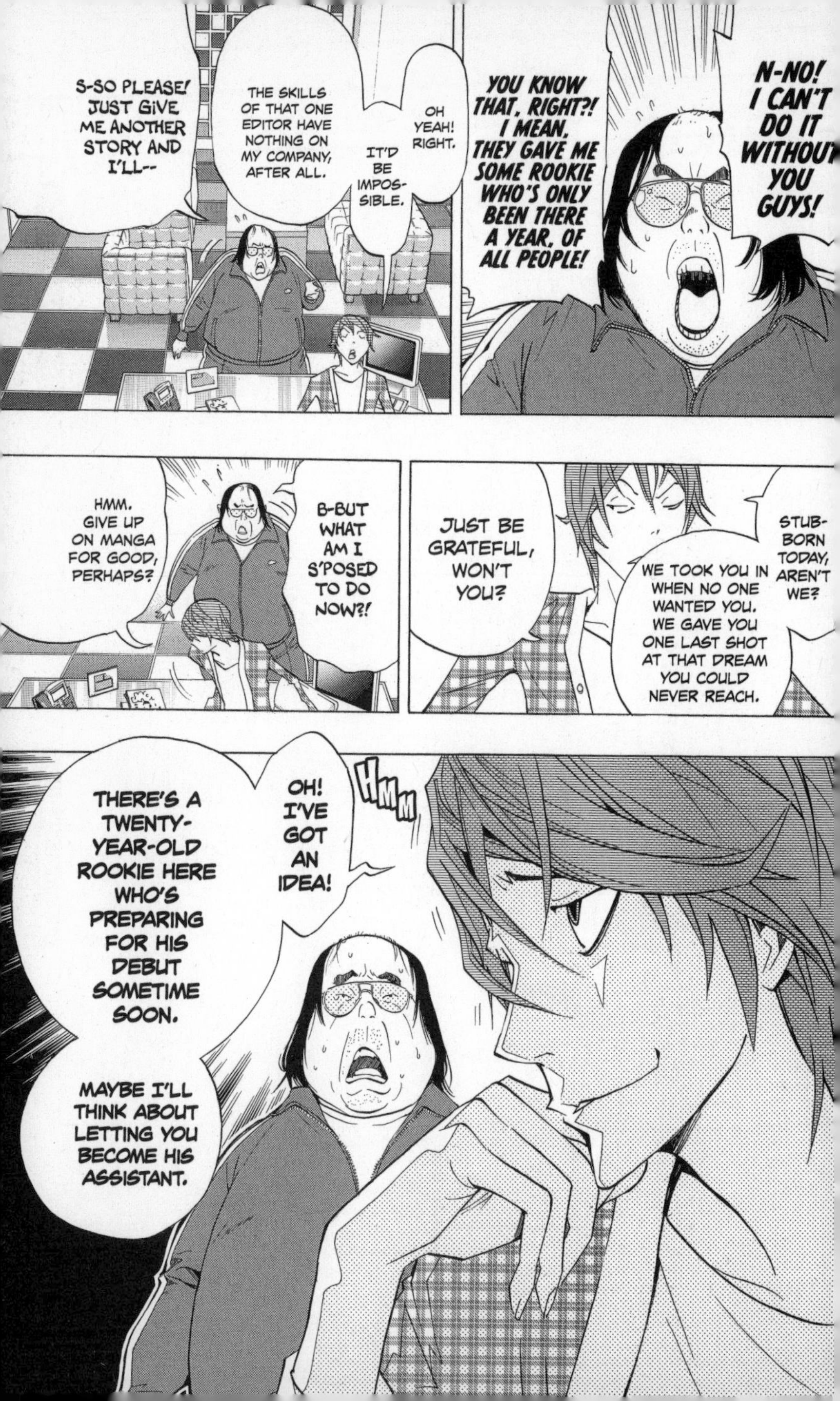
N-NO! I CAN'T DO IT WITHOUT YOU GUYS!
YOU KNOW THAT, RIGHT?! I MEAN, THEY GAVE ME SOME ROOKIE WHO'S ONLY BEEN THERE A YEAR, OF ALL PEOPLE!
OH YEAH! RIGHT.
IT'D BE IMPOSSIBLE.
THE SKILLS OF THAT ONE EDITOR HAVE NOTHING ON MY COMPANY, AFTER ALL.
S-SO PLEASE! JUST GIVE ME ANOTHER STORY AND I'LL--
STUBBORN TODAY, AREN'T WE?
WE TOOK YOU IN WHEN NO ONE WANTED YOU. WE GAVE YOU ONE LAST SHOT AT THAT DREAM YOU COULD NEVER REACH.
JUST BE GRATEFUL, WON'T YOU?
B-BUT WHAT AM I S'POSED TO DO NOW?!
HMM. GIVE UP ON MANGA FOR GOOD, PERHAPS?
HMM
OH! I'VE GOT AN IDEA!
THERE'S A TWENTY-YEAR-OLD ROOKIE HERE WHO'S PREPARING FOR HIS DEBUT SOMETIME SOON.
MAYBE I'LL THINK ABOUT LETTING YOU BECOME HIS ASSISTANT.

OHBA'S STORYBOARD

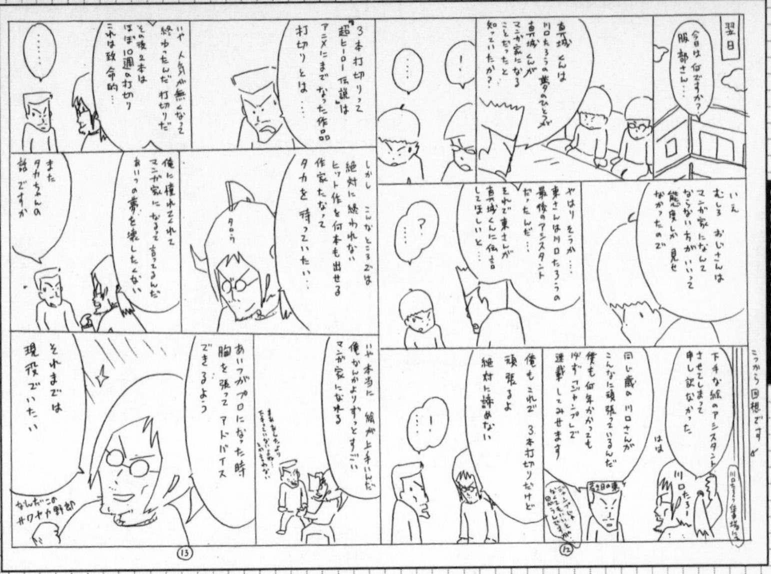
翌日
今日は何ですか? 服部さん…
真城くんは川口たろうの夢のひとつがマンガ家になることだったと知っていたか?
!
…
いえ むしろおじさんはマンガ家になんてならない方がいいって態度しか見せなかったので
やはりそうか… 東さんは川口たろうの最後のアシスタントだったんだ… それで東さんが真城くんに伝言してほしいと…
?
…
ここから回想です
下手な絵のアシスタントさせてしまって申し訳なかった
はは
川口たろー
川口たろう仕事場にて
同じ歳の川口さんがこんなに頑張っているんだ 僕も何年かかっても必ず「ジャンプ」で連載してみせます
俺もこれで3本打切りだけど頑張るよ 絶対に諦めない
…!
3本打切りって「超ヒーロー伝説」はアニメにまでなった作品。打切りとは…
いや 人気が無くなって終わったんだ 打切りだ その後2本はほぼ10週の打切り これは致命的…
……
しかし こんなところでは絶対に終われない ヒット作を何本も出せる作家になってタカを待っていたい…
タロウ
俺に憧れてくれてマンガ家になるって言ってるんだ あいつの夢を壊したくない
また タカちゃんの話ですか
いや本当に絵が上手いんだ 俺なんかよりずっとすごいマンガ家になれる
あいつがプロになった時 胸を張ってアドバイスできるよう
それまでは現役でいたい
12
13

OBATA'S STORYBOARD

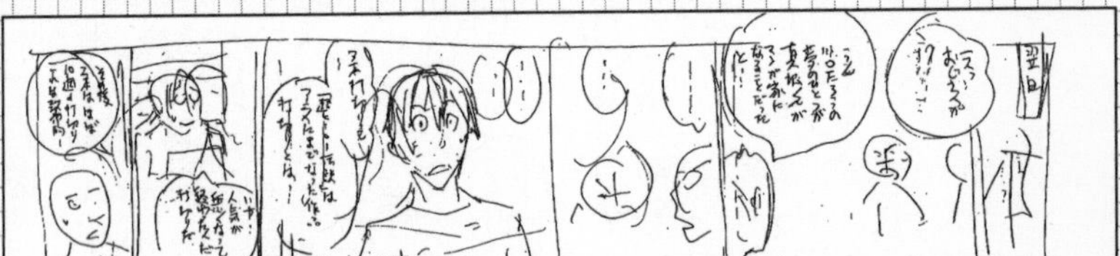

COMPLETE!

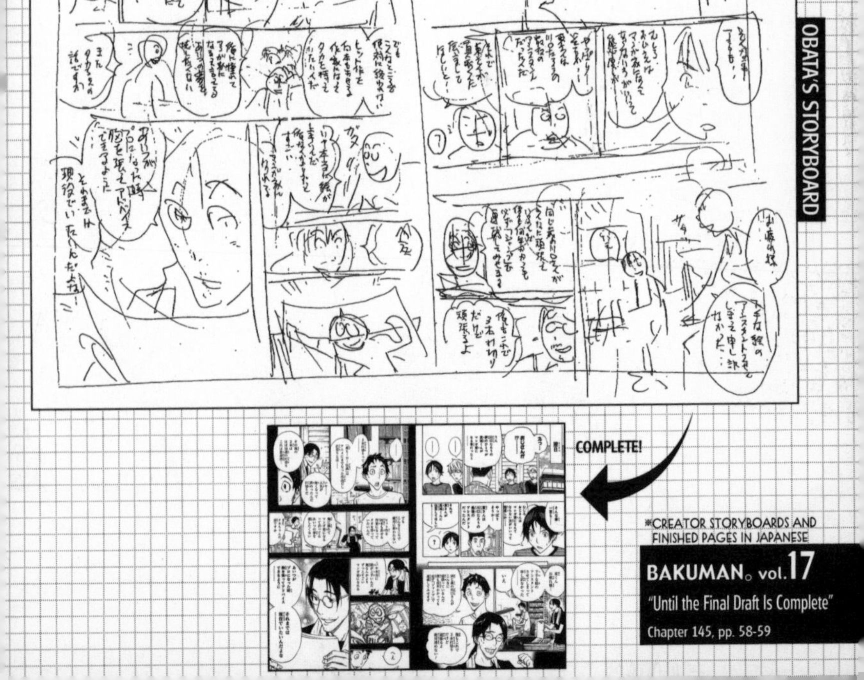

※CREATOR STORYBOARDS AND FINISHED PAGES IN JAPANESE

BAKUMAN。vol.17

"Until the Final Draft Is Complete"

Chapter 145, pp. 58-59

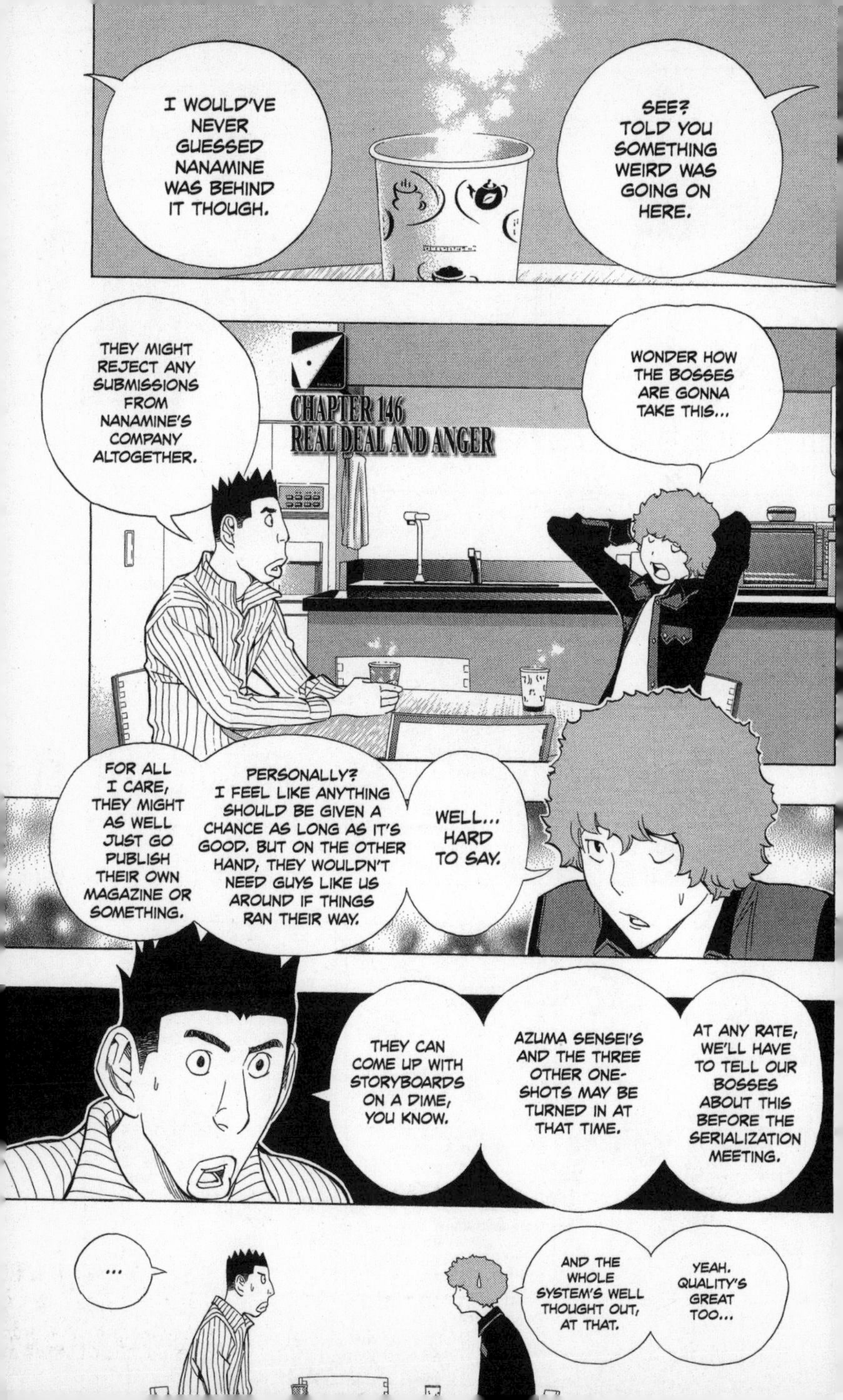
SEE? TOLD YOU SOMETHING WEIRD WAS GOING ON HERE.
I WOULD'VE NEVER GUESSED NANAMINE WAS BEHIND IT THOUGH.
CHAPTER 146 REAL DEAL AND ANGER
WONDER HOW THE BOSSES ARE GONNA TAKE THIS...
THEY MIGHT REJECT ANY SUBMISSIONS FROM NANAMINE'S COMPANY ALTOGETHER.
WELL... HARD TO SAY.
PERSONALLY? I FEEL LIKE ANYTHING SHOULD BE GIVEN A CHANCE AS LONG AS IT'S GOOD. BUT ON THE OTHER HAND, THEY WOULDN'T NEED GUYS LIKE US AROUND IF THINGS RAN THEIR WAY.
FOR ALL I CARE, THEY MIGHT AS WELL JUST GO PUBLISH THEIR OWN MAGAZINE OR SOMETHING.
AT ANY RATE, WE'LL HAVE TO TELL OUR BOSSES ABOUT THIS BEFORE THE SERIALIZATION MEETING.
AZUMA SENSEI'S AND THE THREE OTHER ONE-SHOTS MAY BE TURNED IN AT THAT TIME.
THEY CAN COME UP WITH STORYBOARDS ON A DIME, YOU KNOW.
YEAH. QUALITY'S GREAT TOO...
AND THE WHOLE SYSTEM'S WELL THOUGHT OUT, AT THAT.
...

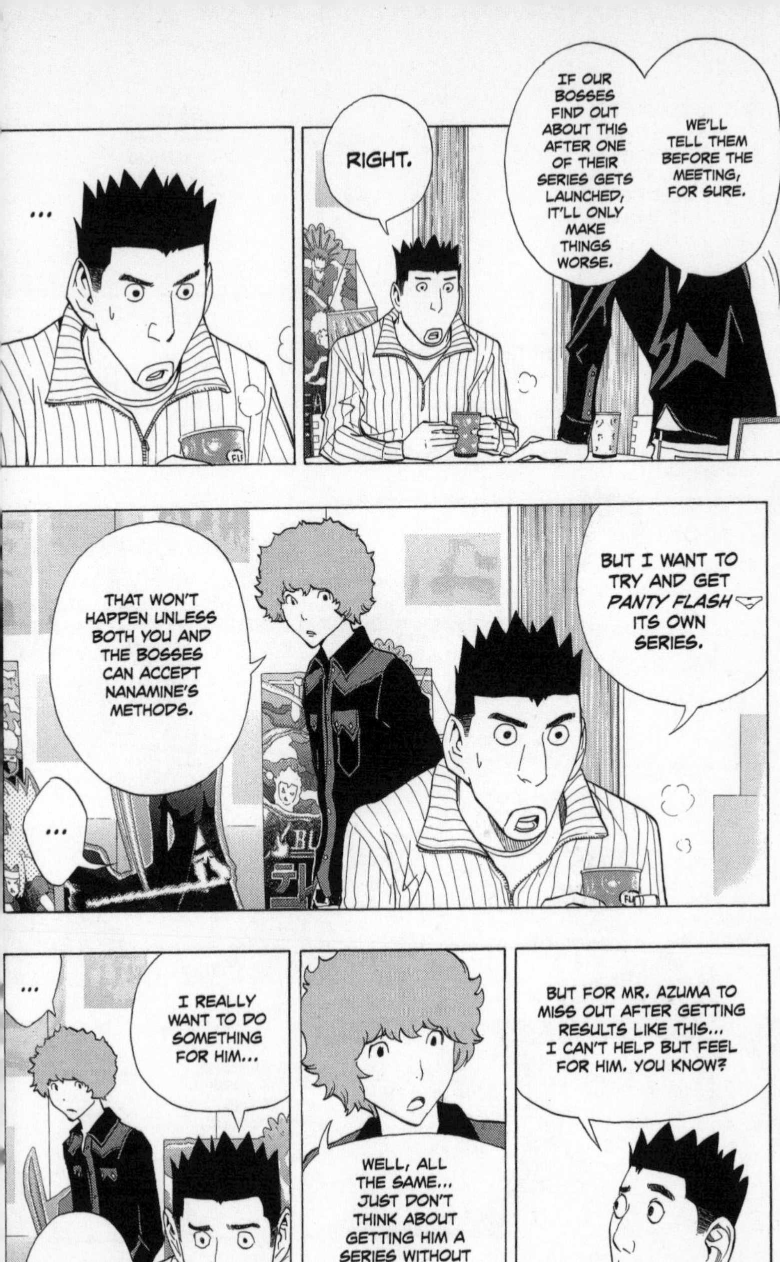
KLAK
WE'LL TELL THEM BEFORE THE MEETING, FOR SURE.
IF OUR BOSSES FIND OUT ABOUT THIS AFTER ONE OF THEIR SERIES GETS LAUNCHED, IT'LL ONLY MAKE THINGS WORSE.
RIGHT.
...
BUT I WANT TO TRY AND GET *PANTY FLASH* ITS OWN SERIES.
THAT WON'T HAPPEN UNLESS BOTH YOU AND THE BOSSES CAN ACCEPT NANAMINE'S METHODS.
...
BUT FOR MR. AZUMA TO MISS OUT AFTER GETTING RESULTS LIKE THIS... I CAN'T HELP BUT FEEL FOR HIM. YOU KNOW?
WELL, ALL THE SAME... JUST DON'T THINK ABOUT GETTING HIM A SERIES WITHOUT LETTING THE BOSSES KNOW FIRST.
I REALLY WANT TO DO SOMETHING FOR HIM...
...
MR. AZUMA ...

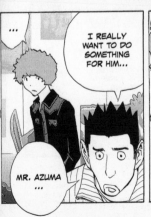

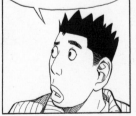

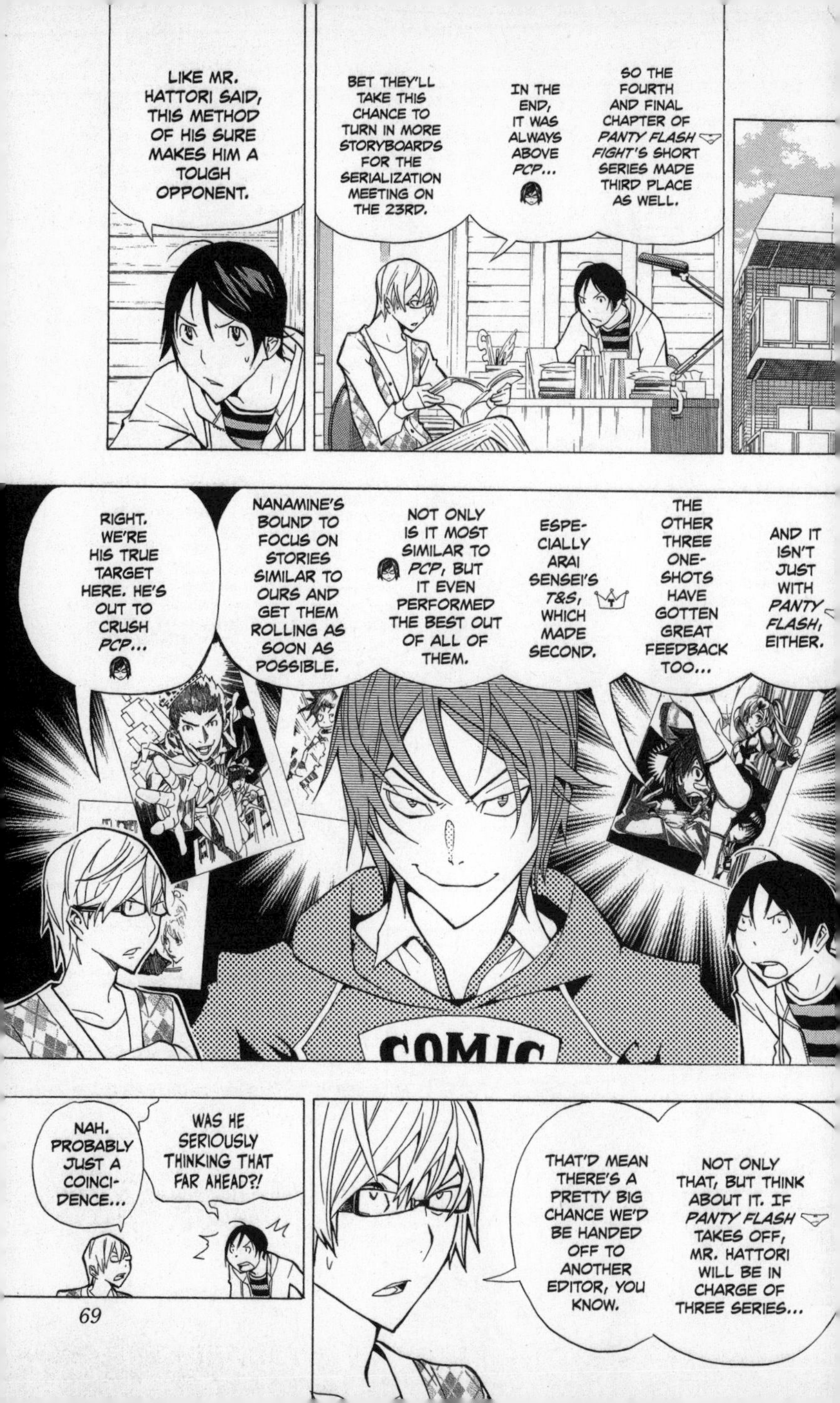
SO THE FOURTH AND FINAL CHAPTER OF PANTY FLASH FIGHT'S SHORT SERIES MADE THIRD PLACE AS WELL.
IN THE END, IT WAS ALWAYS ABOVE PCP...
BET THEY'LL TAKE THIS CHANCE TO TURN IN MORE STORYBOARDS FOR THE SERIALIZATION MEETING ON THE 23RD.
LIKE MR. HATTORI SAID, THIS METHOD OF HIS SURE MAKES HIM A TOUGH OPPONENT.
AND IT ISN'T JUST WITH PANTY FLASH, EITHER.
THE OTHER THREE ONE-SHOTS HAVE GOTTEN GREAT FEEDBACK TOO...
ESPECIALLY ARAI SENSEI'S T&S, WHICH MADE SECOND.
NOT ONLY IS IT MOST SIMILAR TO PCP, BUT IT EVEN PERFORMED THE BEST OUT OF ALL OF THEM.
NANAMINE'S BOUND TO FOCUS ON STORIES SIMILAR TO OURS AND GET THEM ROLLING AS SOON AS POSSIBLE.
RIGHT. WE'RE HIS TRUE TARGET HERE. HE'S OUT TO CRUSH PCP...
COMIC
NOT ONLY THAT, BUT THINK ABOUT IT. IF PANTY FLASH TAKES OFF, MR. HATTORI WILL BE IN CHARGE OF THREE SERIES...
THAT'D MEAN THERE'S A PRETTY BIG CHANCE WE'D BE HANDED OFF TO ANOTHER EDITOR, YOU KNOW.
WAS HE SERIOUSLY THINKING THAT FAR AHEAD?!
NAH. PROBABLY JUST A COINCI-DENCE...

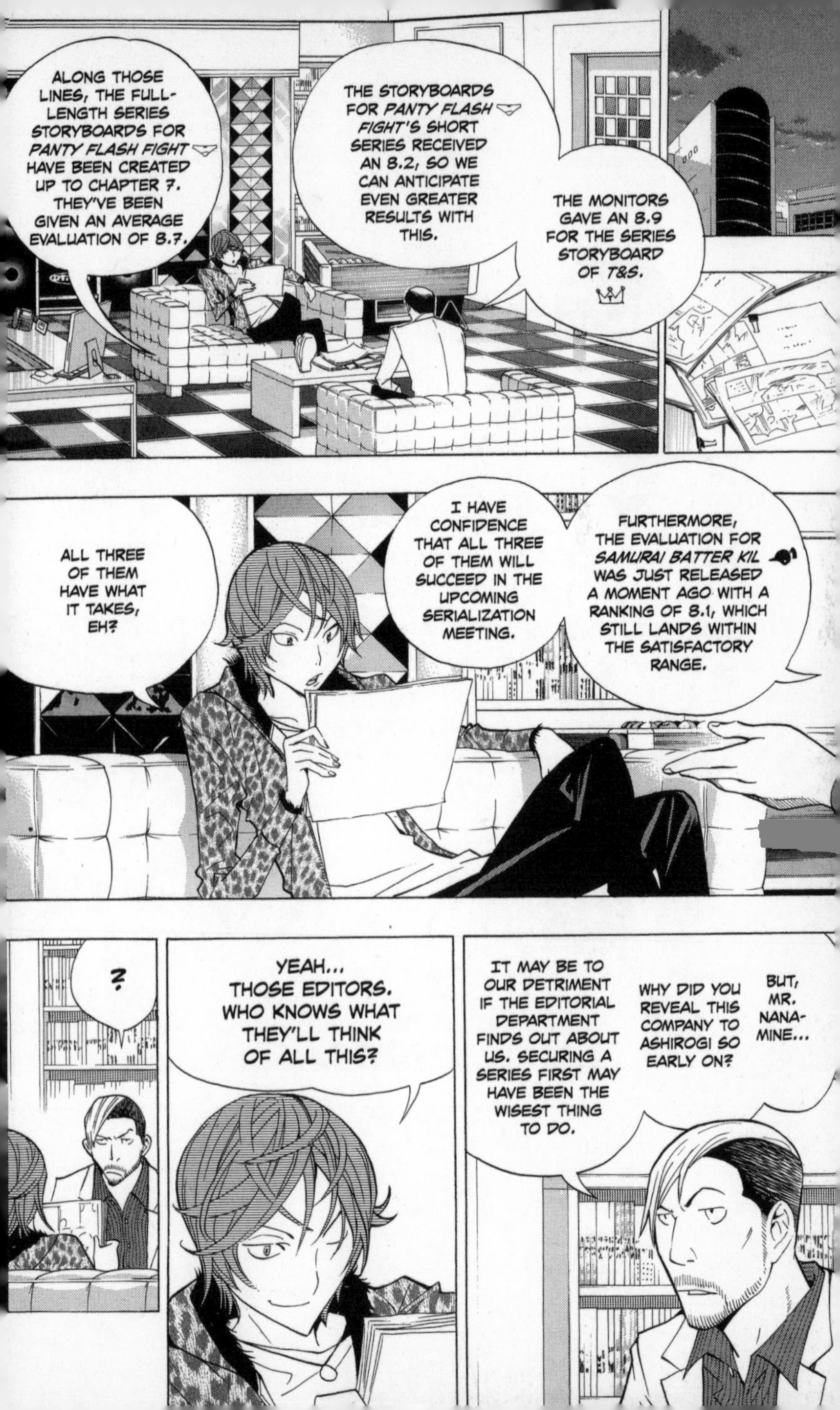

THE MONITORS GAVE AN 8.9 FOR THE SERIES STORYBOARD OF T&S.
THE STORYBOARDS FOR *PANTY FLASH FIGHT*'S SHORT SERIES RECEIVED AN 8.2, SO WE CAN ANTICIPATE EVEN GREATER RESULTS WITH THIS.
ALONG THOSE LINES, THE FULL-LENGTH SERIES STORYBOARDS FOR *PANTY FLASH FIGHT* HAVE BEEN CREATED UP TO CHAPTER 7. THEY'VE BEEN GIVEN AN AVERAGE EVALUATION OF 8.7.
FURTHERMORE, THE EVALUATION FOR *SAMURAI BATTER KIL* WAS JUST RELEASED A MOMENT AGO WITH A RANKING OF 8.1, WHICH STILL LANDS WITHIN THE SATISFACTORY RANGE.
I HAVE CONFIDENCE THAT ALL THREE OF THEM WILL SUCCEED IN THE UPCOMING SERIALIZATION MEETING.
ALL THREE OF THEM HAVE WHAT IT TAKES, EH?
BUT, MR. NANAMINE...
WHY DID YOU REVEAL THIS COMPANY TO ASHIROGI SO EARLY ON?
IT MAY BE TO OUR DETRIMENT IF THE EDITORIAL DEPARTMENT FINDS OUT ABOUT US. SECURING A SERIES FIRST MAY HAVE BEEN THE WISEST THING TO DO.
YEAH... THOSE EDITORS. WHO KNOWS WHAT THEY'LL THINK OF ALL THIS?
?

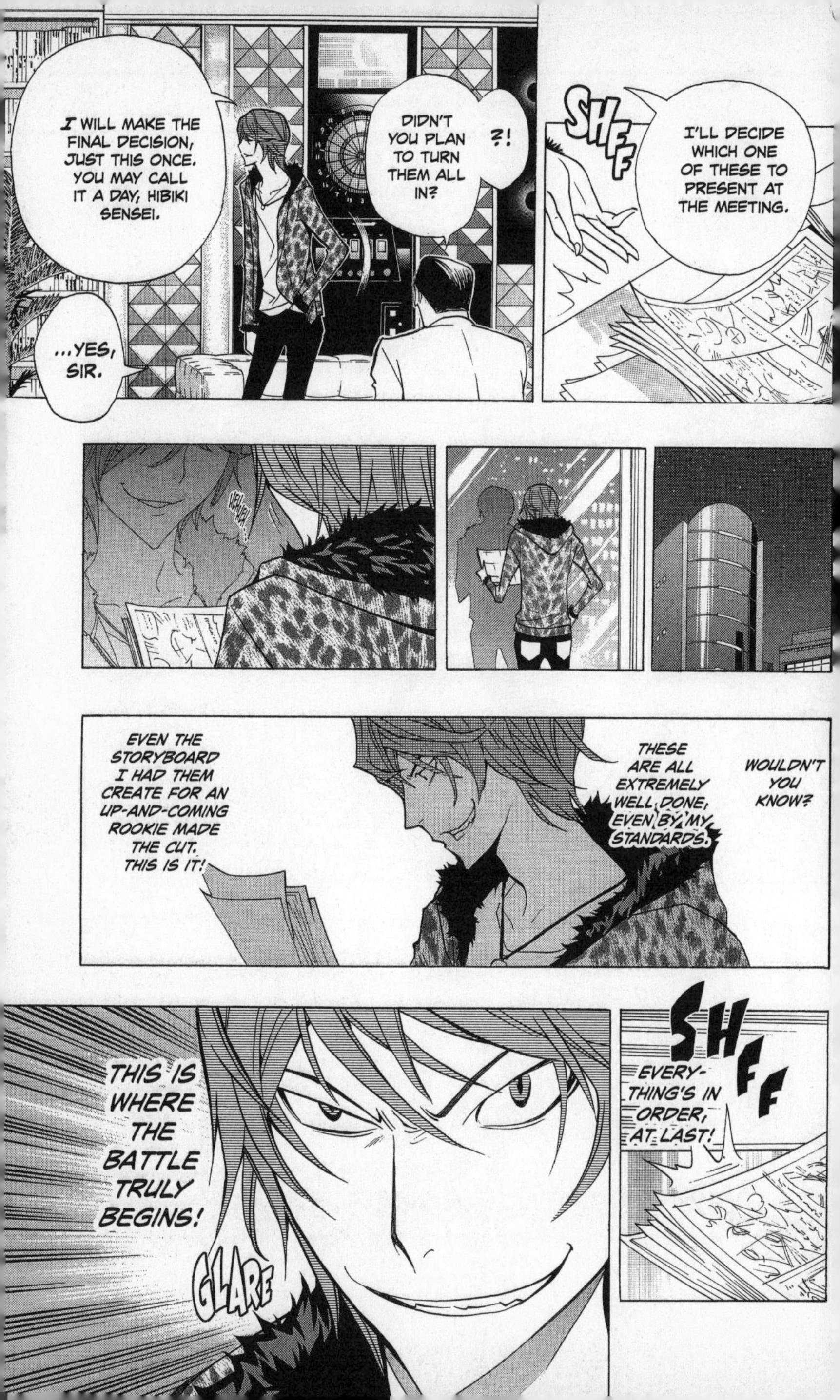
SHFF
I'LL DECIDE WHICH ONE OF THESE TO PRESENT AT THE MEETING.
DIDN'T YOU PLAN TO TURN THEM ALL IN?
?!
I WILL MAKE THE FINAL DECISION, JUST THIS ONCE. YOU MAY CALL IT A DAY, HIBIKI SENSEI.
...YES, SIR.
HEH HEH...
WOULDN'T YOU KNOW?
THESE ARE ALL EXTREMELY WELL DONE, EVEN BY MY STANDARDS.
EVEN THE STORYBOARD I HAD THEM CREATE FOR AN UP-AND-COMING ROOKIE MADE THE CUT. THIS IS IT!
SHFF
EVERY-THING'S IN ORDER, AT LAST!
THIS IS WHERE THE BATTLE TRULY BEGINS!
GLARE

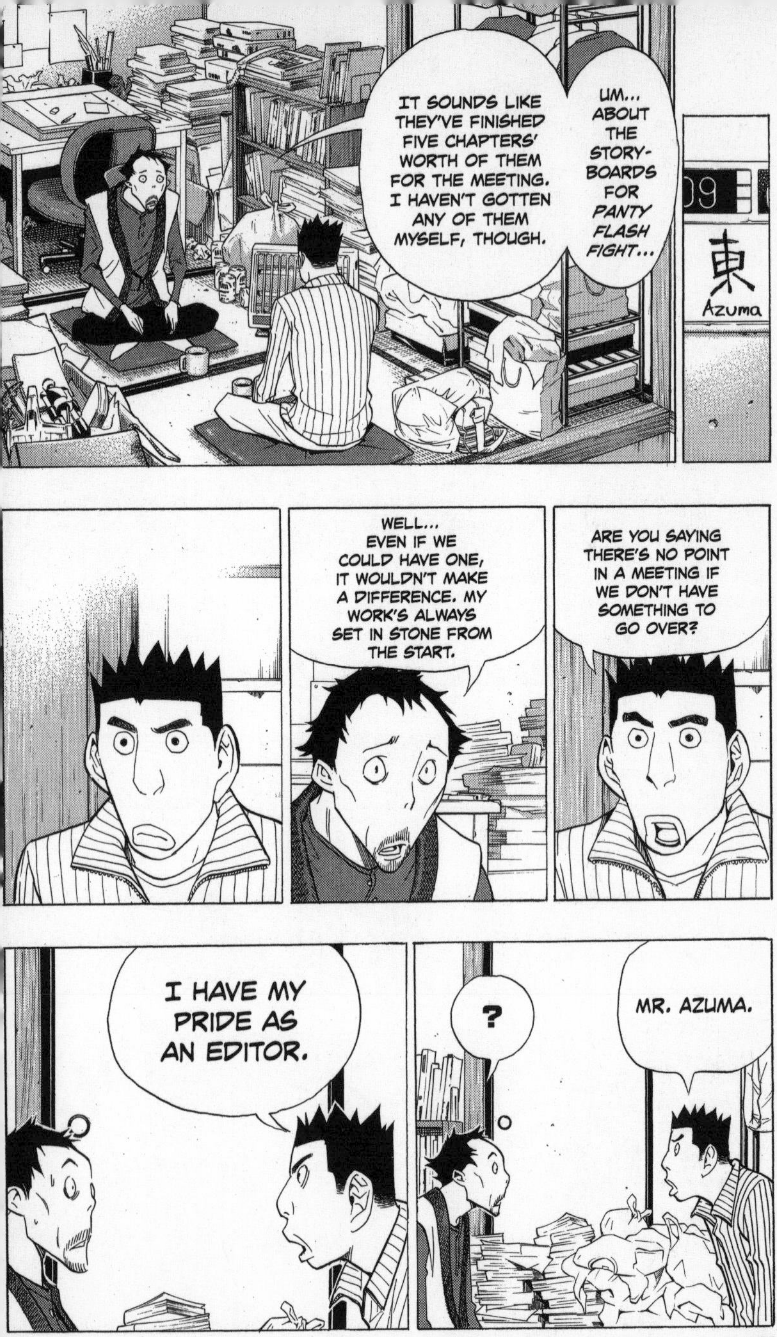
東
Azuma
UM... ABOUT THE STORYBOARDS FOR PANTY FLASH FIGHT...
IT SOUNDS LIKE THEY'VE FINISHED FIVE CHAPTERS' WORTH OF THEM FOR THE MEETING. I HAVEN'T GOTTEN ANY OF THEM MYSELF, THOUGH.
ARE YOU SAYING THERE'S NO POINT IN A MEETING IF WE DON'T HAVE SOMETHING TO GO OVER?
WELL... EVEN IF WE COULD HAVE ONE, IT WOULDN'T MAKE A DIFFERENCE. MY WORK'S ALWAYS SET IN STONE FROM THE START.
MR. AZUMA.
?
I HAVE MY PRIDE AS AN EDITOR.

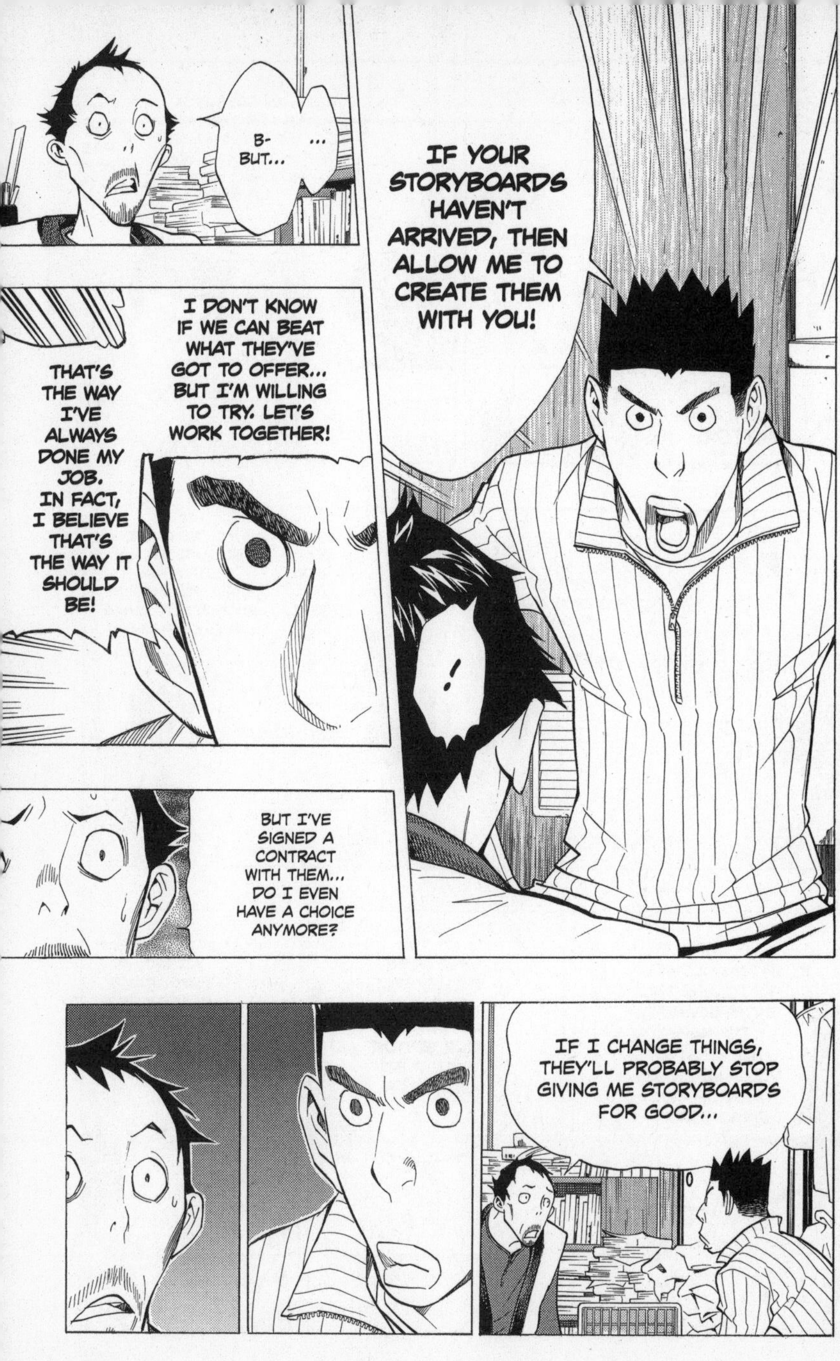
IF YOUR STORYBOARDS HAVEN'T ARRIVED, THEN ALLOW ME TO CREATE THEM WITH YOU!
B-BUT...
...
I DON'T KNOW IF WE CAN BEAT WHAT THEY'VE GOT TO OFFER... BUT I'M WILLING TO TRY. LET'S WORK TOGETHER!
THAT'S THE WAY I'VE ALWAYS DONE MY JOB. IN FACT, I BELIEVE THAT'S THE WAY IT SHOULD BE!
!
BUT I'VE SIGNED A CONTRACT WITH THEM... DO I EVEN HAVE A CHOICE ANYMORE?
IF I CHANGE THINGS, THEY'LL PROBABLY STOP GIVING ME STORYBOARDS FOR GOOD...

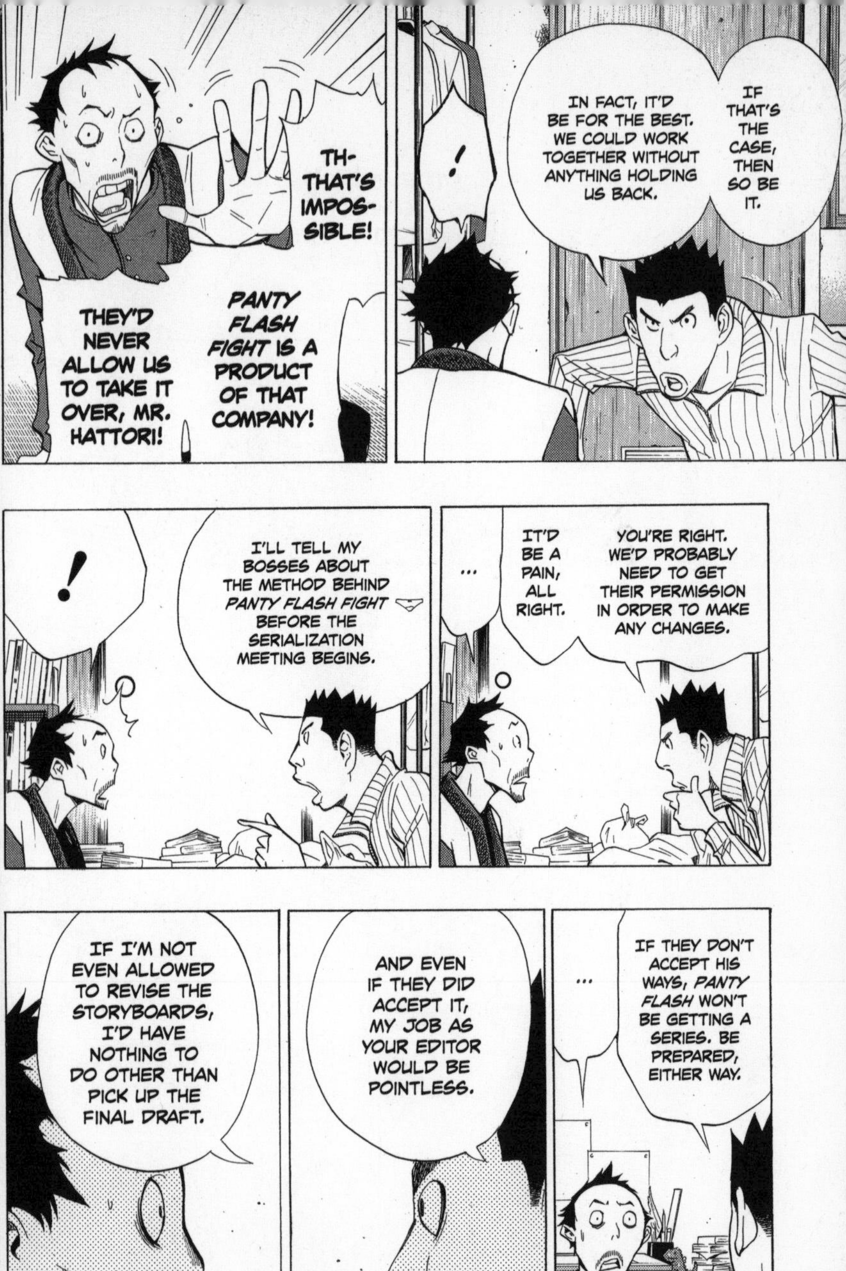
IF THAT'S THE CASE, THEN SO BE IT.
IN FACT, IT'D BE FOR THE BEST. WE COULD WORK TOGETHER WITHOUT ANYTHING HOLDING US BACK.
!
TH-THAT'S IMPOSSIBLE!
PANTY FLASH FIGHT IS A PRODUCT OF THAT COMPANY!
THEY'D NEVER ALLOW US TO TAKE IT OVER, MR. HATTORI!
YOU'RE RIGHT. WE'D PROBABLY NEED TO GET THEIR PERMISSION IN ORDER TO MAKE ANY CHANGES.
IT'D BE A PAIN, ALL RIGHT.
...
I'LL TELL MY BOSSES ABOUT THE METHOD BEHIND *PANTY FLASH FIGHT* BEFORE THE SERIALIZATION MEETING BEGINS.
!
IF THEY DON'T ACCEPT HIS WAYS, *PANTY FLASH* WON'T BE GETTING A SERIES. BE PREPARED, EITHER WAY.
...
AND EVEN IF THEY DID ACCEPT IT, MY JOB AS YOUR EDITOR WOULD BE POINTLESS.
IF I'M NOT EVEN ALLOWED TO REVISE THE STORYBOARDS, I'D HAVE NOTHING TO DO OTHER THAN PICK UP THE FINAL DRAFT.

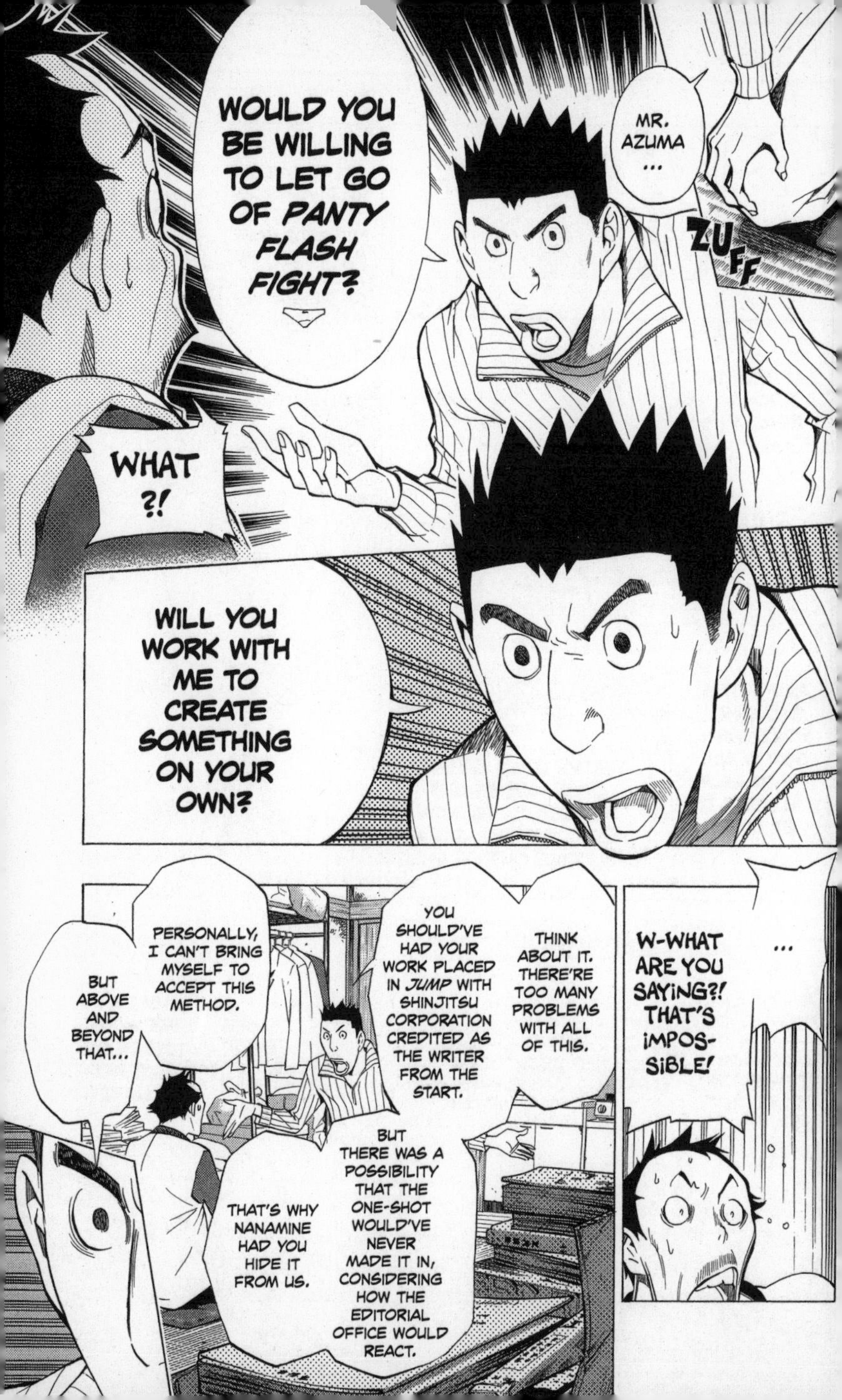

MR. AZUMA ...
ZUFF
WOULD YOU BE WILLING TO LET GO OF *PANTY FLASH FIGHT*?
WHAT ?!
WILL YOU WORK WITH ME TO CREATE SOMETHING ON YOUR OWN?
...
W-WHAT ARE YOU SAYING?! THAT'S IMPOSSIBLE!
THINK ABOUT IT. THERE'RE TOO MANY PROBLEMS WITH ALL OF THIS.
YOU SHOULD'VE HAD YOUR WORK PLACED IN *JUMP* WITH SHINJITSU CORPORATION CREDITED AS THE WRITER FROM THE START.
BUT THERE WAS A POSSIBILITY THAT THE ONE-SHOT WOULD'VE NEVER MADE IT IN, CONSIDERING HOW THE EDITORIAL OFFICE WOULD REACT.
THAT'S WHY NANAMINE HAD YOU HIDE IT FROM US.
PERSONALLY, I CAN'T BRING MYSELF TO ACCEPT THIS METHOD.
BUT ABOVE AND BEYOND THAT...

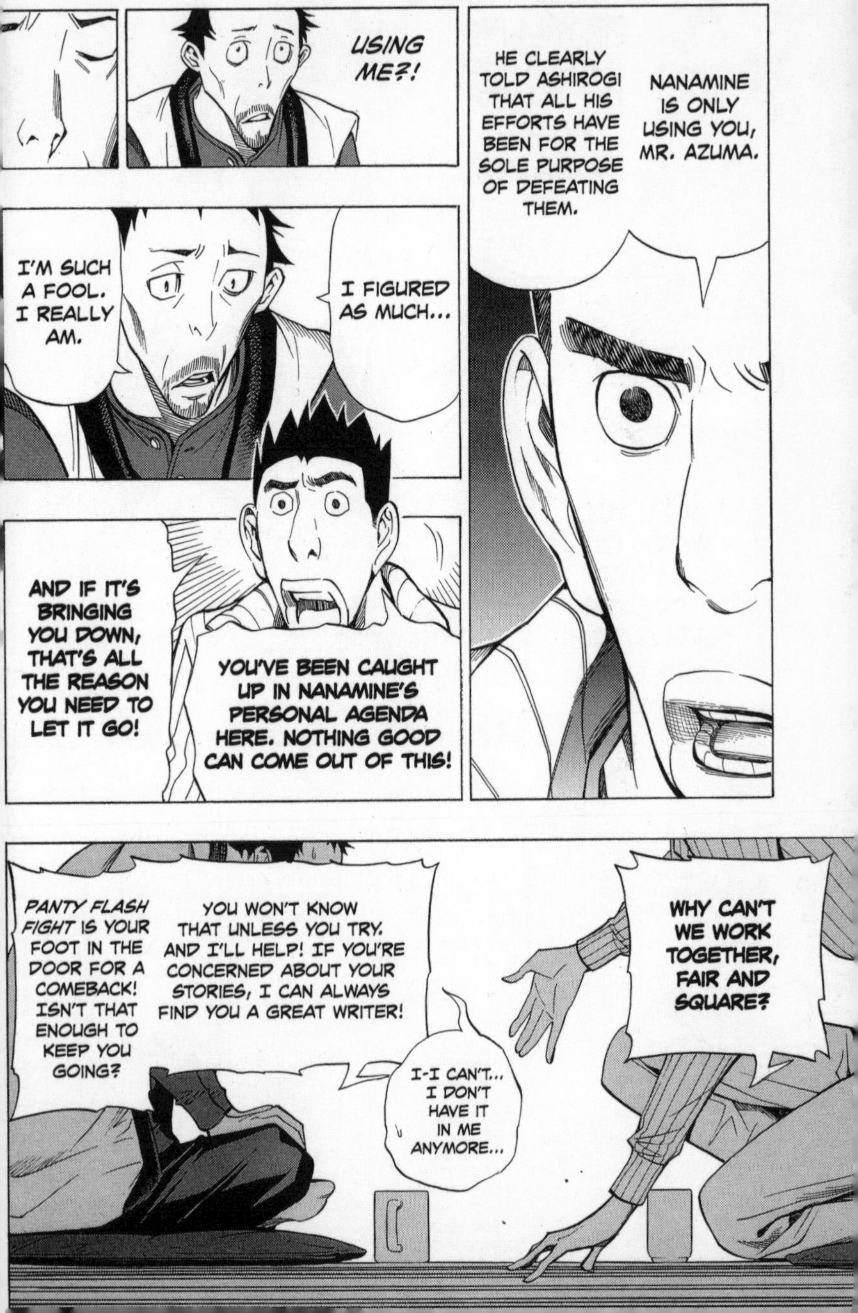
NANAMINE IS ONLY USING YOU, MR. AZUMA.
HE CLEARLY TOLD ASHIROGI THAT ALL HIS EFFORTS HAVE BEEN FOR THE SOLE PURPOSE OF DEFEATING THEM.
USING ME?!
I FIGURED AS MUCH...
I'M SUCH A FOOL. I REALLY AM.
YOU'VE BEEN CAUGHT UP IN NANAMINE'S PERSONAL AGENDA HERE. NOTHING GOOD CAN COME OUT OF THIS!
AND IF IT'S BRINGING YOU DOWN, THAT'S ALL THE REASON YOU NEED TO LET IT GO!
WHY CAN'T WE WORK TOGETHER, FAIR AND SQUARE?
I-I CAN'T... I DON'T HAVE IT IN ME ANYMORE...
YOU WON'T KNOW THAT UNLESS YOU TRY. AND I'LL HELP! IF YOU'RE CONCERNED ABOUT YOUR STORIES, I CAN ALWAYS FIND YOU A GREAT WRITER!
PANTY FLASH FIGHT IS YOUR FOOT IN THE DOOR FOR A COMEBACK! ISN'T THAT ENOUGH TO KEEP YOU GOING?

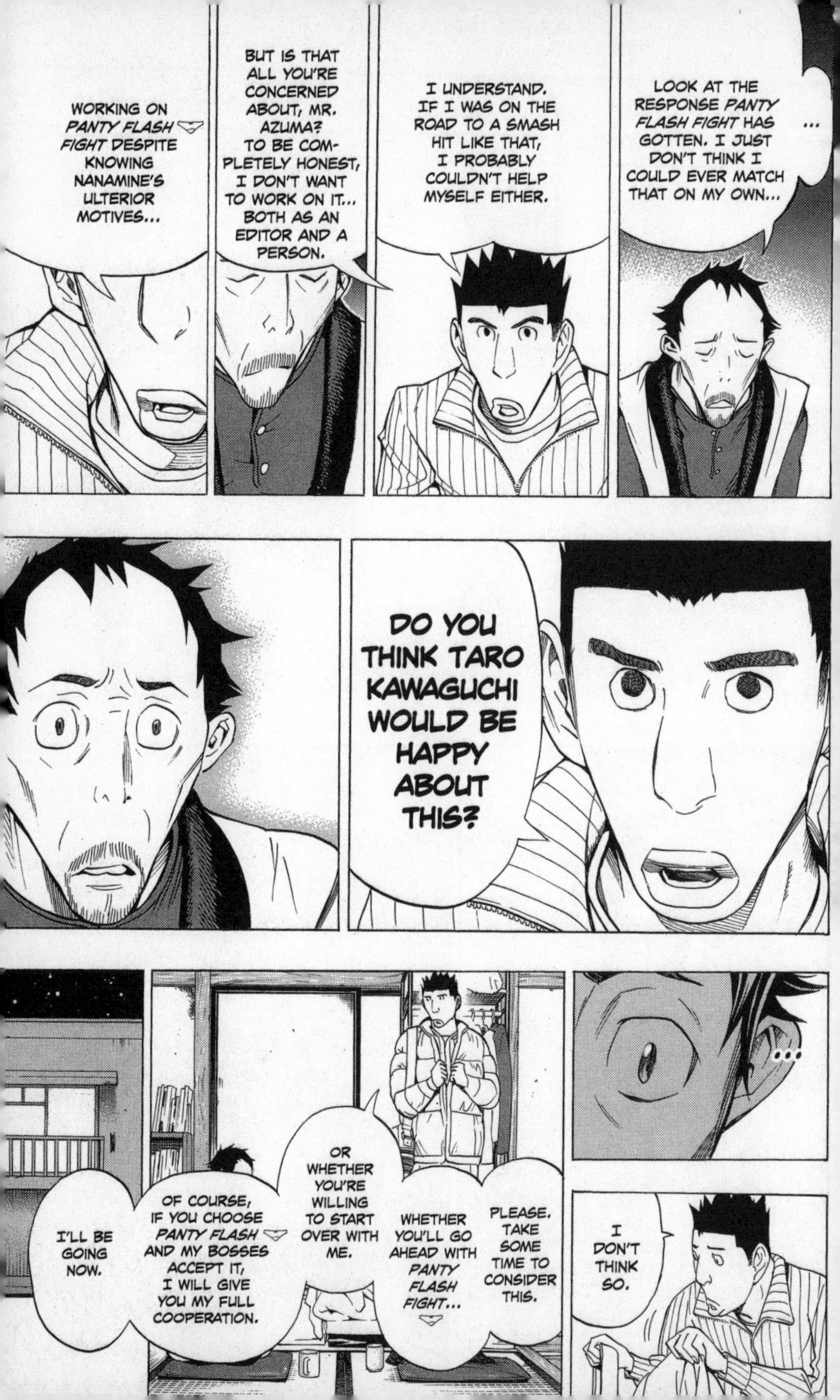
...
LOOK AT THE RESPONSE PANTY FLASH FIGHT HAS GOTTEN. I JUST DON'T THINK I COULD EVER MATCH THAT ON MY OWN...
I UNDERSTAND. IF I WAS ON THE ROAD TO A SMASH HIT LIKE THAT, I PROBABLY COULDN'T HELP MYSELF EITHER.
BUT IS THAT ALL YOU'RE CONCERNED ABOUT, MR. AZUMA? TO BE COMPLETELY HONEST, I DON'T WANT TO WORK ON IT... BOTH AS AN EDITOR AND A PERSON.
WORKING ON PANTY FLASH FIGHT DESPITE KNOWING NANAMINE'S ULTERIOR MOTIVES...
DO YOU THINK TARO KAWAGUCHI WOULD BE HAPPY ABOUT THIS?
...
I DON'T THINK SO.
PLEASE. TAKE SOME TIME TO CONSIDER THIS.
WHETHER YOU'LL GO AHEAD WITH PANTY FLASH FIGHT...
OR WHETHER YOU'RE WILLING TO START OVER WITH ME.
OF COURSE, IF YOU CHOOSE PANTY FLASH AND MY BOSSES ACCEPT IT, I WILL GIVE YOU MY FULL COOPERATION.
I'LL BE GOING NOW.

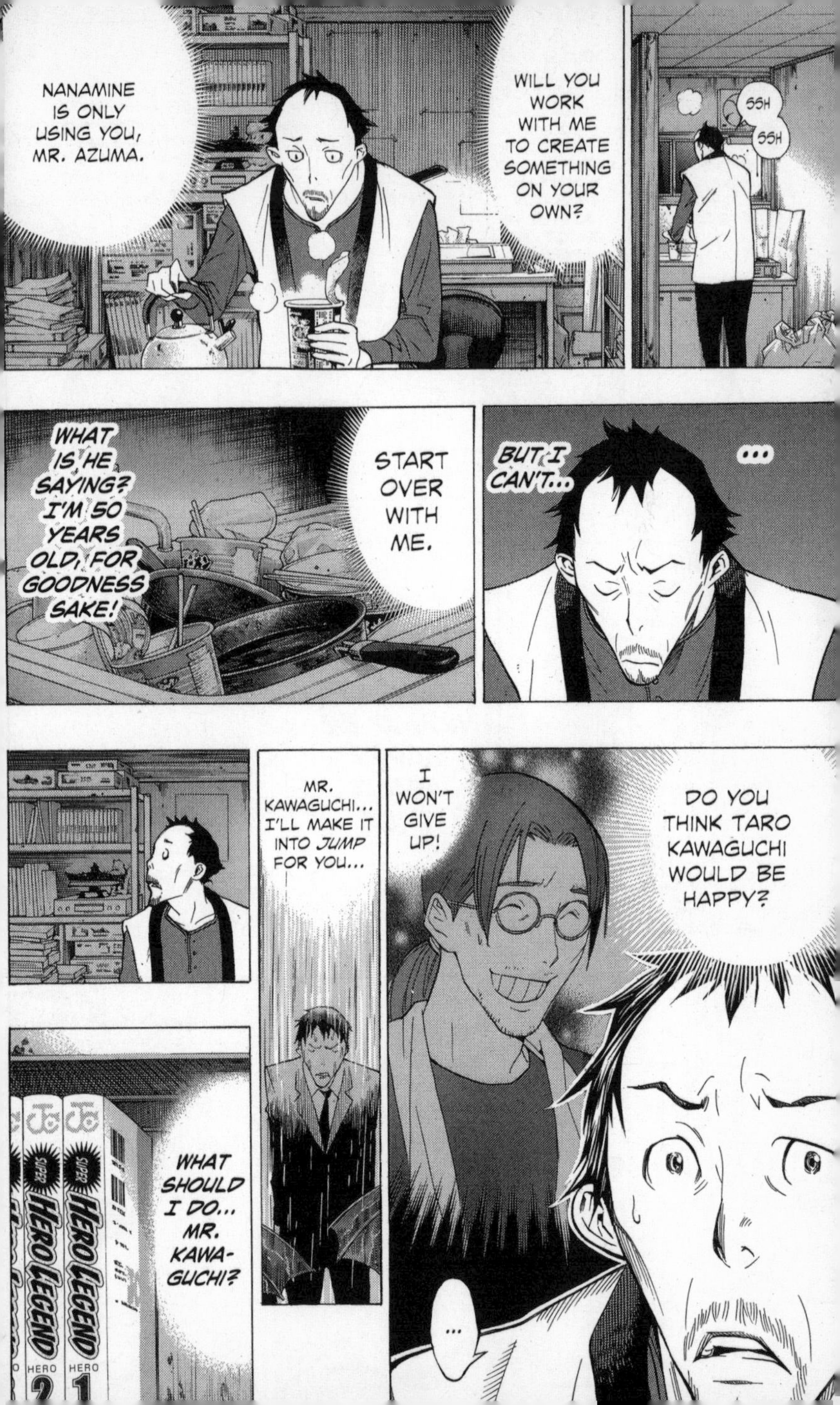
SSH
SSH
WILL YOU WORK WITH ME TO CREATE SOMETHING ON YOUR OWN?
NANAMINE IS ONLY USING YOU, MR. AZUMA.
...
BUT I CAN'T...
START OVER WITH ME.
WHAT IS HE SAYING? I'M 50 YEARS OLD, FOR GOODNESS SAKE!
DO YOU THINK TARO KAWAGUCHI WOULD BE HAPPY?
I WON'T GIVE UP!
...
MR. KAWAGUCHI... I'LL MAKE IT INTO *JUMP* FOR YOU...
WHAT SHOULD I DO... MR. KAWAGUCHI?
SUPER HERO LEGEND
HERO 1
HERO 2

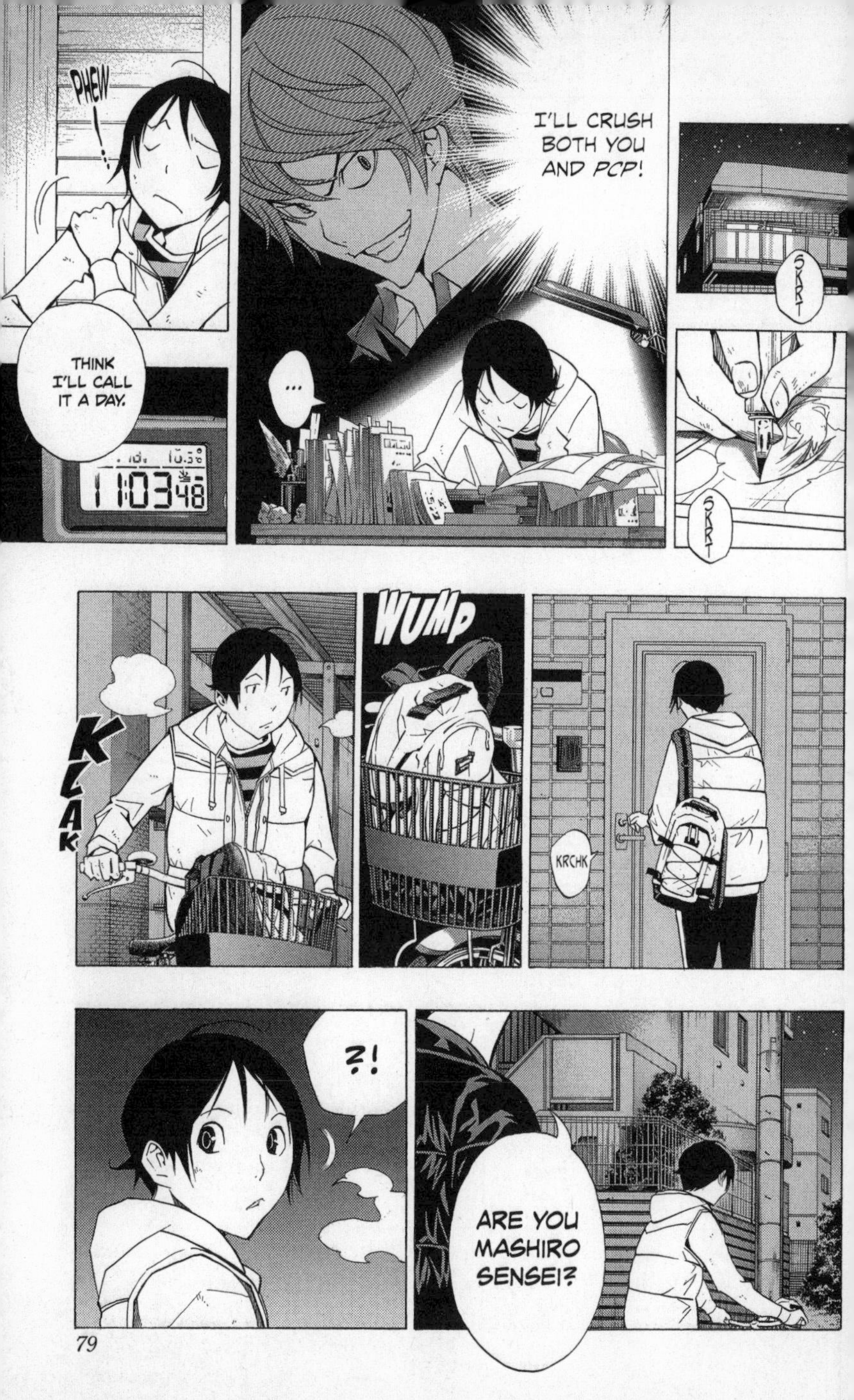
SKRT
SKRT
I'LL CRUSH BOTH YOU AND *PCP*!
...
PHEW
THINK I'LL CALL IT A DAY.
KRCHK
WUMP
KLAK
ARE YOU MASHIRO SENSEI?
?!

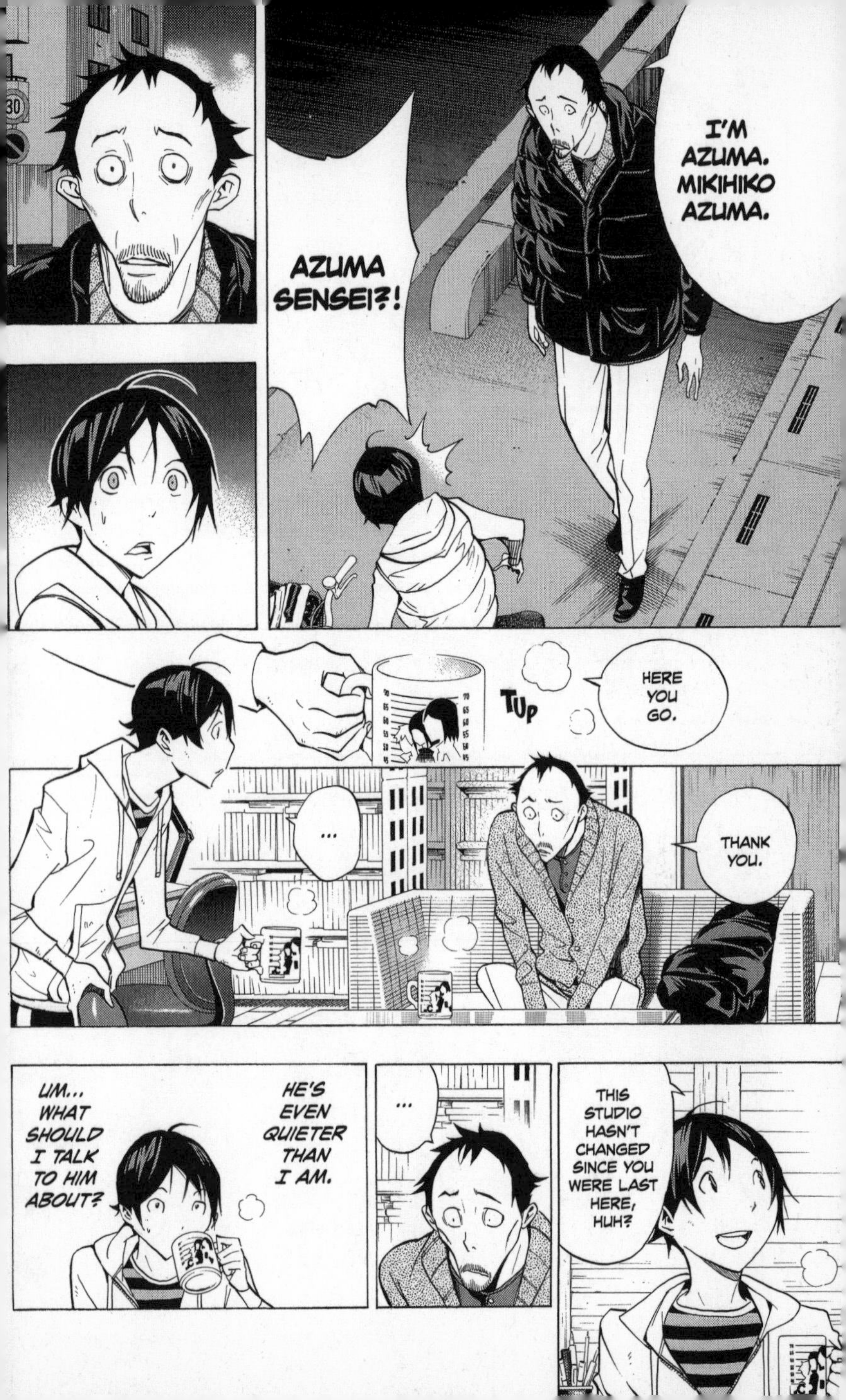
I'M AZUMA. MIKIHIKO AZUMA.
AZUMA SENSEI?!
TUP
HERE YOU GO.
THANK YOU.
...
THIS STUDIO HASN'T CHANGED SINCE YOU WERE LAST HERE, HUH?
...
HE'S EVEN QUIETER THAN I AM.
UM... WHAT SHOULD I TALK TO HIM ABOUT?

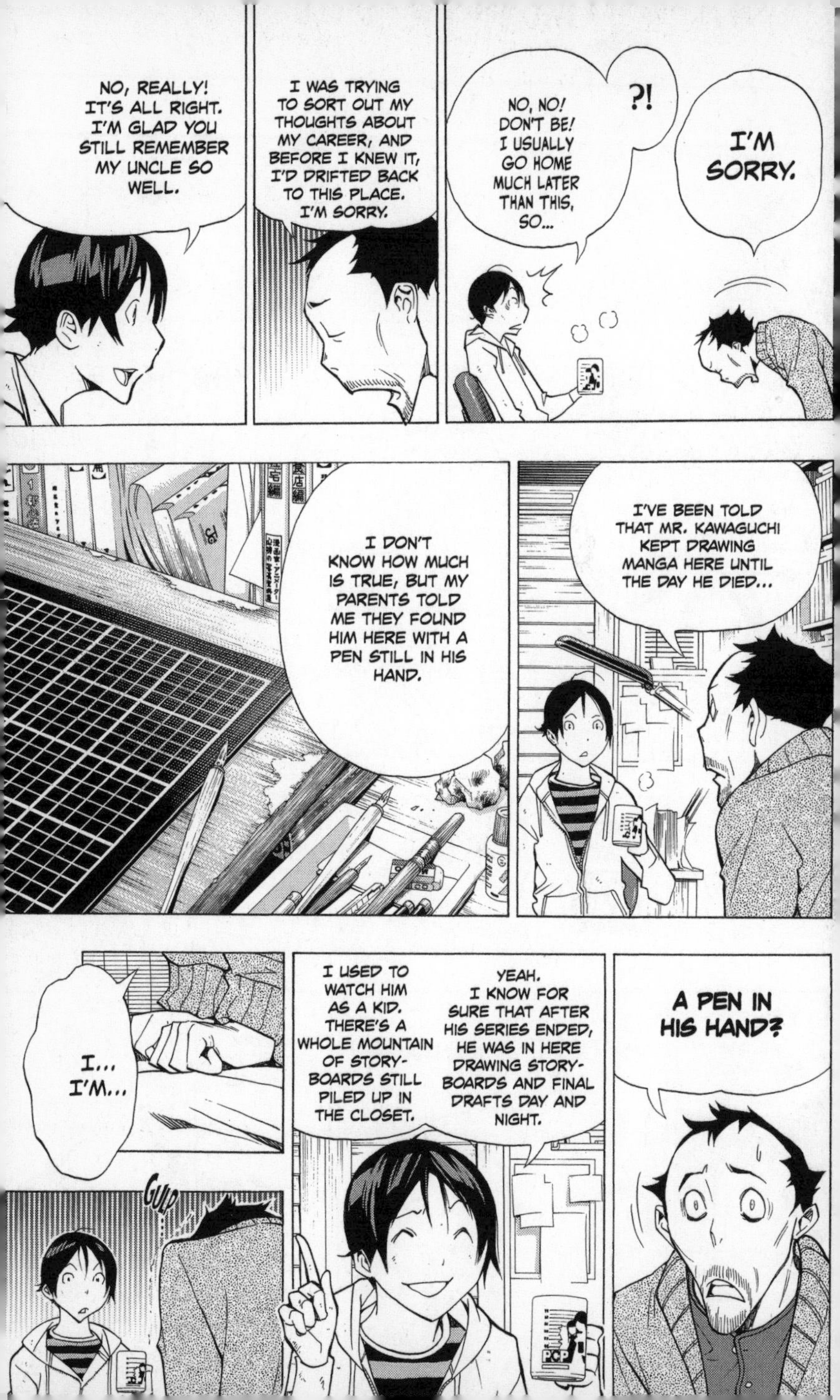
I'M SORRY.
?!
NO, NO! DON'T BE! I USUALLY GO HOME MUCH LATER THAN THIS, SO...
I WAS TRYING TO SORT OUT MY THOUGHTS ABOUT MY CAREER, AND BEFORE I KNEW IT, I'D DRIFTED BACK TO THIS PLACE. I'M SORRY.
NO, REALLY! IT'S ALL RIGHT. I'M GLAD YOU STILL REMEMBER MY UNCLE SO WELL.
I'VE BEEN TOLD THAT MR. KAWAGUCHI KEPT DRAWING MANGA HERE UNTIL THE DAY HE DIED...
I DON'T KNOW HOW MUCH IS TRUE, BUT MY PARENTS TOLD ME THEY FOUND HIM HERE WITH A PEN STILL IN HIS HAND.
A PEN IN HIS HAND?
YEAH. I KNOW FOR SURE THAT AFTER HIS SERIES ENDED, HE WAS IN HERE DRAWING STORY-BOARDS AND FINAL DRAFTS DAY AND NIGHT.
I USED TO WATCH HIM AS A KID. THERE'S A WHOLE MOUNTAIN OF STORY-BOARDS STILL PILED UP IN THE CLOSET.
PCP
I... I'M...
GULP

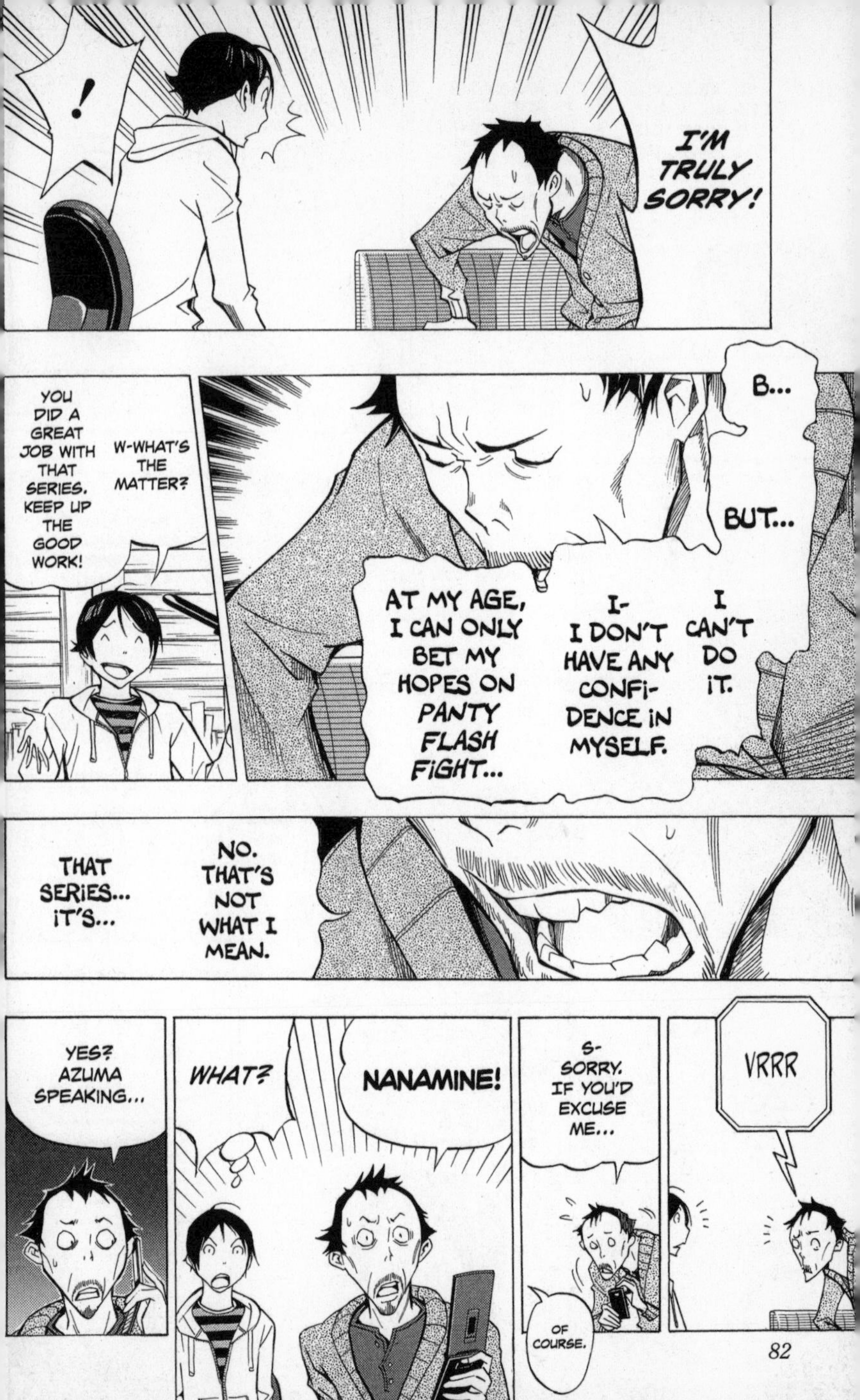

I'M TRULY SORRY!
!
B...
BUT...
I CAN'T DO IT.
I- I DON'T HAVE ANY CONFIDENCE IN MYSELF.
AT MY AGE, I CAN ONLY BET MY HOPES ON PANTY FLASH FIGHT...
W-WHAT'S THE MATTER?
YOU DID A GREAT JOB WITH THAT SERIES. KEEP UP THE GOOD WORK!
NO. THAT'S NOT WHAT I MEAN.
THAT SERIES... IT'S...
VRRR
S-SORRY. IF YOU'D EXCUSE ME...
OF COURSE.
NANAMINE!
WHAT?
YES? AZUMA SPEAKING...

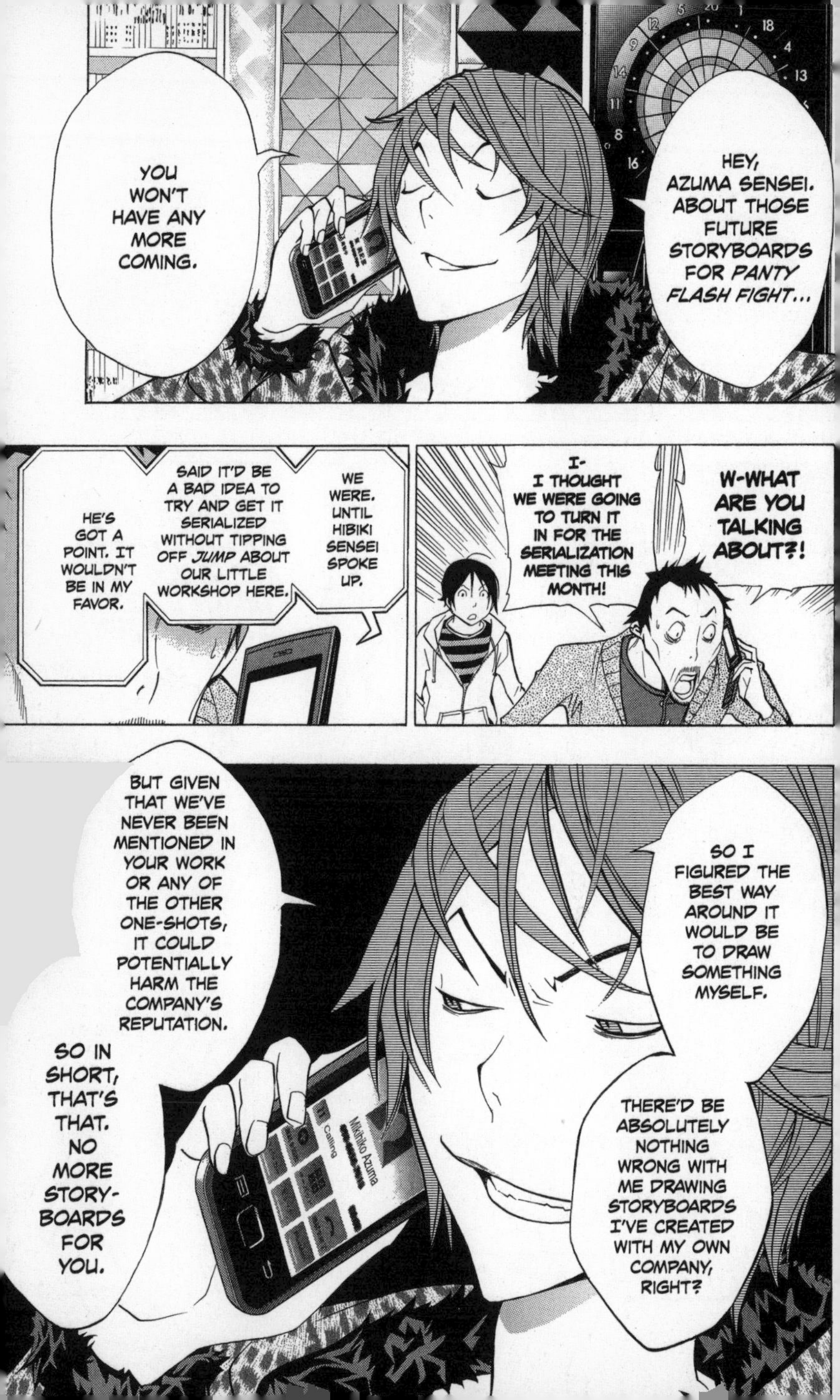

HEY, AZUMA SENSEI. ABOUT THOSE FUTURE STORYBOARDS FOR *PANTY FLASH FIGHT*...
YOU WON'T HAVE ANY MORE COMING.
W-WHAT ARE YOU TALKING ABOUT?!
I- I THOUGHT WE WERE GOING TO TURN IT IN FOR THE SERIALIZATION MEETING THIS MONTH!
WE WERE. UNTIL HIBIKI SENSEI SPOKE UP.
SAID IT'D BE A BAD IDEA TO TRY AND GET IT SERIALIZED WITHOUT TIPPING OFF *JUMP* ABOUT OUR LITTLE WORKSHOP HERE.
HE'S GOT A POINT. IT WOULDN'T BE IN MY FAVOR.
BUT GIVEN THAT WE'VE NEVER BEEN MENTIONED IN YOUR WORK OR ANY OF THE OTHER ONE-SHOTS, IT COULD POTENTIALLY HARM THE COMPANY'S REPUTATION.
SO I FIGURED THE BEST WAY AROUND IT WOULD BE TO DRAW SOMETHING MYSELF.
THERE'D BE ABSOLUTELY NOTHING WRONG WITH ME DRAWING STORYBOARDS I'VE CREATED WITH MY OWN COMPANY, RIGHT?
SO IN SHORT, THAT'S THAT. NO MORE STORY-BOARDS FOR YOU.

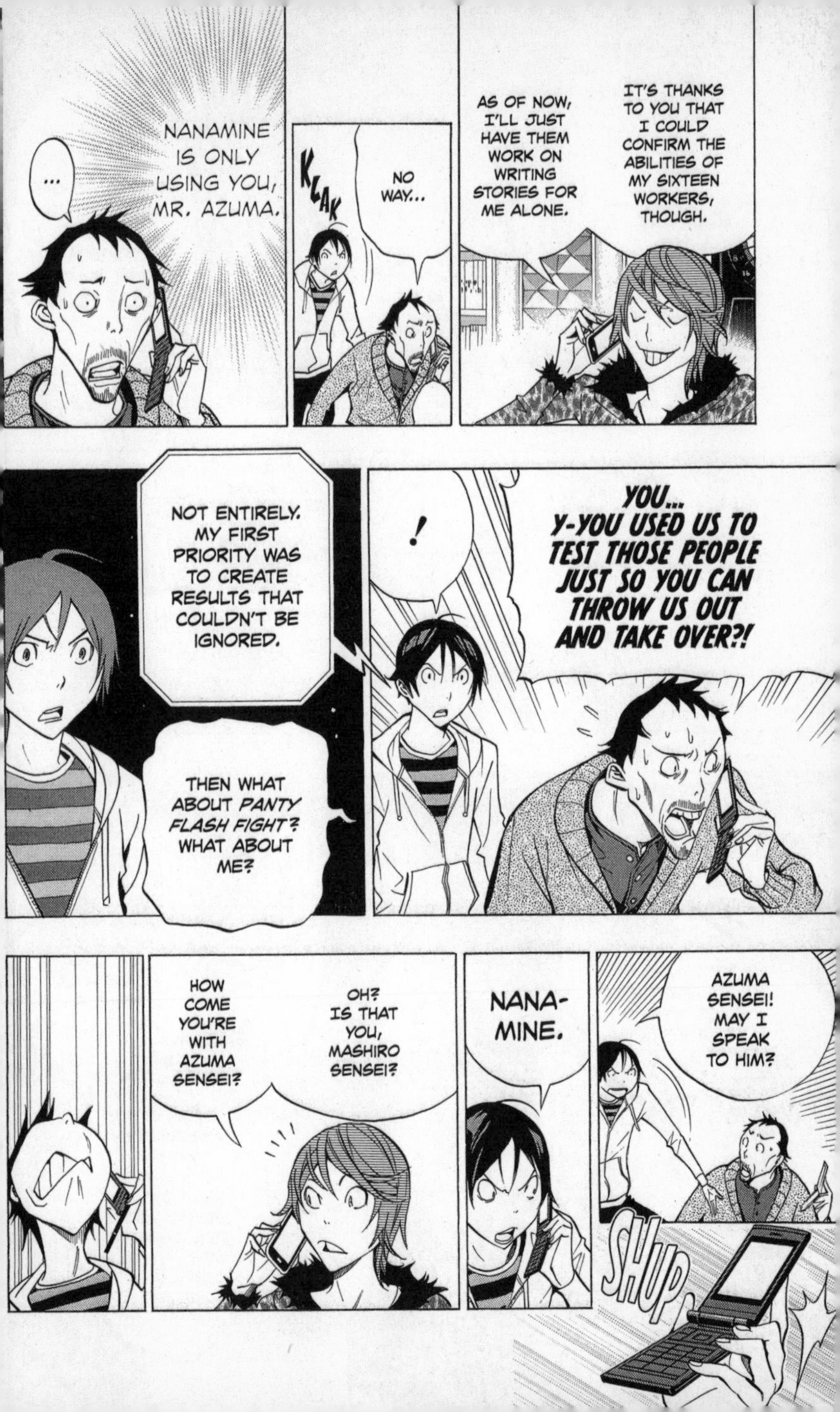
IT'S THANKS TO YOU THAT I COULD CONFIRM THE ABILITIES OF MY SIXTEEN WORKERS, THOUGH.
AS OF NOW, I'LL JUST HAVE THEM WORK ON WRITING STORIES FOR ME ALONE.
NO WAY...
KLAK
NANAMINE IS ONLY USING YOU, MR. AZUMA.
...
YOU... Y-YOU USED US TO TEST THOSE PEOPLE JUST SO YOU CAN THROW US OUT AND TAKE OVER?!
!
NOT ENTIRELY. MY FIRST PRIORITY WAS TO CREATE RESULTS THAT COULDN'T BE IGNORED.
THEN WHAT ABOUT *PANTY FLASH FIGHT*? WHAT ABOUT ME?
AZUMA SENSEI! MAY I SPEAK TO HIM?
SHUP
NANA-MINE.
OH? IS THAT YOU, MASHIRO SENSEI?
HOW COME YOU'RE WITH AZUMA SENSEI?

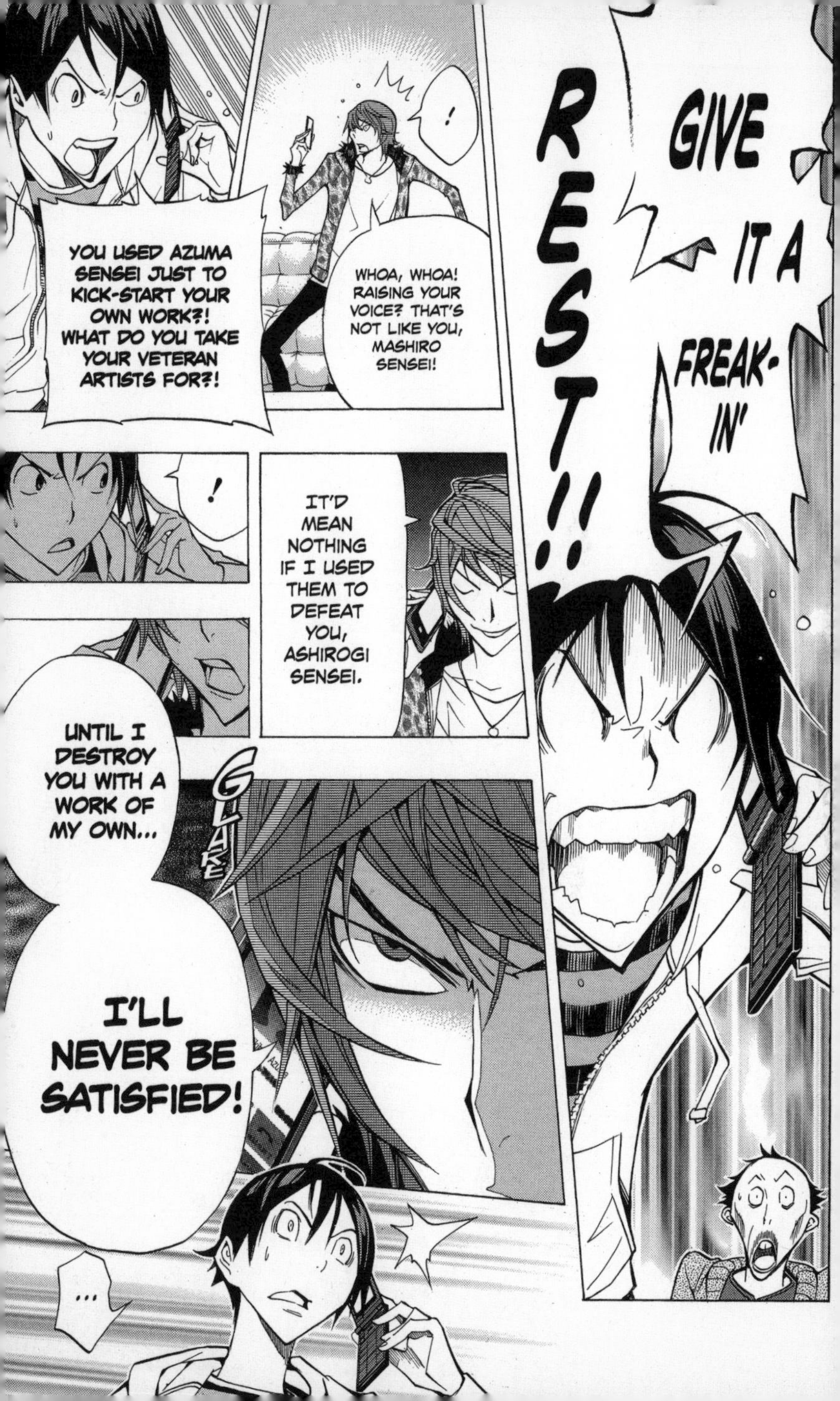
GIVE IT A FREAKIN' REST!!
!
WHOA, WHOA! RAISING YOUR VOICE? THAT'S NOT LIKE YOU, MASHIRO SENSEI!
YOU USED AZUMA SENSEI JUST TO KICK-START YOUR OWN WORK?! WHAT DO YOU TAKE YOUR VETERAN ARTISTS FOR?!
IT'D MEAN NOTHING IF I USED THEM TO DEFEAT YOU, ASHIROGI SENSEI.
!
GLARE
UNTIL I DESTROY YOU WITH A WORK OF MY OWN...
I'LL NEVER BE SATISFIED!
...

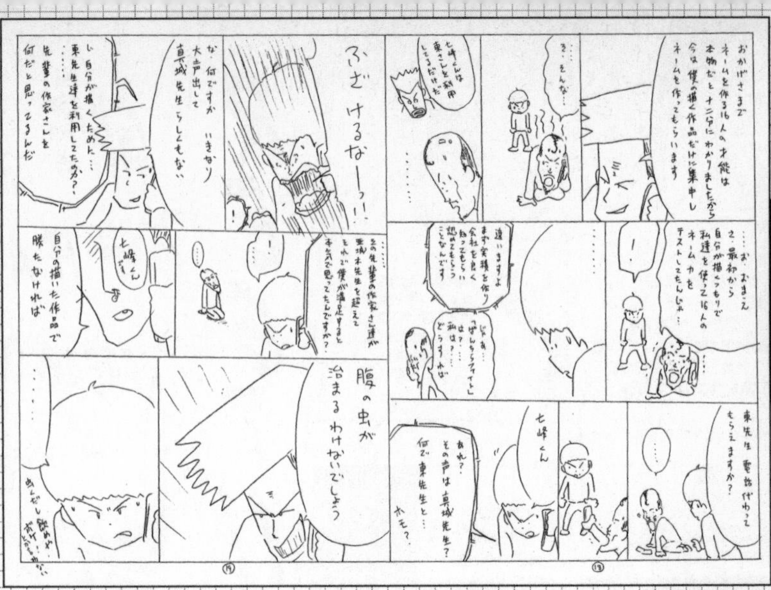

おかげさまで ネームを作る16人の才能は本物だとナニゲにわかりましたから 今は僕の描く作品だけに集中しネームを作ってもらいます
き・・・ そんな・・・
七峰くんは東さんを利用しているだけだ
・・・・・・
お・・・ おまえ 最初から自分が描くつもりで私達を使って16人のネーム力をテストしてたんじゃ・・・
!
・・・・・・
違いますよ まず実績を作り会社を良く知ってもらい認めてもらうことなんです
じゃあ・・・
は? 私は? どうすれば
東先生 電話代わってもらえますか?
・・・
七峰くん
あれ? その声は真城先生? 何で東先生と・・・ ホモ?
ふざけるなーっ!!
!
な・何ですか いきなり大声出して 真城先生らしくもない
じ 自分が描くために・・・ 東先生達を利用してたのか? ・・・・・・ 先輩の作家さんを何だと思ってるんだ
その先輩の作家さん達が 真城先生を超えるとかで僕が満足すると本気で思ってたんですか?
!
・・・
七峰くん
自分の描いた作品で勝たなければ
腹の虫が治まるわけないでしょう
・・・・・・
⑲
⑱

OHBA'S STORYBOARD

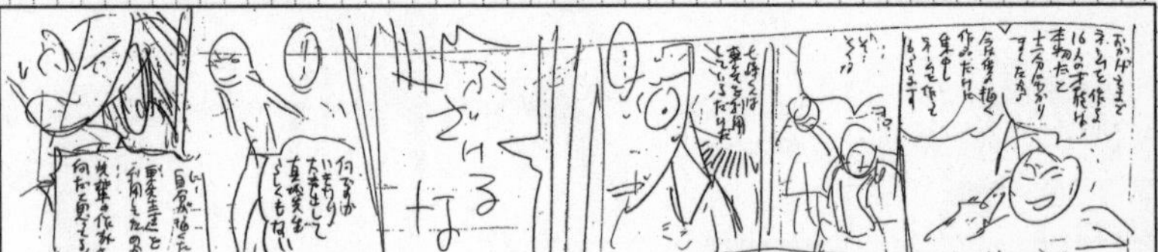

ふざけるなーっ
腹の虫が治まるわけないでしょう

OBATA'S STORYBOARD

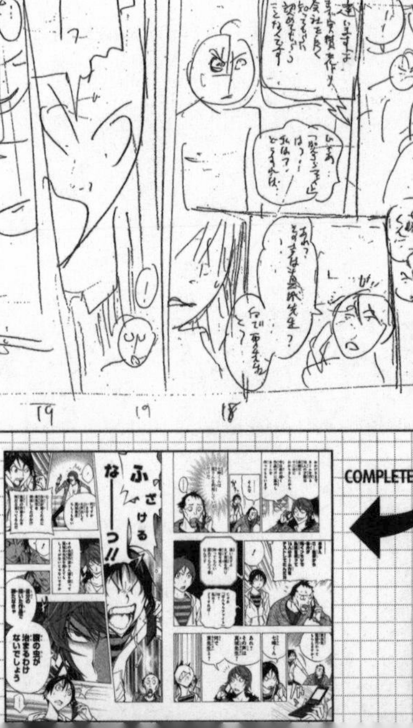

ふざけるなーっ!!
腹の虫が治まるわけないでしょう

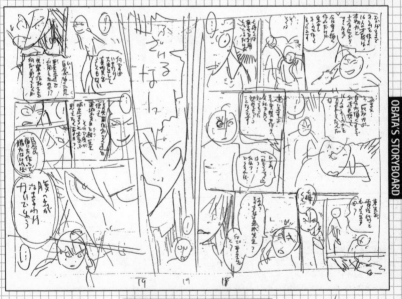

COMPLETE!

※CREATOR STORYBOARDS AND FINISHED PAGES IN JAPANESE

BAKUMAN。vol.17

"Until the Final Draft Is Complete"

Chapter 146, pp. 84-85

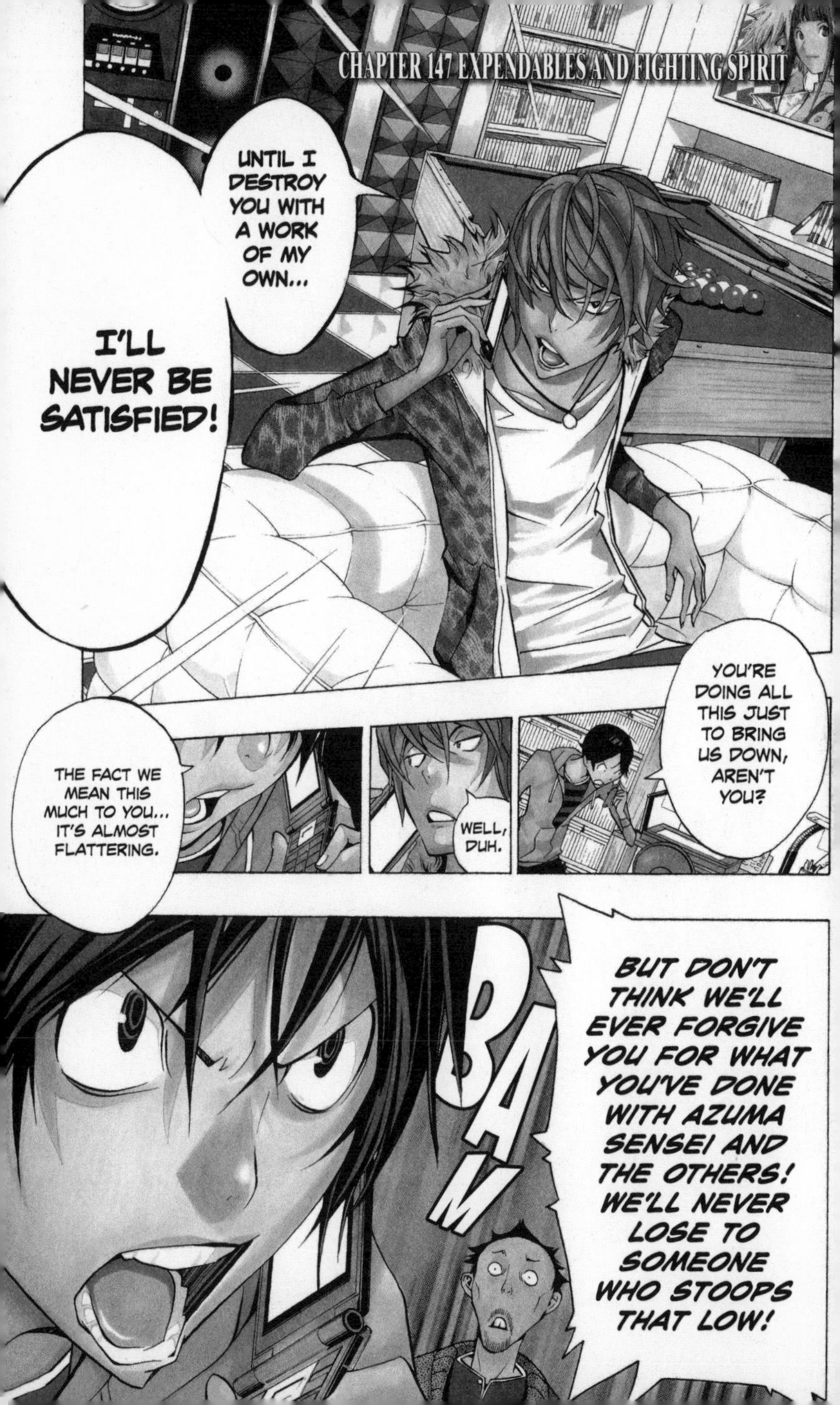
CHAPTER 147 EXPENDABLES AND FIGHTING SPIRIT
UNTIL I DESTROY YOU WITH A WORK OF MY OWN...
I'LL NEVER BE SATISFIED!
YOU'RE DOING ALL THIS JUST TO BRING US DOWN, AREN'T YOU?
WELL, DUH.
THE FACT WE MEAN THIS MUCH TO YOU... IT'S ALMOST FLATTERING.
BAM
BUT DON'T THINK WE'LL EVER FORGIVE YOU FOR WHAT YOU'VE DONE WITH AZUMA SENSEI AND THE OTHERS! WE'LL NEVER LOSE TO SOMEONE WHO STOOPS THAT LOW!

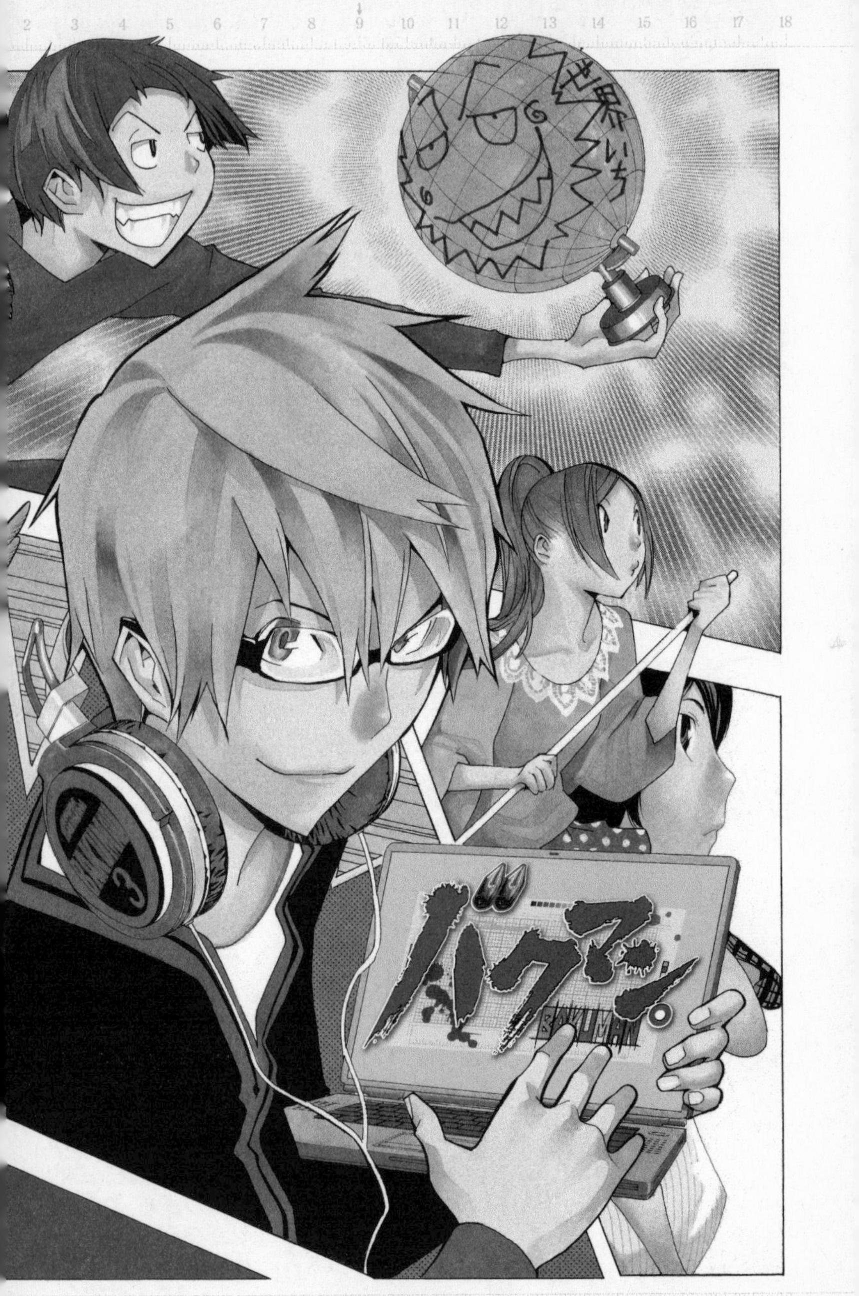
世界いち
バクマン。
BAKUMAN

CHAPTER 147
EXPENDABLES AND FIGHTING SPIRIT

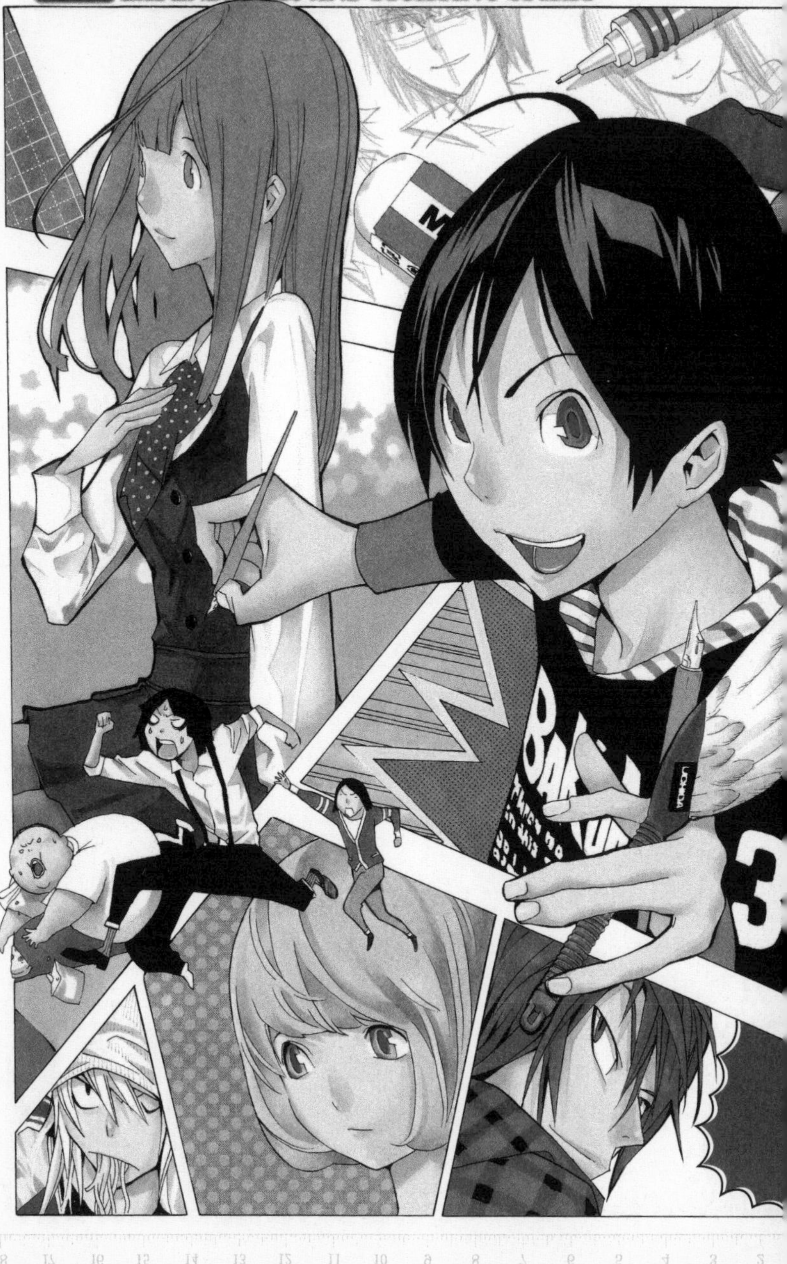

BAKUMAN。

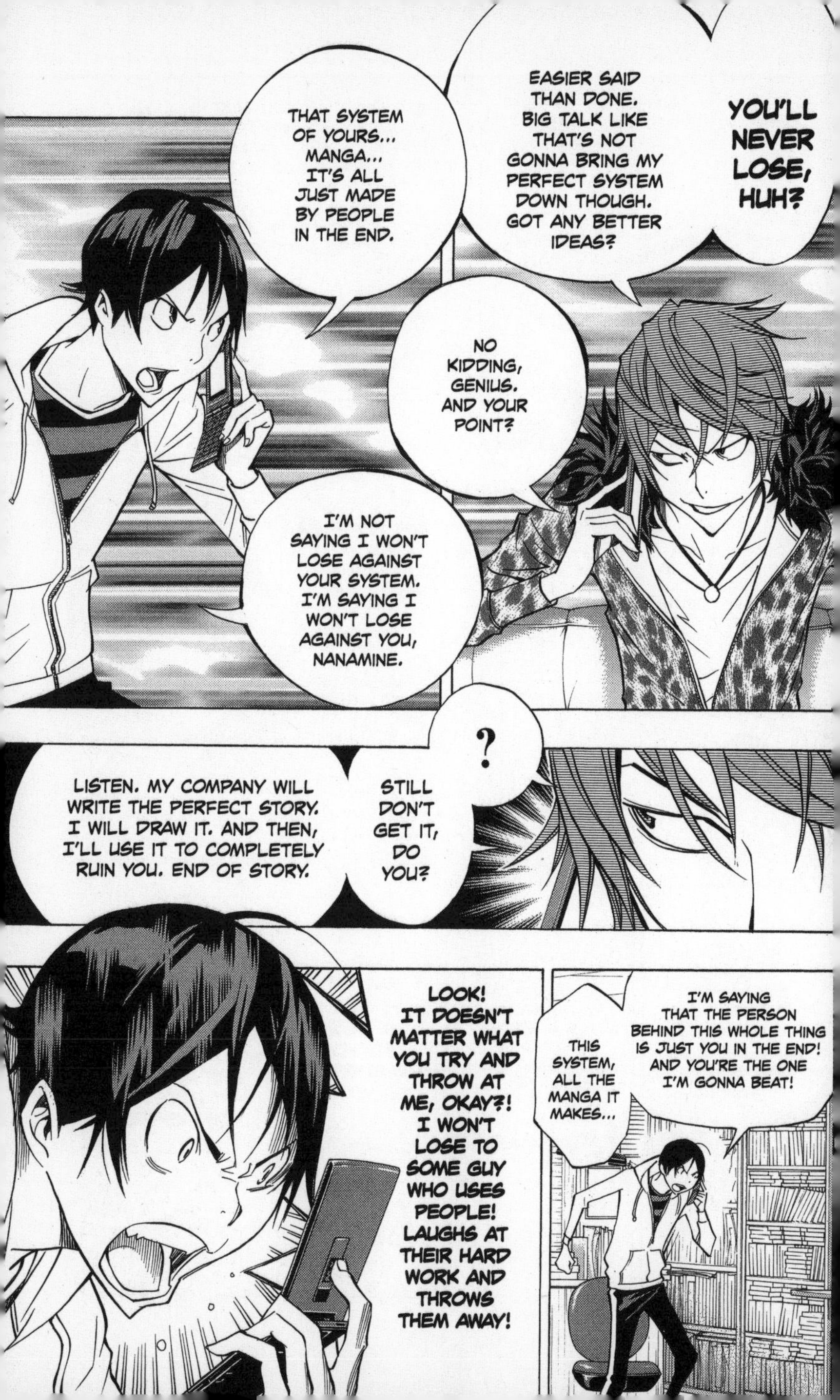
YOU'LL NEVER LOSE, HUH?
EASIER SAID THAN DONE. BIG TALK LIKE THAT'S NOT GONNA BRING MY PERFECT SYSTEM DOWN THOUGH. GOT ANY BETTER IDEAS?
THAT SYSTEM OF YOURS... MANGA... IT'S ALL JUST MADE BY PEOPLE IN THE END.
NO KIDDING, GENIUS. AND YOUR POINT?
I'M NOT SAYING I WON'T LOSE AGAINST YOUR SYSTEM. I'M SAYING I WON'T LOSE AGAINST YOU, NANAMINE.
?
STILL DON'T GET IT, DO YOU?
LISTEN. MY COMPANY WILL WRITE THE PERFECT STORY. I WILL DRAW IT. AND THEN, I'LL USE IT TO COMPLETELY RUIN YOU. END OF STORY.
I'M SAYING THAT THE PERSON BEHIND THIS WHOLE THING IS JUST YOU IN THE END! AND YOU'RE THE ONE I'M GONNA BEAT!
THIS SYSTEM, ALL THE MANGA IT MAKES...
LOOK! IT DOESN'T MATTER WHAT YOU TRY AND THROW AT ME, OKAY?! I WON'T LOSE TO SOME GUY WHO USES PEOPLE! LAUGHS AT THEIR HARD WORK AND THROWS THEM AWAY!

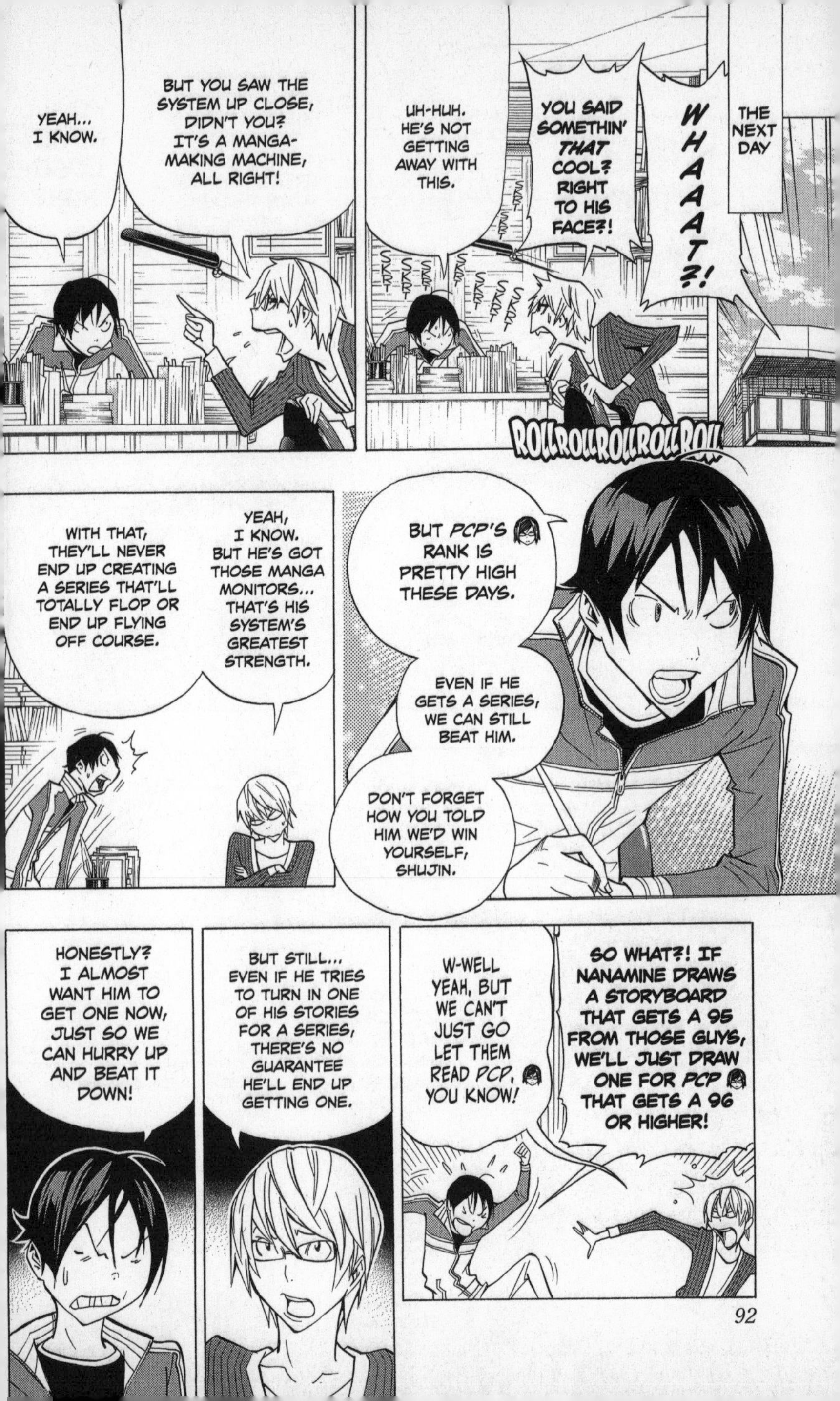
THE NEXT DAY
WHAAAAT?!
YOU SAID SOMETHIN' *THAT* COOL? RIGHT TO HIS FACE?!
SKRT SKRT SKRT
SKRT SKRT SKRT SKRT SKRT SKRT SKRT
UH-HUH. HE'S NOT GETTING AWAY WITH THIS.
BUT YOU SAW THE SYSTEM UP CLOSE, DIDN'T YOU? IT'S A MANGA-MAKING MACHINE, ALL RIGHT!
YEAH... I KNOW.
ROLLROLLROLLROLLROLL
BUT *PCP'S* RANK IS PRETTY HIGH THESE DAYS.
EVEN IF HE GETS A SERIES, WE CAN STILL BEAT HIM.
DON'T FORGET HOW YOU TOLD HIM WE'D WIN YOURSELF, SHUJIN.
YEAH, I KNOW. BUT HE'S GOT THOSE MANGA MONITORS... THAT'S HIS SYSTEM'S GREATEST STRENGTH.
WITH THAT, THEY'LL NEVER END UP CREATING A SERIES THAT'LL TOTALLY FLOP OR END UP FLYING OFF COURSE.
SO WHAT?! IF NANAMINE DRAWS A STORYBOARD THAT GETS A 95 FROM THOSE GUYS, WE'LL JUST DRAW ONE FOR *PCP* THAT GETS A 96 OR HIGHER!
W-WELL YEAH, BUT WE CAN'T JUST GO LET THEM READ *PCP*, YOU KNOW!
BUT STILL... EVEN IF HE TRIES TO TURN IN ONE OF HIS STORIES FOR A SERIES, THERE'S NO GUARANTEE HE'LL END UP GETTING ONE.
HONESTLY? I ALMOST WANT HIM TO GET ONE NOW, JUST SO WE CAN HURRY UP AND BEAT IT DOWN!

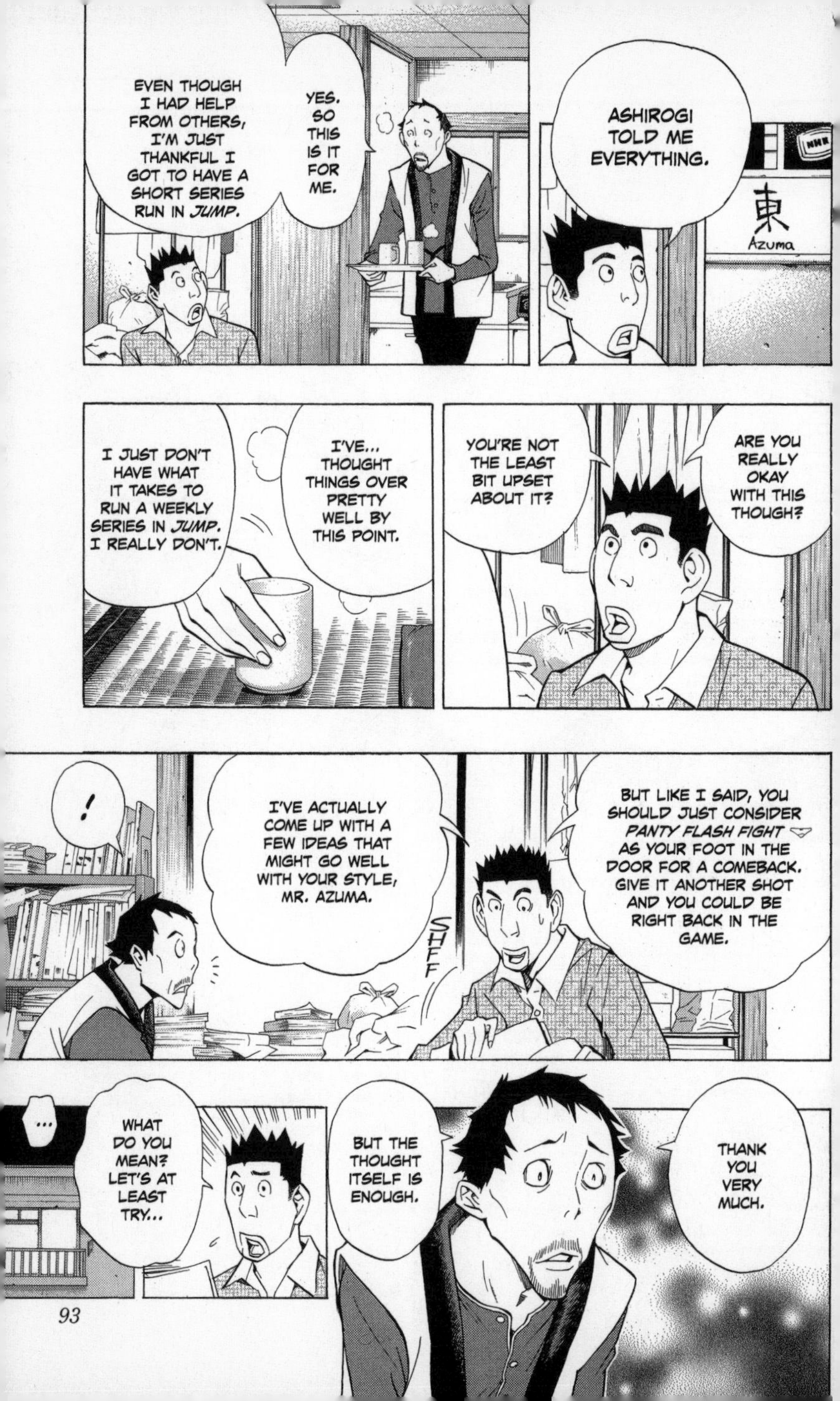
ASHIROGI TOLD ME EVERYTHING.
東
Azuma
YES. SO THIS IS IT FOR ME.
EVEN THOUGH I HAD HELP FROM OTHERS, I'M JUST THANKFUL I GOT TO HAVE A SHORT SERIES RUN IN *JUMP*.
ARE YOU REALLY OKAY WITH THIS THOUGH?
YOU'RE NOT THE LEAST BIT UPSET ABOUT IT?
I'VE... THOUGHT THINGS OVER PRETTY WELL BY THIS POINT.
I JUST DON'T HAVE WHAT IT TAKES TO RUN A WEEKLY SERIES IN *JUMP*. I REALLY DON'T.
BUT LIKE I SAID, YOU SHOULD JUST CONSIDER *PANTY FLASH FIGHT* AS YOUR FOOT IN THE DOOR FOR A COMEBACK. GIVE IT ANOTHER SHOT AND YOU COULD BE RIGHT BACK IN THE GAME.
SHFF
I'VE ACTUALLY COME UP WITH A FEW IDEAS THAT MIGHT GO WELL WITH YOUR STYLE, MR. AZUMA.
!
THANK YOU VERY MUCH.
BUT THE THOUGHT ITSELF IS ENOUGH.
WHAT DO YOU MEAN? LET'S AT LEAST TRY...
...

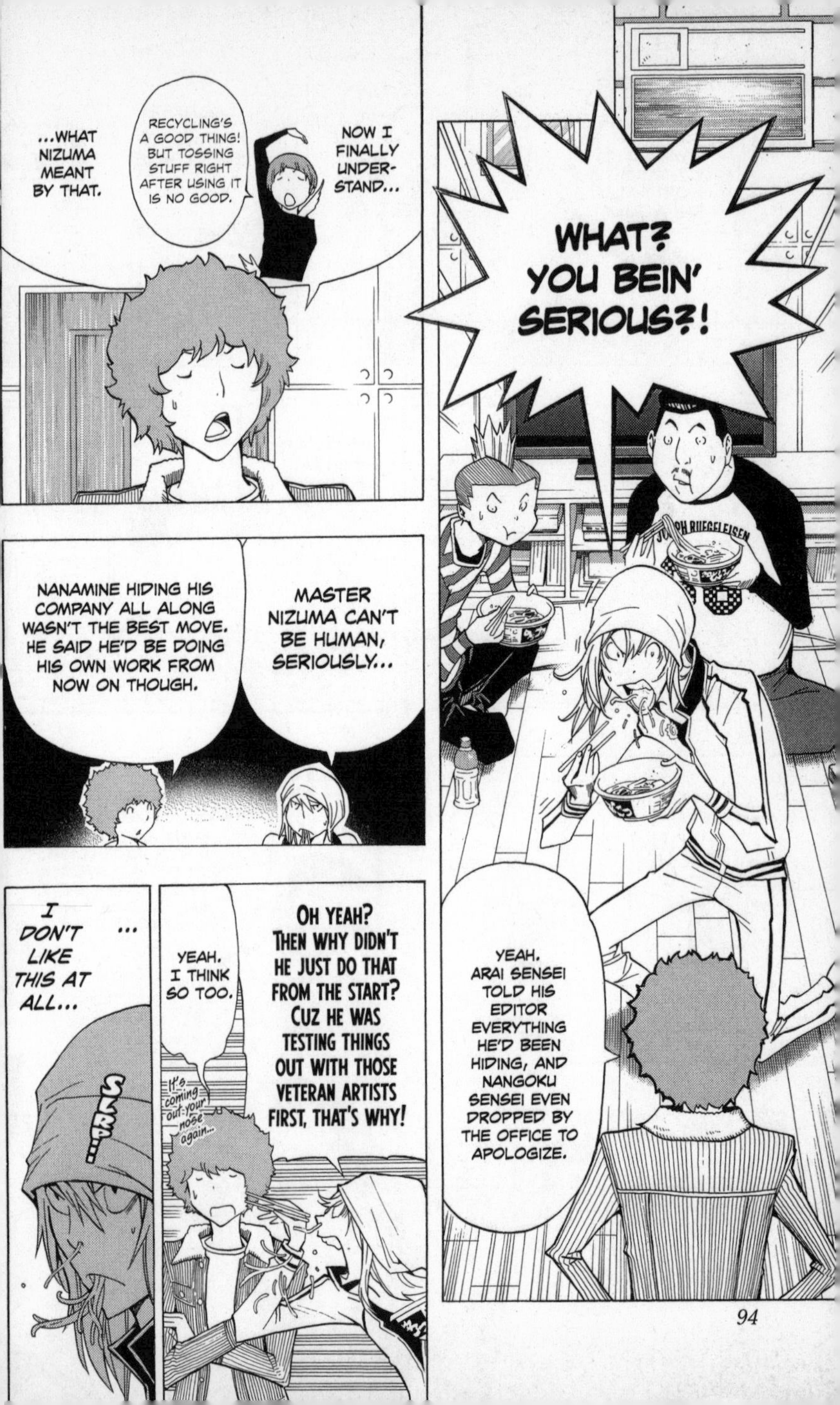
WHAT? YOU BEIN' SERIOUS?!
YEAH. ARAI SENSEI TOLD HIS EDITOR EVERYTHING HE'D BEEN HIDING, AND NANGOKU SENSEI EVEN DROPPED BY THE OFFICE TO APOLOGIZE.
NOW I FINALLY UNDER-STAND...
RECYCLING'S A GOOD THING! BUT TOSSING STUFF RIGHT AFTER USING IT IS NO GOOD.
...WHAT NIZUMA MEANT BY THAT.
MASTER NIZUMA CAN'T BE HUMAN, SERIOUSLY...
NANAMINE HIDING HIS COMPANY ALL ALONG WASN'T THE BEST MOVE. HE SAID HE'D BE DOING HIS OWN WORK FROM NOW ON THOUGH.
OH YEAH? THEN WHY DIDN'T HE JUST DO THAT FROM THE START? CUZ HE WAS TESTING THINGS OUT WITH THOSE VETERAN ARTISTS FIRST, THAT'S WHY!
YEAH. I THINK SO TOO.
It's coming out your nose again...
...
I DON'T LIKE THIS AT ALL...
SLRP...

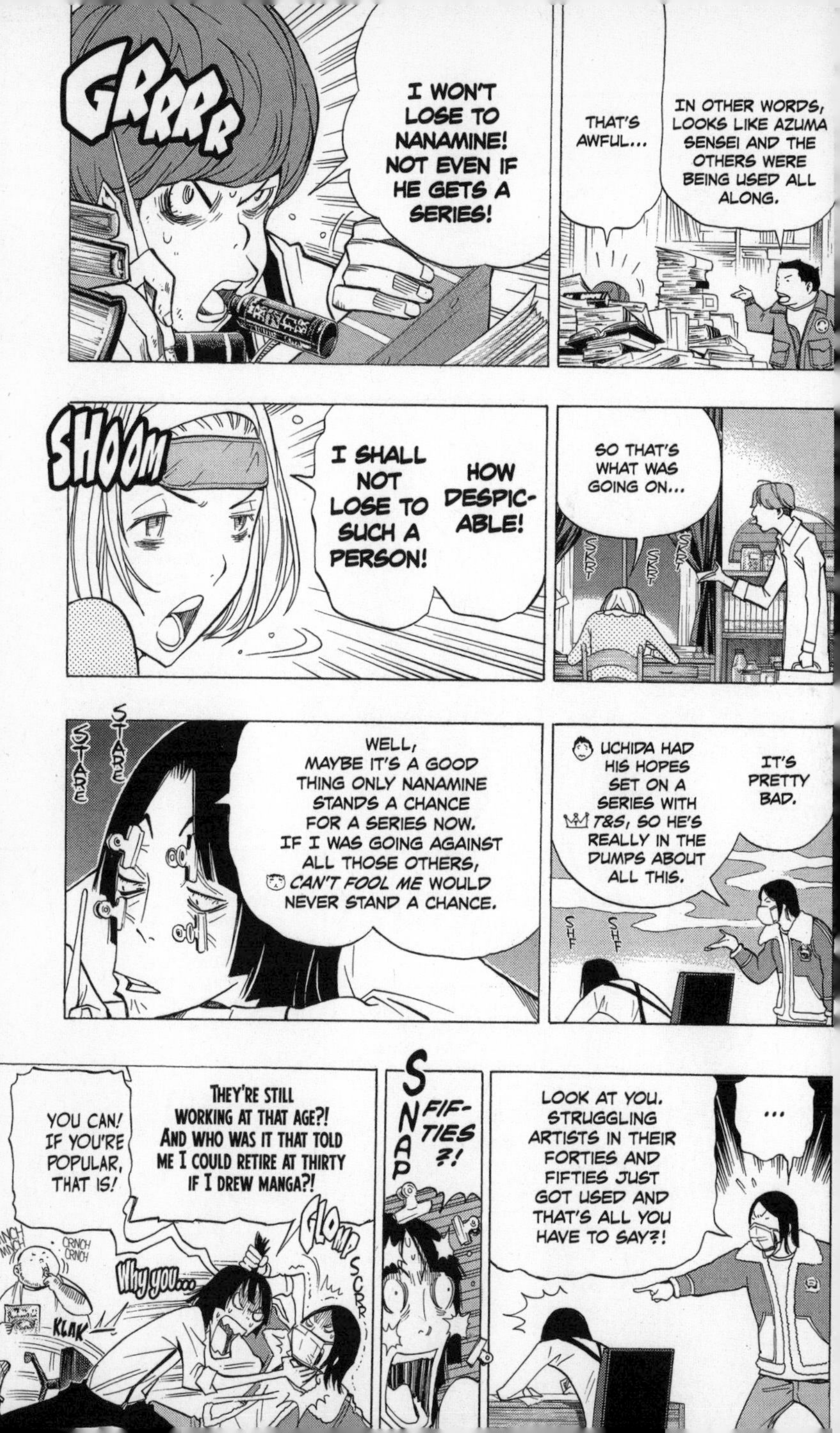
IN OTHER WORDS, LOOKS LIKE AZUMA SENSEI AND THE OTHERS WERE BEING USED ALL ALONG.
THAT'S AWFUL...
I WON'T LOSE TO NANAMINE! NOT EVEN IF HE GETS A SERIES!
GRRRR
SO THAT'S WHAT WAS GOING ON...
SKRT SKRT SKRT
HOW DESPICABLE!
I SHALL NOT LOSE TO SUCH A PERSON!
SHOOM
IT'S PRETTY BAD.
UCHIDA HAD HIS HOPES SET ON A SERIES WITH T&S, SO HE'S REALLY IN THE DUMPS ABOUT ALL THIS.
SHF SHF
STARE STARE
WELL, MAYBE IT'S A GOOD THING ONLY NANAMINE STANDS A CHANCE FOR A SERIES NOW. IF I WAS GOING AGAINST ALL THOSE OTHERS, CAN'T FOOL ME WOULD NEVER STAND A CHANCE.
...
LOOK AT YOU. STRUGGLING ARTISTS IN THEIR FORTIES AND FIFTIES JUST GOT USED AND THAT'S ALL YOU HAVE TO SAY?!
SNAP
FIF-TIES?!
THEY'RE STILL WORKING AT THAT AGE?! AND WHO WAS IT THAT TOLD ME I COULD RETIRE AT THIRTY IF I DREW MANGA?!
YOU CAN! IF YOU'RE POPULAR, THAT IS!
GLOMP
SCRR
Why you...
MNCH MNCH
CRNCH CRNCH
KLAK

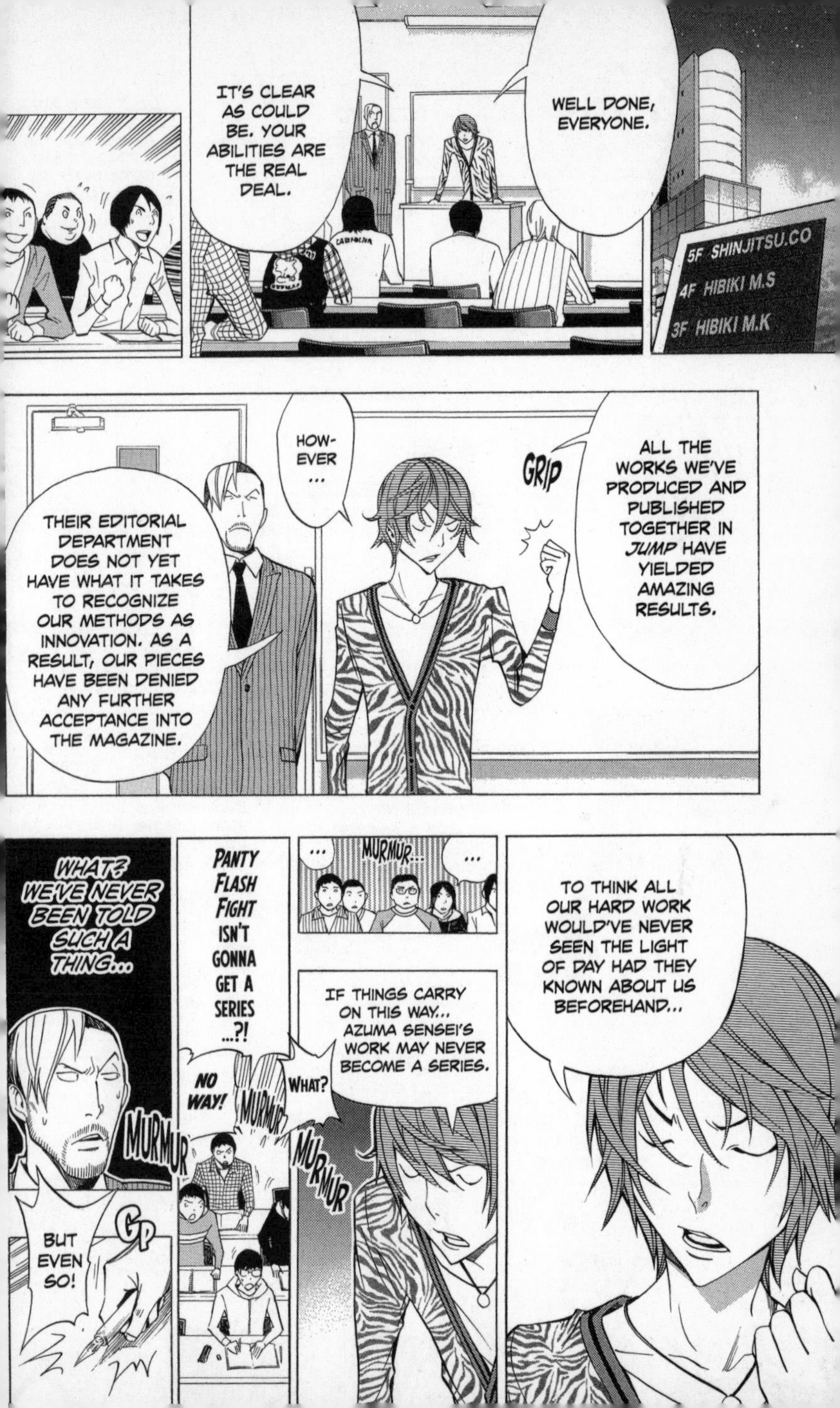
5F SHINJITSU.CO
4F HIBIKI M.S
3F HIBIKI M.K
WELL DONE, EVERYONE.
IT'S CLEAR AS COULD BE. YOUR ABILITIES ARE THE REAL DEAL.
ALL THE WORKS WE'VE PRODUCED AND PUBLISHED TOGETHER IN *JUMP* HAVE YIELDED AMAZING RESULTS.
GRIP
HOW-EVER ...
THEIR EDITORIAL DEPARTMENT DOES NOT YET HAVE WHAT IT TAKES TO RECOGNIZE OUR METHODS AS INNOVATION. AS A RESULT, OUR PIECES HAVE BEEN DENIED ANY FURTHER ACCEPTANCE INTO THE MAGAZINE.
TO THINK ALL OUR HARD WORK WOULD'VE NEVER SEEN THE LIGHT OF DAY HAD THEY KNOWN ABOUT US BEFOREHAND...
...
MURMUR...
...
IF THINGS CARRY ON THIS WAY... AZUMA SENSEI'S WORK MAY NEVER BECOME A SERIES.
MURMUR
WHAT?
NO WAY!
MURMUR
PANTY FLASH FIGHT ISN'T GONNA GET A SERIES ...?!
WHAT? WE'VE NEVER BEEN TOLD SUCH A THING...
MURMUR
GP
BUT EVEN SO!

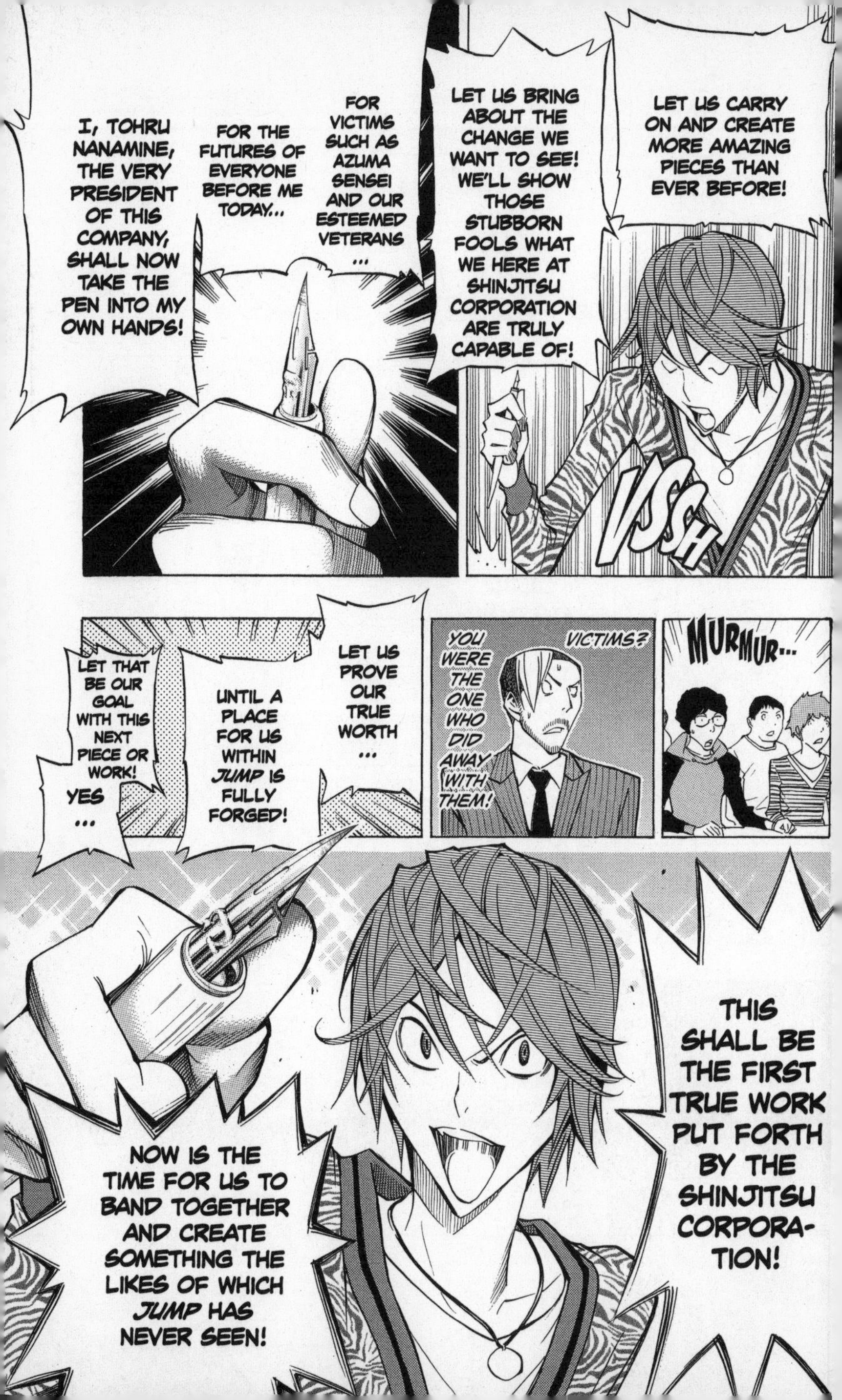
LET US CARRY ON AND CREATE MORE AMAZING PIECES THAN EVER BEFORE!
LET US BRING ABOUT THE CHANGE WE WANT TO SEE! WE'LL SHOW THOSE STUBBORN FOOLS WHAT WE HERE AT SHINJITSU CORPORATION ARE TRULY CAPABLE OF!
VSSH
FOR VICTIMS SUCH AS AZUMA SENSEI AND OUR ESTEEMED VETERANS...
FOR THE FUTURES OF EVERYONE BEFORE ME TODAY...
I, TOHRU NANAMINE, THE VERY PRESIDENT OF THIS COMPANY, SHALL NOW TAKE THE PEN INTO MY OWN HANDS!
MURMUR...
VICTIMS?
YOU WERE THE ONE WHO DID AWAY WITH THEM!
LET US PROVE OUR TRUE WORTH...
UNTIL A PLACE FOR US WITHIN *JUMP* IS FULLY FORGED!
LET THAT BE OUR GOAL WITH THIS NEXT PIECE OR WORK! YES...
THIS SHALL BE THE FIRST TRUE WORK PUT FORTH BY THE SHINJITSU CORPORA-TION!
NOW IS THE TIME FOR US TO BAND TOGETHER AND CREATE SOMETHING THE LIKES OF WHICH *JUMP* HAS NEVER SEEN!

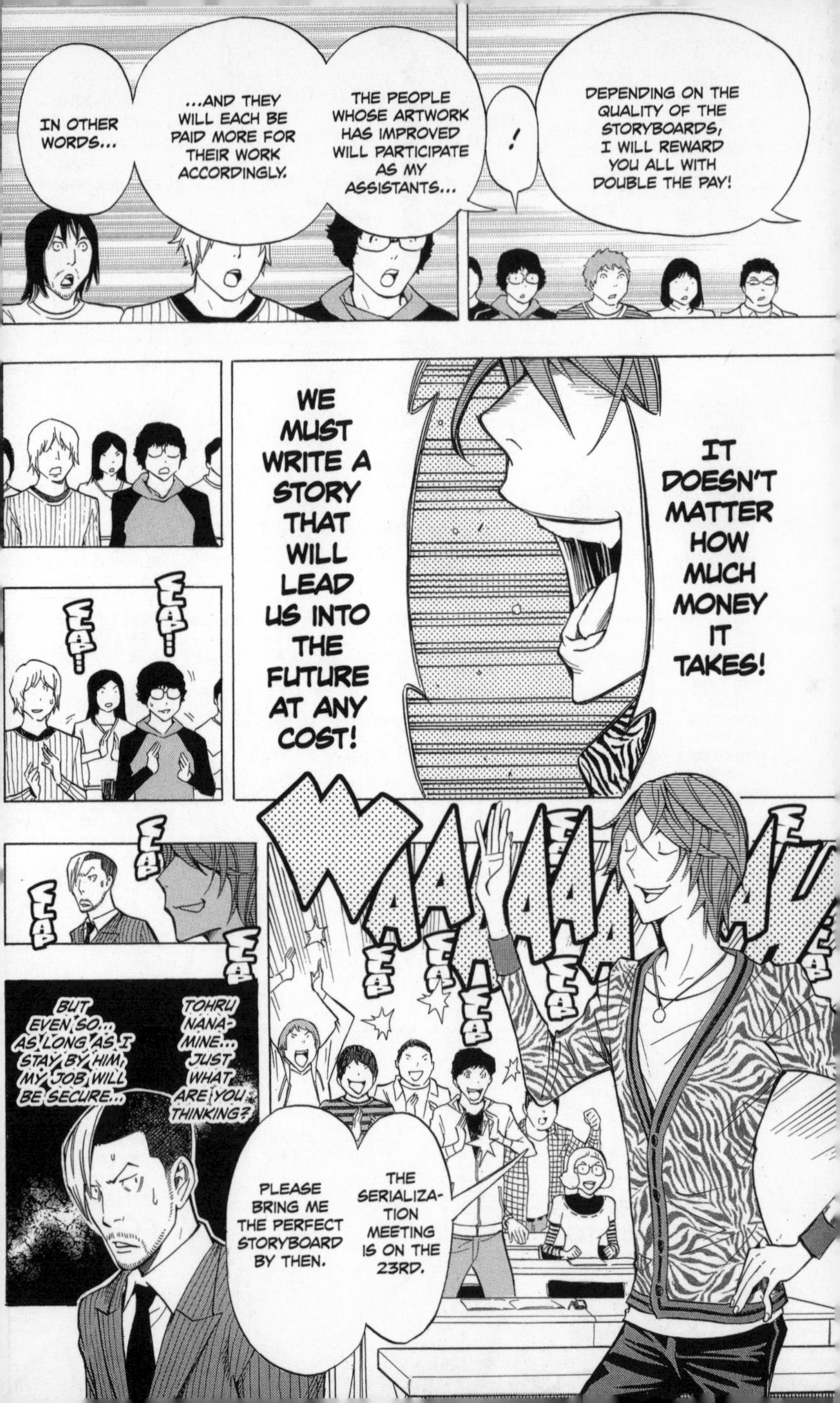
DEPENDING ON THE QUALITY OF THE STORYBOARDS, I WILL REWARD YOU ALL WITH DOUBLE THE PAY!
!
THE PEOPLE WHOSE ARTWORK HAS IMPROVED WILL PARTICIPATE AS MY ASSISTANTS...
...AND THEY WILL EACH BE PAID MORE FOR THEIR WORK ACCORDINGLY.
IN OTHER WORDS...
IT DOESN'T MATTER HOW MUCH MONEY IT TAKES!
WE MUST WRITE A STORY THAT WILL LEAD US INTO THE FUTURE AT ANY COST!
CLAP!!
CLAP!!
WAAAAAH
CLAP
CLAP
CLAP
CLAP
CLAP
CLAP
THE SERIALIZATION MEETING IS ON THE 23RD.
PLEASE BRING ME THE PERFECT STORYBOARD BY THEN.
CLAP
CLAP
CLAP
TOHRU NANAMINE... JUST WHAT ARE YOU THINKING?
BUT EVEN SO... AS LONG AS I STAY BY HIM, MY JOB WILL BE SECURE...

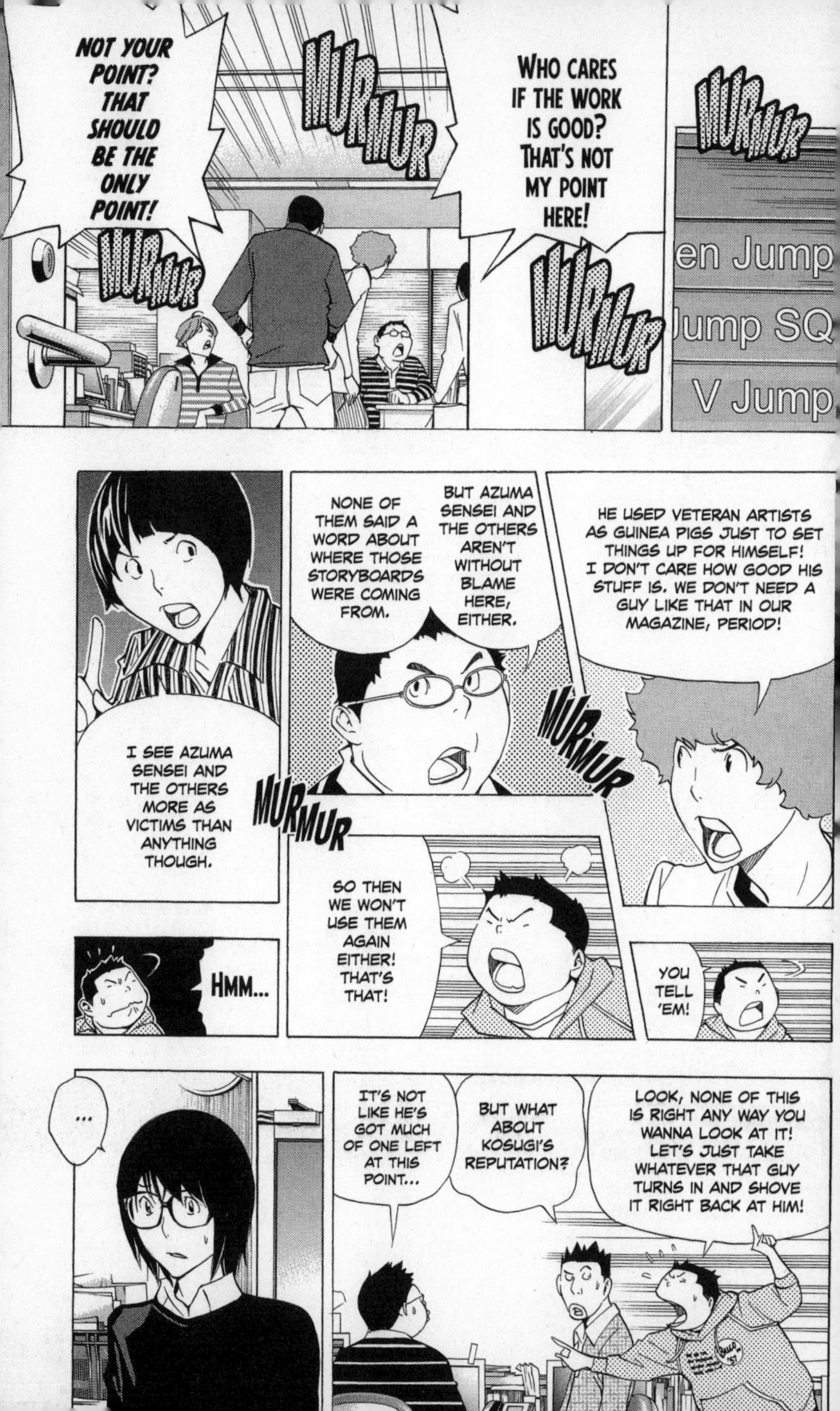

MURMUR
en Jump
Jump SQ
V Jump
WHO CARES IF THE WORK IS GOOD? THAT'S NOT MY POINT HERE!
MURMUR
MURMUR
NOT YOUR POINT? THAT SHOULD BE THE ONLY POINT!
MURMUR
HE USED VETERAN ARTISTS AS GUINEA PIGS JUST TO SET THINGS UP FOR HIMSELF! I DON'T CARE HOW GOOD HIS STUFF IS. WE DON'T NEED A GUY LIKE THAT IN OUR MAGAZINE, PERIOD!
MURMUR
BUT AZUMA SENSEI AND THE OTHERS AREN'T WITHOUT BLAME HERE, EITHER.
NONE OF THEM SAID A WORD ABOUT WHERE THOSE STORYBOARDS WERE COMING FROM.
MURMUR
I SEE AZUMA SENSEI AND THE OTHERS MORE AS VICTIMS THAN ANYTHING THOUGH.
YOU TELL 'EM!
SO THEN WE WON'T USE THEM AGAIN EITHER! THAT'S THAT!
HMM...
LOOK, NONE OF THIS IS RIGHT ANY WAY YOU WANNA LOOK AT IT! LET'S JUST TAKE WHATEVER THAT GUY TURNS IN AND SHOVE IT RIGHT BACK AT HIM!
BUT WHAT ABOUT KOSUGI'S REPUTATION?
IT'S NOT LIKE HE'S GOT MUCH OF ONE LEFT AT THIS POINT...
...

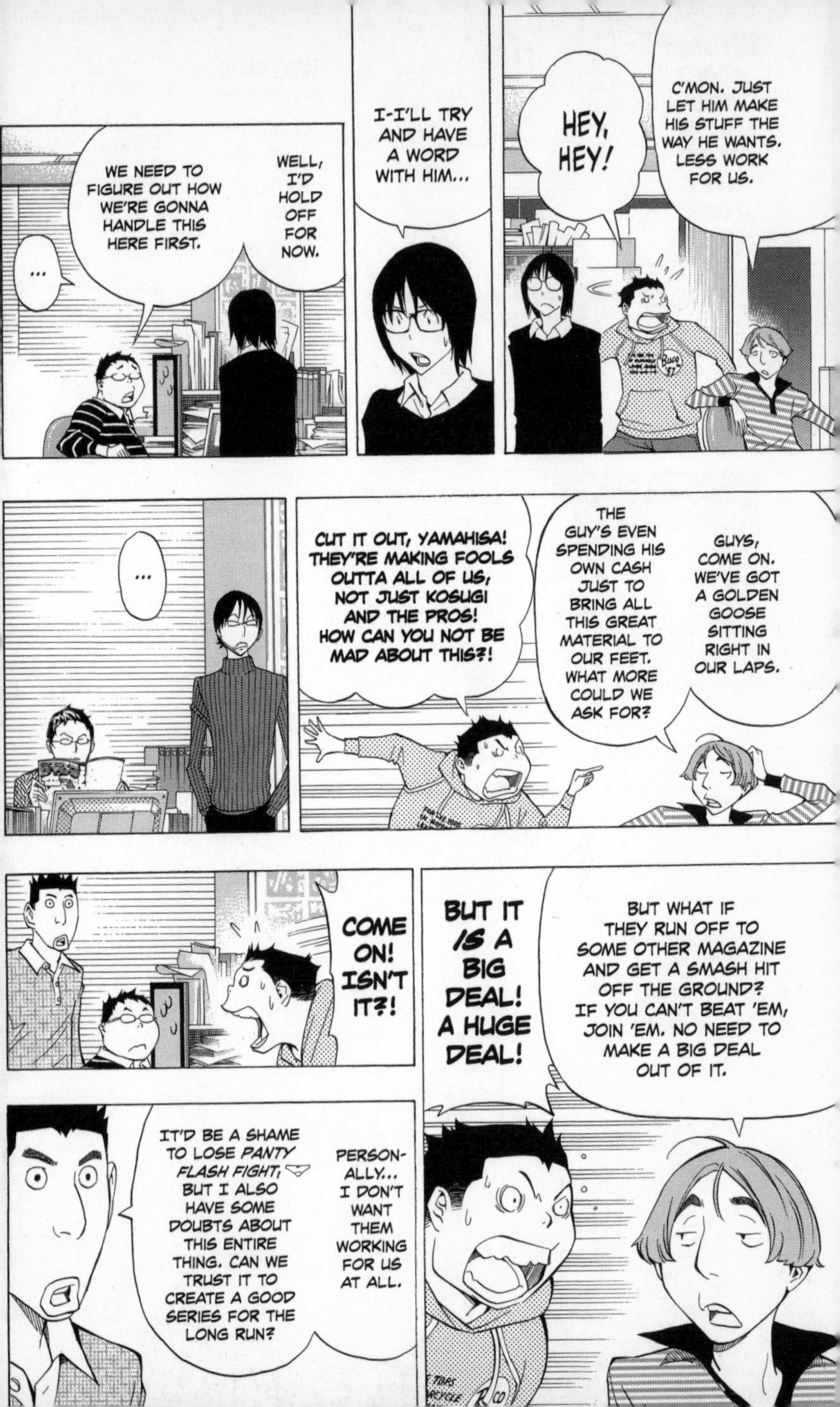
C'MON. JUST LET HIM MAKE HIS STUFF THE WAY HE WANTS. LESS WORK FOR US.
HEY, HEY!
I-I'LL TRY AND HAVE A WORD WITH HIM...
WELL, I'D HOLD OFF FOR NOW.
WE NEED TO FIGURE OUT HOW WE'RE GONNA HANDLE THIS HERE FIRST.
...
GUYS, COME ON. WE'VE GOT A GOLDEN GOOSE SITTING RIGHT IN OUR LAPS.
THE GUY'S EVEN SPENDING HIS OWN CASH JUST TO BRING ALL THIS GREAT MATERIAL TO OUR FEET. WHAT MORE COULD WE ASK FOR?
CUT IT OUT, YAMAHISA! THEY'RE MAKING FOOLS OUTTA ALL OF US, NOT JUST KOSUGI AND THE PROS! HOW CAN YOU NOT BE MAD ABOUT THIS?!
...
BUT WHAT IF THEY RUN OFF TO SOME OTHER MAGAZINE AND GET A SMASH HIT OFF THE GROUND? IF YOU CAN'T BEAT 'EM, JOIN 'EM. NO NEED TO MAKE A BIG DEAL OUT OF IT.
BUT IT *IS* A BIG DEAL! A HUGE DEAL!
COME ON! ISN'T IT?!
PERSON-ALLY... I DON'T WANT THEM WORKING FOR US AT ALL.
IT'D BE A SHAME TO LOSE *PANTY FLASH FIGHT*, BUT I ALSO HAVE SOME DOUBTS ABOUT THIS ENTIRE THING. CAN WE TRUST IT TO CREATE A GOOD SERIES FOR THE LONG RUN?

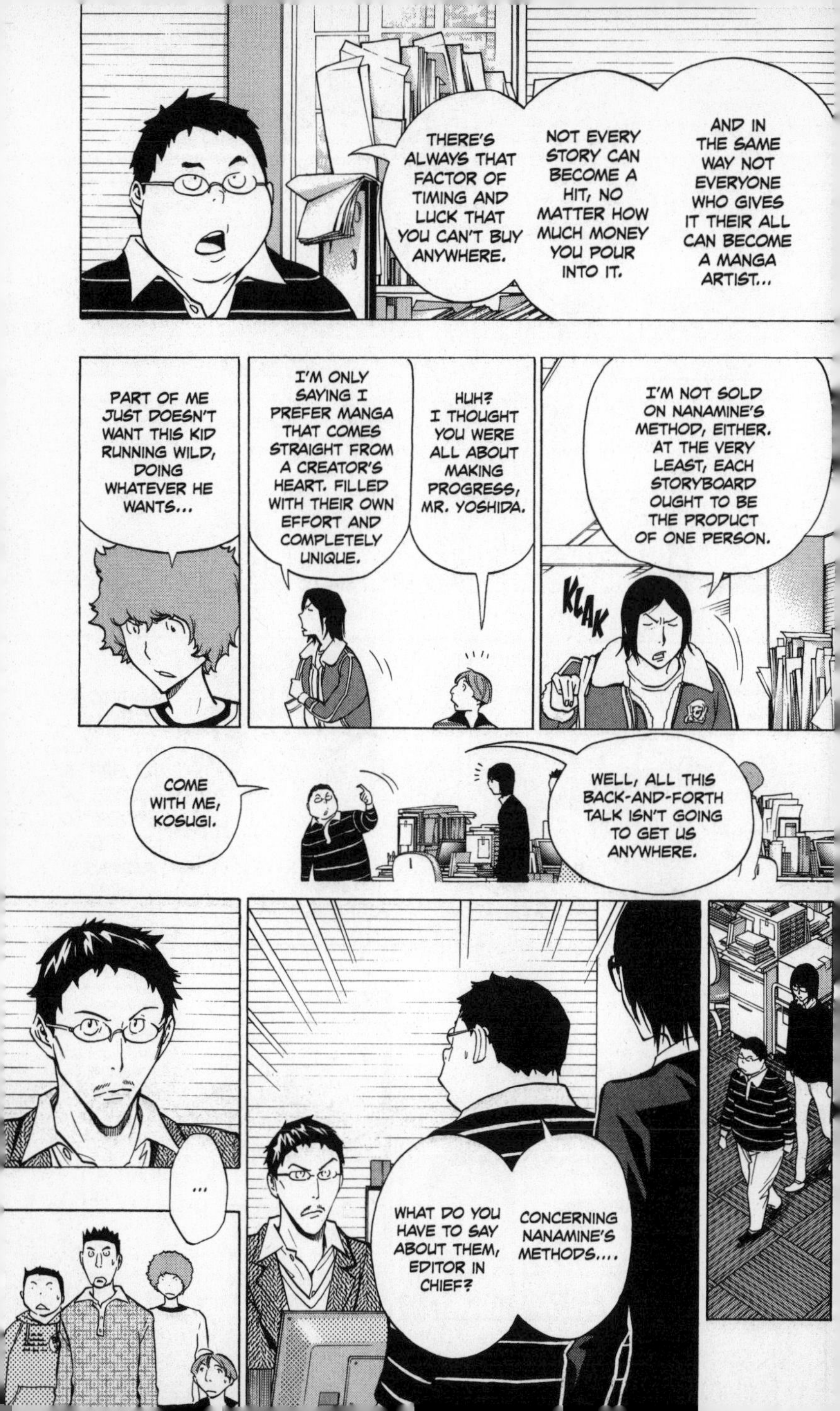
AND IN THE SAME WAY NOT EVERYONE WHO GIVES IT THEIR ALL CAN BECOME A MANGA ARTIST...
NOT EVERY STORY CAN BECOME A HIT, NO MATTER HOW MUCH MONEY YOU POUR INTO IT.
THERE'S ALWAYS THAT FACTOR OF TIMING AND LUCK THAT YOU CAN'T BUY ANYWHERE.
I'M NOT SOLD ON NANAMINE'S METHOD, EITHER. AT THE VERY LEAST, EACH STORYBOARD OUGHT TO BE THE PRODUCT OF ONE PERSON.
KLAK
HUH? I THOUGHT YOU WERE ALL ABOUT MAKING PROGRESS, MR. YOSHIDA.
I'M ONLY SAYING I PREFER MANGA THAT COMES STRAIGHT FROM A CREATOR'S HEART. FILLED WITH THEIR OWN EFFORT AND COMPLETELY UNIQUE.
PART OF ME JUST DOESN'T WANT THIS KID RUNNING WILD, DOING WHATEVER HE WANTS...
WELL, ALL THIS BACK-AND-FORTH TALK ISN'T GOING TO GET US ANYWHERE.
COME WITH ME, KOSUGI.
CONCERNING NANAMINE'S METHODS....
WHAT DO YOU HAVE TO SAY ABOUT THEM, EDITOR IN CHIEF?
...

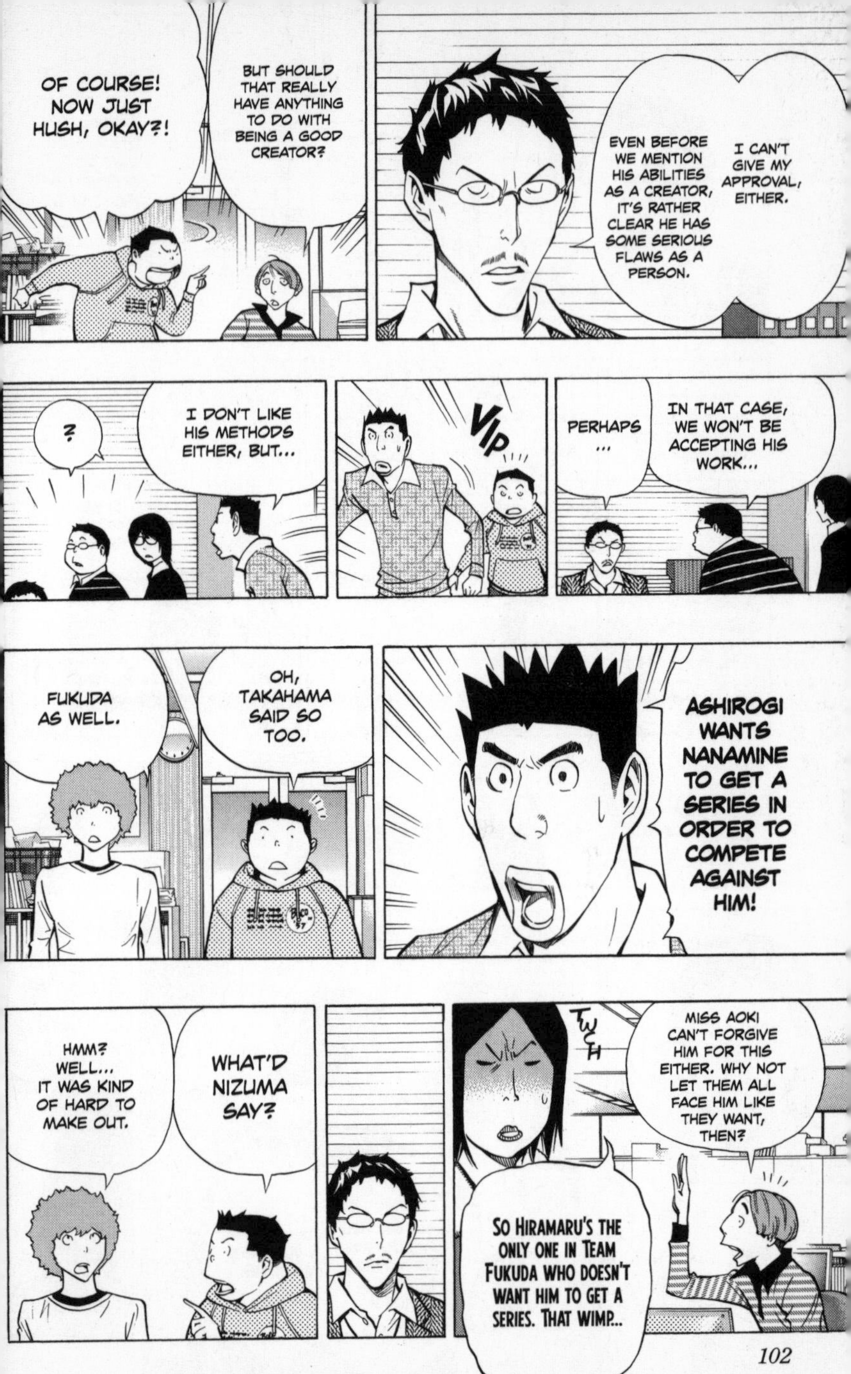
I CAN'T GIVE MY APPROVAL, EITHER.
EVEN BEFORE WE MENTION HIS ABILITIES AS A CREATOR, IT'S RATHER CLEAR HE HAS SOME SERIOUS FLAWS AS A PERSON.
BUT SHOULD THAT REALLY HAVE ANYTHING TO DO WITH BEING A GOOD CREATOR?
OF COURSE! NOW JUST HUSH, OKAY?!
IN THAT CASE, WE WON'T BE ACCEPTING HIS WORK...
PERHAPS...
VIP
I DON'T LIKE HIS METHODS EITHER, BUT...
?
ASHIROGI WANTS NANAMINE TO GET A SERIES IN ORDER TO COMPETE AGAINST HIM!
OH, TAKAHAMA SAID SO TOO.
FUKUDA AS WELL.
MISS AOKI CAN'T FORGIVE HIM FOR THIS EITHER. WHY NOT LET THEM ALL FACE HIM LIKE THEY WANT, THEN?
TWCH
SO HIRAMARU'S THE ONLY ONE IN TEAM FUKUDA WHO DOESN'T WANT HIM TO GET A SERIES. THAT WIMP...
WHAT'D NIZUMA SAY?
HMM? WELL... IT WAS KIND OF HARD TO MAKE OUT.

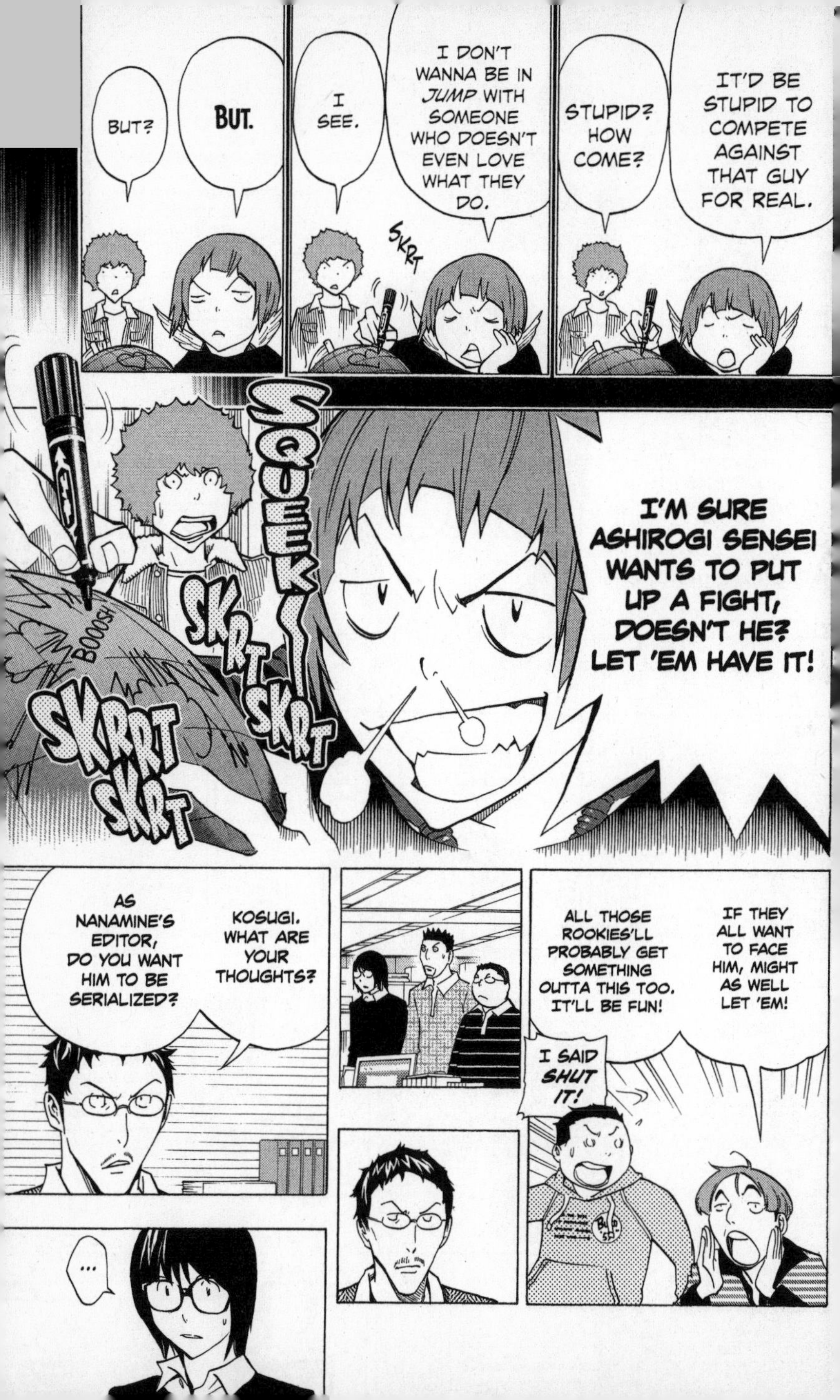
IT'D BE STUPID TO COMPETE AGAINST THAT GUY FOR REAL.
STUPID? HOW COME?
I DON'T WANNA BE IN JUMP WITH SOMEONE WHO DOESN'T EVEN LOVE WHAT THEY DO.
SKRT
I SEE.
BUT.
BUT?
I'M SURE ASHIROGI SENSEI WANTS TO PUT UP A FIGHT, DOESN'T HE? LET 'EM HAVE IT!
SQUEEK
SKRT SKRT
SKRT SKRT
BOOOSH
IF THEY ALL WANT TO FACE HIM, MIGHT AS WELL LET 'EM!
ALL THOSE ROOKIES'LL PROBABLY GET SOMETHING OUTTA THIS TOO. IT'LL BE FUN!
I SAID SHUT IT!
KOSUGI. WHAT ARE YOUR THOUGHTS?
AS NANAMINE'S EDITOR, DO YOU WANT HIM TO BE SERIALIZED?
...

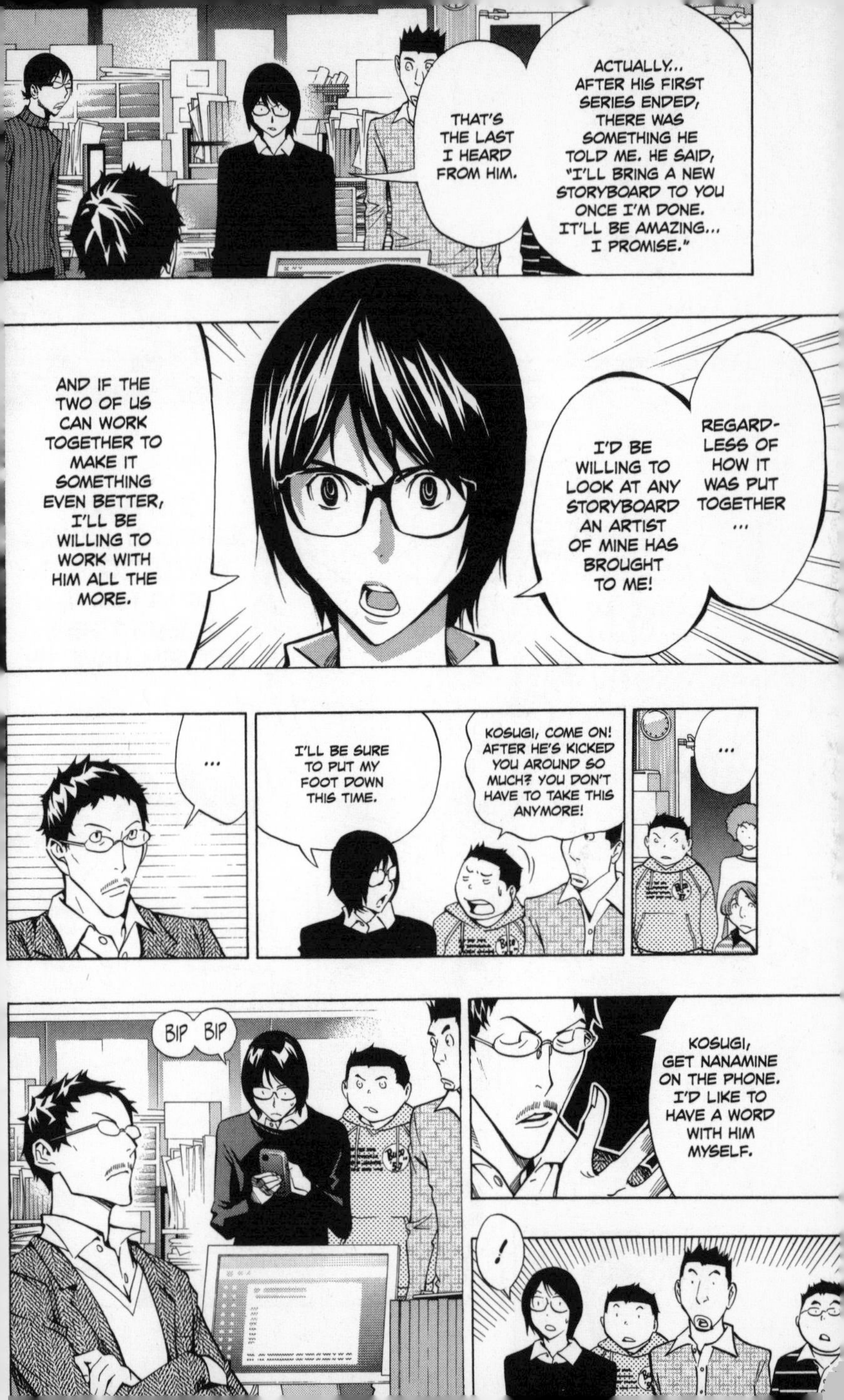
ACTUALLY... AFTER HIS FIRST SERIES ENDED, THERE WAS SOMETHING HE TOLD ME. HE SAID, "I'LL BRING A NEW STORYBOARD TO YOU ONCE I'M DONE. IT'LL BE AMAZING... I PROMISE."
THAT'S THE LAST I HEARD FROM HIM.
REGARD-LESS OF HOW IT WAS PUT TOGETHER ...
I'D BE WILLING TO LOOK AT ANY STORYBOARD AN ARTIST OF MINE HAS BROUGHT TO ME!
AND IF THE TWO OF US CAN WORK TOGETHER TO MAKE IT SOMETHING EVEN BETTER, I'LL BE WILLING TO WORK WITH HIM ALL THE MORE.
...
KOSUGI, COME ON! AFTER HE'S KICKED YOU AROUND SO MUCH? YOU DON'T HAVE TO TAKE THIS ANYMORE!
I'LL BE SURE TO PUT MY FOOT DOWN THIS TIME.
...
KOSUGI, GET NANAMINE ON THE PHONE. I'D LIKE TO HAVE A WORD WITH HIM MYSELF.
!
BIP BIP

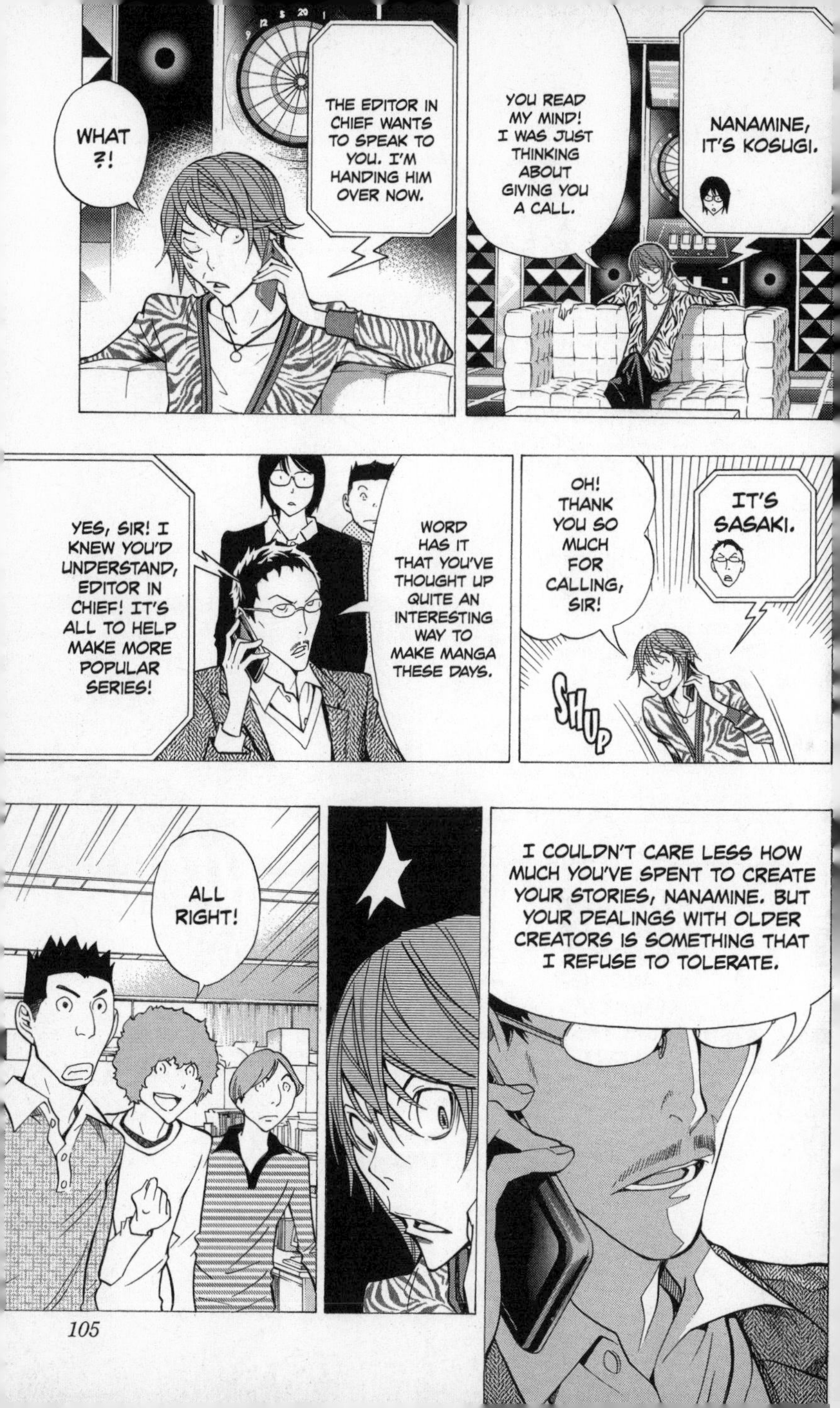

NANAMINE, IT'S KOSUGI.
YOU READ MY MIND! I WAS JUST THINKING ABOUT GIVING YOU A CALL.
THE EDITOR IN CHIEF WANTS TO SPEAK TO YOU. I'M HANDING HIM OVER NOW.
WHAT ?!
IT'S SASAKI.
OH! THANK YOU SO MUCH FOR CALLING, SIR!
SHUP
WORD HAS IT THAT YOU'VE THOUGHT UP QUITE AN INTERESTING WAY TO MAKE MANGA THESE DAYS.
YES, SIR! I KNEW YOU'D UNDERSTAND, EDITOR IN CHIEF! IT'S ALL TO HELP MAKE MORE POPULAR SERIES!
I COULDN'T CARE LESS HOW MUCH YOU'VE SPENT TO CREATE YOUR STORIES, NANAMINE. BUT YOUR DEALINGS WITH OLDER CREATORS IS SOMETHING THAT I REFUSE TO TOLERATE.
ALL RIGHT!

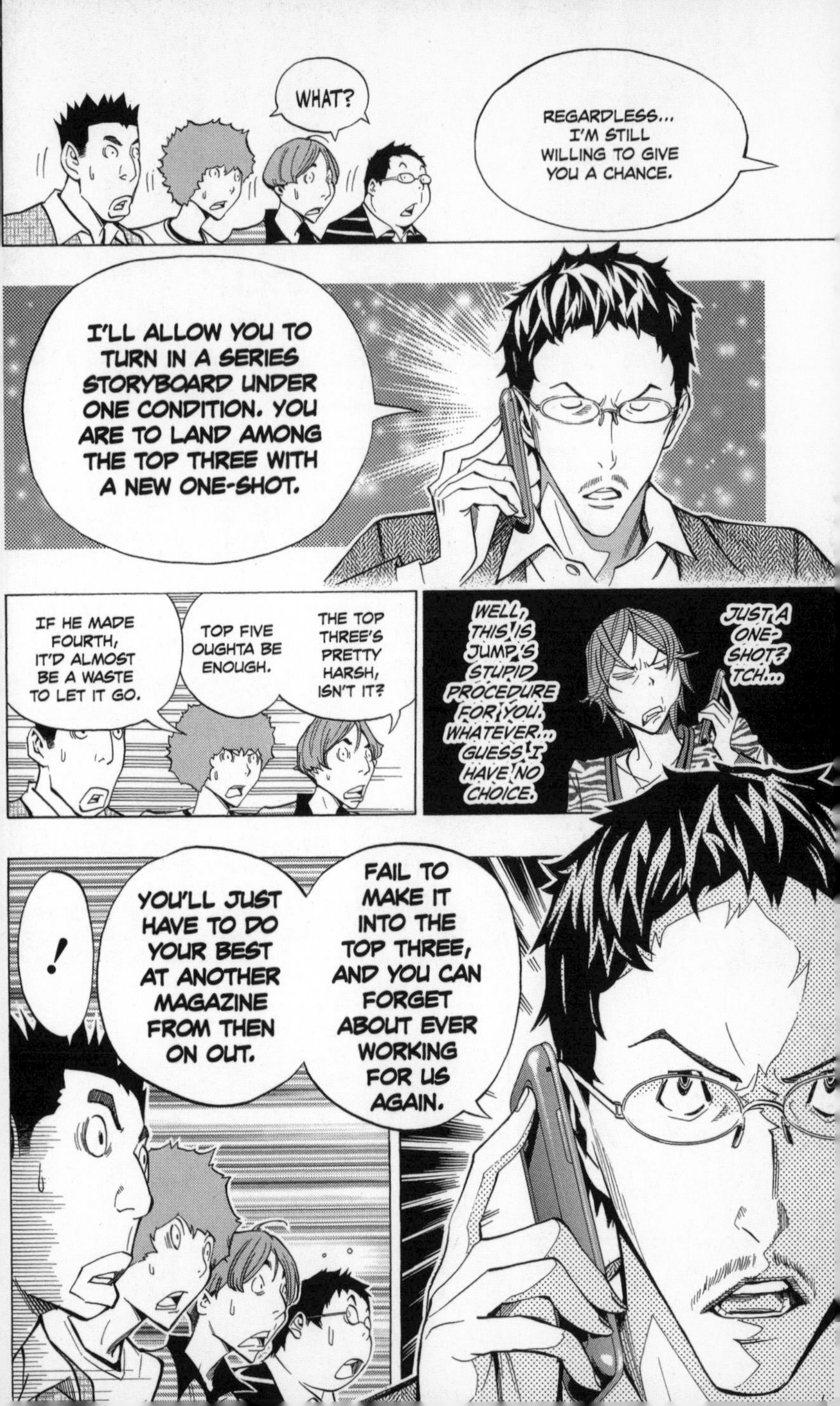
REGARDLESS... I'M STILL WILLING TO GIVE YOU A CHANCE.
WHAT?
I'LL ALLOW YOU TO TURN IN A SERIES STORYBOARD UNDER ONE CONDITION. YOU ARE TO LAND AMONG THE TOP THREE WITH A NEW ONE-SHOT.
JUST A ONE-SHOT? TCH...
WELL, THIS IS JUMP'S STUPID PROCEDURE FOR YOU. WHATEVER... GUESS I HAVE NO CHOICE.
THE TOP THREE'S PRETTY HARSH, ISN'T IT?
TOP FIVE OUGHTA BE ENOUGH.
IF HE MADE FOURTH, IT'D ALMOST BE A WASTE TO LET IT GO.
FAIL TO MAKE IT INTO THE TOP THREE, AND YOU CAN FORGET ABOUT EVER WORKING FOR US AGAIN.
YOU'LL JUST HAVE TO DO YOUR BEST AT ANOTHER MAGAZINE FROM THEN ON OUT.
!

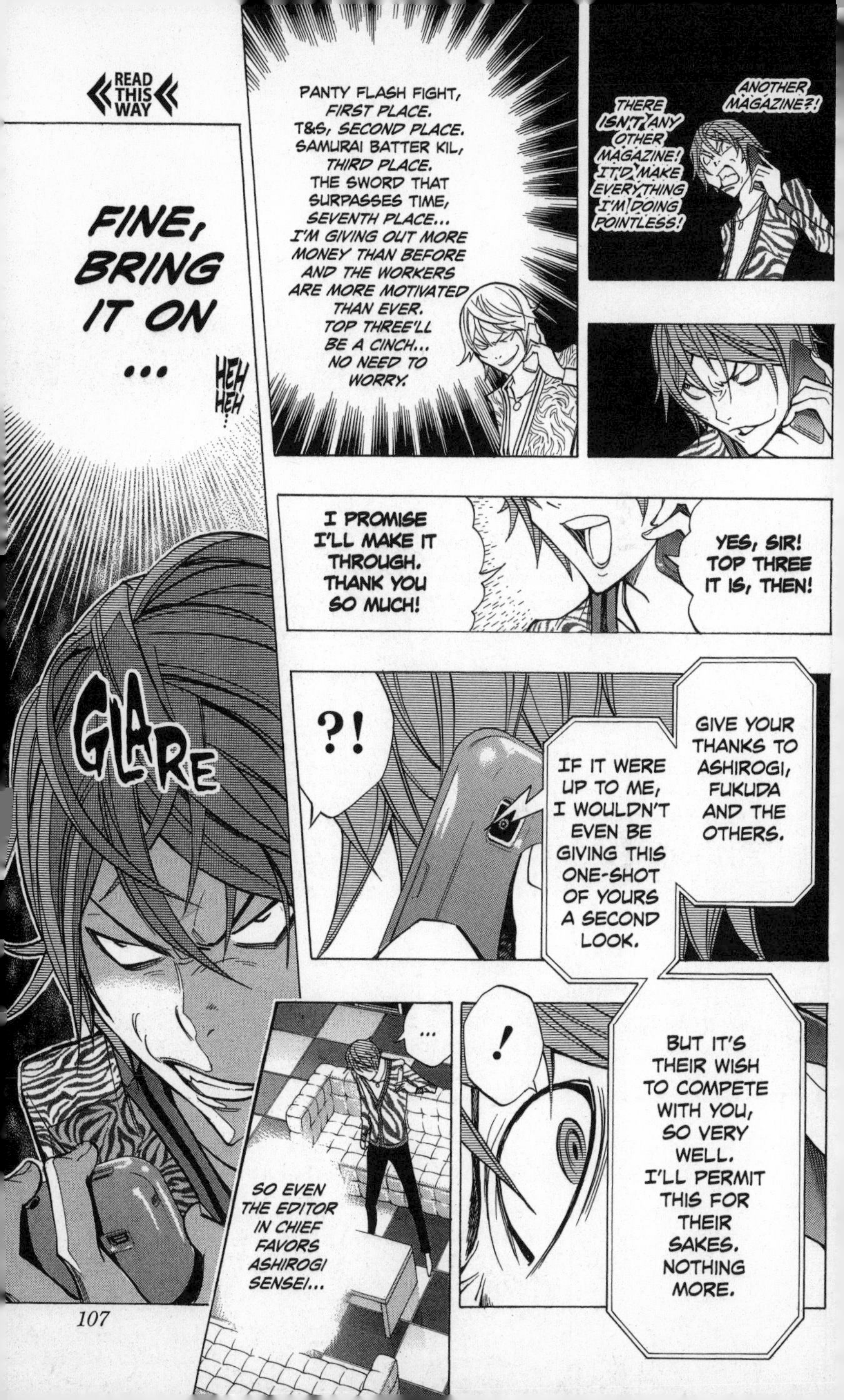
READ THIS WAY
ANOTHER MAGAZINE?!
THERE ISN'T ANY OTHER MAGAZINE! IT'D MAKE EVERYTHING I'M DOING POINTLESS!
PANTY FLASH FIGHT, FIRST PLACE. T&S, SECOND PLACE. SAMURAI BATTER KIL, THIRD PLACE. THE SWORD THAT SURPASSES TIME, SEVENTH PLACE... I'M GIVING OUT MORE MONEY THAN BEFORE AND THE WORKERS ARE MORE MOTIVATED THAN EVER. TOP THREE'LL BE A CINCH... NO NEED TO WORRY.
YES, SIR! TOP THREE IT IS, THEN!
I PROMISE I'LL MAKE IT THROUGH. THANK YOU SO MUCH!
GIVE YOUR THANKS TO ASHIROGI, FUKUDA AND THE OTHERS.
IF IT WERE UP TO ME, I WOULDN'T EVEN BE GIVING THIS ONE-SHOT OF YOURS A SECOND LOOK.
?!
BUT IT'S THEIR WISH TO COMPETE WITH YOU, SO VERY WELL. I'LL PERMIT THIS FOR THEIR SAKES. NOTHING MORE.
!
...
SO EVEN THE EDITOR IN CHIEF FAVORS ASHIROGI SENSEI...
FINE, BRING IT ON ...
HEH HEH
GLARE

OHBA'S STORYBOARD

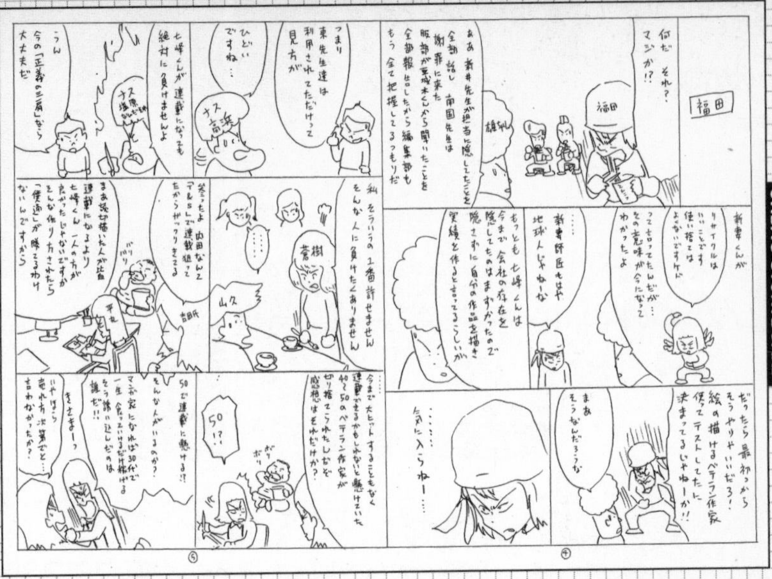
福田
何だ それ？ マジか!?
福田
雄二
ああ 新井先生が担当に隠してたことを全部話し 南国先生は謝罪に来た 服部が東城木くんから聞いたことを全部報告したから編集部も もう全て把握してるつもりだ
新妻くんが リサイクルはいいことです 使い捨てはよくないですケド って言ってたんだが… その意味が今になってわかったよ
…… 新妻師匠もはや 地球人じゃねーな
もっとも 七峰くんは 今まで会社の存在を隠してたのはまずかったので 隠さずに 自分の作品を描き 実績を作ると言ってるらしいが
だったら最初っから そうやりゃいいだろ! 絵の描けるベテラン作家 使ってテストしてたに 決まってるじゃねーか!!
まあ そうなんだろうな
…… 気に入らねー…
つまり 東先生達は 利用されてただけって 見方が
ひどい ですね…
ナス 高浜
七峰くんが連載になっても 絶対に負けませんよ
ナス 塩原
うん 今の「正義の三肩」なら 大丈夫だ
私 そういうの 1番許せません そんな人に負けたくありません
蒼樹
……
山久
参ったよ 内田なんて「アルS」で連載狙ってたからガックリきてる
バリ バリ
吉田氏
まあ読切描いた人が沢山連載になるより 七峰くん一人の方が 良かったじゃないですか そんな作り方されたら「僕達」が勝てるわけないんですから
平丸
…… 今まで大ヒットすることもなく 連載できるかもしれないと懸けていた 40や50のベテラン作家が 切り捨てられたしなぞ 感想はそれだけか？
50 !?
ボリ ボリ
50で連載に懸ける!? そんなんがいるのか？
マンガ家になれば30代で 一生食っていけるだけ稼げる そう誘い込んだのは 誰だ!!
きさまーっ
いやほら 売れ方次第でと… 言わなかったか？
⑤
④

OBATA'S STORYBOARD

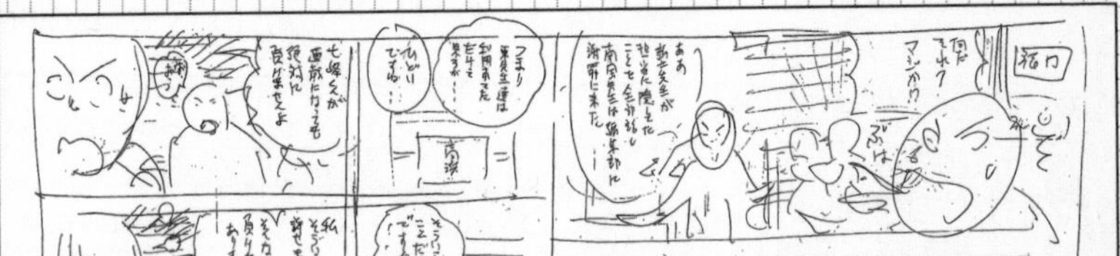
HIRAMARU
5
4

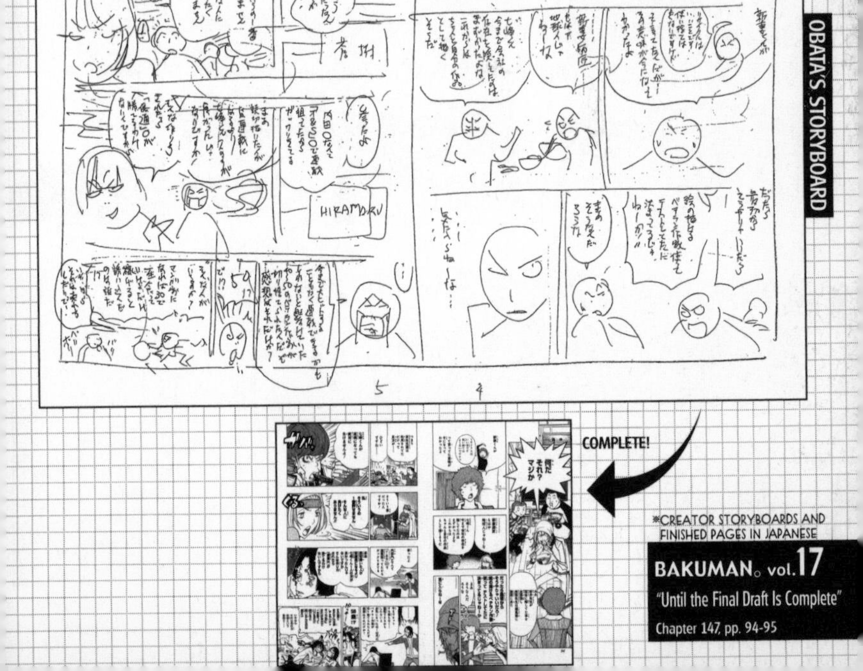
何だ それ？ マジか

COMPLETE!

※CREATOR STORYBOARDS AND FINISHED PAGES IN JAPANESE

BAKUMAN。 vol.17

"Until the Final Draft Is Complete"

Chapter 147, pp. 94-95

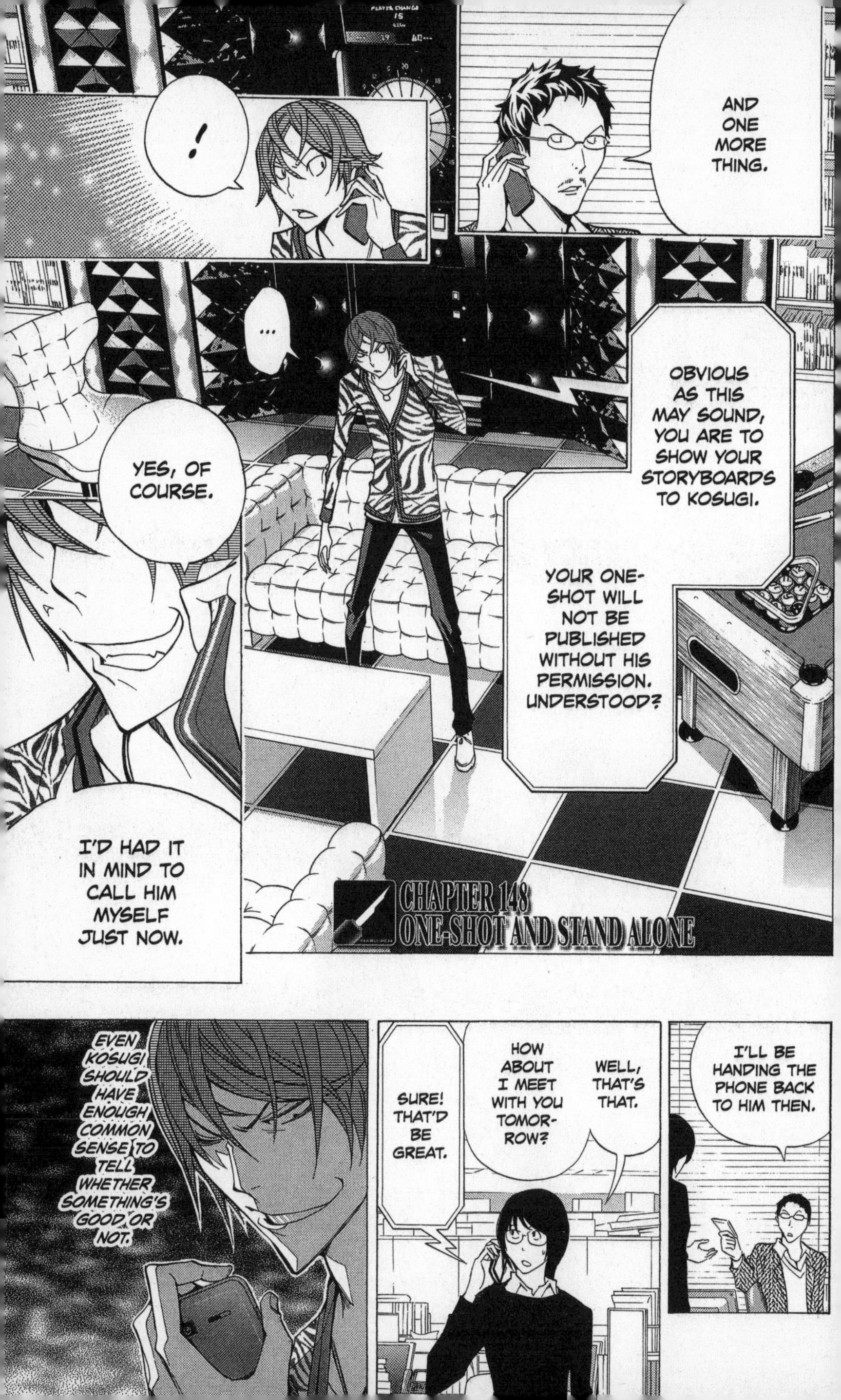
AND ONE MORE THING.
!
OBVIOUS AS THIS MAY SOUND, YOU ARE TO SHOW YOUR STORYBOARDS TO KOSUGI.
YOUR ONE-SHOT WILL NOT BE PUBLISHED WITHOUT HIS PERMISSION. UNDERSTOOD?
...
CHAPTER 148
ONE-SHOT AND STAND ALONE
YES, OF COURSE.
I'D HAD IT IN MIND TO CALL HIM MYSELF JUST NOW.
I'LL BE HANDING THE PHONE BACK TO HIM THEN.
WELL, THAT'S THAT.
HOW ABOUT I MEET WITH YOU TOMORROW?
SURE! THAT'D BE GREAT.
EVEN KOSUGI SHOULD HAVE ENOUGH COMMON SENSE TO TELL WHETHER SOMETHING'S GOOD OR NOT.

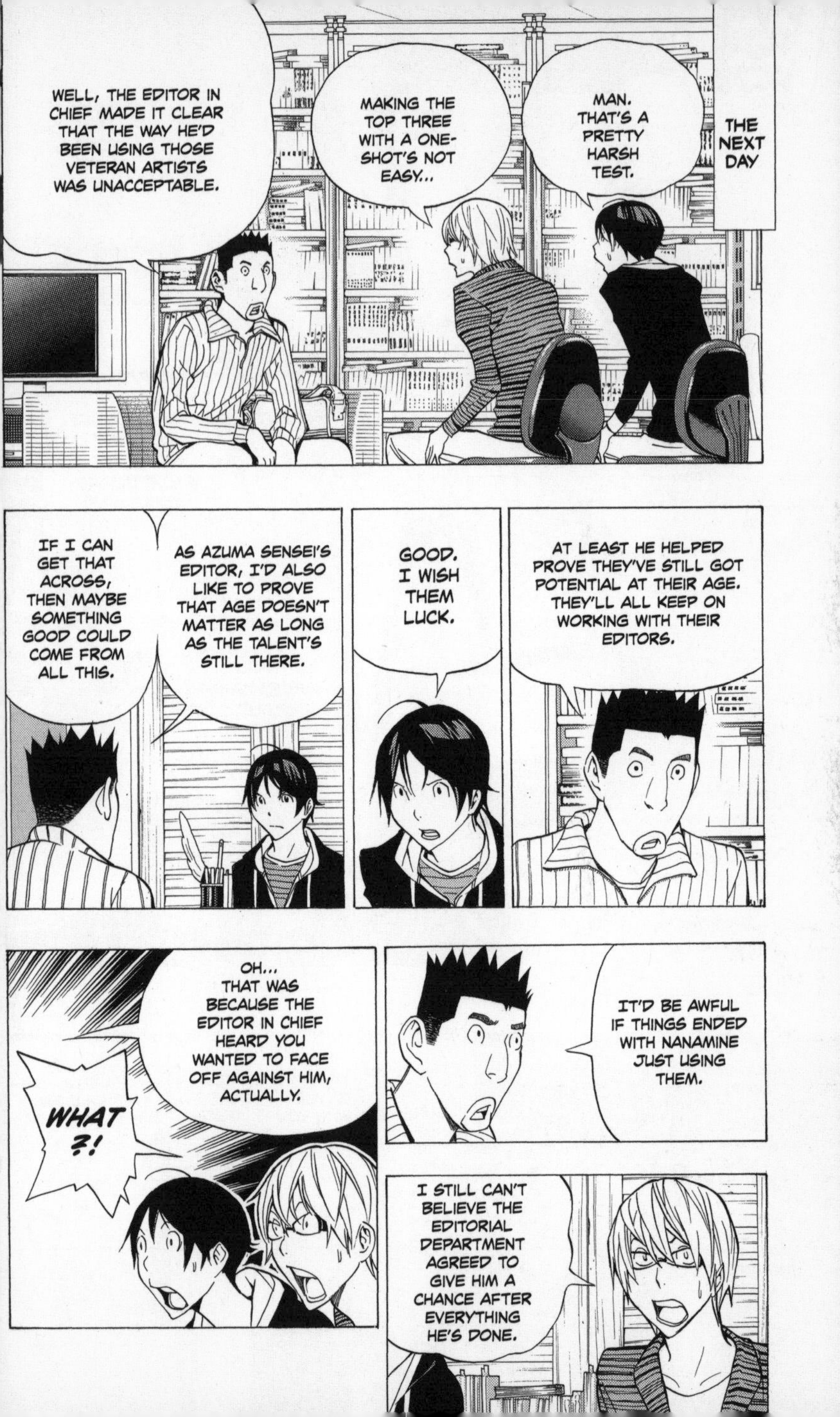
THE NEXT DAY
MAN. THAT'S A PRETTY HARSH TEST.
MAKING THE TOP THREE WITH A ONE-SHOT'S NOT EASY...
WELL, THE EDITOR IN CHIEF MADE IT CLEAR THAT THE WAY HE'D BEEN USING THOSE VETERAN ARTISTS WAS UNACCEPTABLE.
AT LEAST HE HELPED PROVE THEY'VE STILL GOT POTENTIAL AT THEIR AGE. THEY'LL ALL KEEP ON WORKING WITH THEIR EDITORS.
GOOD. I WISH THEM LUCK.
AS AZUMA SENSEI'S EDITOR, I'D ALSO LIKE TO PROVE THAT AGE DOESN'T MATTER AS LONG AS THE TALENT'S STILL THERE.
IF I CAN GET THAT ACROSS, THEN MAYBE SOMETHING GOOD COULD COME FROM ALL THIS.
IT'D BE AWFUL IF THINGS ENDED WITH NANAMINE JUST USING THEM.
I STILL CAN'T BELIEVE THE EDITORIAL DEPARTMENT AGREED TO GIVE HIM A CHANCE AFTER EVERYTHING HE'S DONE.
OH... THAT WAS BECAUSE THE EDITOR IN CHIEF HEARD YOU WANTED TO FACE OFF AGAINST HIM, ACTUALLY.
WHAT?!

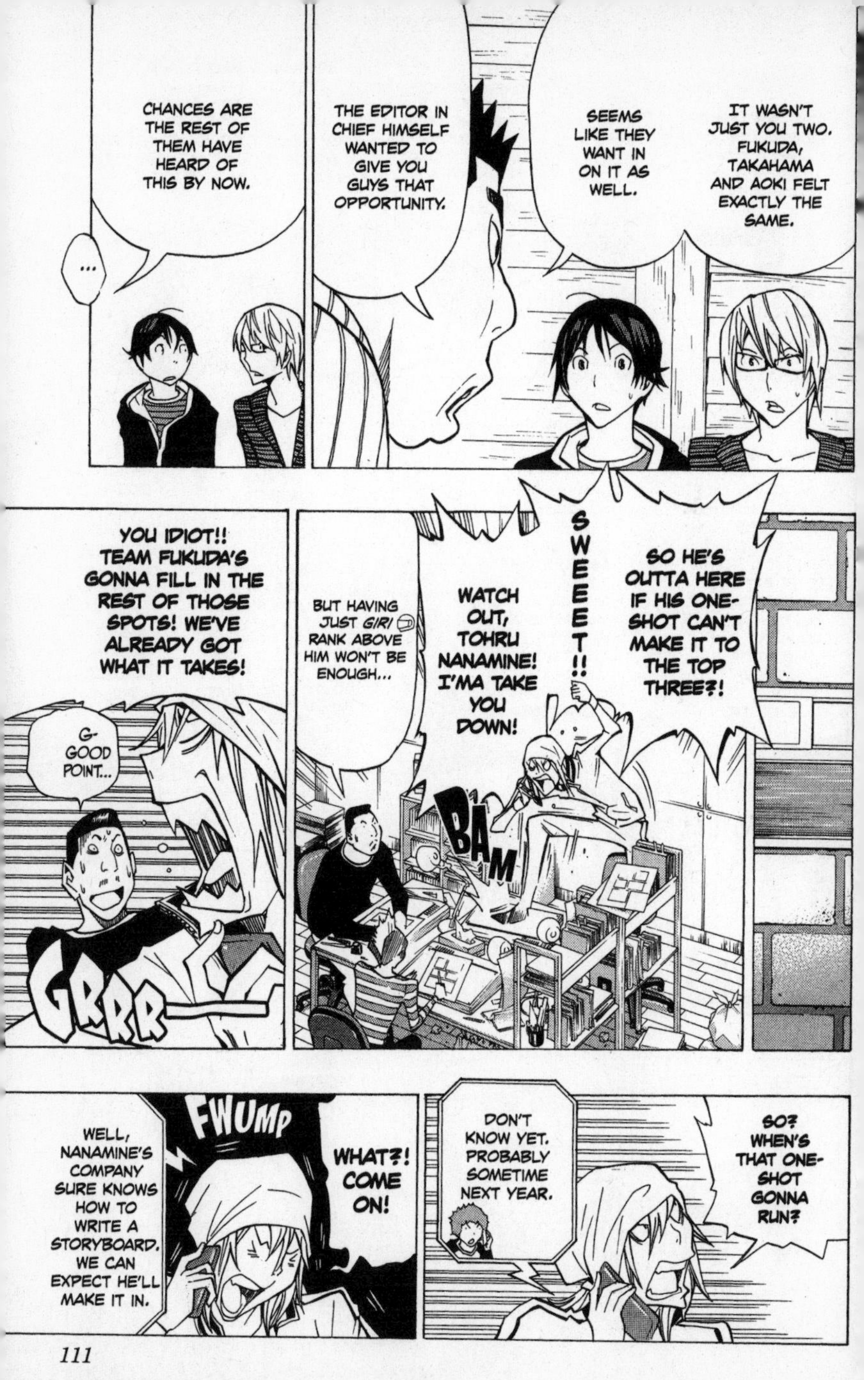
IT WASN'T JUST YOU TWO. FUKUDA, TAKAHAMA AND AOKI FELT EXACTLY THE SAME.
SEEMS LIKE THEY WANT IN ON IT AS WELL.
THE EDITOR IN CHIEF HIMSELF WANTED TO GIVE YOU GUYS THAT OPPORTUNITY.
CHANCES ARE THE REST OF THEM HAVE HEARD OF THIS BY NOW.
...
SO HE'S OUTTA HERE IF HIS ONE-SHOT CAN'T MAKE IT TO THE TOP THREE?!
SWEEEET!!
WATCH OUT, TOHRU NANAMINE! I'MA TAKE YOU DOWN!
BAM
BUT HAVING JUST GIRI RANK ABOVE HIM WON'T BE ENOUGH...
YOU IDIOT!! TEAM FUKUDA'S GONNA FILL IN THE REST OF THOSE SPOTS! WE'VE ALREADY GOT WHAT IT TAKES!
G-GOOD POINT...
GRRR
SO? WHEN'S THAT ONE-SHOT GONNA RUN?
DON'T KNOW YET. PROBABLY SOMETIME NEXT YEAR.
FWUMP
WHAT?! COME ON!
WELL, NANAMINE'S COMPANY SURE KNOWS HOW TO WRITE A STORYBOARD. WE CAN EXPECT HE'LL MAKE IT IN.

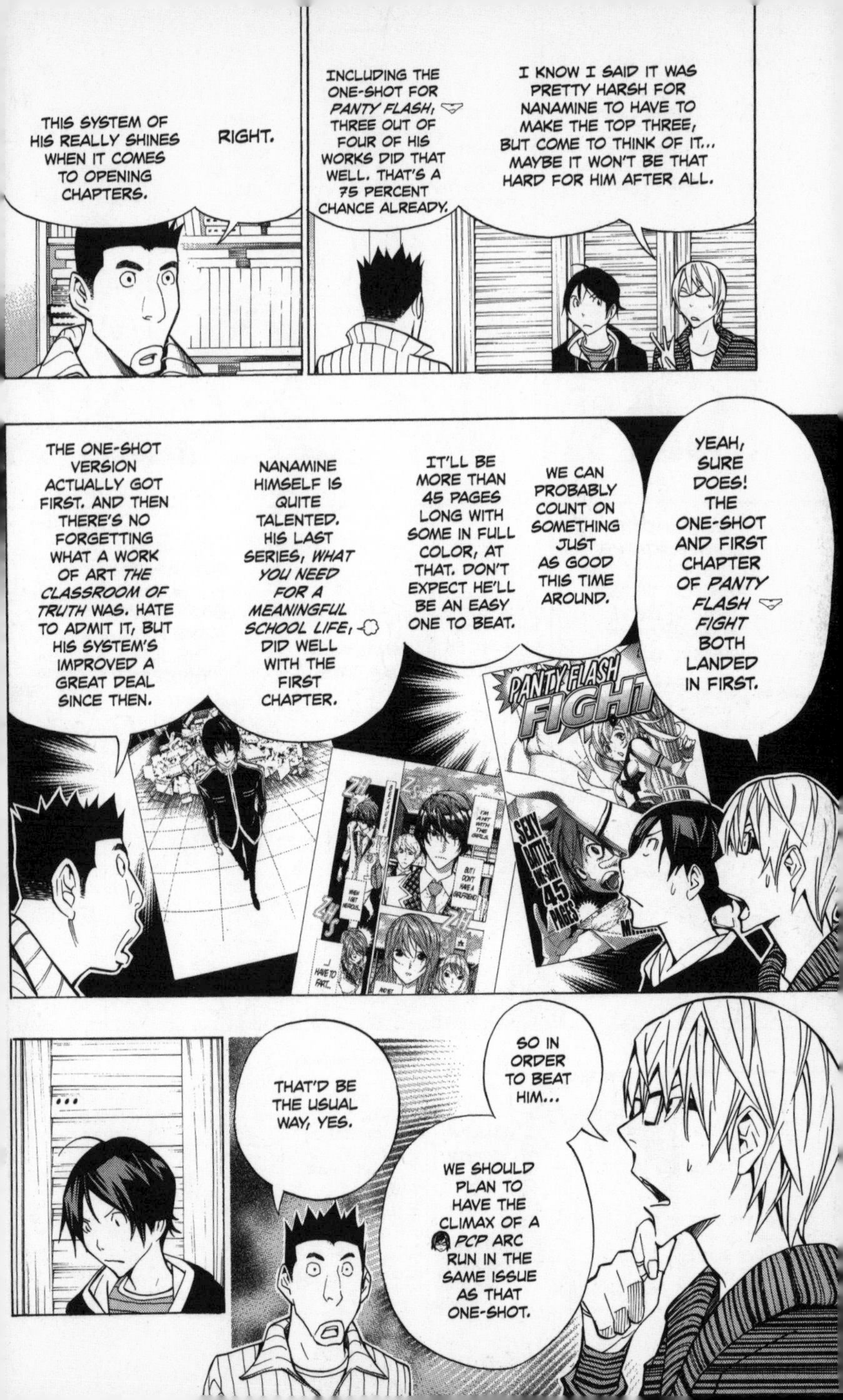
I KNOW I SAID IT WAS PRETTY HARSH FOR NANAMINE TO HAVE TO MAKE THE TOP THREE, BUT COME TO THINK OF IT... MAYBE IT WON'T BE THAT HARD FOR HIM AFTER ALL.
INCLUDING THE ONE-SHOT FOR *PANTY FLASH*, THREE OUT OF FOUR OF HIS WORKS DID THAT WELL. THAT'S A 75 PERCENT CHANCE ALREADY.
RIGHT.
THIS SYSTEM OF HIS REALLY SHINES WHEN IT COMES TO OPENING CHAPTERS.
YEAH, SURE DOES! THE ONE-SHOT AND FIRST CHAPTER OF *PANTY FLASH FIGHT* BOTH LANDED IN FIRST.
WE CAN PROBABLY COUNT ON SOMETHING JUST AS GOOD THIS TIME AROUND.
IT'LL BE MORE THAN 45 PAGES LONG WITH SOME IN FULL COLOR, AT THAT. DON'T EXPECT HE'LL BE AN EASY ONE TO BEAT.
NANAMINE HIMSELF IS QUITE TALENTED. HIS LAST SERIES, *WHAT YOU NEED FOR A MEANINGFUL SCHOOL LIFE*, DID WELL WITH THE FIRST CHAPTER.
THE ONE-SHOT VERSION ACTUALLY GOT FIRST. AND THEN THERE'S NO FORGETTING WHAT A WORK OF ART *THE CLASSROOM OF TRUTH* WAS. HATE TO ADMIT IT, BUT HIS SYSTEM'S IMPROVED A GREAT DEAL SINCE THEN.
PANTY FLASH FIGHT
SEXY BATTLE
45 PAGES
SO IN ORDER TO BEAT HIM...
WE SHOULD PLAN TO HAVE THE CLIMAX OF A *PCP* ARC RUN IN THE SAME ISSUE AS THAT ONE-SHOT.
THAT'D BE THE USUAL WAY, YES.
...

READ THIS WAY

IF THEY DECIDE TO HOLD OFF UNTIL NEXT YEAR, IT COULD RUN AS LATE AS THE END OF FEBRUARY.

CORRECT. IT'S NOT EVEN FINAL THAT HE'LL GET THE ONE-SHOT, BUT I THINK WE CAN ASSUME SO.

MR. HATTORI... THEY HAVEN'T DECIDED WHICH ISSUE TO PUT THAT ONE-SHOT IN YET, RIGHT?

WHAT'S UP, SAIKO?

December

T	F	S
1	2	3
8	9	10
15	16	17
22	23	24
29	30	31

...

?

WHAT IF WE WENT WITH A STAND-ALONE CHAPTER?

THIS TIME, INSTEAD OF AN ARC'S CLIMAX...

YEAH. WE SHOULD HAVE TWO WHOLE WEEKS OFF.

OUR NEW YEAR'S BREAK'S GONNA START SOON, RIGHT?

T	F	
	1	3
	2	
7	8	9	10
14	15	16	17
21	22	23	24
28	29	30	31

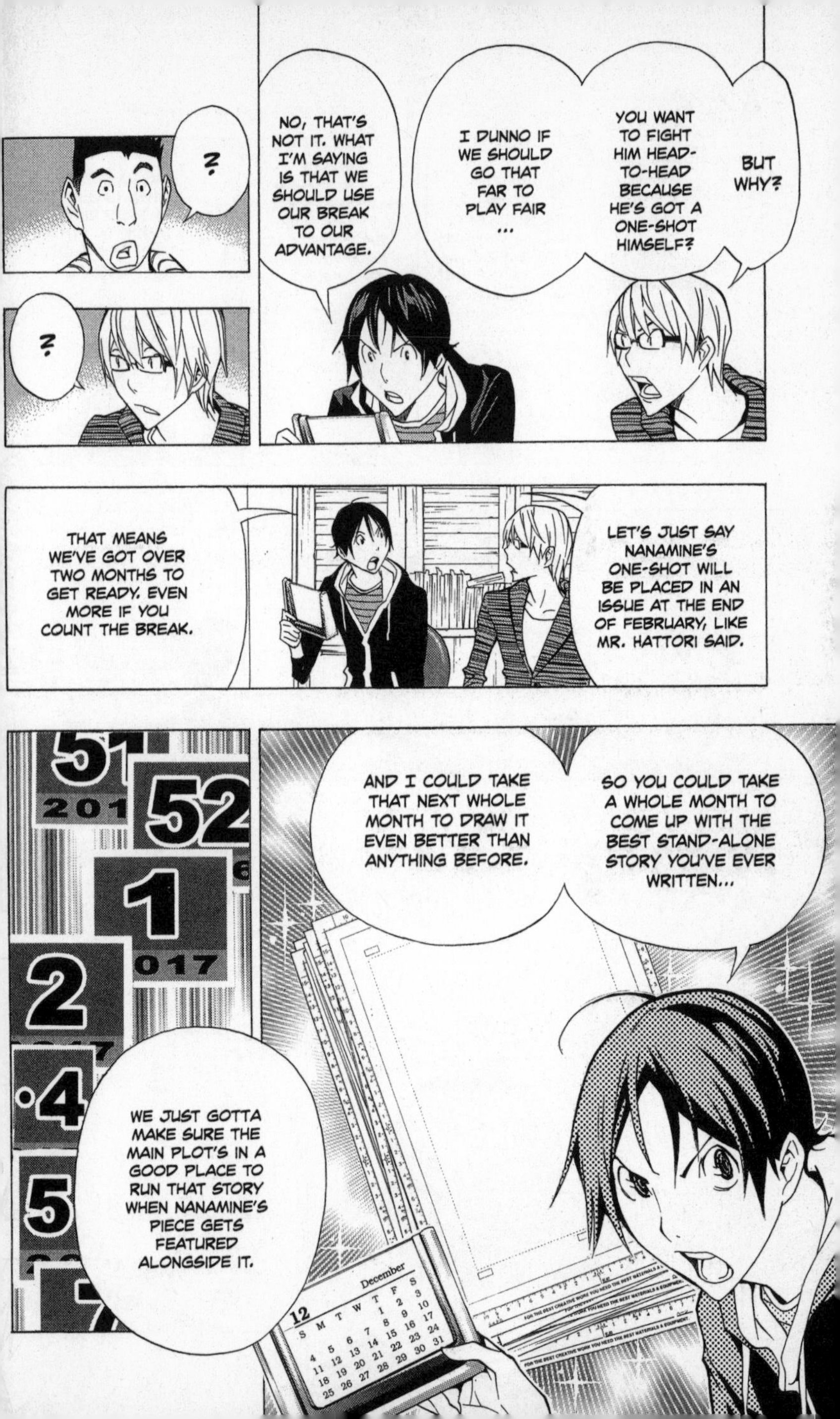
BUT WHY?
YOU WANT TO FIGHT HIM HEAD-TO-HEAD BECAUSE HE'S GOT A ONE-SHOT HIMSELF?
I DUNNO IF WE SHOULD GO THAT FAR TO PLAY FAIR ...
NO, THAT'S NOT IT. WHAT I'M SAYING IS THAT WE SHOULD USE OUR BREAK TO OUR ADVANTAGE.
?
?
LET'S JUST SAY NANAMINE'S ONE-SHOT WILL BE PLACED IN AN ISSUE AT THE END OF FEBRUARY, LIKE MR. HATTORI SAID.
THAT MEANS WE'VE GOT OVER TWO MONTHS TO GET READY. EVEN MORE IF YOU COUNT THE BREAK.
SO YOU COULD TAKE A WHOLE MONTH TO COME UP WITH THE BEST STAND-ALONE STORY YOU'VE EVER WRITTEN...
AND I COULD TAKE THAT NEXT WHOLE MONTH TO DRAW IT EVEN BETTER THAN ANYTHING BEFORE.
WE JUST GOTTA MAKE SURE THE MAIN PLOT'S IN A GOOD PLACE TO RUN THAT STORY WHEN NANAMINE'S PIECE GETS FEATURED ALONGSIDE IT.

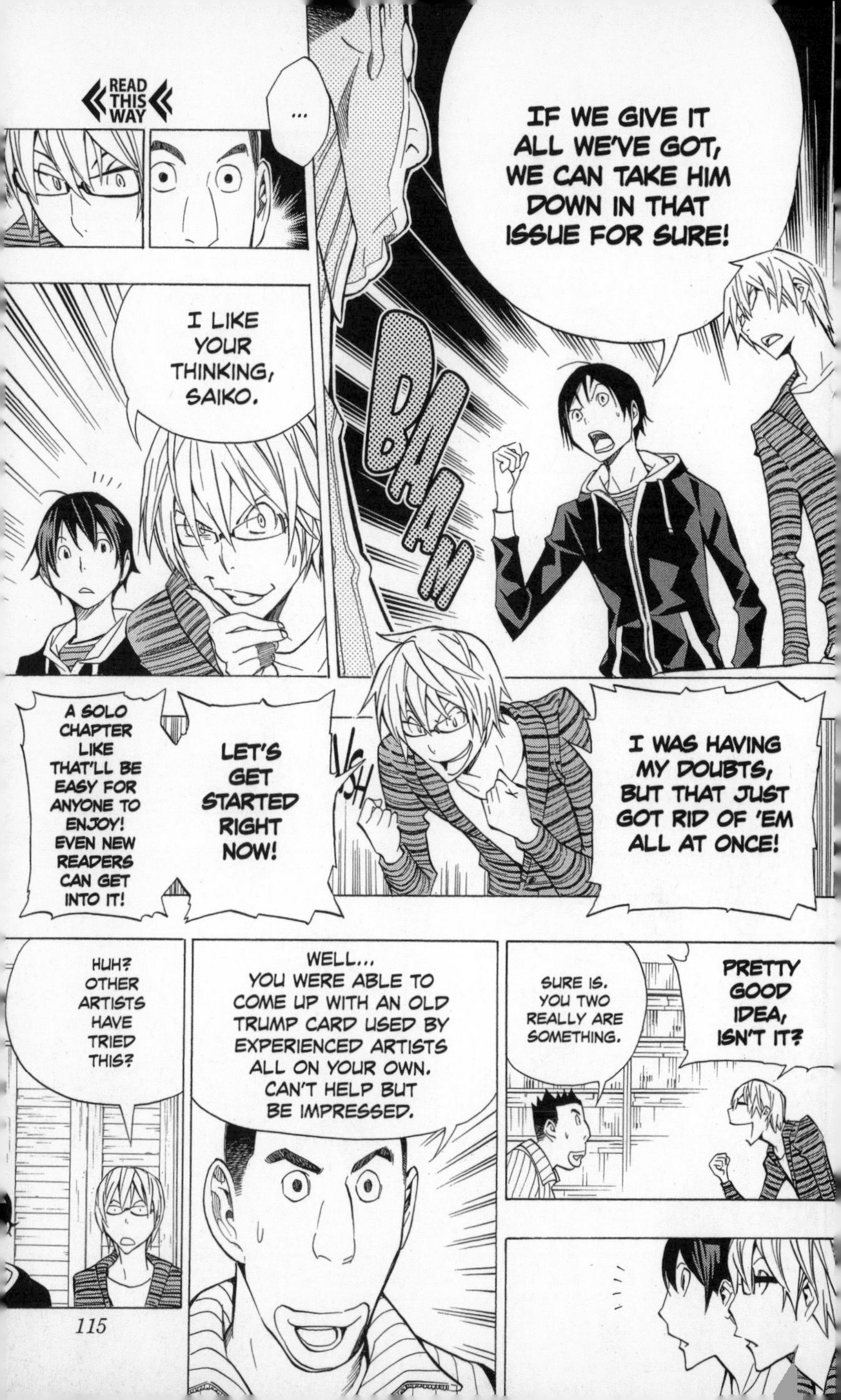
READ THIS WAY
IF WE GIVE IT ALL WE'VE GOT, WE CAN TAKE HIM DOWN IN THAT ISSUE FOR SURE!
BAM
...
I LIKE YOUR THINKING, SAIKO.
I WAS HAVING MY DOUBTS, BUT THAT JUST GOT RID OF 'EM ALL AT ONCE!
LET'S GET STARTED RIGHT NOW!
A SOLO CHAPTER LIKE THAT'LL BE EASY FOR ANYONE TO ENJOY! EVEN NEW READERS CAN GET INTO IT!
PRETTY GOOD IDEA, ISN'T IT?
SURE IS. YOU TWO REALLY ARE SOMETHING.
WELL... YOU WERE ABLE TO COME UP WITH AN OLD TRUMP CARD USED BY EXPERIENCED ARTISTS ALL ON YOUR OWN. CAN'T HELP BUT BE IMPRESSED.
HUH? OTHER ARTISTS HAVE TRIED THIS?

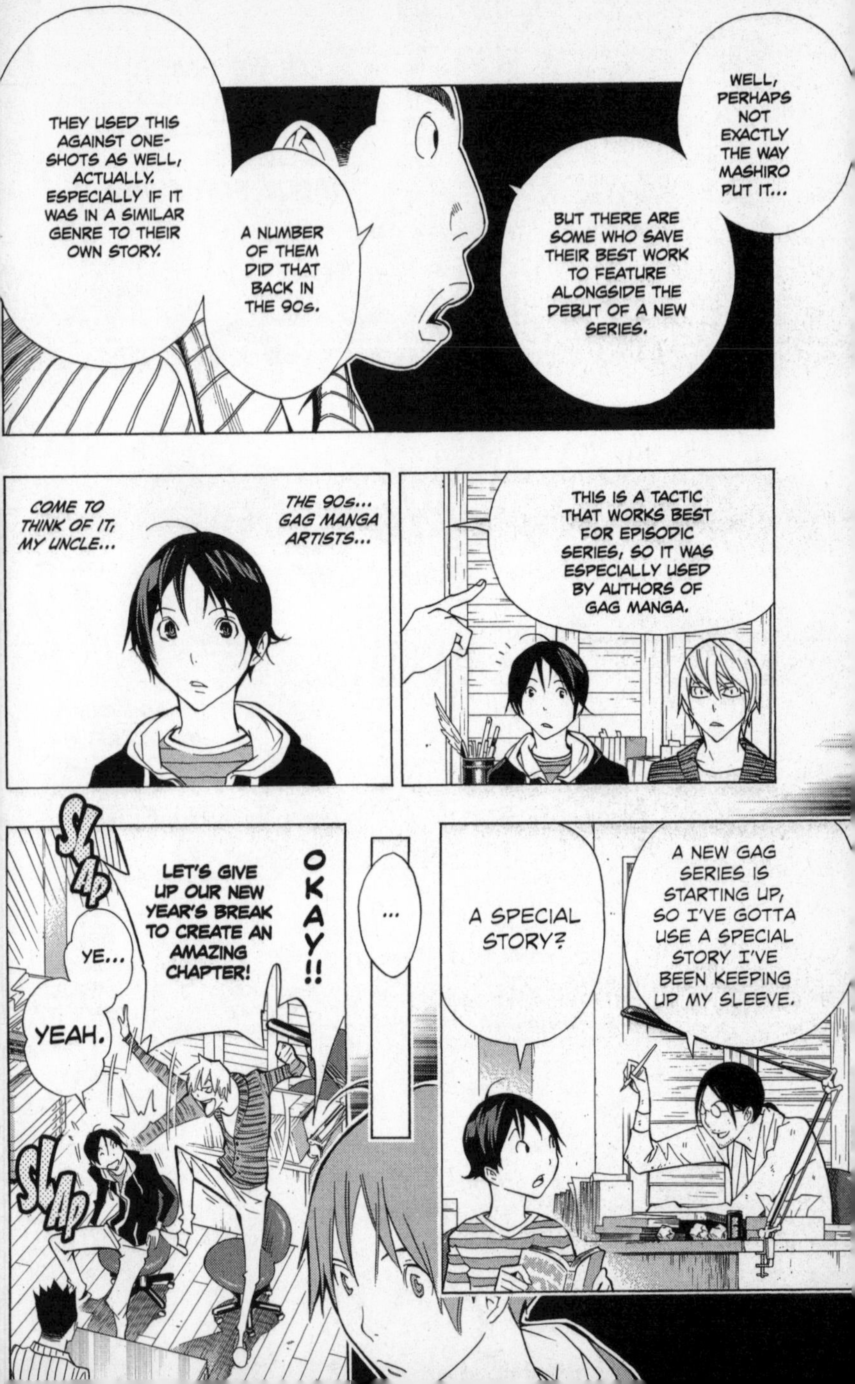
WELL, PERHAPS NOT EXACTLY THE WAY MASHIRO PUT IT...
BUT THERE ARE SOME WHO SAVE THEIR BEST WORK TO FEATURE ALONGSIDE THE DEBUT OF A NEW SERIES.
A NUMBER OF THEM DID THAT BACK IN THE 90s.
THEY USED THIS AGAINST ONE-SHOTS AS WELL, ACTUALLY. ESPECIALLY IF IT WAS IN A SIMILAR GENRE TO THEIR OWN STORY.
THIS IS A TACTIC THAT WORKS BEST FOR EPISODIC SERIES, SO IT WAS ESPECIALLY USED BY AUTHORS OF GAG MANGA.
THE 90s... GAG MANGA ARTISTS...
COME TO THINK OF IT, MY UNCLE...
A NEW GAG SERIES IS STARTING UP, SO I'VE GOTTA USE A SPECIAL STORY I'VE BEEN KEEPING UP MY SLEEVE.
A SPECIAL STORY?
...
OKAY!!
LET'S GIVE UP OUR NEW YEAR'S BREAK TO CREATE AN AMAZING CHAPTER!
SLAP
YE...
YEAH.
SLAP

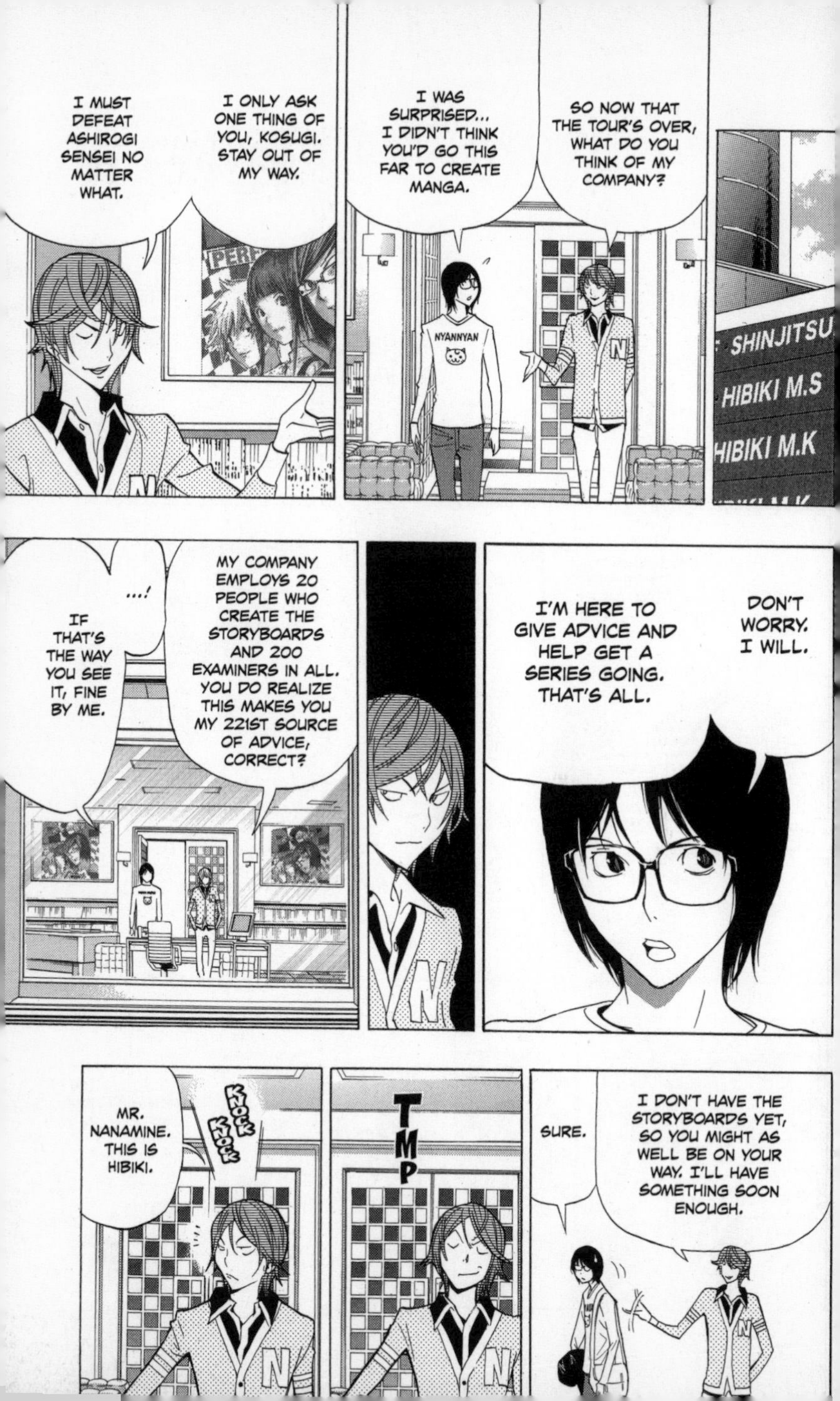
SHINJITSU
HIBIKI M.S
HIBIKI M.K
SO NOW THAT THE TOUR'S OVER, WHAT DO YOU THINK OF MY COMPANY?
I WAS SURPRISED... I DIDN'T THINK YOU'D GO THIS FAR TO CREATE MANGA.
NYANNYAN
I ONLY ASK ONE THING OF YOU, KOSUGI. STAY OUT OF MY WAY.
I MUST DEFEAT ASHIROGI SENSEI NO MATTER WHAT.
DON'T WORRY. I WILL.
I'M HERE TO GIVE ADVICE AND HELP GET A SERIES GOING. THAT'S ALL.
MY COMPANY EMPLOYS 20 PEOPLE WHO CREATE THE STORYBOARDS AND 200 EXAMINERS IN ALL. YOU DO REALIZE THIS MAKES YOU MY 221ST SOURCE OF ADVICE, CORRECT?
...!
IF THAT'S THE WAY YOU SEE IT, FINE BY ME.
I DON'T HAVE THE STORYBOARDS YET, SO YOU MIGHT AS WELL BE ON YOUR WAY. I'LL HAVE SOMETHING SOON ENOUGH.
SURE.
TMP
KNOCK KNOCK
MR. NANAMINE. THIS IS HIBIKI.

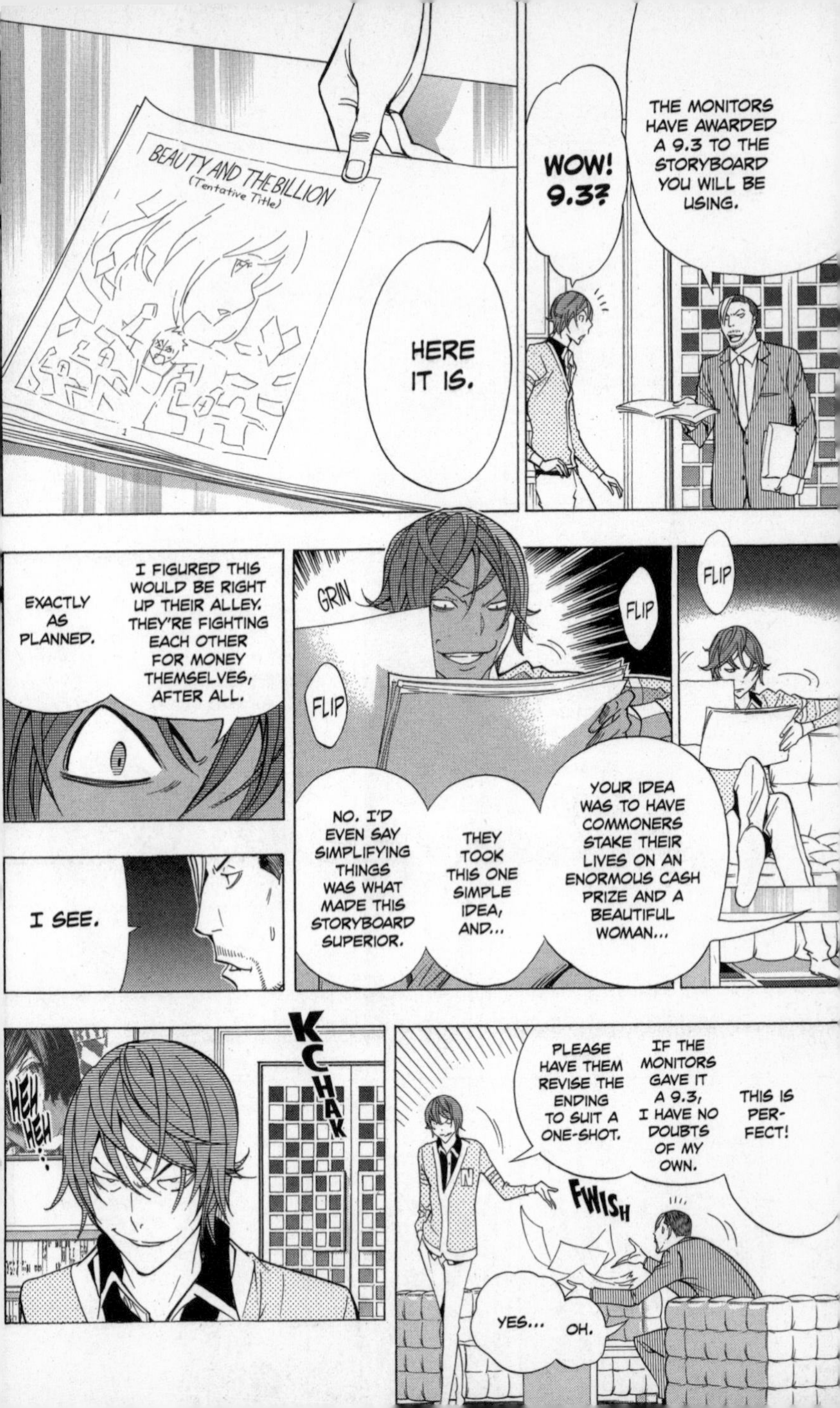
THE MONITORS HAVE AWARDED A 9.3 TO THE STORYBOARD YOU WILL BE USING.
WOW! 9.3?
HERE IT IS.
BEAUTY AND THE BILLION
(Tentative Title)
FLIP
FLIP
YOUR IDEA WAS TO HAVE COMMONERS STAKE THEIR LIVES ON AN ENORMOUS CASH PRIZE AND A BEAUTIFUL WOMAN...
GRIN
FLIP
THEY TOOK THIS ONE SIMPLE IDEA, AND...
NO. I'D EVEN SAY SIMPLIFYING THINGS WAS WHAT MADE THIS STORYBOARD SUPERIOR.
I FIGURED THIS WOULD BE RIGHT UP THEIR ALLEY. THEY'RE FIGHTING EACH OTHER FOR MONEY THEMSELVES, AFTER ALL.
EXACTLY AS PLANNED.
I SEE.
THIS IS PER-FECT!
IF THE MONITORS GAVE IT A 9.3, I HAVE NO DOUBTS OF MY OWN.
PLEASE HAVE THEM REVISE THE ENDING TO SUIT A ONE-SHOT.
FWISH
YES... OH.
KCHAK
HEH HEH...

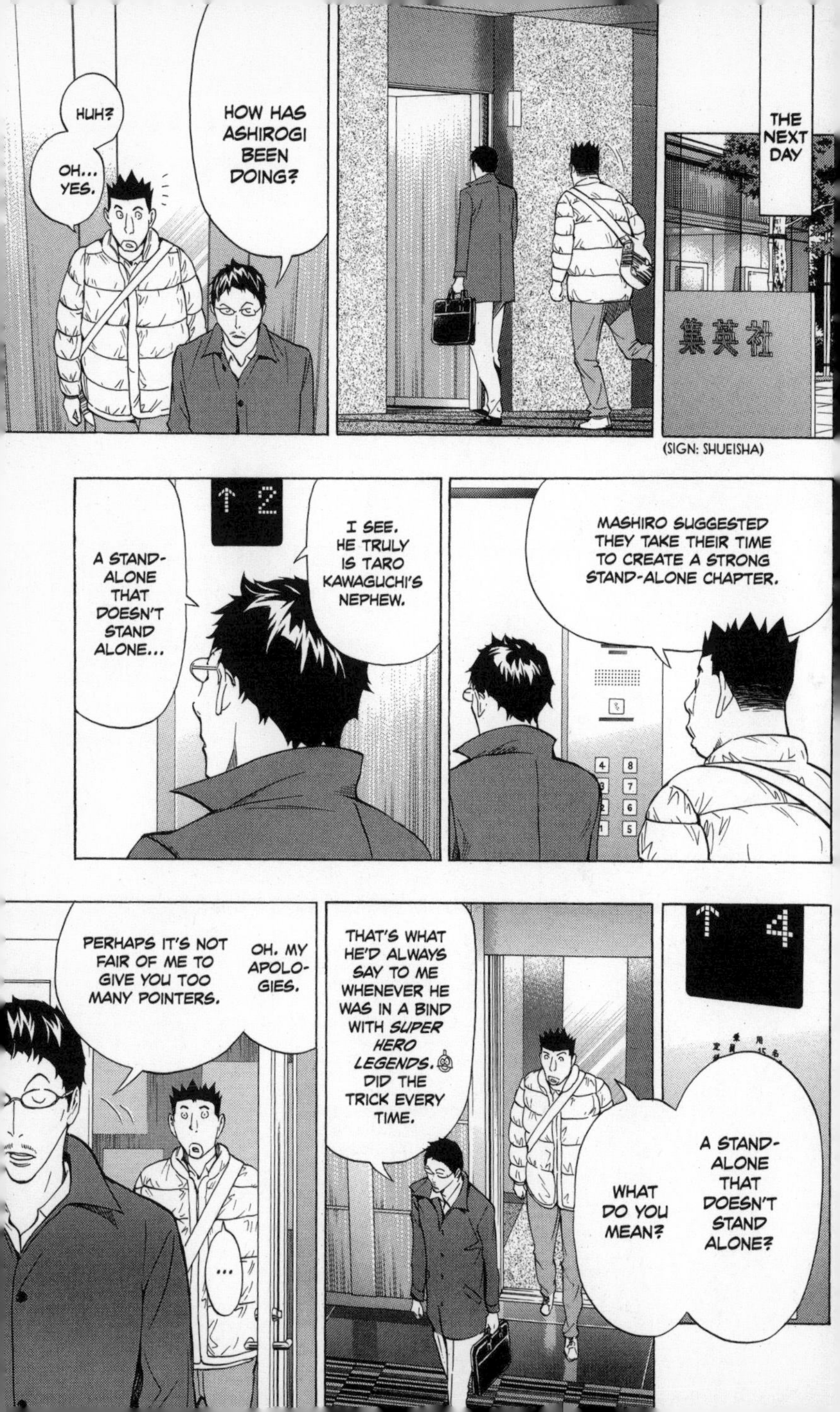
THE NEXT DAY
集英社
HOW HAS ASHIROGI BEEN DOING?
HUH?
OH... YES.
MASHIRO SUGGESTED THEY TAKE THEIR TIME TO CREATE A STRONG STAND-ALONE CHAPTER.
I SEE. HE TRULY IS TARO KAWAGUCHI'S NEPHEW.
A STAND-ALONE THAT DOESN'T STAND ALONE...
A STAND-ALONE THAT DOESN'T STAND ALONE?
WHAT DO YOU MEAN?
THAT'S WHAT HE'D ALWAYS SAY TO ME WHENEVER HE WAS IN A BIND WITH *SUPER HERO LEGENDS.* DID THE TRICK EVERY TIME.
OH. MY APOLOGIES.
PERHAPS IT'S NOT FAIR OF ME TO GIVE YOU TOO MANY POINTERS.
...
(SIGN: SHUEISHA)

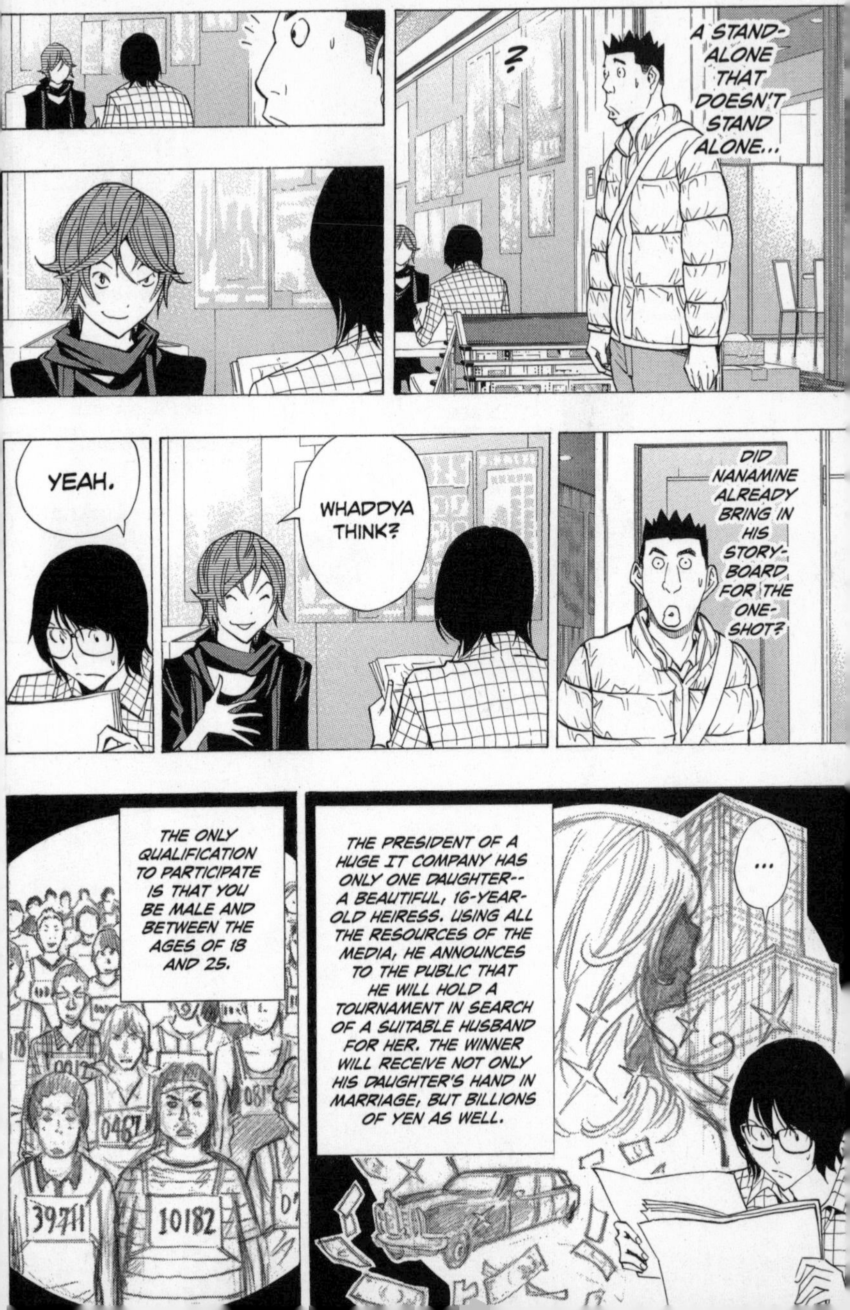
A STAND-ALONE THAT DOESN'T STAND ALONE...
DID NANAMINE ALREADY BRING IN HIS STORY-BOARD FOR THE ONE-SHOT?
WHADDYA THINK?
YEAH.
...
THE PRESIDENT OF A HUGE IT COMPANY HAS ONLY ONE DAUGHTER-- A BEAUTIFUL, 16-YEAR-OLD HEIRESS. USING ALL THE RESOURCES OF THE MEDIA, HE ANNOUNCES TO THE PUBLIC THAT HE WILL HOLD A TOURNAMENT IN SEARCH OF A SUITABLE HUSBAND FOR HER. THE WINNER WILL RECEIVE NOT ONLY HIS DAUGHTER'S HAND IN MARRIAGE, BUT BILLIONS OF YEN AS WELL.
THE ONLY QUALIFICATION TO PARTICIPATE IS THAT YOU BE MALE AND BETWEEN THE AGES OF 18 AND 25.
39711
10182

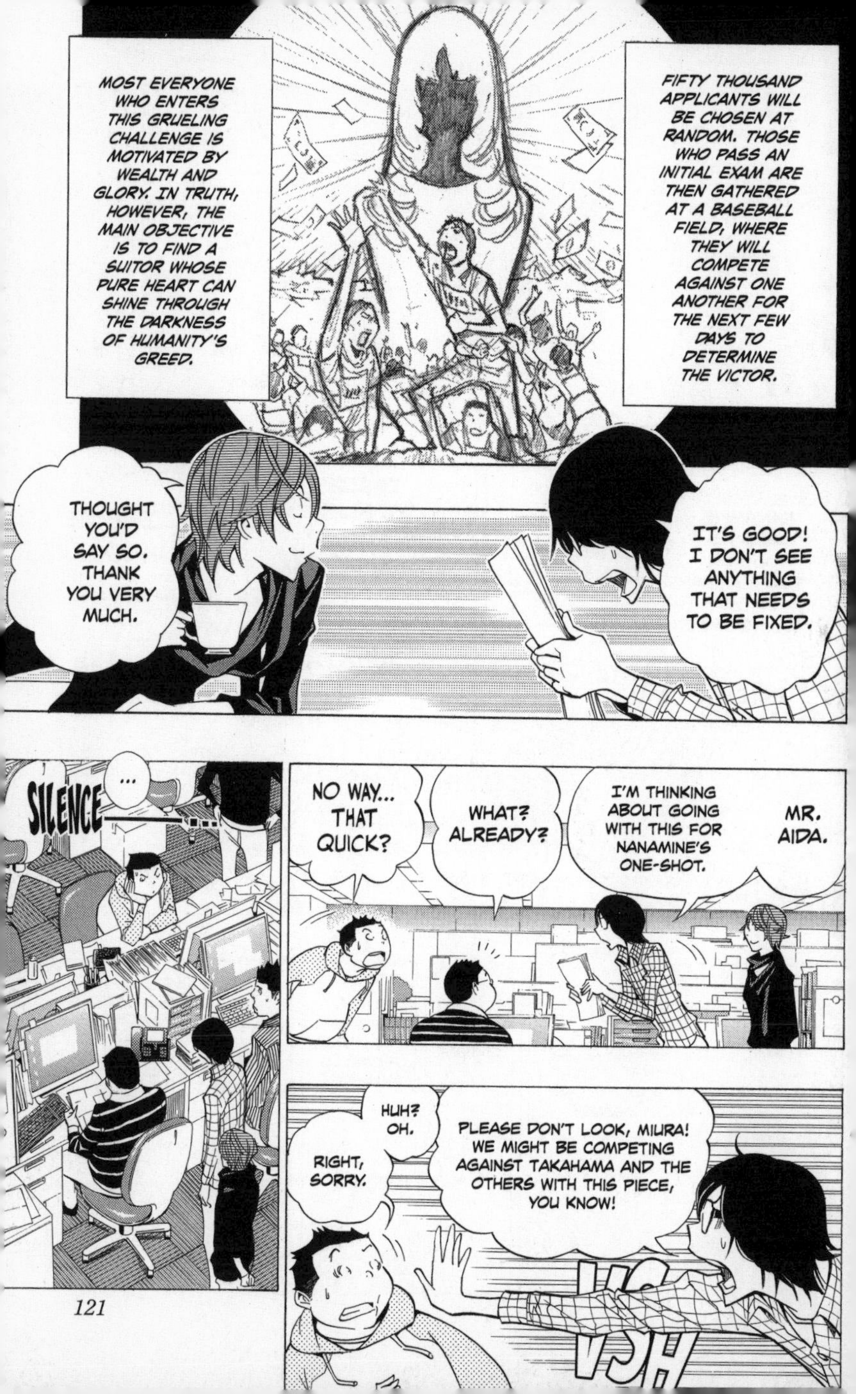

FIFTY THOUSAND APPLICANTS WILL BE CHOSEN AT RANDOM. THOSE WHO PASS AN INITIAL EXAM ARE THEN GATHERED AT A BASEBALL FIELD, WHERE THEY WILL COMPETE AGAINST ONE ANOTHER FOR THE NEXT FEW DAYS TO DETERMINE THE VICTOR.
MOST EVERYONE WHO ENTERS THIS GRUELING CHALLENGE IS MOTIVATED BY WEALTH AND GLORY. IN TRUTH, HOWEVER, THE MAIN OBJECTIVE IS TO FIND A SUITOR WHOSE PURE HEART CAN SHINE THROUGH THE DARKNESS OF HUMANITY'S GREED.
IT'S GOOD! I DON'T SEE ANYTHING THAT NEEDS TO BE FIXED.
THOUGHT YOU'D SAY SO. THANK YOU VERY MUCH.
MR. AIDA.
I'M THINKING ABOUT GOING WITH THIS FOR NANAMINE'S ONE-SHOT.
WHAT? ALREADY?
NO WAY... THAT QUICK?
PLEASE DON'T LOOK, MIURA! WE MIGHT BE COMPETING AGAINST TAKAHAMA AND THE OTHERS WITH THIS PIECE, YOU KNOW!
HUH? OH.
RIGHT, SORRY.
...
SILENCE

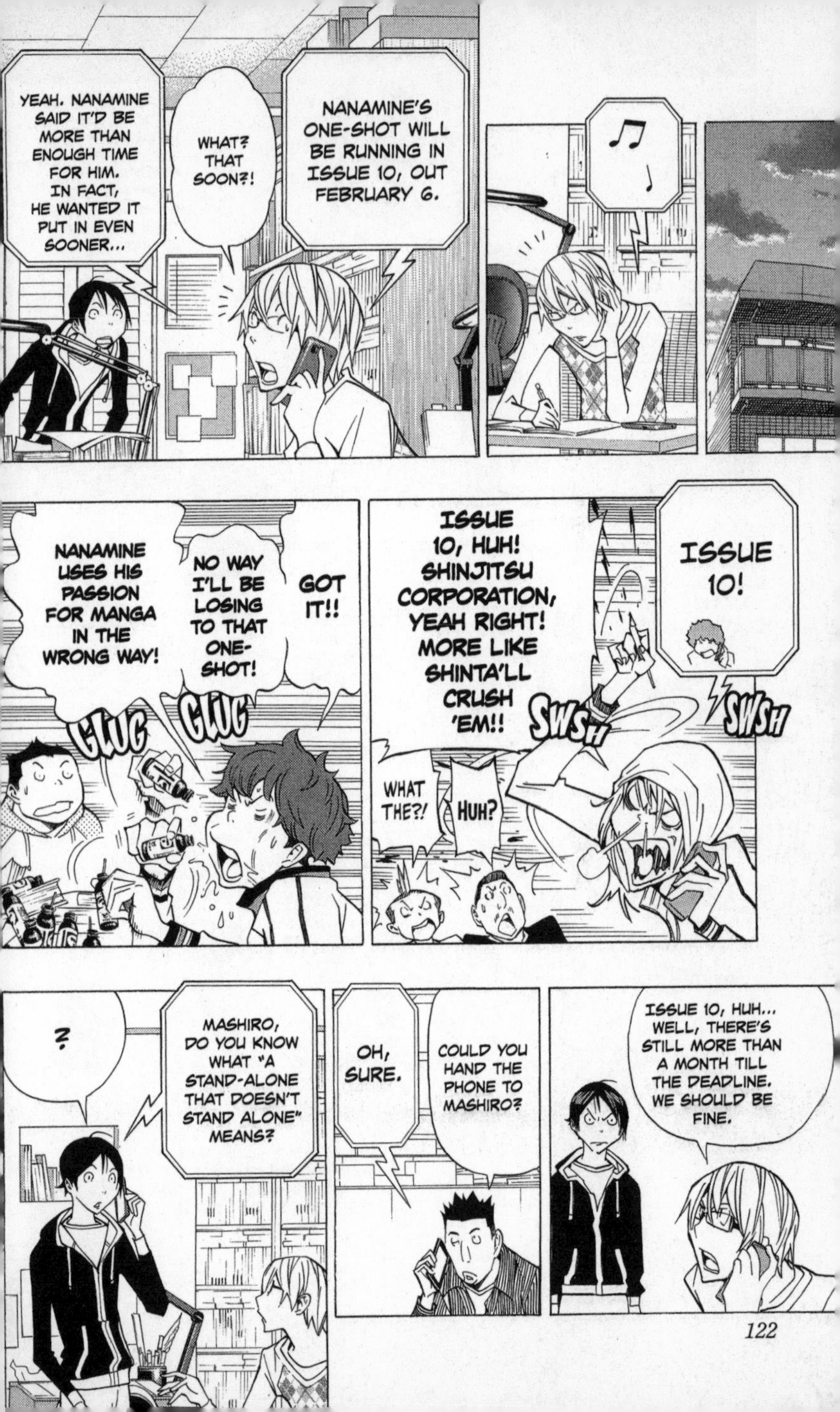
NANAMINE'S ONE-SHOT WILL BE RUNNING IN ISSUE 10, OUT FEBRUARY 6.
WHAT? THAT SOON?!
YEAH. NANAMINE SAID IT'D BE MORE THAN ENOUGH TIME FOR HIM. IN FACT, HE WANTED IT PUT IN EVEN SOONER...
ISSUE 10!
SWSH
ISSUE 10, HUH! SHINJITSU CORPORATION, YEAH RIGHT! MORE LIKE SHINTA'LL CRUSH 'EM!!
SWSH
HUH?
WHAT THE?!
GOT IT!!
NO WAY I'LL BE LOSING TO THAT ONE-SHOT!
NANAMINE USES HIS PASSION FOR MANGA IN THE WRONG WAY!
GLUG
GLUG
ISSUE 10, HUH... WELL, THERE'S STILL MORE THAN A MONTH TILL THE DEADLINE. WE SHOULD BE FINE.
COULD YOU HAND THE PHONE TO MASHIRO?
OH, SURE.
MASHIRO, DO YOU KNOW WHAT "A STAND-ALONE THAT DOESN'T STAND ALONE" MEANS?
?

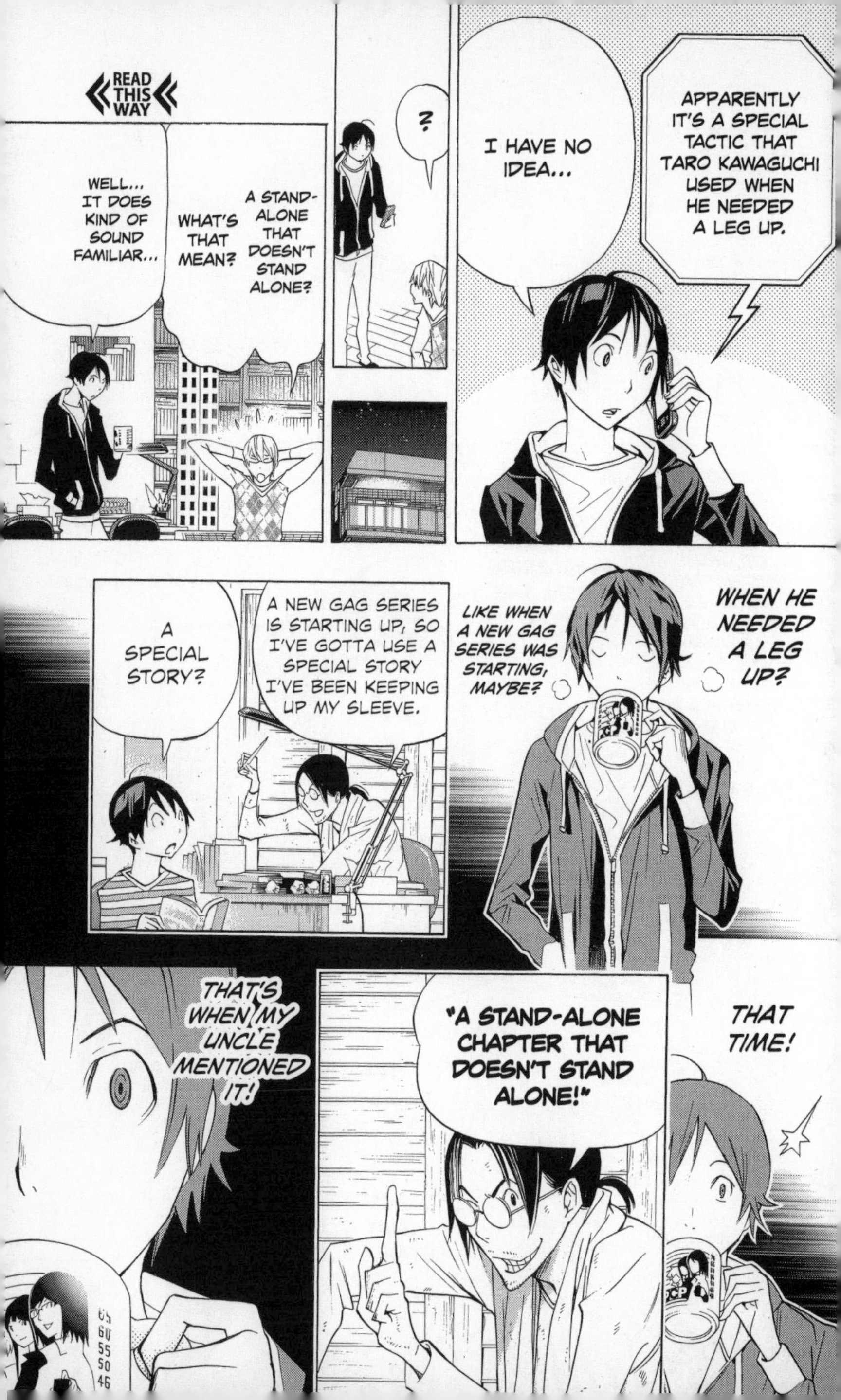
READ THIS WAY
APPARENTLY IT'S A SPECIAL TACTIC THAT TARO KAWAGUCHI USED WHEN HE NEEDED A LEG UP.
I HAVE NO IDEA...
?
A STAND-ALONE THAT DOESN'T STAND ALONE?
WHAT'S THAT MEAN?
WELL... IT DOES KIND OF SOUND FAMILIAR...
WHEN HE NEEDED A LEG UP?
LIKE WHEN A NEW GAG SERIES WAS STARTING, MAYBE?
A NEW GAG SERIES IS STARTING UP, SO I'VE GOTTA USE A SPECIAL STORY I'VE BEEN KEEPING UP MY SLEEVE.
A SPECIAL STORY?
THAT TIME!
"A STAND-ALONE CHAPTER THAT DOESN'T STAND ALONE!"
THAT'S WHEN MY UNCLE MENTIONED IT!

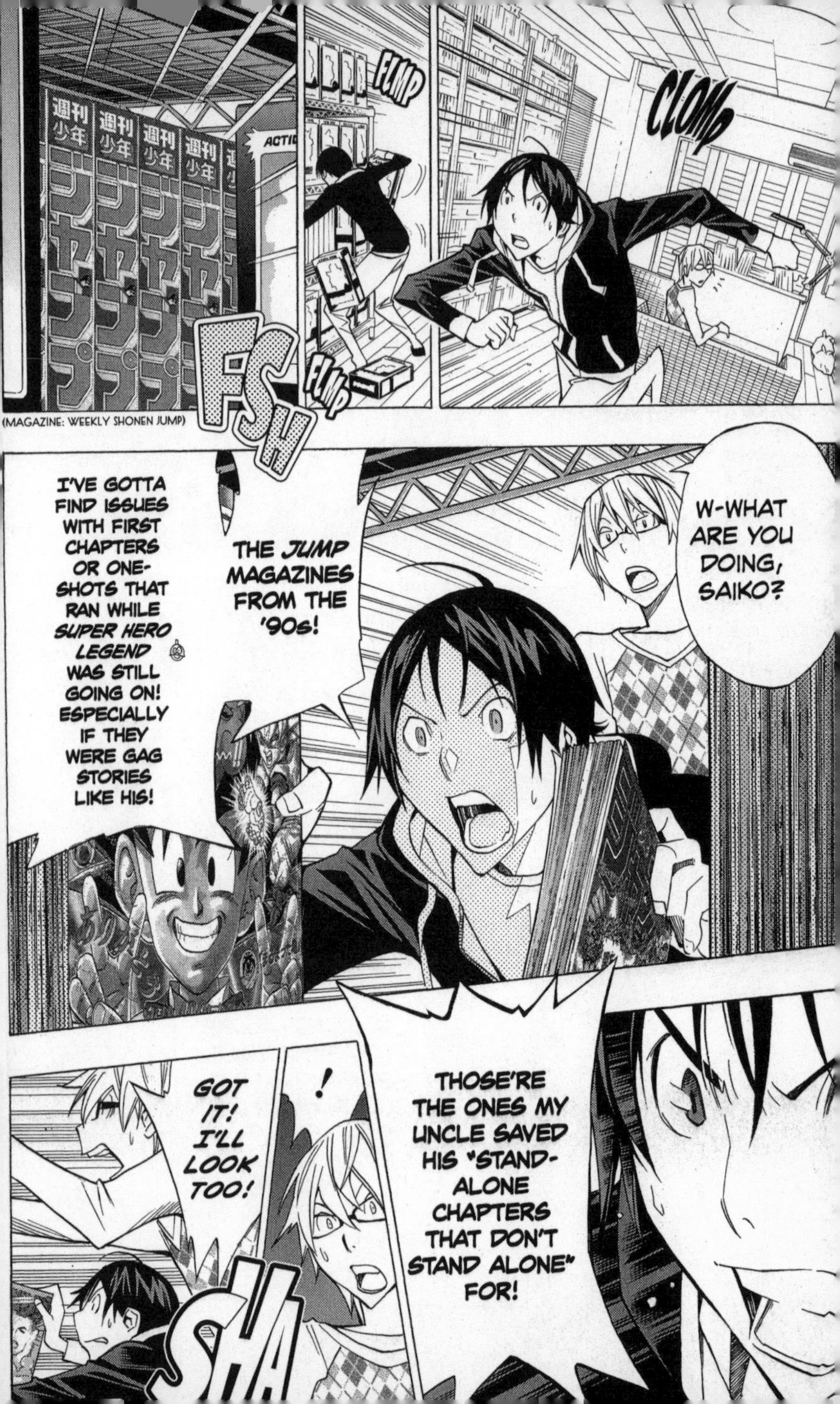
CLOMP
FLMP
FSH
FLMP
週刊少年
(MAGAZINE: WEEKLY SHONEN JUMP)
W-WHAT ARE YOU DOING, SAIKO?
THE *JUMP* MAGAZINES FROM THE '90s!
I'VE GOTTA FIND ISSUES WITH FIRST CHAPTERS OR ONE-SHOTS THAT RAN WHILE *SUPER HERO LEGEND* WAS STILL GOING ON! ESPECIALLY IF THEY WERE GAG STORIES LIKE HIS!
THOSE'RE THE ONES MY UNCLE SAVED HIS "STAND-ALONE CHAPTERS THAT DON'T STAND ALONE" FOR!
!
GOT IT! I'LL LOOK TOO!
SHA

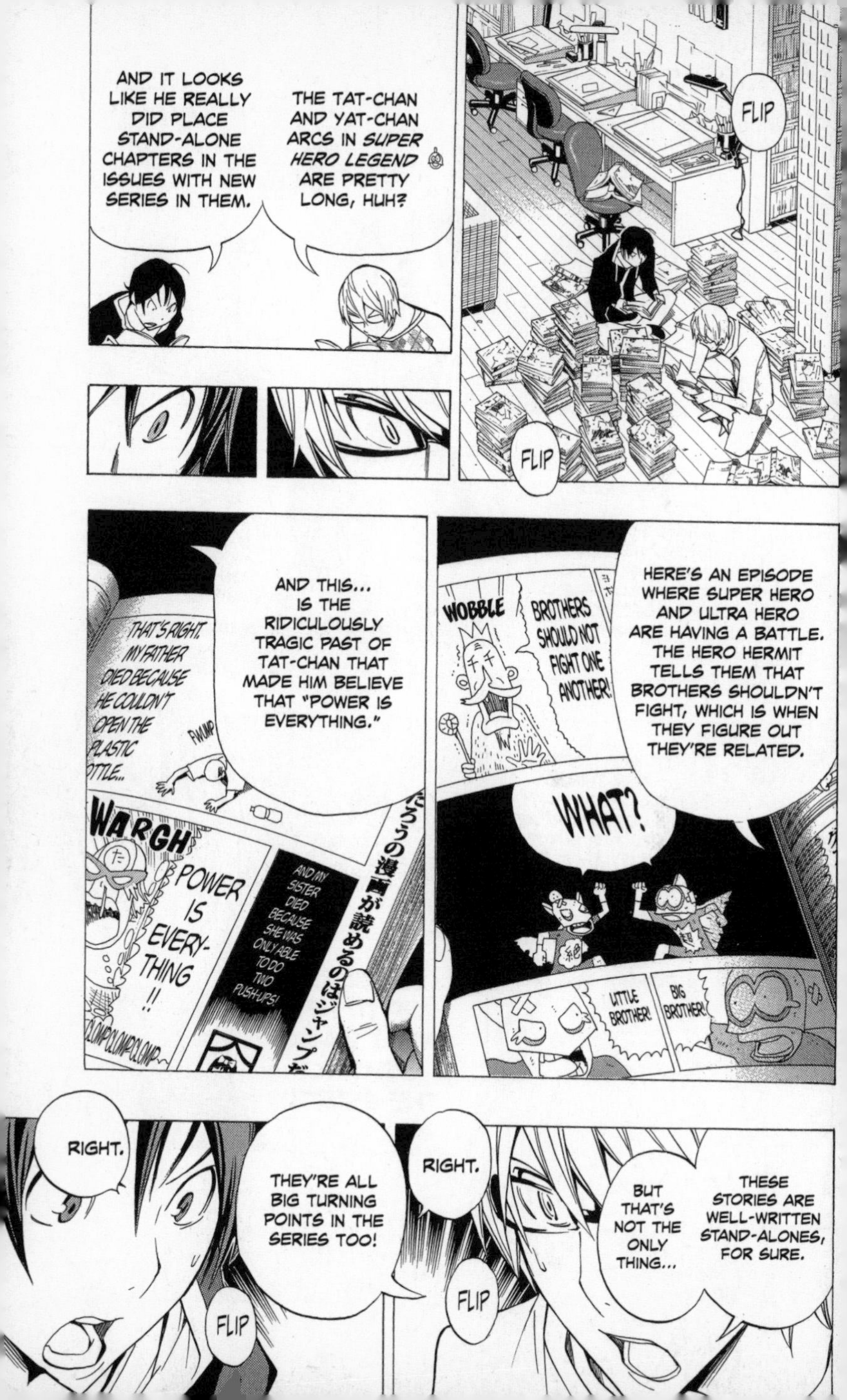
FLIP
FLIP
THE TAT-CHAN AND YAT-CHAN ARCS IN *SUPER HERO LEGEND* ARE PRETTY LONG, HUH?
AND IT LOOKS LIKE HE REALLY DID PLACE STAND-ALONE CHAPTERS IN THE ISSUES WITH NEW SERIES IN THEM.
HERE'S AN EPISODE WHERE SUPER HERO AND ULTRA HERO ARE HAVING A BATTLE. THE HERO HERMIT TELLS THEM THAT BROTHERS SHOULDN'T FIGHT, WHICH IS WHEN THEY FIGURE OUT THEY'RE RELATED.
BROTHERS SHOULD NOT FIGHT ONE ANOTHER!
WOBBLE
WHAT?
BIG BROTHER!
LITTLE BROTHER!
AND THIS... IS THE RIDICULOUSLY TRAGIC PAST OF TAT-CHAN THAT MADE HIM BELIEVE THAT "POWER IS EVERYTHING."
THAT'S RIGHT. MY FATHER DIED BECAUSE HE COULDN'T OPEN THE PLASTIC OTTLE...
FWUMP
たろうの漫画が読めるのはジャンプ
AND MY SISTER DIED BECAUSE SHE WAS ONLY ABLE TO DO TWO PUSH-UPS!
POWER IS EVERYTHING!!
WARGH
CLOMP CLOMP CLOMP
THESE STORIES ARE WELL-WRITTEN STAND-ALONES, FOR SURE.
BUT THAT'S NOT THE ONLY THING...
FLIP
RIGHT.
THEY'RE ALL BIG TURNING POINTS IN THE SERIES TOO!
RIGHT.
FLIP

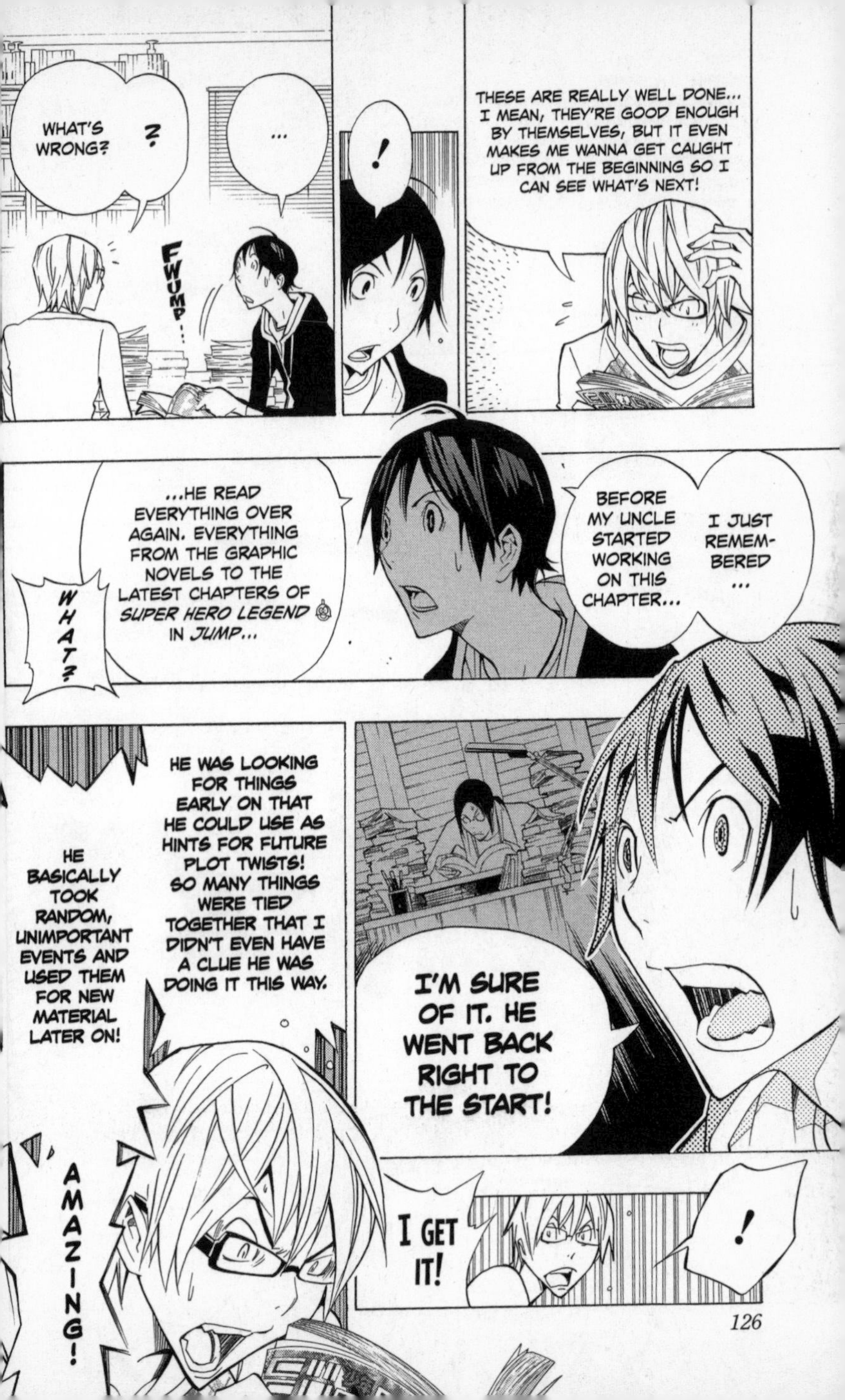
THESE ARE REALLY WELL DONE... I MEAN, THEY'RE GOOD ENOUGH BY THEMSELVES, BUT IT EVEN MAKES ME WANNA GET CAUGHT UP FROM THE BEGINNING SO I CAN SEE WHAT'S NEXT!
!
...
?
WHAT'S WRONG?
FWUMP...
I JUST REMEMBERED...
BEFORE MY UNCLE STARTED WORKING ON THIS CHAPTER...
...HE READ EVERYTHING OVER AGAIN. EVERYTHING FROM THE GRAPHIC NOVELS TO THE LATEST CHAPTERS OF *SUPER HERO LEGEND* IN *JUMP*...
WHAT?
I'M SURE OF IT. HE WENT BACK RIGHT TO THE START!
HE WAS LOOKING FOR THINGS EARLY ON THAT HE COULD USE AS HINTS FOR FUTURE PLOT TWISTS! SO MANY THINGS WERE TIED TOGETHER THAT I DIDN'T EVEN HAVE A CLUE HE WAS DOING IT THIS WAY.
HE BASICALLY TOOK RANDOM, UNIMPORTANT EVENTS AND USED THEM FOR NEW MATERIAL LATER ON!
!
I GET IT!
AMAZING!

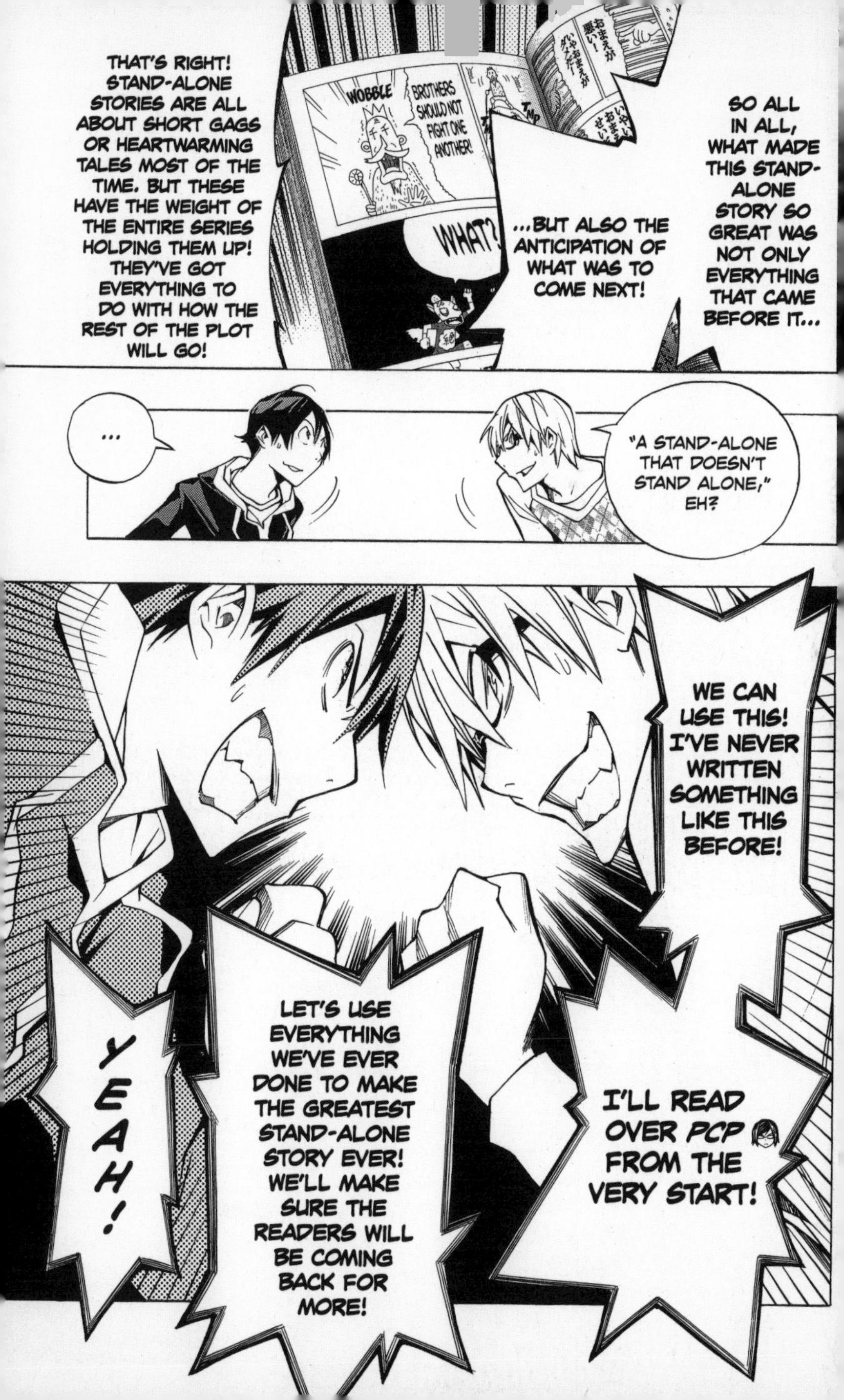
SO ALL IN ALL, WHAT MADE THIS STAND-ALONE STORY SO GREAT WAS NOT ONLY EVERYTHING THAT CAME BEFORE IT...
...BUT ALSO THE ANTICIPATION OF WHAT WAS TO COME NEXT!
おまえが悪い!
いやおまえがダメだー
WOBBLE
BROTHERS SHOULD NOT FIGHT ONE ANOTHER!
WHAT?!
THAT'S RIGHT! STAND-ALONE STORIES ARE ALL ABOUT SHORT GAGS OR HEARTWARMING TALES MOST OF THE TIME. BUT THESE HAVE THE WEIGHT OF THE ENTIRE SERIES HOLDING THEM UP! THEY'VE GOT EVERYTHING TO DO WITH HOW THE REST OF THE PLOT WILL GO!
"A STAND-ALONE THAT DOESN'T STAND ALONE," EH?
...
WE CAN USE THIS! I'VE NEVER WRITTEN SOMETHING LIKE THIS BEFORE!
I'LL READ OVER *PCP* FROM THE VERY START!
LET'S USE EVERYTHING WE'VE EVER DONE TO MAKE THE GREATEST STAND-ALONE STORY EVER! WE'LL MAKE SURE THE READERS WILL BE COMING BACK FOR MORE!
YEAH!

OHBA'S STORYBOARD

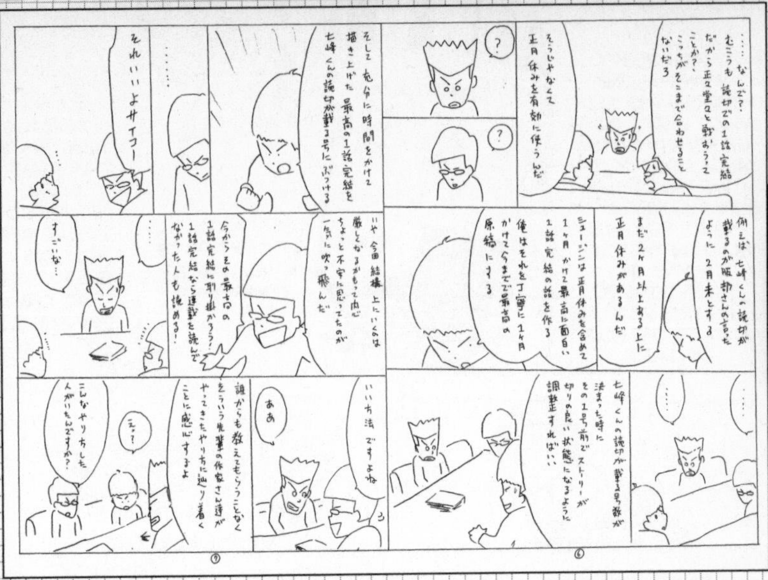
……なんで？むこうも読切での1話完結だから正々堂々と戦おうってことか？こっちがそこまで合わせることないだろ
そうじゃなくて正月休みを有効に使うんだ
？
？
例えば七峰くんの読切が載るのが服部さんの言ったように2月末とする
まだ2ヶ月以上ある上に正月休みがあるんだ
シュージンは正月休みを含めて1ヶ月かけて最高に面白い1話完結の話を作る
俺はそれを丁寧に1ヶ月かけて今までで最高の原稿にする
……
……
七峰くんの読切が載る号数が決まった時にその1号前でストーリーが切りの良い状態になるように調整すればいい
そして充分に時間をかけて描き上げた最高の1話完結を七峰くんの読切が載る号にぶつける
……
それいいよサイコー
……
いや今回結構上にいくのは厳しくなるかもって内心ちょっと不安に思ってたのが一気に吹っ飛んだ
今からその最高の1話完結に取り掛かろう！1話完結なら連載を読んでなかった人も読める！
……
すごいな…
いい方法ですよね
ああ
誰からも教えてもらうことなくそういう先輩の作家さん達がやってきたやり方に辿り着くことに感心するよ
えっ？
こんなやり方した人がいたんですか？

OBATA'S STORYBOARD

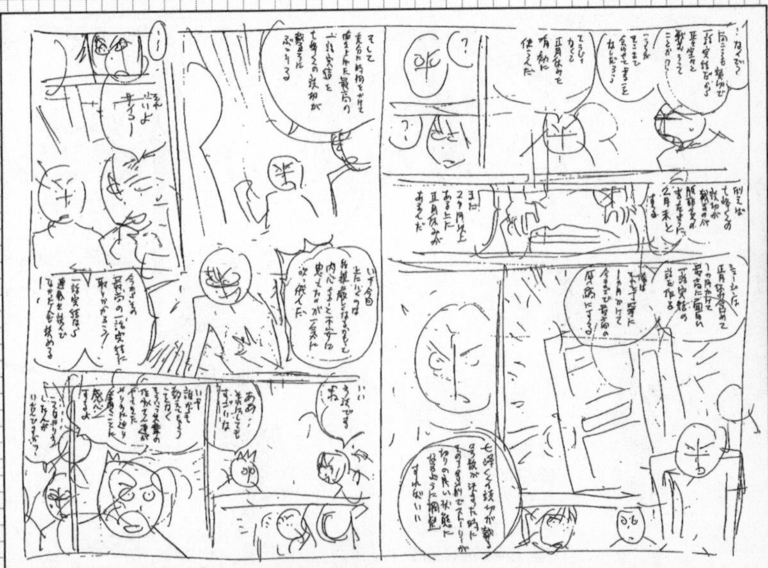

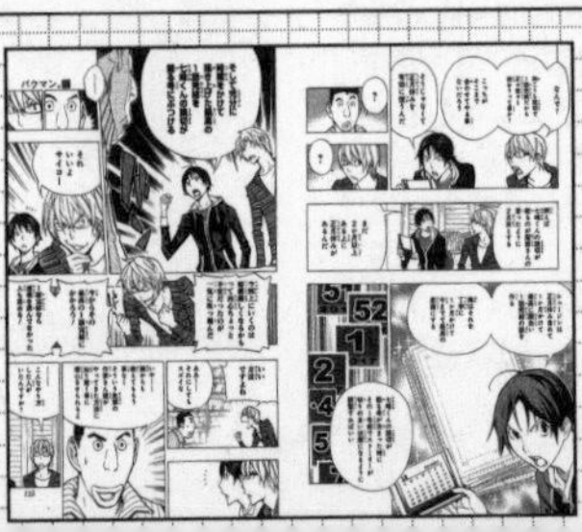

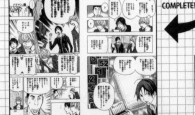

COMPLETE!

※CREATOR STORYBOARDS AND FINISHED PAGES IN JAPANESE

BAKUMAN。 vol.17

"Until the Final Draft Is Complete"

Chapter 148, pp. 114-115

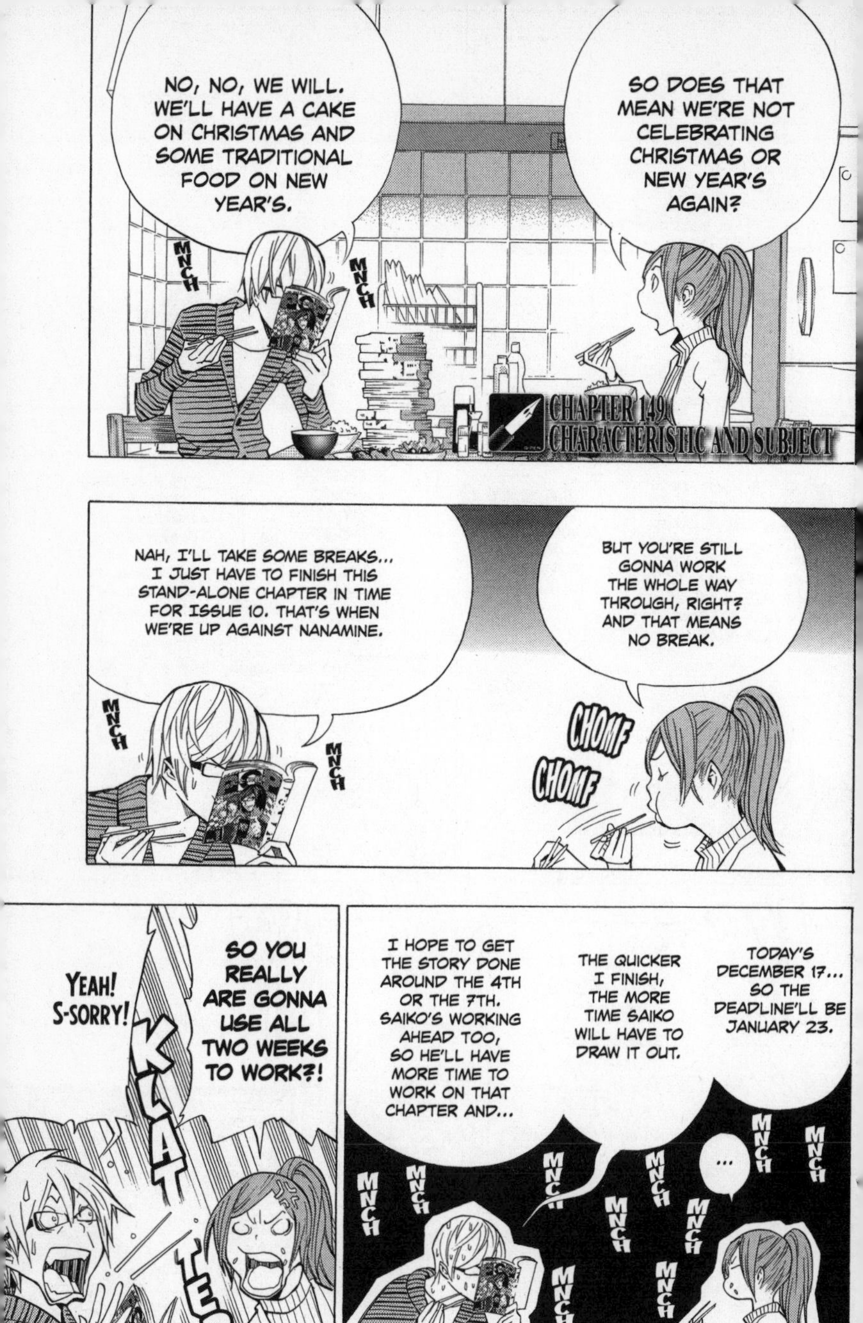
SO DOES THAT MEAN WE'RE NOT CELEBRATING CHRISTMAS OR NEW YEAR'S AGAIN?
NO, NO, WE WILL. WE'LL HAVE A CAKE ON CHRISTMAS AND SOME TRADITIONAL FOOD ON NEW YEAR'S.
MNCH
MNCH
CHAPTER 149: CHARACTERISTIC AND SUBJECT
BUT YOU'RE STILL GONNA WORK THE WHOLE WAY THROUGH, RIGHT? AND THAT MEANS NO BREAK.
CHOMF
CHOMF
NAH, I'LL TAKE SOME BREAKS... I JUST HAVE TO FINISH THIS STAND-ALONE CHAPTER IN TIME FOR ISSUE 10. THAT'S WHEN WE'RE UP AGAINST NANAMINE.
MNCH
MNCH
TODAY'S DECEMBER 17... SO THE DEADLINE'LL BE JANUARY 23.
THE QUICKER I FINISH, THE MORE TIME SAIKO WILL HAVE TO DRAW IT OUT.
I HOPE TO GET THE STORY DONE AROUND THE 4TH OR THE 7TH. SAIKO'S WORKING AHEAD TOO, SO HE'LL HAVE MORE TIME TO WORK ON THAT CHAPTER AND...
...
MNCH
MNCH
MNCH
MNCH
SO YOU REALLY ARE GONNA USE ALL TWO WEEKS TO WORK?!
YEAH! S-SORRY!
KLATTER

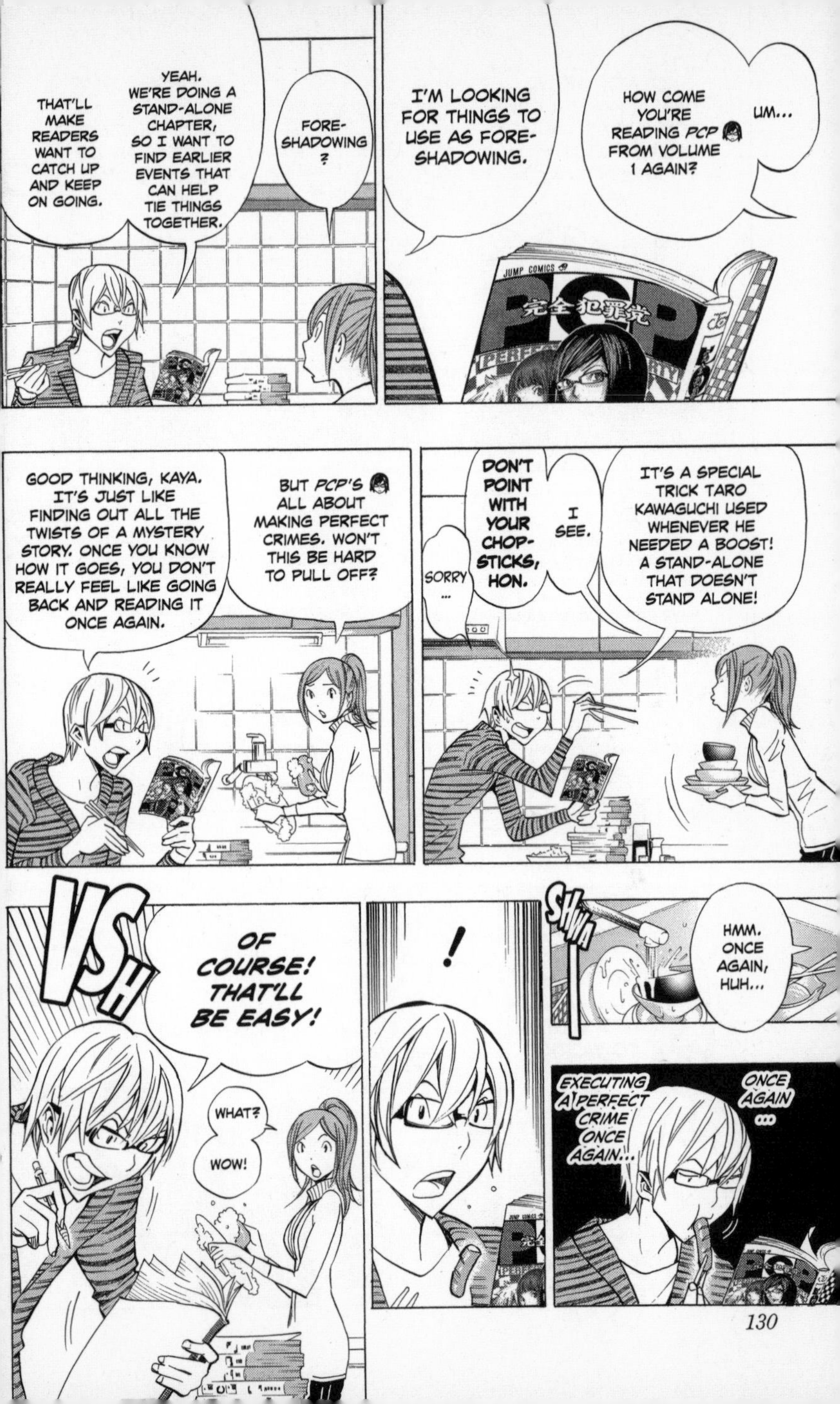

UM...
HOW COME YOU'RE READING *PCP* FROM VOLUME 1 AGAIN?
JUMP COMICS
完全犯罪党
I'M LOOKING FOR THINGS TO USE AS FORE-SHADOWING.
FORE-SHADOWING?
YEAH. WE'RE DOING A STAND-ALONE CHAPTER, SO I WANT TO FIND EARLIER EVENTS THAT CAN HELP TIE THINGS TOGETHER.
THAT'LL MAKE READERS WANT TO CATCH UP AND KEEP ON GOING.
IT'S A SPECIAL TRICK TARO KAWAGUCHI USED WHENEVER HE NEEDED A BOOST! A STAND-ALONE THAT DOESN'T STAND ALONE!
I SEE.
DON'T POINT WITH YOUR CHOP-STICKS, HON.
SORRY...
BUT *PCP*'S ALL ABOUT MAKING PERFECT CRIMES. WON'T THIS BE HARD TO PULL OFF?
GOOD THINKING, KAYA. IT'S JUST LIKE FINDING OUT ALL THE TWISTS OF A MYSTERY STORY. ONCE YOU KNOW HOW IT GOES, YOU DON'T REALLY FEEL LIKE GOING BACK AND READING IT ONCE AGAIN.
SHWA
HMM. ONCE AGAIN, HUH...
ONCE AGAIN...
EXECUTING A PERFECT CRIME ONCE AGAIN...
!
VSH
OF COURSE! THAT'LL BE EASY!
WHAT?
WOW!

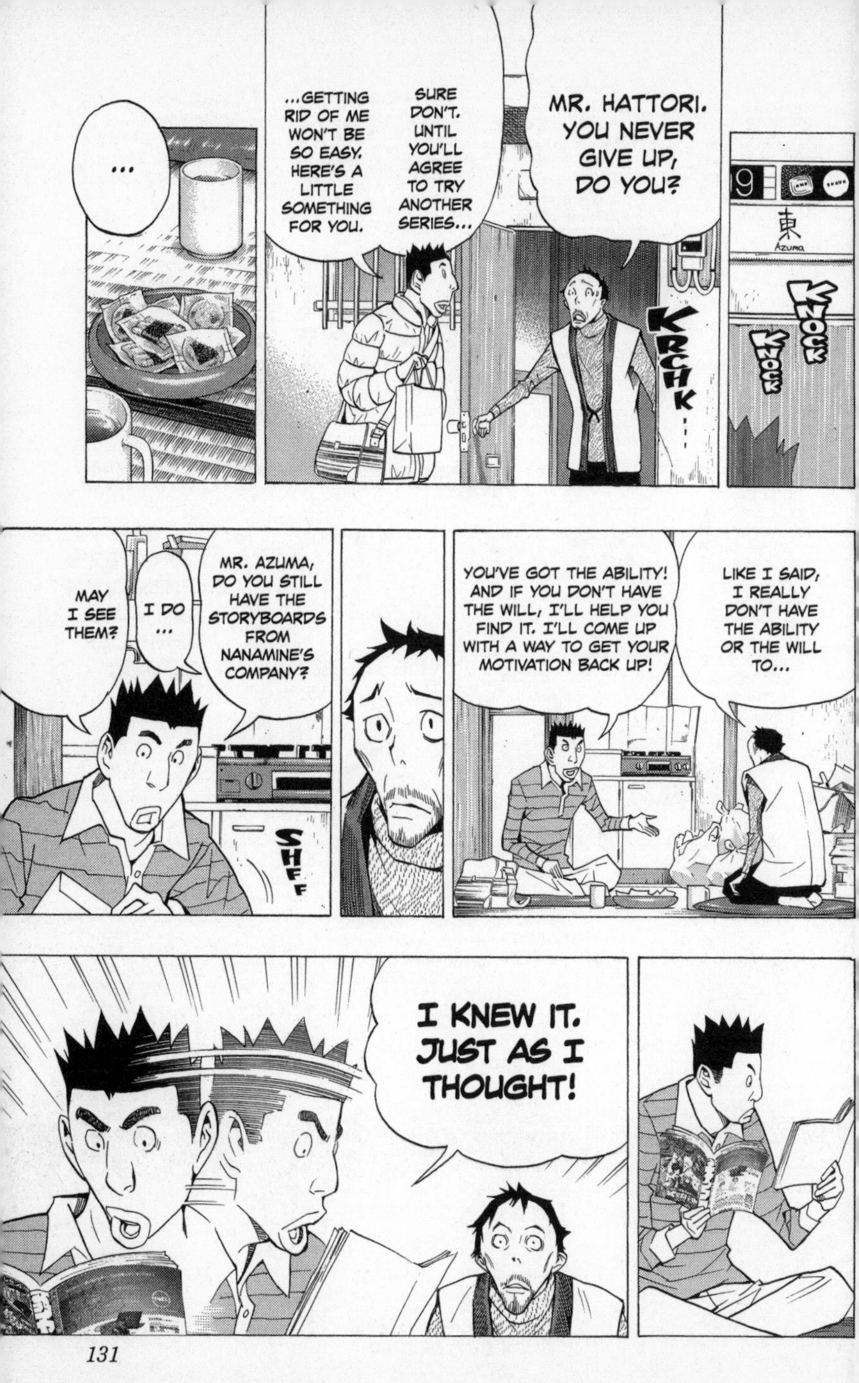
KNOCK
KNOCK
東
Azuma
MR. HATTORI. YOU NEVER GIVE UP, DO YOU?
KRCHK...
SURE DON'T. UNTIL YOU'LL AGREE TO TRY ANOTHER SERIES...
...GETTING RID OF ME WON'T BE SO EASY. HERE'S A LITTLE SOMETHING FOR YOU.
...
LIKE I SAID, I REALLY DON'T HAVE THE ABILITY OR THE WILL TO...
YOU'VE GOT THE ABILITY! AND IF YOU DON'T HAVE THE WILL, I'LL HELP YOU FIND IT. I'LL COME UP WITH A WAY TO GET YOUR MOTIVATION BACK UP!
MR. AZUMA, DO YOU STILL HAVE THE STORYBOARDS FROM NANAMINE'S COMPANY?
I DO ...
MAY I SEE THEM?
SHFF
I KNEW IT. JUST AS I THOUGHT!

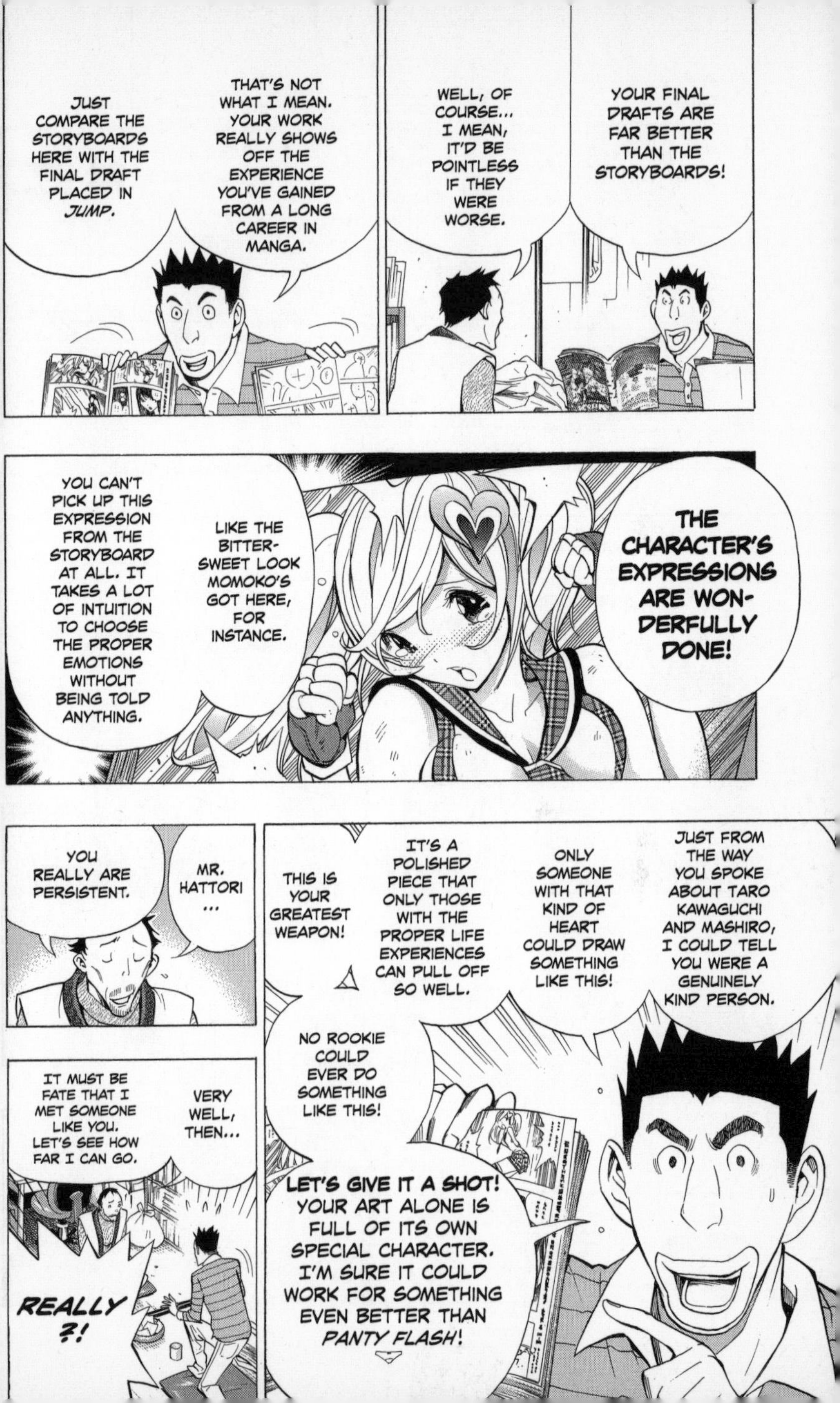
YOUR FINAL DRAFTS ARE FAR BETTER THAN THE STORYBOARDS!
WELL, OF COURSE... I MEAN, IT'D BE POINTLESS IF THEY WERE WORSE.
THAT'S NOT WHAT I MEAN. YOUR WORK REALLY SHOWS OFF THE EXPERIENCE YOU'VE GAINED FROM A LONG CAREER IN MANGA.
JUST COMPARE THE STORYBOARDS HERE WITH THE FINAL DRAFT PLACED IN *JUMP*.
THE CHARACTER'S EXPRESSIONS ARE WONDERFULLY DONE!
LIKE THE BITTERSWEET LOOK MOMOKO'S GOT HERE, FOR INSTANCE.
YOU CAN'T PICK UP THIS EXPRESSION FROM THE STORYBOARD AT ALL. IT TAKES A LOT OF INTUITION TO CHOOSE THE PROPER EMOTIONS WITHOUT BEING TOLD ANYTHING.
JUST FROM THE WAY YOU SPOKE ABOUT TARO KAWAGUCHI AND MASHIRO, I COULD TELL YOU WERE A GENUINELY KIND PERSON.
ONLY SOMEONE WITH THAT KIND OF HEART COULD DRAW SOMETHING LIKE THIS!
IT'S A POLISHED PIECE THAT ONLY THOSE WITH THE PROPER LIFE EXPERIENCES CAN PULL OFF SO WELL.
THIS IS YOUR GREATEST WEAPON!
NO ROOKIE COULD EVER DO SOMETHING LIKE THIS!
LET'S GIVE IT A SHOT! YOUR ART ALONE IS FULL OF ITS OWN SPECIAL CHARACTER. I'M SURE IT COULD WORK FOR SOMETHING EVEN BETTER THAN *PANTY FLASH*!
MR. HATTORI...
YOU REALLY ARE PERSISTENT.
VERY WELL, THEN...
IT MUST BE FATE THAT I MET SOMEONE LIKE YOU. LET'S SEE HOW FAR I CAN GO.
REALLY ?!

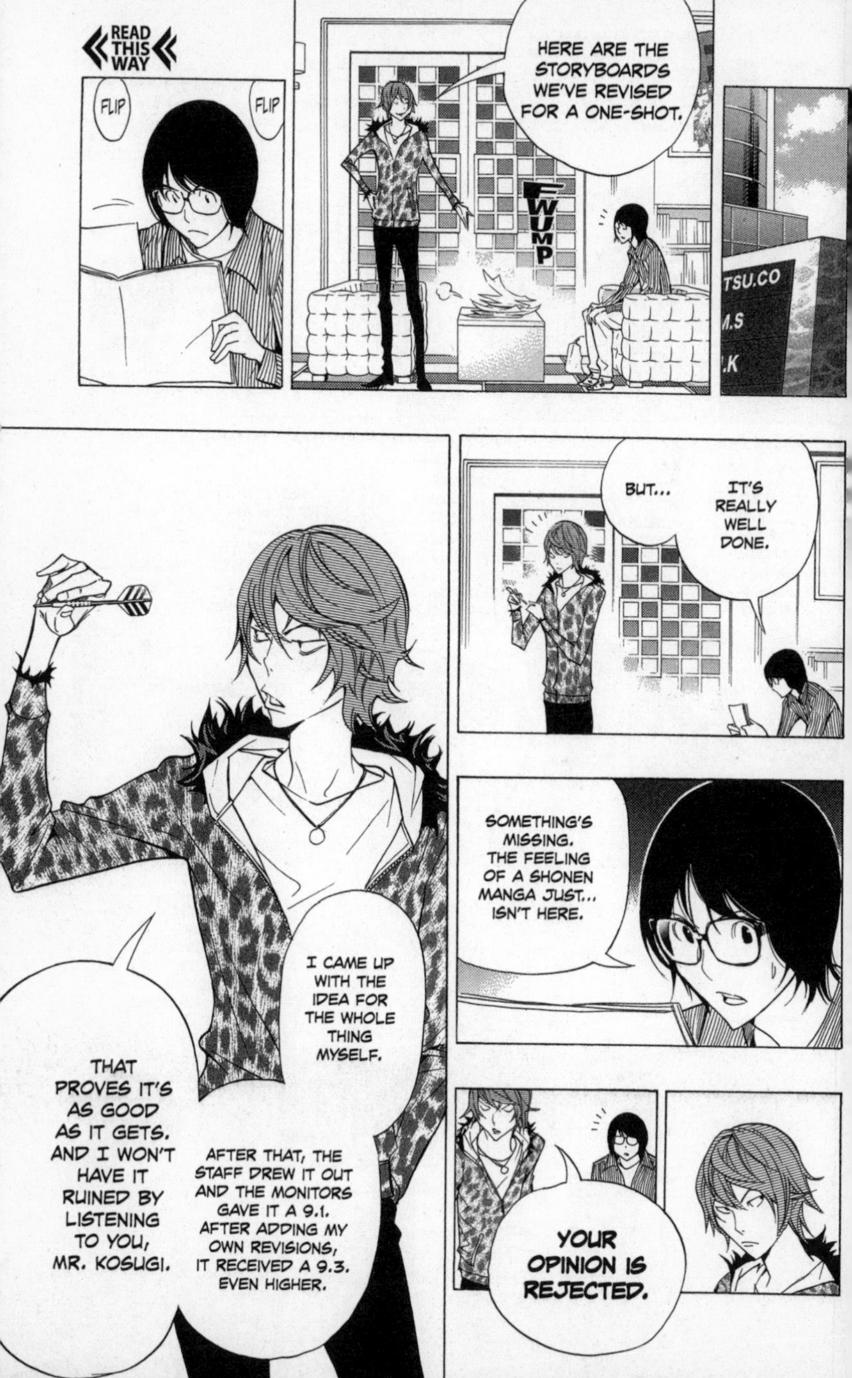
READ THIS WAY
TSU.CO
M.S
.K
HERE ARE THE STORYBOARDS WE'VE REVISED FOR A ONE-SHOT.
FWUMP
FLIP
FLIP
IT'S REALLY WELL DONE.
BUT...
SOMETHING'S MISSING. THE FEELING OF A SHONEN MANGA JUST... ISN'T HERE.
YOUR OPINION IS REJECTED.
I CAME UP WITH THE IDEA FOR THE WHOLE THING MYSELF.
AFTER THAT, THE STAFF DREW IT OUT AND THE MONITORS GAVE IT A 9.1. AFTER ADDING MY OWN REVISIONS, IT RECEIVED A 9.3. EVEN HIGHER.
THAT PROVES IT'S AS GOOD AS IT GETS. AND I WON'T HAVE IT RUINED BY LISTENING TO YOU, MR. KOSUGI.

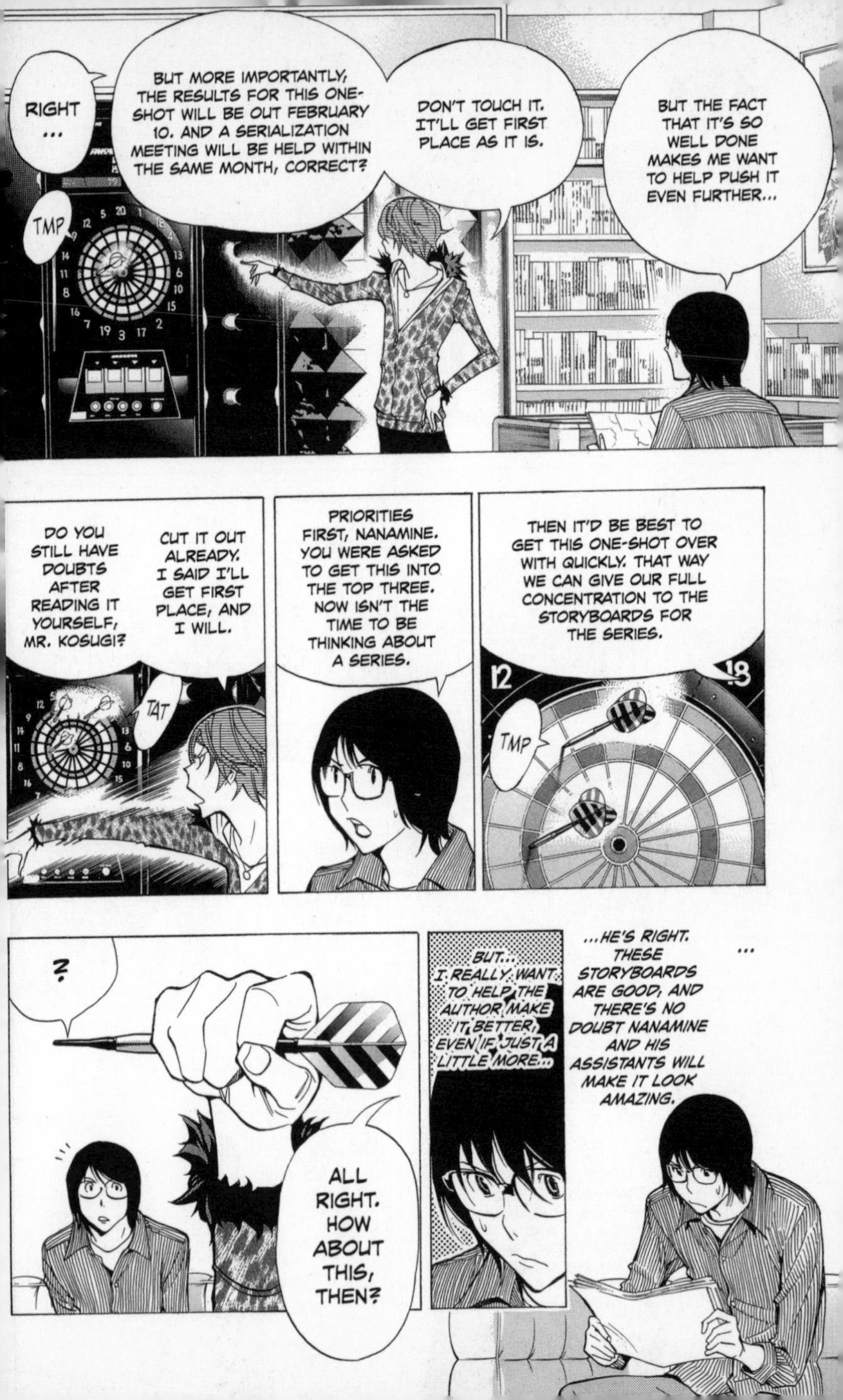
BUT THE FACT THAT IT'S SO WELL DONE MAKES ME WANT TO HELP PUSH IT EVEN FURTHER...
DON'T TOUCH IT. IT'LL GET FIRST PLACE AS IT IS.
BUT MORE IMPORTANTLY, THE RESULTS FOR THIS ONE-SHOT WILL BE OUT FEBRUARY 10. AND A SERIALIZATION MEETING WILL BE HELD WITHIN THE SAME MONTH, CORRECT?
RIGHT...
TMP
THEN IT'D BE BEST TO GET THIS ONE-SHOT OVER WITH QUICKLY. THAT WAY WE CAN GIVE OUR FULL CONCENTRATION TO THE STORYBOARDS FOR THE SERIES.
TMP
PRIORITIES FIRST, NANAMINE. YOU WERE ASKED TO GET THIS INTO THE TOP THREE. NOW ISN'T THE TIME TO BE THINKING ABOUT A SERIES.
CUT IT OUT ALREADY. I SAID I'LL GET FIRST PLACE, AND I WILL.
DO YOU STILL HAVE DOUBTS AFTER READING IT YOURSELF, MR. KOSUGI?
TAT
...HE'S RIGHT. THESE STORYBOARDS ARE GOOD, AND THERE'S NO DOUBT NANAMINE AND HIS ASSISTANTS WILL MAKE IT LOOK AMAZING.
...
BUT... I REALLY WANT TO HELP THE AUTHOR MAKE IT BETTER, EVEN IF JUST A LITTLE MORE...
?
ALL RIGHT. HOW ABOUT THIS, THEN?

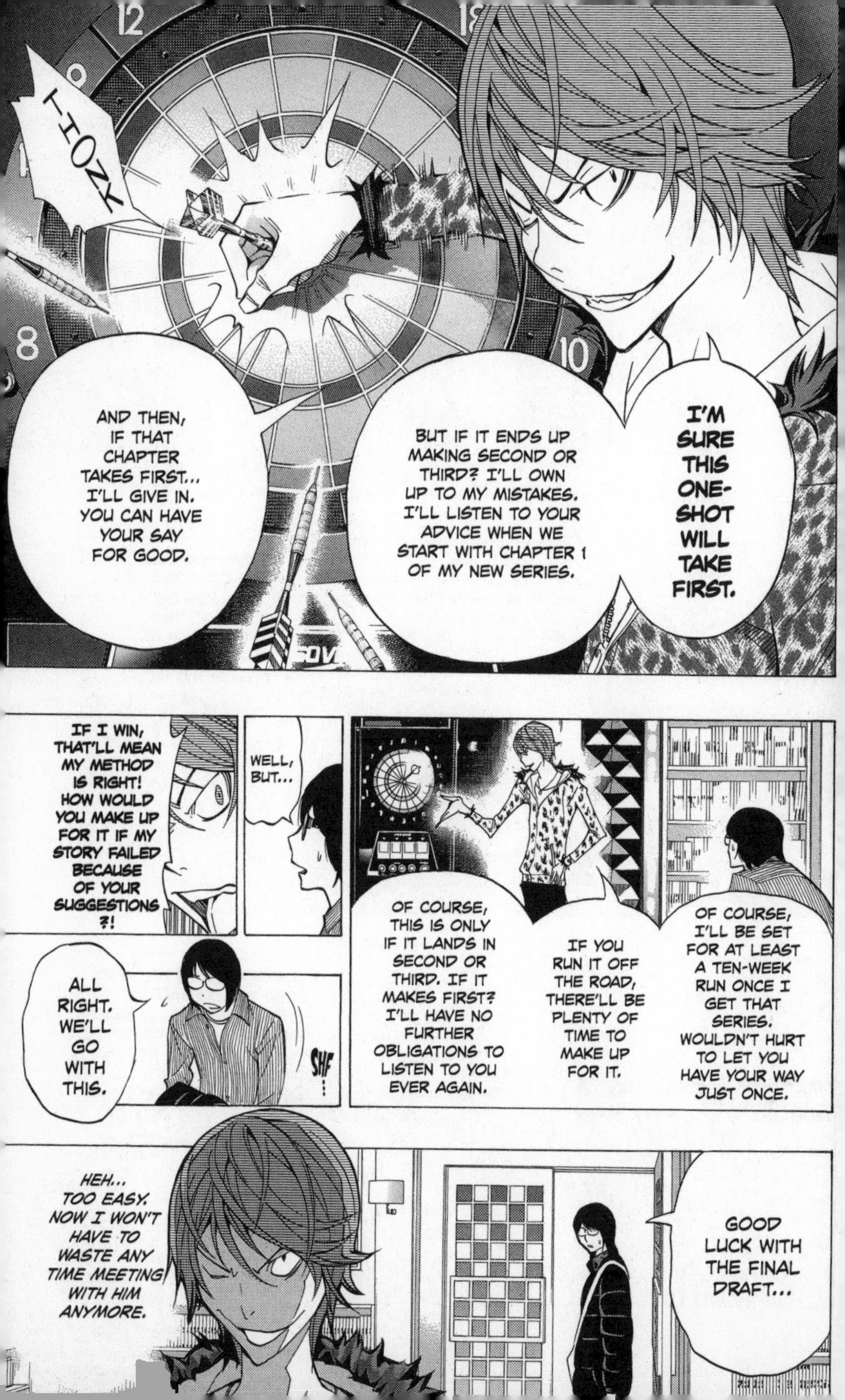
I'M SURE THIS ONE-SHOT WILL TAKE FIRST.
BUT IF IT ENDS UP MAKING SECOND OR THIRD? I'LL OWN UP TO MY MISTAKES. I'LL LISTEN TO YOUR ADVICE WHEN WE START WITH CHAPTER 1 OF MY NEW SERIES.
AND THEN, IF THAT CHAPTER TAKES FIRST... I'LL GIVE IN. YOU CAN HAVE YOUR SAY FOR GOOD.
THONK
OF COURSE, I'LL BE SET FOR AT LEAST A TEN-WEEK RUN ONCE I GET THAT SERIES. WOULDN'T HURT TO LET YOU HAVE YOUR WAY JUST ONCE.
IF YOU RUN IT OFF THE ROAD, THERE'LL BE PLENTY OF TIME TO MAKE UP FOR IT.
OF COURSE, THIS IS ONLY IF IT LANDS IN SECOND OR THIRD. IF IT MAKES FIRST? I'LL HAVE NO FURTHER OBLIGATIONS TO LISTEN TO YOU EVER AGAIN.
WELL, BUT...
IF I WIN, THAT'LL MEAN MY METHOD IS RIGHT! HOW WOULD YOU MAKE UP FOR IT IF MY STORY FAILED BECAUSE OF YOUR SUGGESTIONS?!
ALL RIGHT. WE'LL GO WITH THIS.
SHF
GOOD LUCK WITH THE FINAL DRAFT...
HEH... TOO EASY. NOW I WON'T HAVE TO WASTE ANY TIME MEETING WITH HIM ANYMORE.

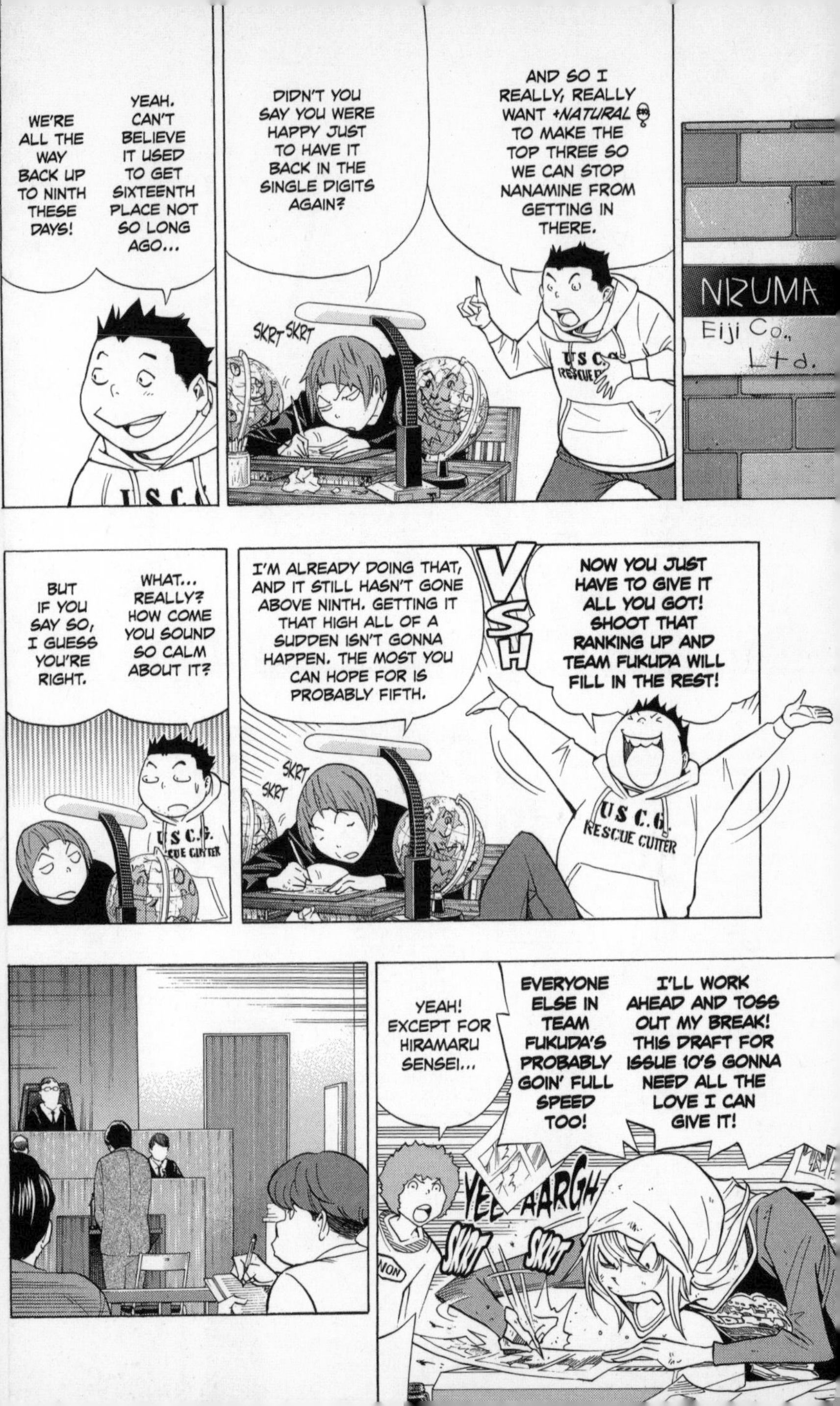
NIZUMA
Eiji Co., Ltd.
AND SO I REALLY, REALLY WANT +NATURAL TO MAKE THE TOP THREE SO WE CAN STOP NANAMINE FROM GETTING IN THERE.
DIDN'T YOU SAY YOU WERE HAPPY JUST TO HAVE IT BACK IN THE SINGLE DIGITS AGAIN?
SKRT SKRT
YEAH. CAN'T BELIEVE IT USED TO GET SIXTEENTH PLACE NOT SO LONG AGO...
WE'RE ALL THE WAY BACK UP TO NINTH THESE DAYS!
NOW YOU JUST HAVE TO GIVE IT ALL YOU GOT! SHOOT THAT RANKING UP AND TEAM FUKUDA WILL FILL IN THE REST!
VSH
I'M ALREADY DOING THAT, AND IT STILL HASN'T GONE ABOVE NINTH. GETTING IT THAT HIGH ALL OF A SUDDEN ISN'T GONNA HAPPEN. THE MOST YOU CAN HOPE FOR IS PROBABLY FIFTH.
SKRT
SKRT
WHAT... REALLY? HOW COME YOU SOUND SO CALM ABOUT IT?
BUT IF YOU SAY SO, I GUESS YOU'RE RIGHT.
I'LL WORK AHEAD AND TOSS OUT MY BREAK! THIS DRAFT FOR ISSUE 10'S GONNA NEED ALL THE LOVE I CAN GIVE IT!
EVERYONE ELSE IN TEAM FUKUDA'S PROBABLY GOIN' FULL SPEED TOO!
YEAH! EXCEPT FOR HIRAMARU SENSEI...
YEE AARGH
SKRT
SKRT
NON

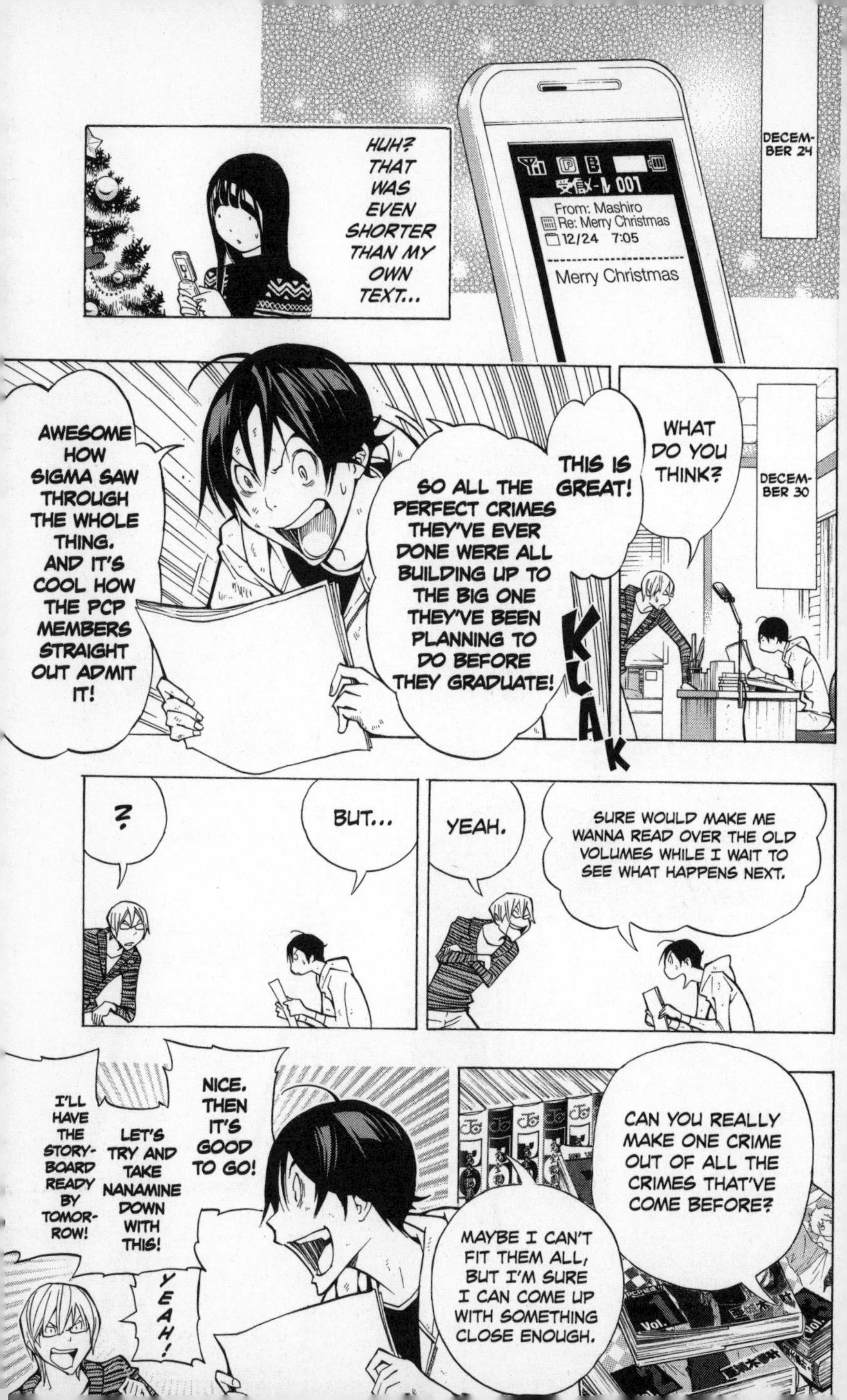
DECEMBER 24
受信メール 001
From: Mashiro
Re: Merry Christmas
12/24 7:05
Merry Christmas
HUH? THAT WAS EVEN SHORTER THAN MY OWN TEXT...
DECEMBER 30
WHAT DO YOU THINK?
KLAK
THIS IS GREAT!
SO ALL THE PERFECT CRIMES THEY'VE EVER DONE WERE ALL BUILDING UP TO THE BIG ONE THEY'VE BEEN PLANNING TO DO BEFORE THEY GRADUATE!
AWESOME HOW SIGMA SAW THROUGH THE WHOLE THING. AND IT'S COOL HOW THE PCP MEMBERS STRAIGHT OUT ADMIT IT!
SURE WOULD MAKE ME WANNA READ OVER THE OLD VOLUMES WHILE I WAIT TO SEE WHAT HAPPENS NEXT.
YEAH.
BUT...
?
CAN YOU REALLY MAKE ONE CRIME OUT OF ALL THE CRIMES THAT'VE COME BEFORE?
MAYBE I CAN'T FIT THEM ALL, BUT I'M SURE I CAN COME UP WITH SOMETHING CLOSE ENOUGH.
NICE. THEN IT'S GOOD TO GO!
LET'S TRY AND TAKE NANAMINE DOWN WITH THIS!
I'LL HAVE THE STORYBOARD READY BY TOMORROW!
YEAH!

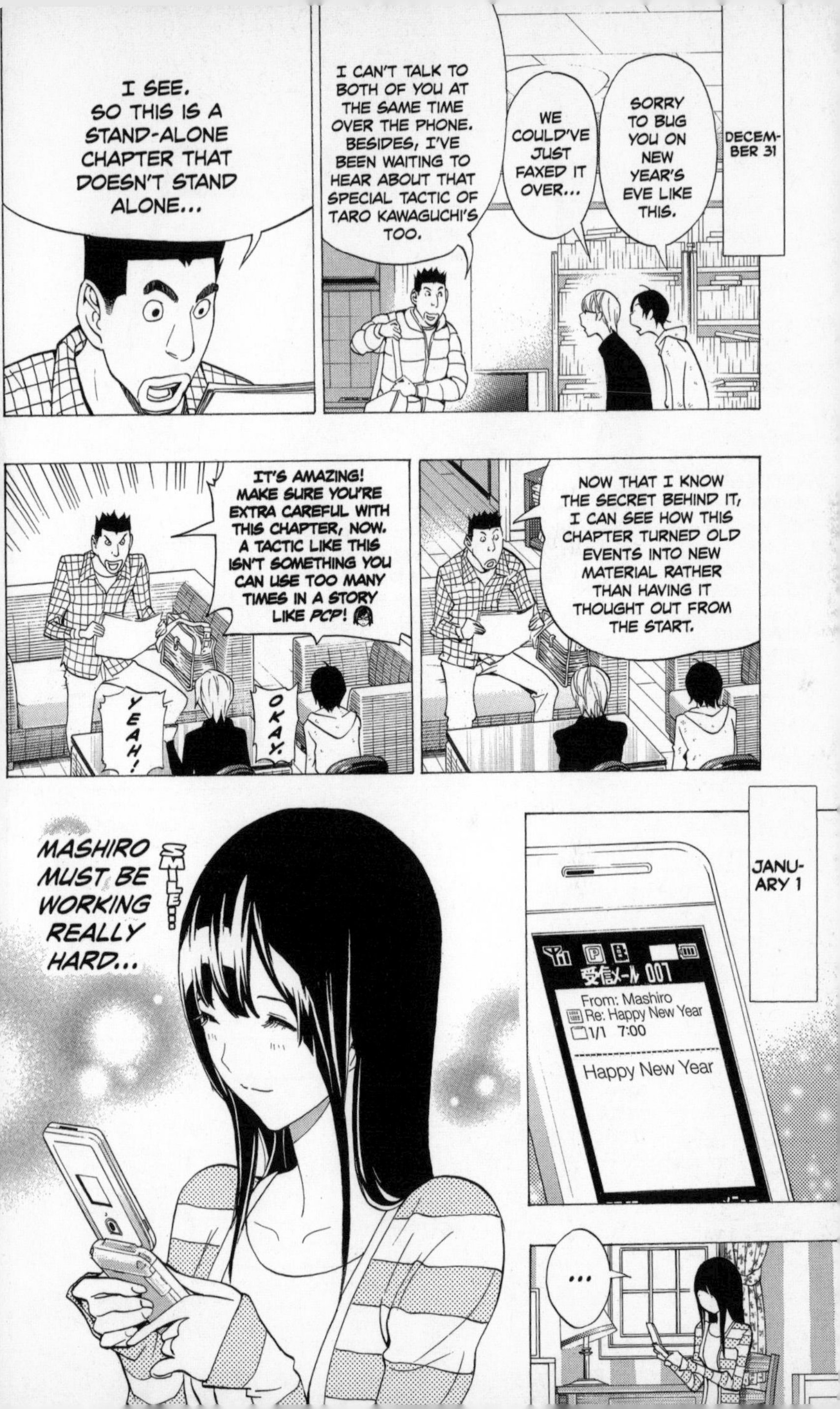
DECEMBER 31
SORRY TO BUG YOU ON NEW YEAR'S EVE LIKE THIS.
WE COULD'VE JUST FAXED IT OVER...
I CAN'T TALK TO BOTH OF YOU AT THE SAME TIME OVER THE PHONE. BESIDES, I'VE BEEN WAITING TO HEAR ABOUT THAT SPECIAL TACTIC OF TARO KAWAGUCHI'S TOO.
I SEE. SO THIS IS A STAND-ALONE CHAPTER THAT DOESN'T STAND ALONE...
NOW THAT I KNOW THE SECRET BEHIND IT, I CAN SEE HOW THIS CHAPTER TURNED OLD EVENTS INTO NEW MATERIAL RATHER THAN HAVING IT THOUGHT OUT FROM THE START.
IT'S AMAZING! MAKE SURE YOU'RE EXTRA CAREFUL WITH THIS CHAPTER, NOW. A TACTIC LIKE THIS ISN'T SOMETHING YOU CAN USE TOO MANY TIMES IN A STORY LIKE PCP!
OKAY.
YEAH!
JANUARY 1
受信メール 007
From: Mashiro
Re: Happy New Year
1/1 7:00
Happy New Year
...
MASHIRO MUST BE WORKING REALLY HARD...
SMILE...

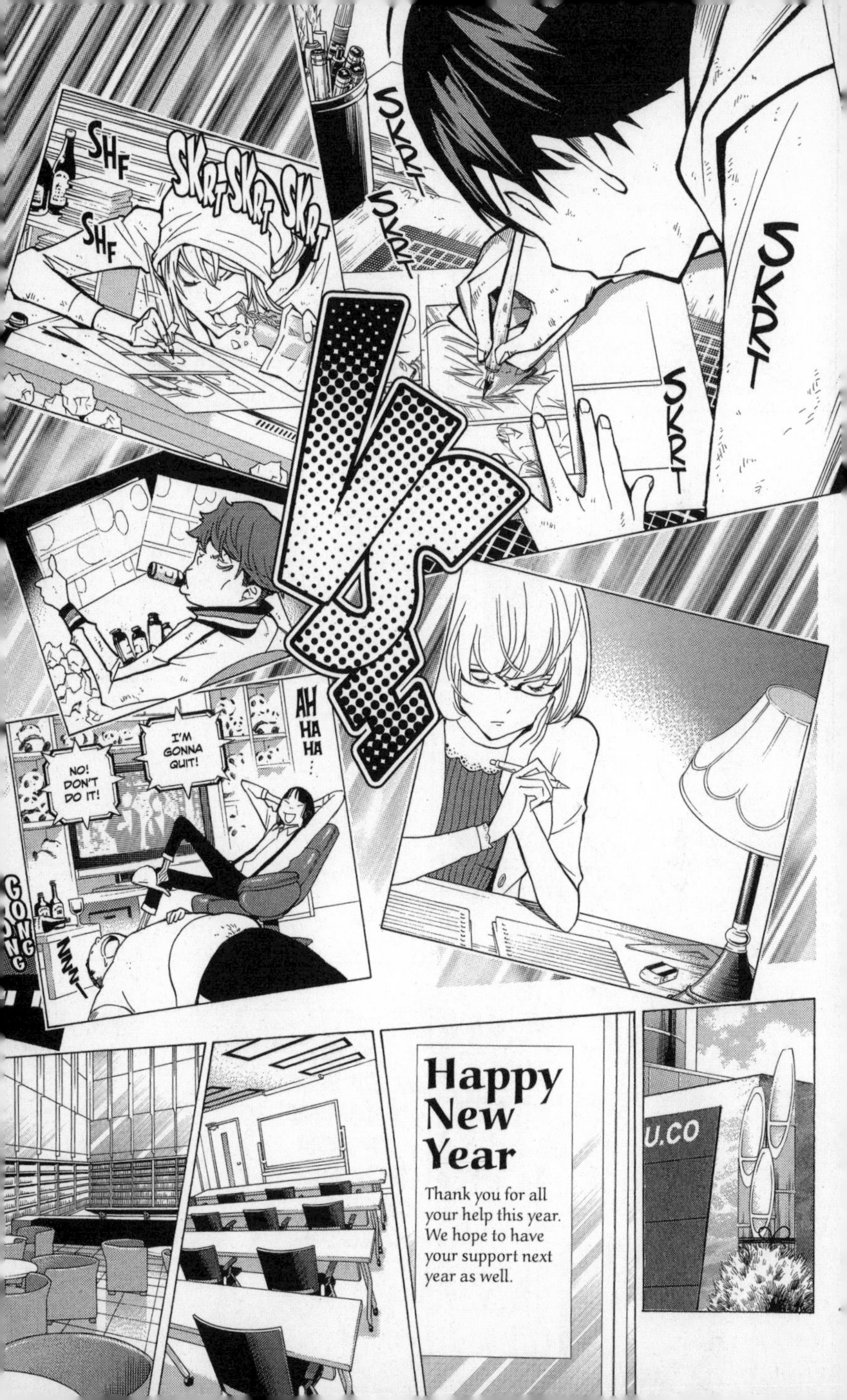
SKRT
SKRT
SKRT
SKRT
SKRT-SKRT SKRT
SHF
SHF
AH HA HA
I'M GONNA QUIT!
NO! DON'T DO IT!
GONG
GONG
ZZZ
U.CO
Happy New Year
Thank you for all your help this year. We hope to have your support next year as well.

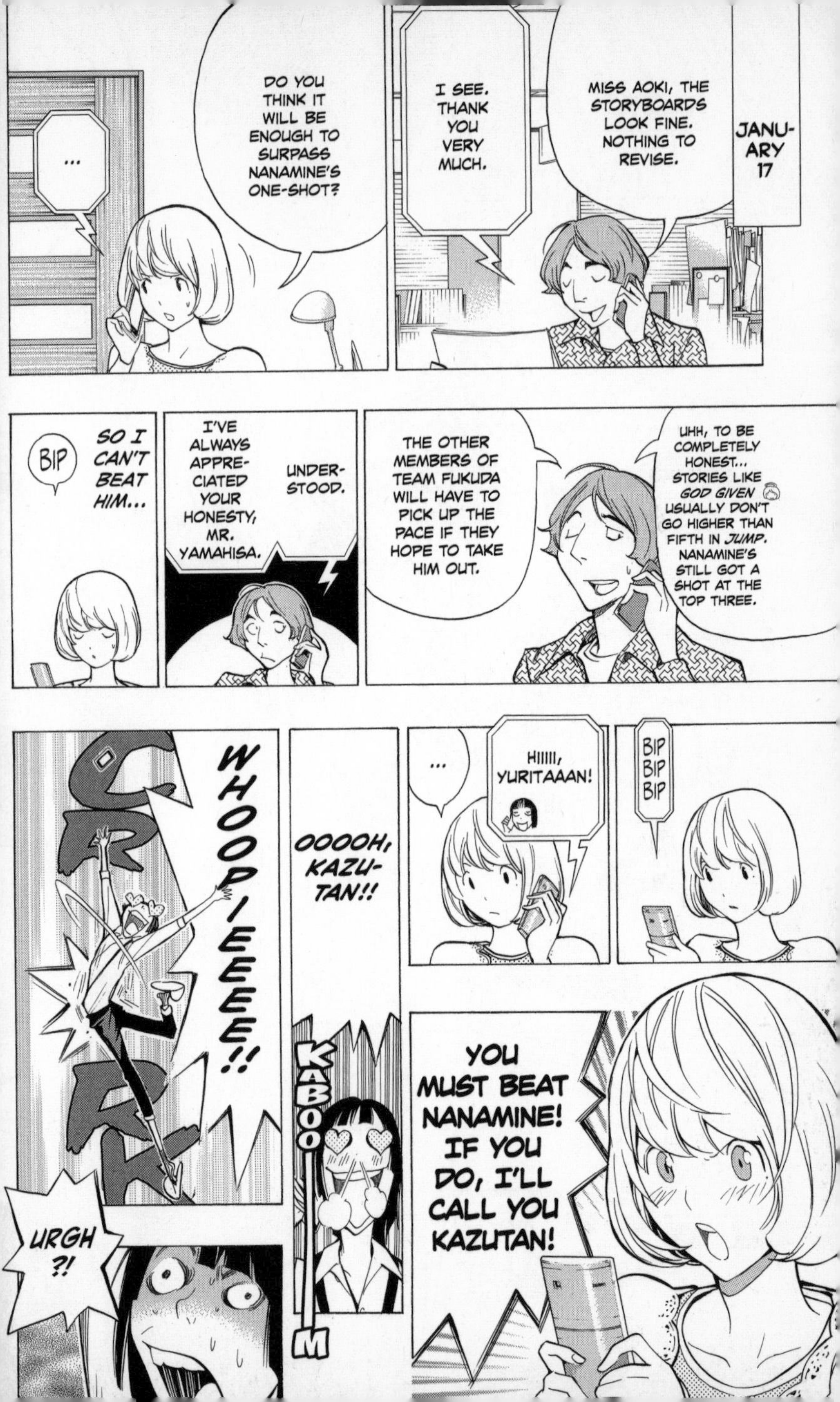
JANUARY 17
MISS AOKI, THE STORYBOARDS LOOK FINE. NOTHING TO REVISE.
I SEE. THANK YOU VERY MUCH.
DO YOU THINK IT WILL BE ENOUGH TO SURPASS NANAMINE'S ONE-SHOT?
...
UHH, TO BE COMPLETELY HONEST... STORIES LIKE *GOD GIVEN* USUALLY DON'T GO HIGHER THAN FIFTH IN *JUMP*. NANAMINE'S STILL GOT A SHOT AT THE TOP THREE.
THE OTHER MEMBERS OF TEAM FUKUDA WILL HAVE TO PICK UP THE PACE IF THEY HOPE TO TAKE HIM OUT.
UNDERSTOOD.
I'VE ALWAYS APPRECIATED YOUR HONESTY, MR. YAMAHISA.
SO I CAN'T BEAT HIM...
BIP
BIP BIP BIP
HIIII, YURITAAAN!
...
YOU MUST BEAT NANAMINE! IF YOU DO, I'LL CALL YOU KAZUTAN!
OOOOH, KAZUTAN!!
KABOOOM
WHOOPIEEEE!!
URGH ?!

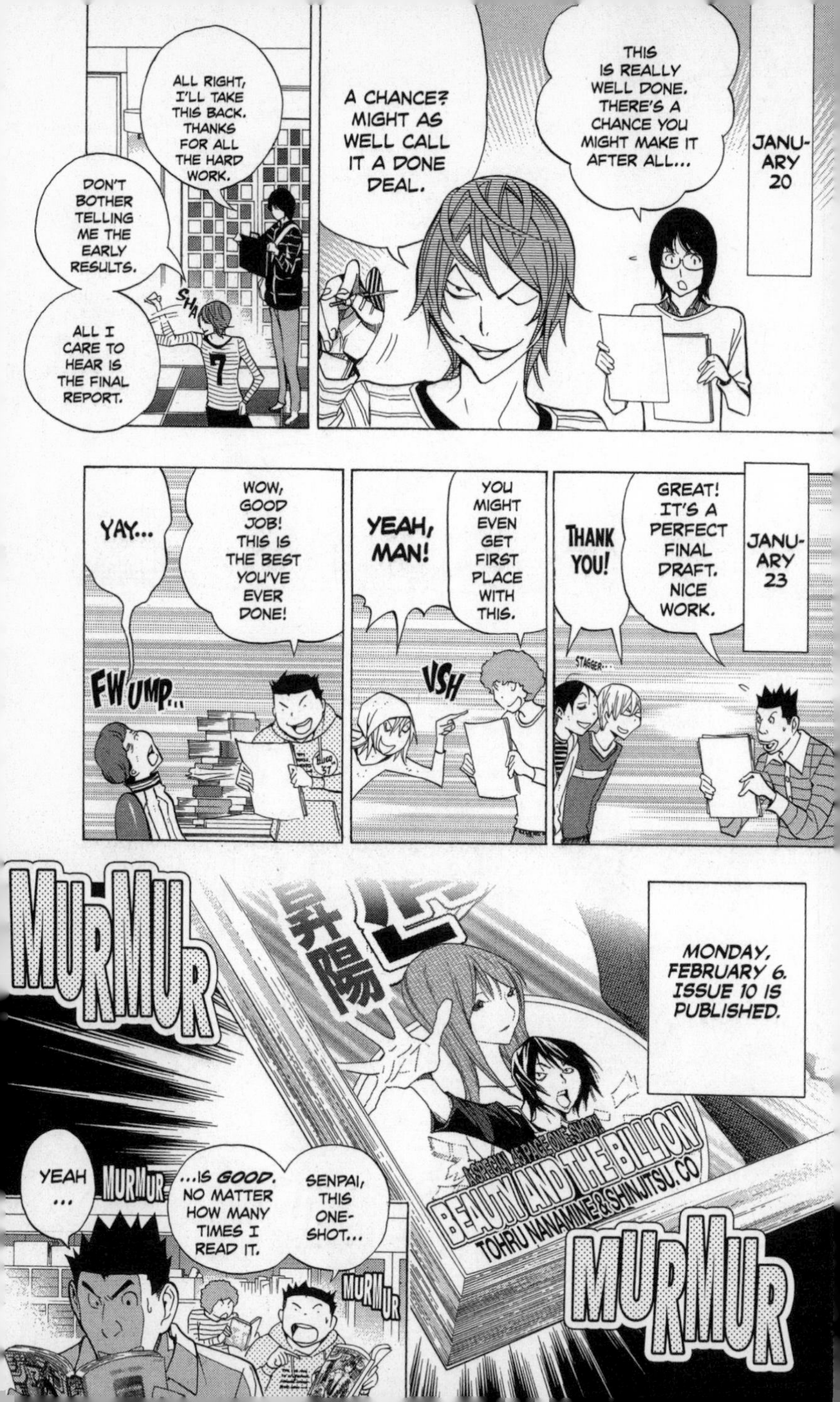
JANUARY 20
THIS IS REALLY WELL DONE. THERE'S A CHANCE YOU MIGHT MAKE IT AFTER ALL...
A CHANCE? MIGHT AS WELL CALL IT A DONE DEAL.
ALL RIGHT, I'LL TAKE THIS BACK. THANKS FOR ALL THE HARD WORK.
DON'T BOTHER TELLING ME THE EARLY RESULTS.
SHA
ALL I CARE TO HEAR IS THE FINAL REPORT.
JANUARY 23
GREAT! IT'S A PERFECT FINAL DRAFT. NICE WORK.
THANK YOU!
STAGGER...
YOU MIGHT EVEN GET FIRST PLACE WITH THIS.
YEAH, MAN!
VSH
WOW, GOOD JOB! THIS IS THE BEST YOU'VE EVER DONE!
YAY...
FWUMP...
MONDAY, FEBRUARY 6. ISSUE 10 IS PUBLISHED.
昇陽
BEAUTY AND THE BILLION
TOHRU NANAMINE & SHINJITSU.CO
MURMUR
SENPAI, THIS ONE-SHOT...
...IS GOOD. NO MATTER HOW MANY TIMES I READ IT.
MURMUR
YEAH ...
MURMUR
MURMUR

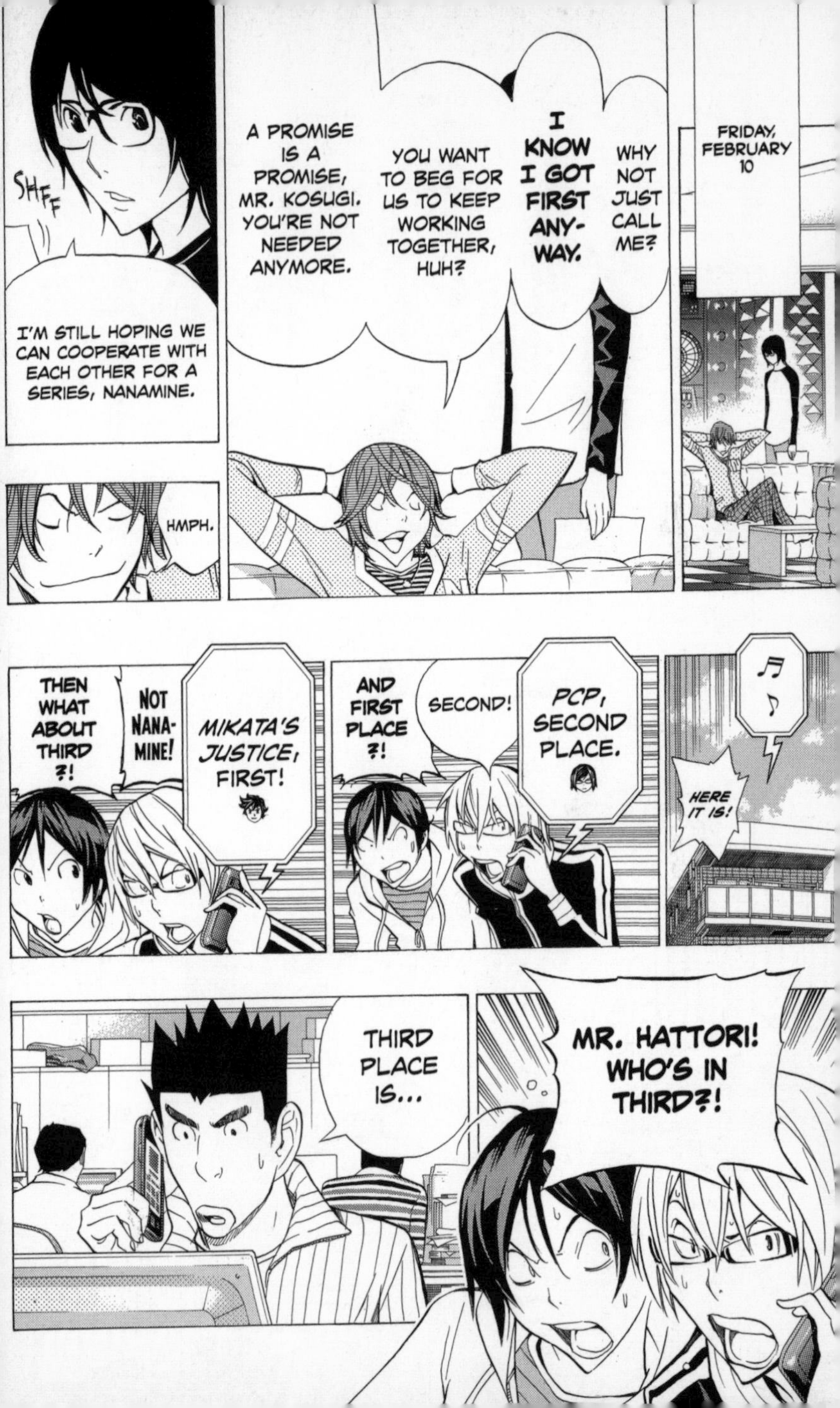
FRIDAY, FEBRUARY 10
WHY NOT JUST CALL ME?
I KNOW I GOT FIRST ANYWAY.
YOU WANT TO BEG FOR US TO KEEP WORKING TOGETHER, HUH?
A PROMISE IS A PROMISE, MR. KOSUGI. YOU'RE NOT NEEDED ANYMORE.
SHFF
I'M STILL HOPING WE CAN COOPERATE WITH EACH OTHER FOR A SERIES, NANAMINE.
HMPH.
♫ ♪
HERE IT IS!
PCP, SECOND PLACE.
SECOND!
AND FIRST PLACE?!
MIKATA'S JUSTICE, FIRST!
NOT NANAMINE!
THEN WHAT ABOUT THIRD?!
MR. HATTORI! WHO'S IN THIRD?!
THIRD PLACE IS...

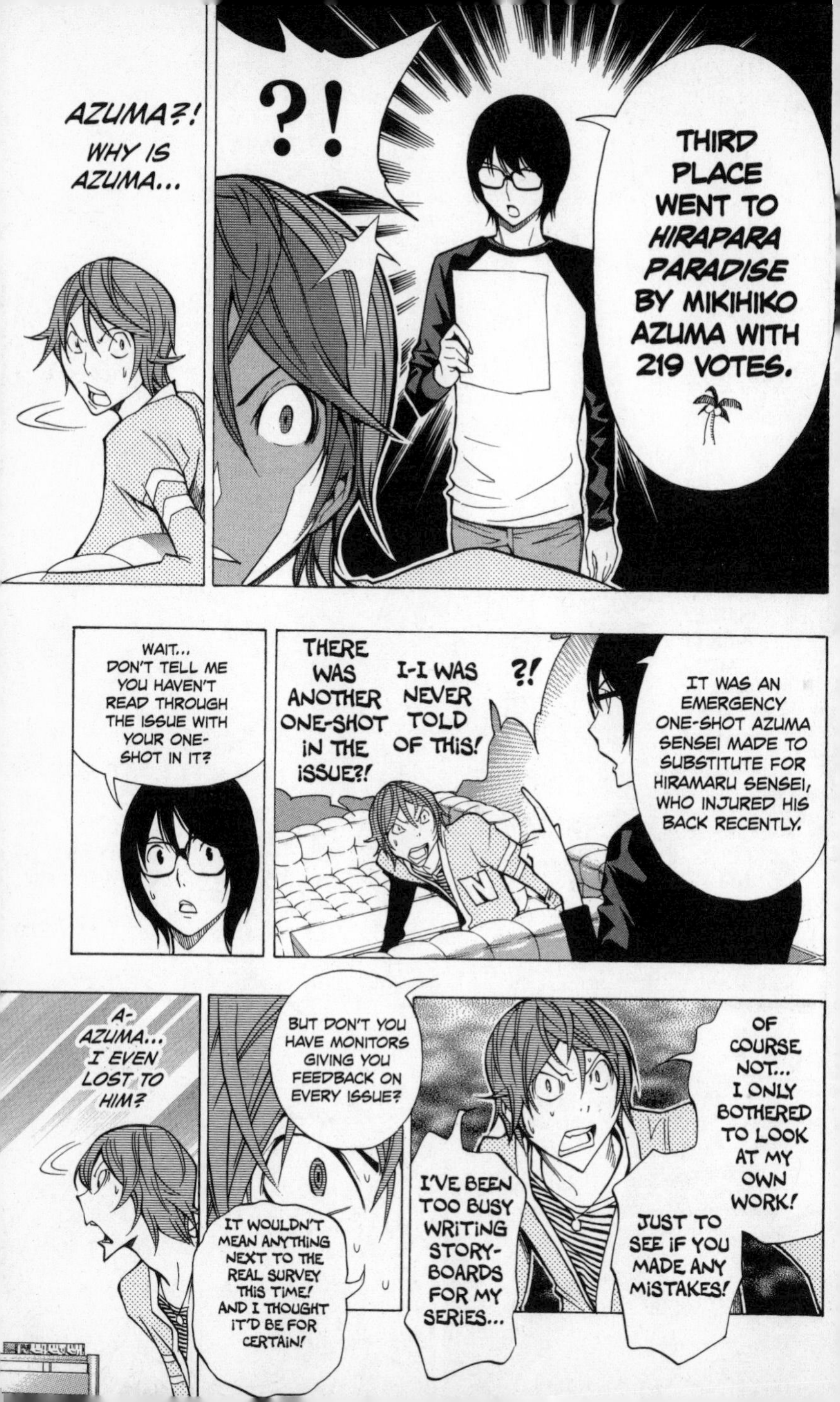
THIRD PLACE WENT TO *HIRAPARA PARADISE* BY MIKIHIKO AZUMA WITH 219 VOTES.
?!
AZUMA?! WHY IS AZUMA...
IT WAS AN EMERGENCY ONE-SHOT AZUMA SENSEI MADE TO SUBSTITUTE FOR HIRAMARU SENSEI, WHO INJURED HIS BACK RECENTLY.
?!
I-I WAS NEVER TOLD OF THIS!
THERE WAS ANOTHER ONE-SHOT IN THE ISSUE?!
WAIT... DON'T TELL ME YOU HAVEN'T READ THROUGH THE ISSUE WITH YOUR ONE-SHOT IN IT?
OF COURSE NOT... I ONLY BOTHERED TO LOOK AT MY OWN WORK!
JUST TO SEE IF YOU MADE ANY MISTAKES!
I'VE BEEN TOO BUSY WRITING STORY-BOARDS FOR MY SERIES...
BUT DON'T YOU HAVE MONITORS GIVING YOU FEEDBACK ON EVERY ISSUE?
IT WOULDN'T MEAN ANYTHING NEXT TO THE REAL SURVEY THIS TIME! AND I THOUGHT IT'D BE FOR CERTAIN!
A- AZUMA... I EVEN LOST TO HIM?

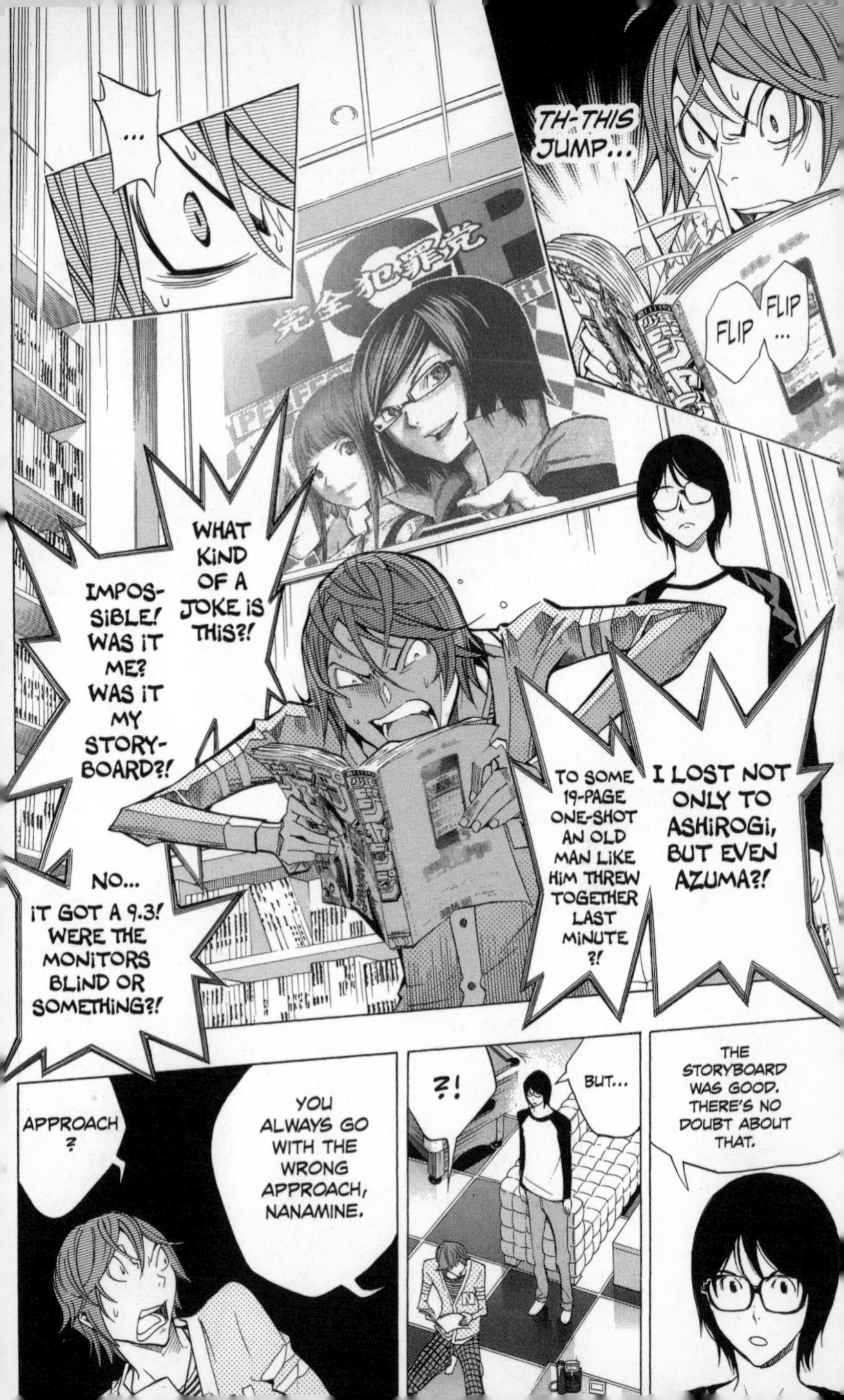
TH-THIS JUMP...
FLIP FLIP ...
...
完全犯罪党
I LOST NOT ONLY TO ASHIROGI, BUT EVEN AZUMA?!
TO SOME 19-PAGE ONE-SHOT AN OLD MAN LIKE HIM THREW TOGETHER LAST MINUTE?!
WHAT KIND OF A JOKE IS THIS?!
IMPOSSIBLE! WAS IT ME? WAS IT MY STORYBOARD?!
NO... IT GOT A 9.3! WERE THE MONITORS BLIND OR SOMETHING?!
THE STORYBOARD WAS GOOD. THERE'S NO DOUBT ABOUT THAT.
BUT...
?!
YOU ALWAYS GO WITH THE WRONG APPROACH, NANAMINE.
APPROACH?

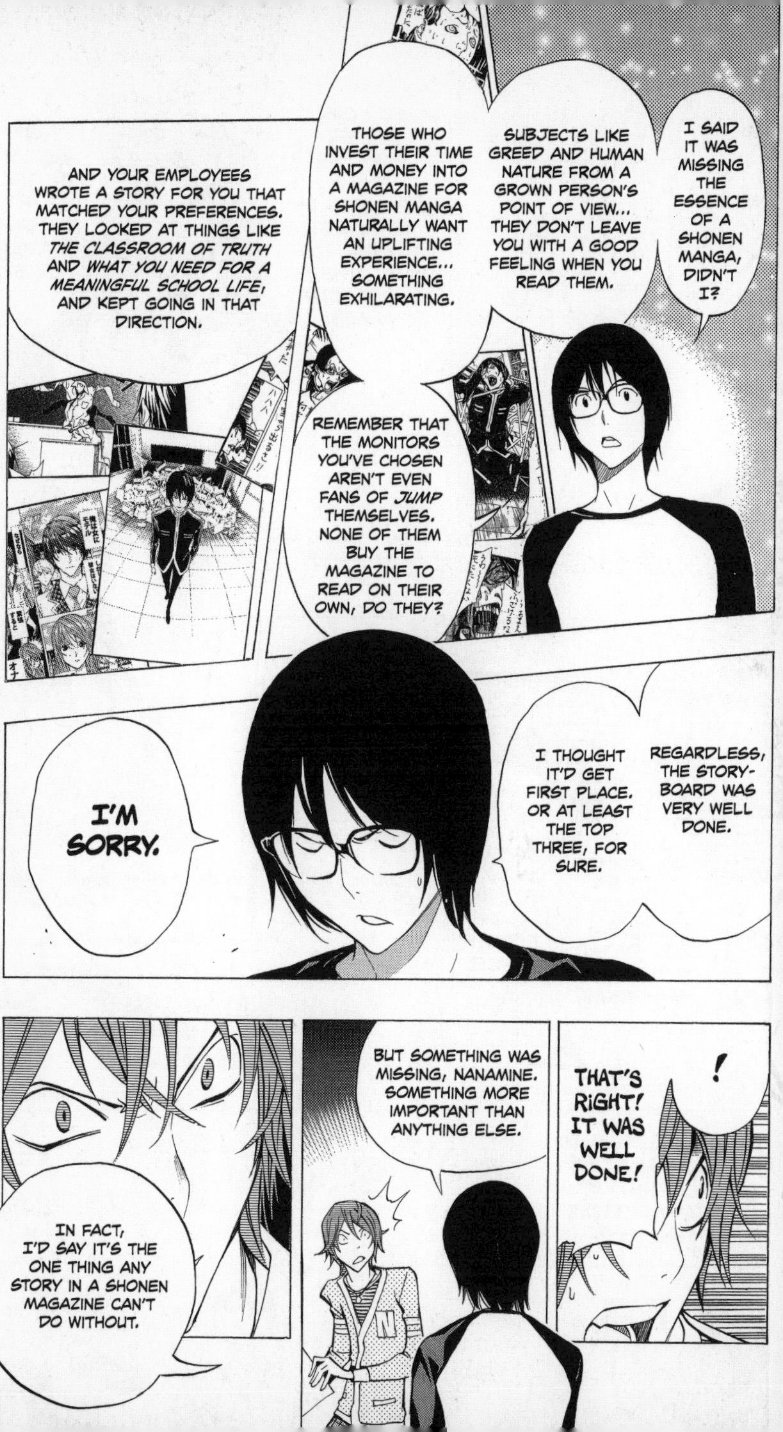
I SAID IT WAS MISSING THE ESSENCE OF A SHONEN MANGA, DIDN'T I?
SUBJECTS LIKE GREED AND HUMAN NATURE FROM A GROWN PERSON'S POINT OF VIEW... THEY DON'T LEAVE YOU WITH A GOOD FEELING WHEN YOU READ THEM.
THOSE WHO INVEST THEIR TIME AND MONEY INTO A MAGAZINE FOR SHONEN MANGA NATURALLY WANT AN UPLIFTING EXPERIENCE... SOMETHING EXHILARATING.
REMEMBER THAT THE MONITORS YOU'VE CHOSEN AREN'T EVEN FANS OF *JUMP* THEMSELVES. NONE OF THEM BUY THE MAGAZINE TO READ ON THEIR OWN, DO THEY?
AND YOUR EMPLOYEES WROTE A STORY FOR YOU THAT MATCHED YOUR PREFERENCES. THEY LOOKED AT THINGS LIKE *THE CLASSROOM OF TRUTH* AND *WHAT YOU NEED FOR A MEANINGFUL SCHOOL LIFE*, AND KEPT GOING IN THAT DIRECTION.
REGARDLESS, THE STORY-BOARD WAS VERY WELL DONE.
I THOUGHT IT'D GET FIRST PLACE. OR AT LEAST THE TOP THREE, FOR SURE.
I'M SORRY.
!
THAT'S RIGHT! IT WAS WELL DONE!
BUT SOMETHING WAS MISSING, NANAMINE. SOMETHING MORE IMPORTANT THAN ANYTHING ELSE.
IN FACT, I'D SAY IT'S THE ONE THING ANY STORY IN A SHONEN MAGAZINE CAN'T DO WITHOUT.

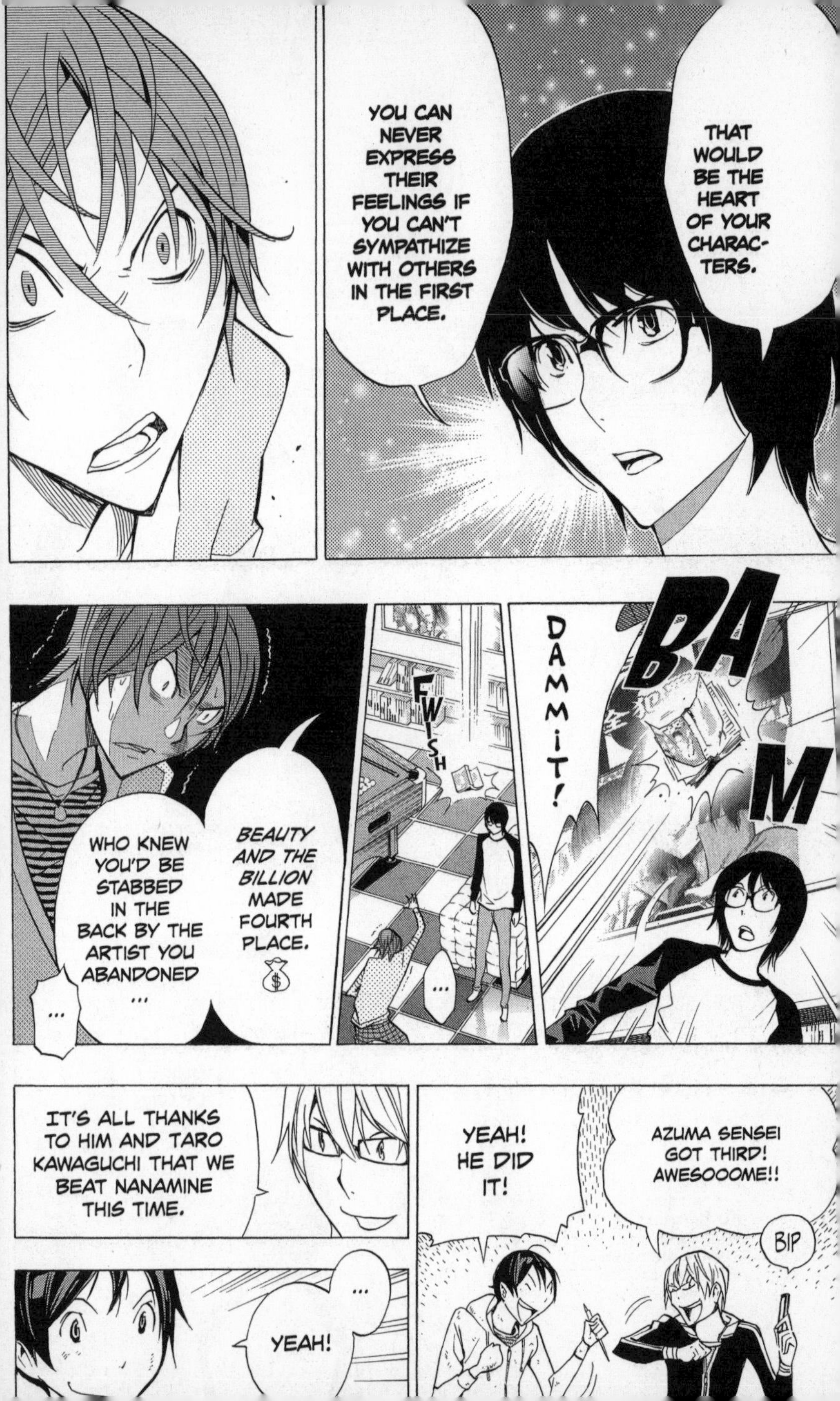
THAT WOULD BE THE HEART OF YOUR CHARAC-TERS.
YOU CAN NEVER EXPRESS THEIR FEELINGS IF YOU CAN'T SYMPATHIZE WITH OTHERS IN THE FIRST PLACE.
BAM
DAMMIT!
FWISH
...
BEAUTY AND THE BILLION MADE FOURTH PLACE.
WHO KNEW YOU'D BE STABBED IN THE BACK BY THE ARTIST YOU ABANDONED ...
...
AZUMA SENSEI GOT THIRD! AWESOOOME!!
YEAH! HE DID IT!
BIP
IT'S ALL THANKS TO HIM AND TARO KAWAGUCHI THAT WE BEAT NANAMINE THIS TIME.
... YEAH!

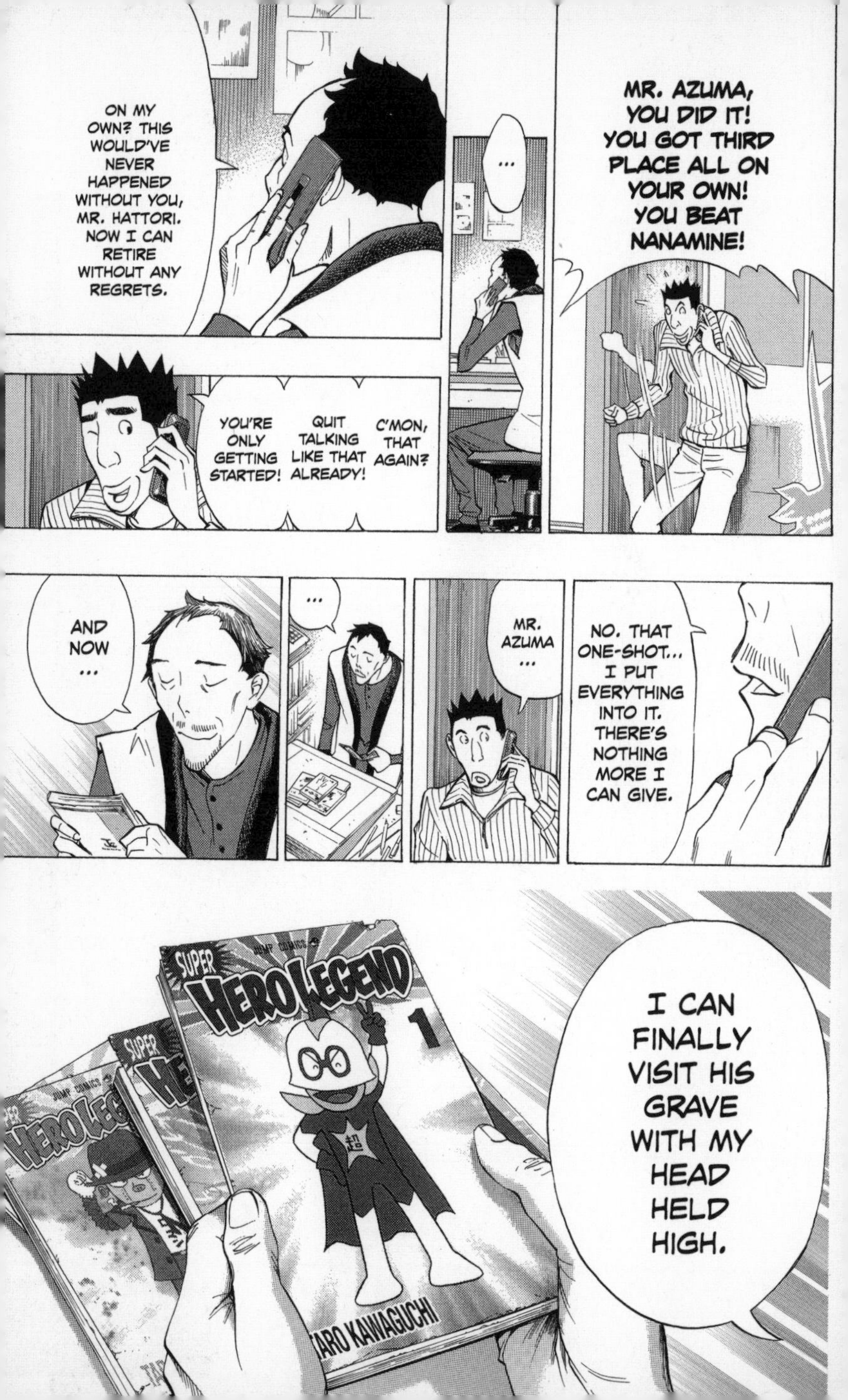
MR. AZUMA, YOU DID IT! YOU GOT THIRD PLACE ALL ON YOUR OWN! YOU BEAT NANAMINE!
...
ON MY OWN? THIS WOULD'VE NEVER HAPPENED WITHOUT YOU, MR. HATTORI. NOW I CAN RETIRE WITHOUT ANY REGRETS.
C'MON, THAT AGAIN?
QUIT TALKING LIKE THAT ALREADY!
YOU'RE ONLY GETTING STARTED!
NO. THAT ONE-SHOT... I PUT EVERYTHING INTO IT. THERE'S NOTHING MORE I CAN GIVE.
MR. AZUMA ...
...
AND NOW ...
I CAN FINALLY VISIT HIS GRAVE WITH MY HEAD HELD HIGH.
SUPER HERO LEGEND
1
TARO KAWAGUCHI

OHBA'S STORYBOARD

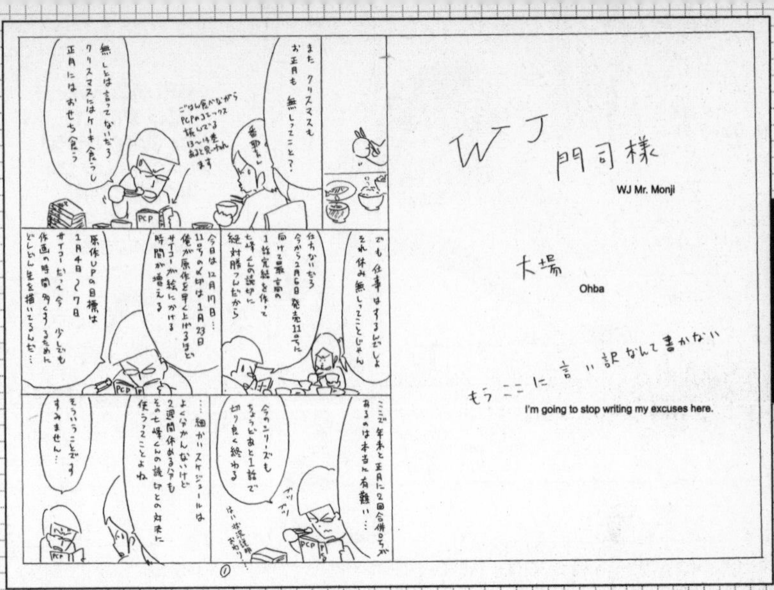
WJ 門司様
WJ Mr. Monji
大場
Ohba
もうここに言い訳なんて書かない
I'm going to stop writing my excuses here.
またクリスマスもお正月も無しってこと?
無しとは言ってないだろ クリスマスにはケーキ食うし正月にはおせち食う
でも仕事はするんでしょ それ休み無しってことじゃん
仕方ないだろ 今から2月6日発売11号に向けて最高の1話完結を作って七峰くんの読切に絶対勝つんだから
今日は12月17日… 11号の〆切は1月23日 俺が原作を早く上げるほどサイコーが絵にかける時間が増える
原作UPの目標は1月4日〜7日
ここで年末と正月に2回合併号があるのは本当に有難い…
今のシリーズもちょうどあと1話で切り良く終わる
…細かいスケジュールはよくわかんないけど 2週間休めるハズの七峰くんの読切との対決に使うってことよね
そういうことです すみません…

OBATA'S STORYBOARD

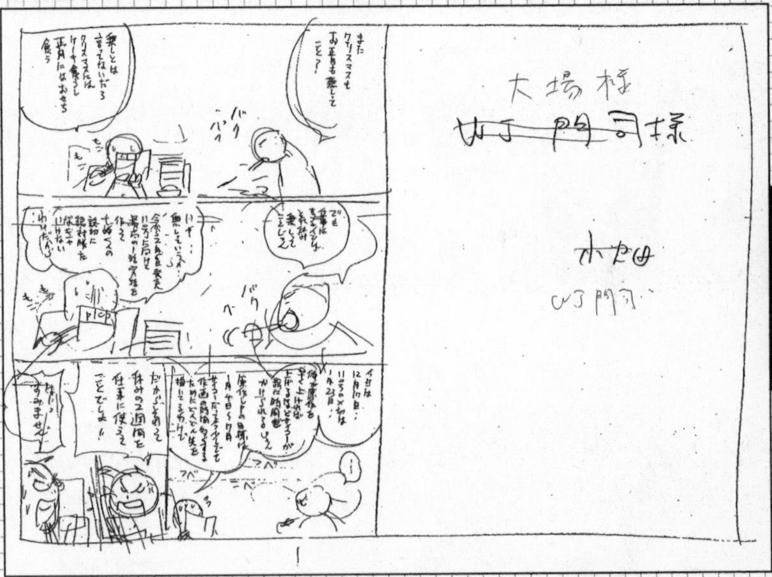
大場様
WJ 門司様
小畑
WJ門司
またクリスマスもお正月も無しってこと?
無しとは言ってないだろ クリスマスはケーキ食うし正月にはおせち食う
バクバク
すみません

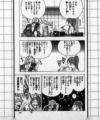

COMPLETE!

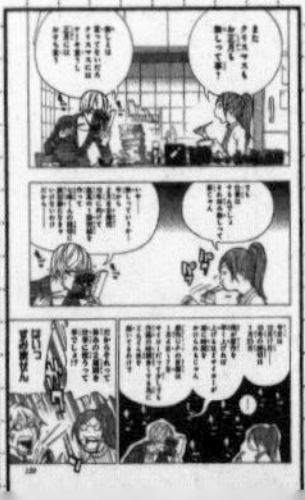

※CREATOR STORYBOARDS AND FINISHED PAGES IN JAPANESE

BAKUMAN。 vol.17
"Until the Final Draft Is Complete"
Chapter 149, pp. 129

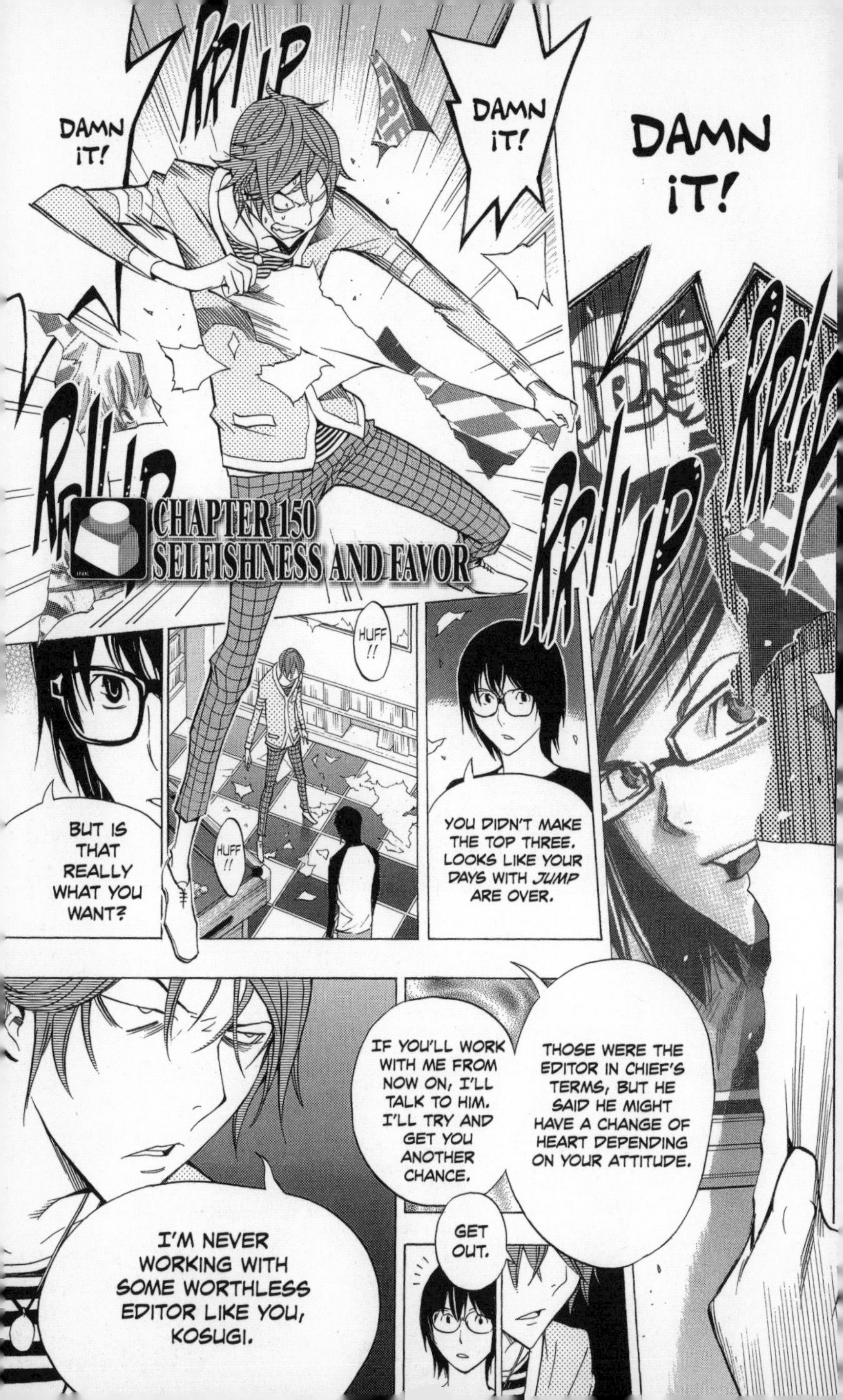

DAMN IT!
DAMN IT!
DAMN IT!
CHAPTER 150
SELFISHNESS AND FAVOR
YOU DIDN'T MAKE THE TOP THREE. LOOKS LIKE YOUR DAYS WITH *JUMP* ARE OVER.
HUFF !!
HUFF !!
BUT IS THAT REALLY WHAT YOU WANT?
THOSE WERE THE EDITOR IN CHIEF'S TERMS, BUT HE SAID HE MIGHT HAVE A CHANGE OF HEART DEPENDING ON YOUR ATTITUDE.
IF YOU'LL WORK WITH ME FROM NOW ON, I'LL TALK TO HIM. I'LL TRY AND GET YOU ANOTHER CHANCE.
GET OUT.
I'M NEVER WORKING WITH SOME WORTHLESS EDITOR LIKE YOU, KOSUGI.

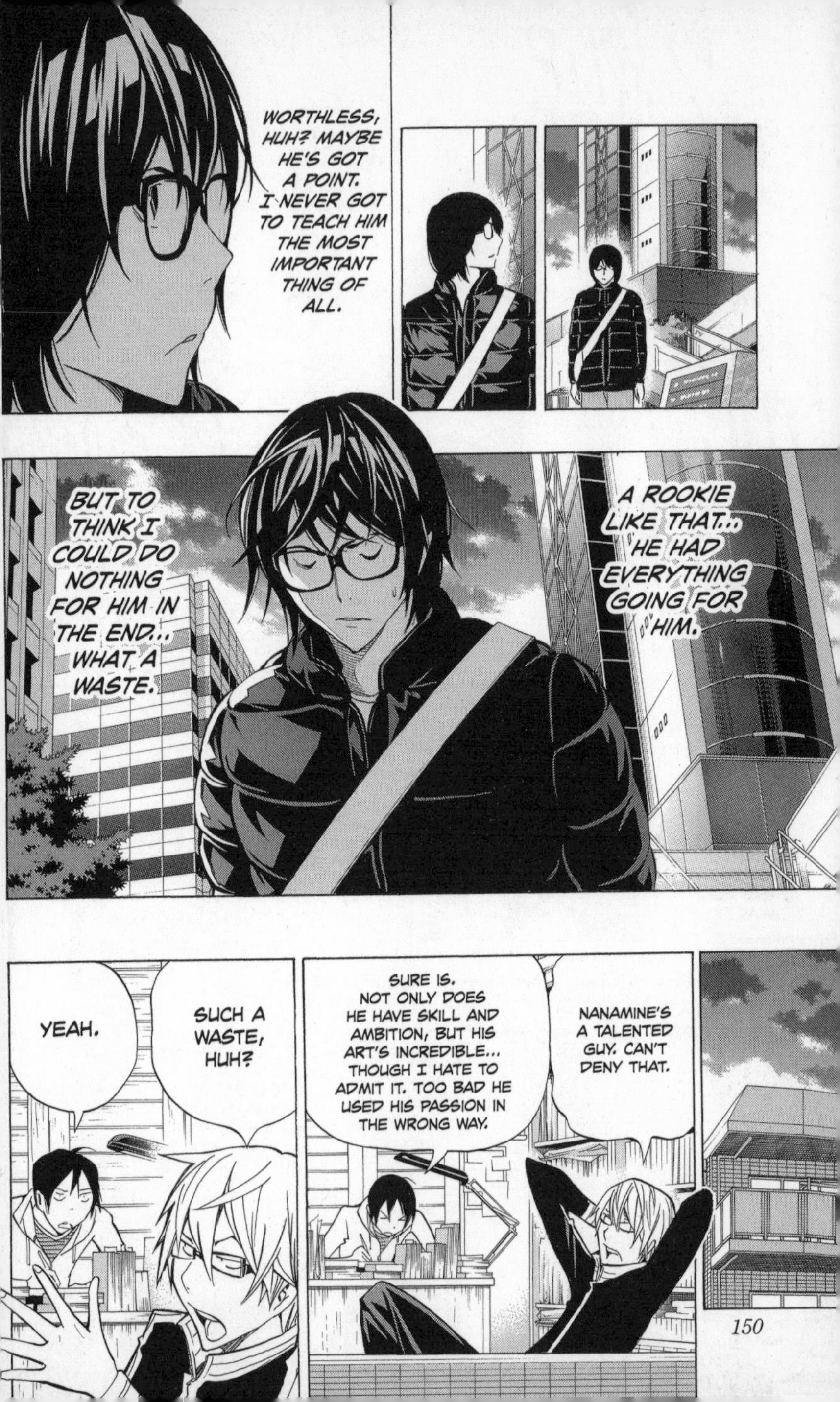
WORTHLESS, HUH? MAYBE HE'S GOT A POINT. I NEVER GOT TO TEACH HIM THE MOST IMPORTANT THING OF ALL.
A ROOKIE LIKE THAT... HE HAD EVERYTHING GOING FOR HIM.
BUT TO THINK I COULD DO NOTHING FOR HIM IN THE END... WHAT A WASTE.
NANAMINE'S A TALENTED GUY. CAN'T DENY THAT.
SURE IS. NOT ONLY DOES HE HAVE SKILL AND AMBITION, BUT HIS ART'S INCREDIBLE... THOUGH I HATE TO ADMIT IT. TOO BAD HE USED HIS PASSION IN THE WRONG WAY.
SUCH A WASTE, HUH?
YEAH.

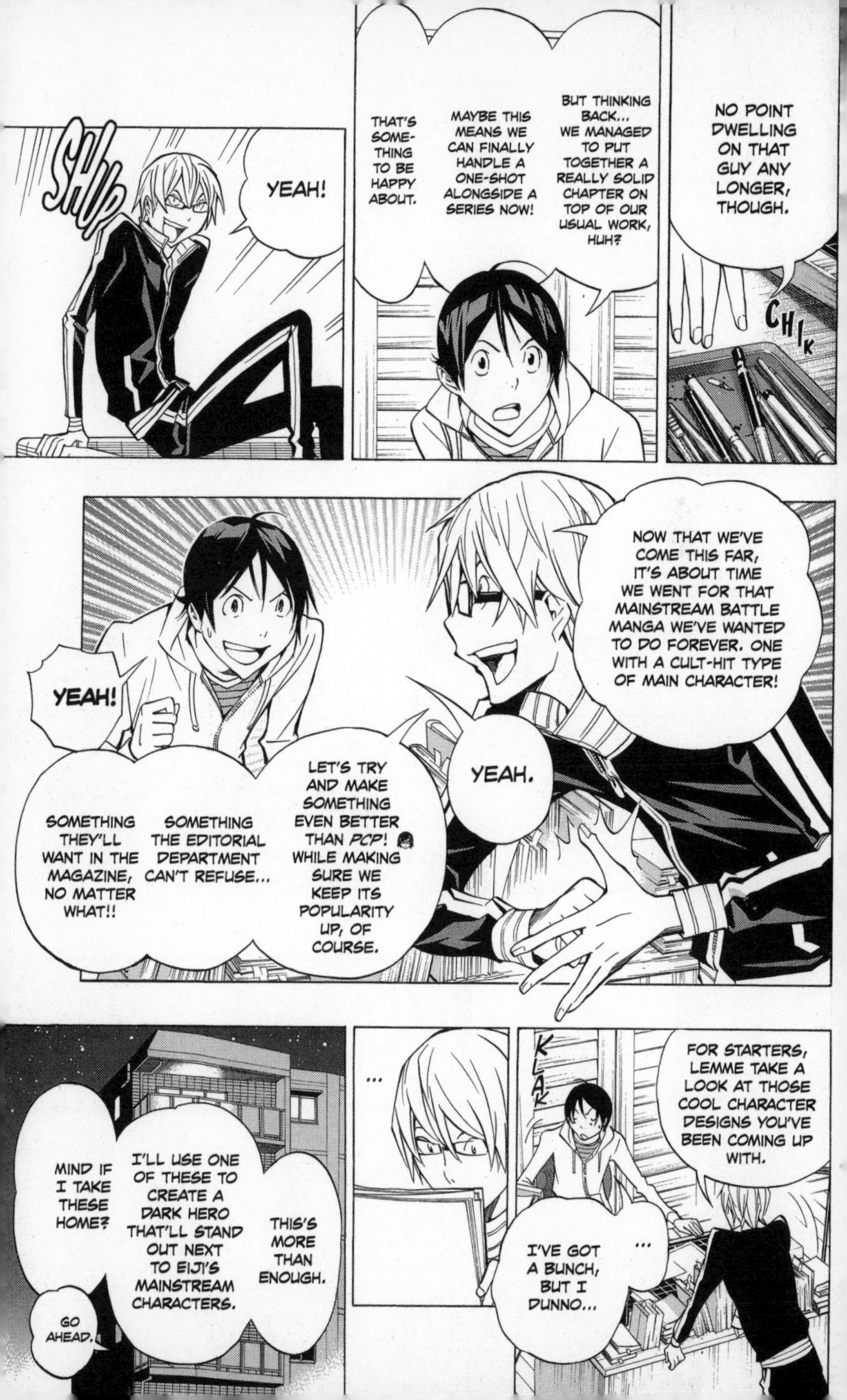
NO POINT DWELLING ON THAT GUY ANY LONGER, THOUGH.
CHIK
BUT THINKING BACK... WE MANAGED TO PUT TOGETHER A REALLY SOLID CHAPTER ON TOP OF OUR USUAL WORK, HUH?
MAYBE THIS MEANS WE CAN FINALLY HANDLE A ONE-SHOT ALONGSIDE A SERIES NOW!
THAT'S SOME-THING TO BE HAPPY ABOUT.
SHUP
YEAH!
NOW THAT WE'VE COME THIS FAR, IT'S ABOUT TIME WE WENT FOR THAT MAINSTREAM BATTLE MANGA WE'VE WANTED TO DO FOREVER. ONE WITH A CULT-HIT TYPE OF MAIN CHARACTER!
YEAH!
YEAH.
LET'S TRY AND MAKE SOMETHING EVEN BETTER THAN *PCP*! WHILE MAKING SURE WE KEEP ITS POPULARITY UP, OF COURSE.
SOMETHING THE EDITORIAL DEPARTMENT CAN'T REFUSE...
SOMETHING THEY'LL WANT IN THE MAGAZINE, NO MATTER WHAT!!
FOR STARTERS, LEMME TAKE A LOOK AT THOSE COOL CHARACTER DESIGNS YOU'VE BEEN COMING UP WITH.
KLAK
...
...
I'VE GOT A BUNCH, BUT I DUNNO...
THIS'S MORE THAN ENOUGH.
I'LL USE ONE OF THESE TO CREATE A DARK HERO THAT'LL STAND OUT NEXT TO EIJI'S MAINSTREAM CHARACTERS.
MIND IF I TAKE THESE HOME?
GO AHEAD.

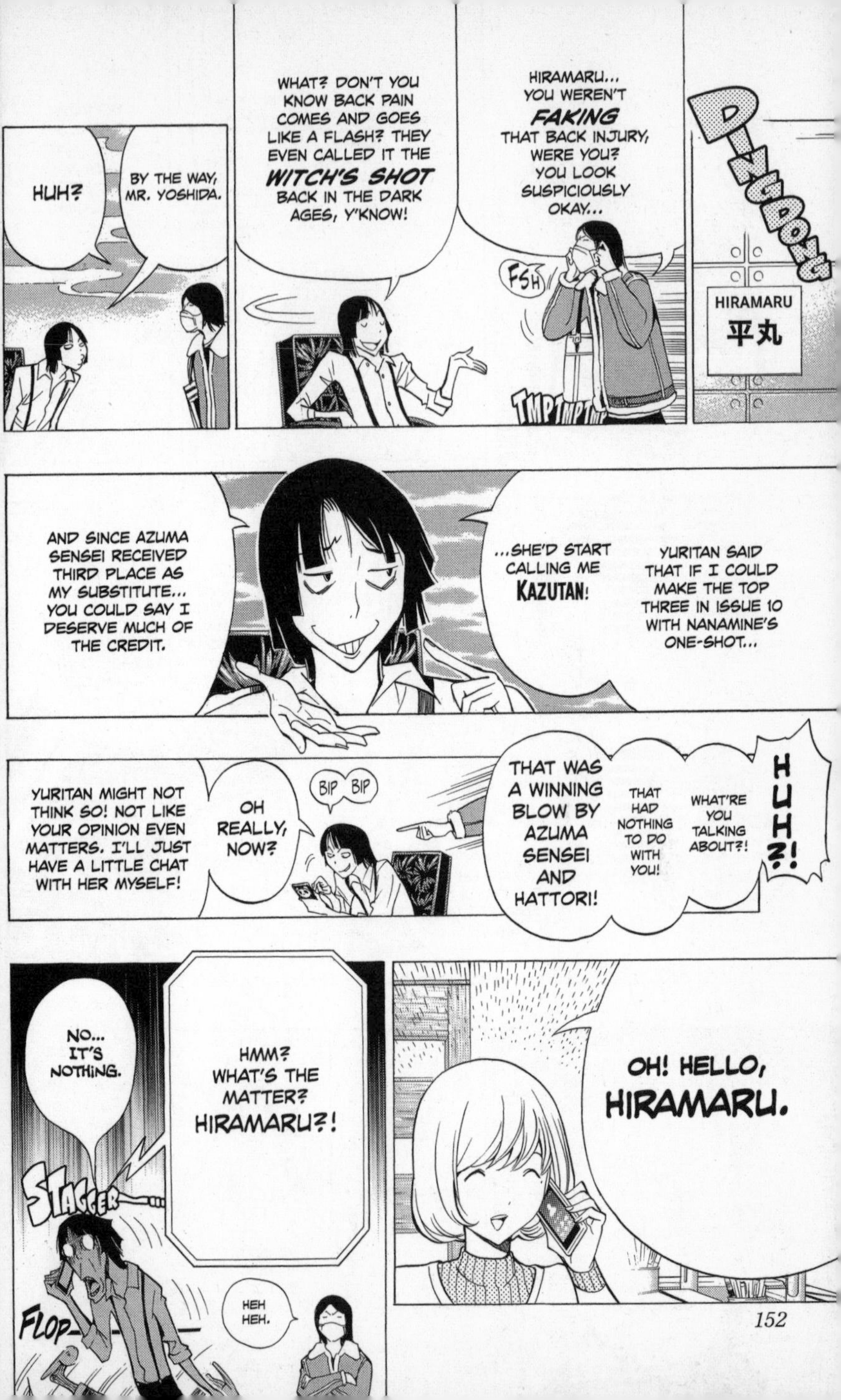
DING DONG
HIRAMARU
平丸
HIRAMARU... YOU WEREN'T FAKING THAT BACK INJURY, WERE YOU? YOU LOOK SUSPICIOUSLY OKAY...
FSH
TMP TMP TMP
WHAT? DON'T YOU KNOW BACK PAIN COMES AND GOES LIKE A FLASH? THEY EVEN CALLED IT THE WITCH'S SHOT BACK IN THE DARK AGES, Y'KNOW!
BY THE WAY, MR. YOSHIDA.
HUH?
YURITAN SAID THAT IF I COULD MAKE THE TOP THREE IN ISSUE 10 WITH NANAMINE'S ONE-SHOT...
...SHE'D START CALLING ME KAZUTAN!
AND SINCE AZUMA SENSEI RECEIVED THIRD PLACE AS MY SUBSTITUTE... YOU COULD SAY I DESERVE MUCH OF THE CREDIT.
HUH?!
WHAT'RE YOU TALKING ABOUT?!
THAT HAD NOTHING TO DO WITH YOU!
THAT WAS A WINNING BLOW BY AZUMA SENSEI AND HATTORI!
BIP BIP
OH REALLY, NOW?
YURITAN MIGHT NOT THINK SO! NOT LIKE YOUR OPINION EVEN MATTERS. I'LL JUST HAVE A LITTLE CHAT WITH HER MYSELF!
OH! HELLO, HIRAMARU.
HMM? WHAT'S THE MATTER? HIRAMARU?!
NO... IT'S NOTHING.
STAGGER
FLOP
HEH HEH.

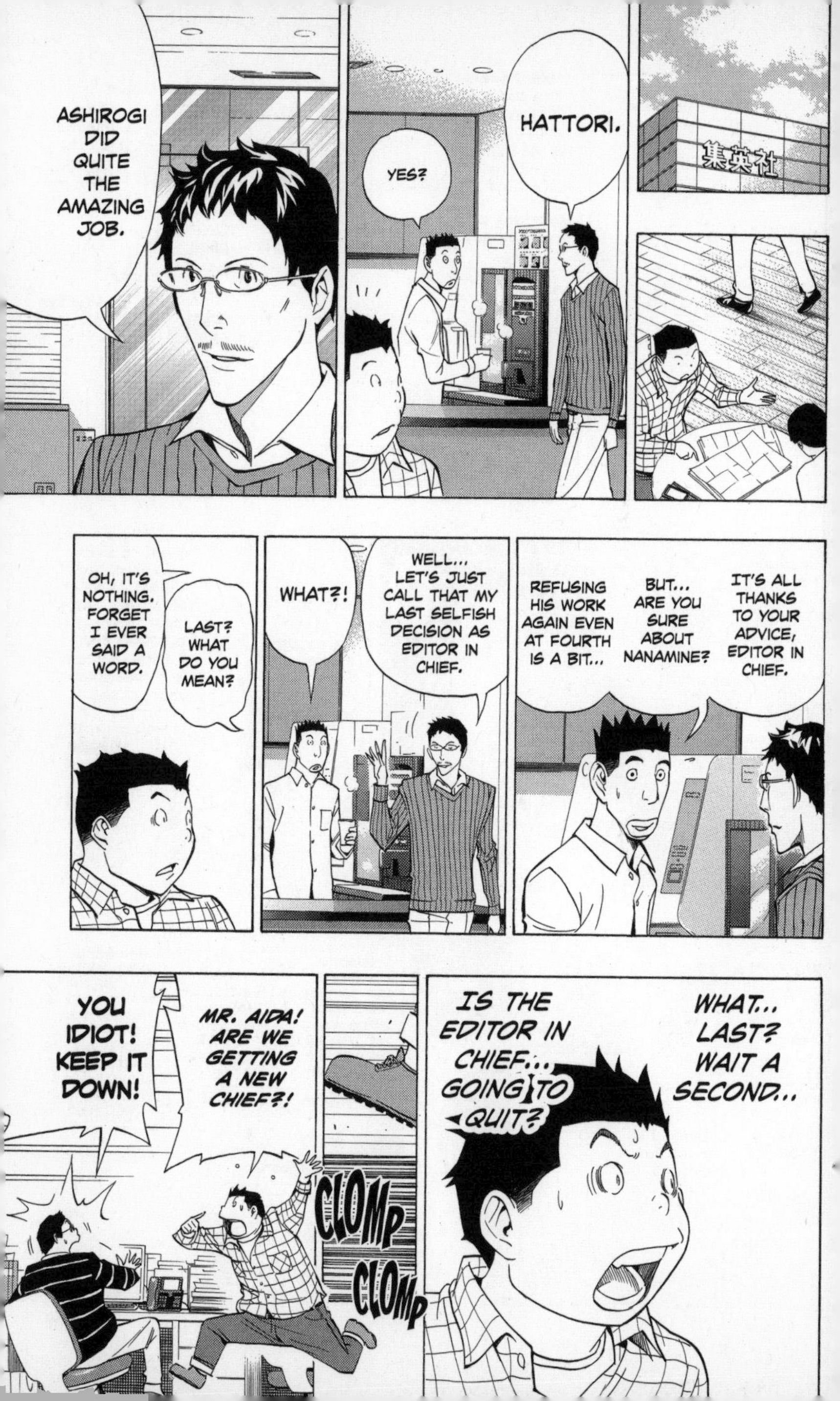
集英社
HATTORI.
YES?
ASHIROGI DID QUITE THE AMAZING JOB.
IT'S ALL THANKS TO YOUR ADVICE, EDITOR IN CHIEF.
BUT... ARE YOU SURE ABOUT NANAMINE?
REFUSING HIS WORK AGAIN EVEN AT FOURTH IS A BIT...
WELL... LET'S JUST CALL THAT MY LAST SELFISH DECISION AS EDITOR IN CHIEF.
WHAT?!
LAST? WHAT DO YOU MEAN?
OH, IT'S NOTHING. FORGET I EVER SAID A WORD.
WHAT... LAST? WAIT A SECOND...
IS THE EDITOR IN CHIEF... GOING TO QUIT?
CLOMP
CLOMP
CLOMP
MR. AIDA! ARE WE GETTING A NEW CHIEF?!
YOU IDIOT! KEEP IT DOWN!

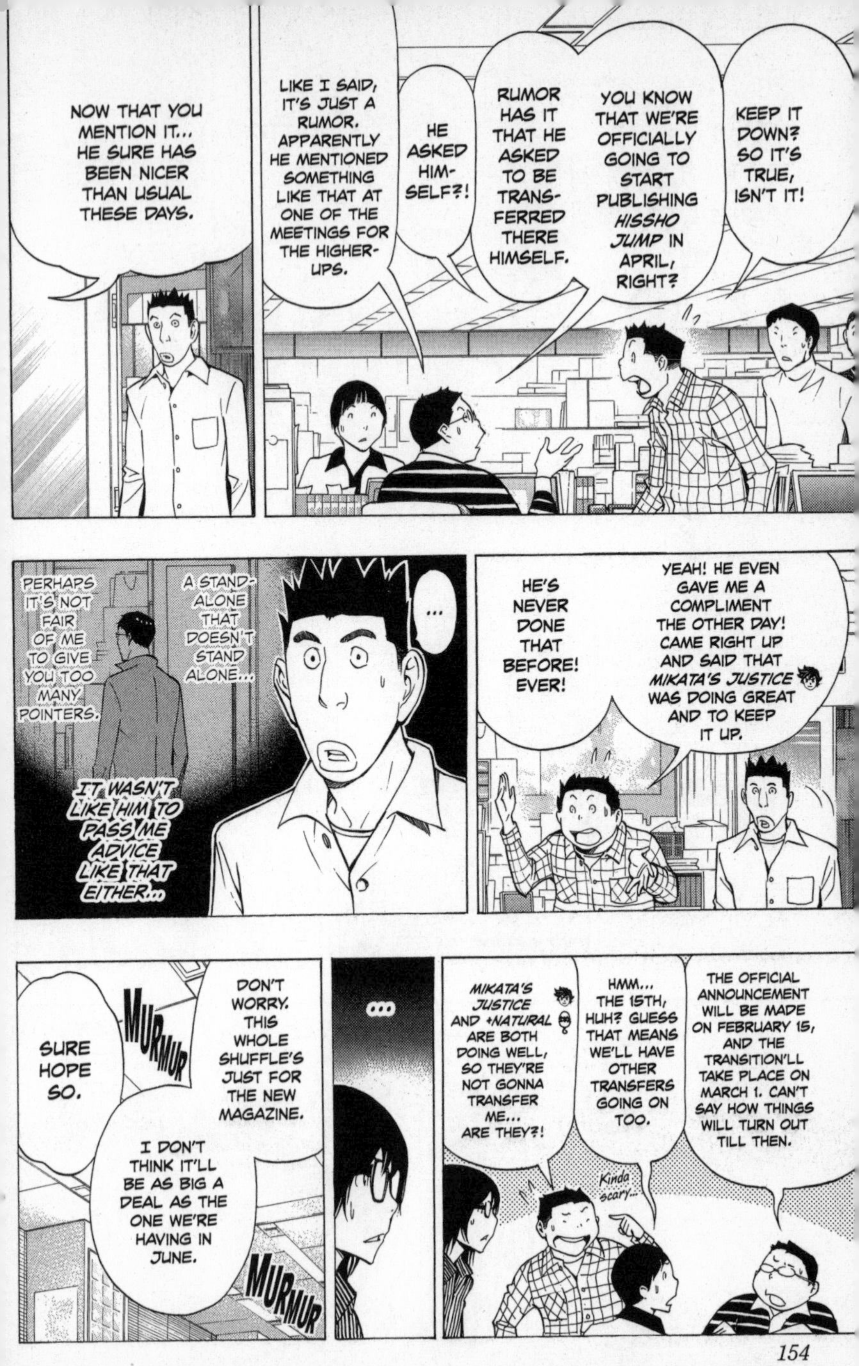

KEEP IT DOWN? SO IT'S TRUE, ISN'T IT!
YOU KNOW THAT WE'RE OFFICIALLY GOING TO START PUBLISHING *HISSHO JUMP* IN APRIL, RIGHT?
RUMOR HAS IT THAT HE ASKED TO BE TRANS-FERRED THERE HIMSELF.
HE ASKED HIM-SELF?!
LIKE I SAID, IT'S JUST A RUMOR. APPARENTLY HE MENTIONED SOMETHING LIKE THAT AT ONE OF THE MEETINGS FOR THE HIGHER-UPS.
NOW THAT YOU MENTION IT... HE SURE HAS BEEN NICER THAN USUAL THESE DAYS.
YEAH! HE EVEN GAVE ME A COMPLIMENT THE OTHER DAY! CAME RIGHT UP AND SAID THAT *MIKATA'S JUSTICE* WAS DOING GREAT AND TO KEEP IT UP.
HE'S NEVER DONE THAT BEFORE! EVER!
...
A STAND-ALONE THAT DOESN'T STAND ALONE...
PERHAPS IT'S NOT FAIR OF ME TO GIVE YOU TOO MANY POINTERS.
IT WASN'T LIKE HIM TO PASS ME ADVICE LIKE THAT EITHER...
THE OFFICIAL ANNOUNCEMENT WILL BE MADE ON FEBRUARY 15, AND THE TRANSITION'LL TAKE PLACE ON MARCH 1. CAN'T SAY HOW THINGS WILL TURN OUT TILL THEN.
HMM... THE 15TH, HUH? GUESS THAT MEANS WE'LL HAVE OTHER TRANSFERS GOING ON TOO.
Kinda scary...
MIKATA'S JUSTICE AND *+NATURAL* ARE BOTH DOING WELL, SO THEY'RE NOT GONNA TRANSFER ME... ARE THEY?!
...
DON'T WORRY. THIS WHOLE SHUFFLE'S JUST FOR THE NEW MAGAZINE.
MURMUR
SURE HOPE SO.
I DON'T THINK IT'LL BE AS BIG A DEAL AS THE ONE WE'RE HAVING IN JUNE.
MURMUR

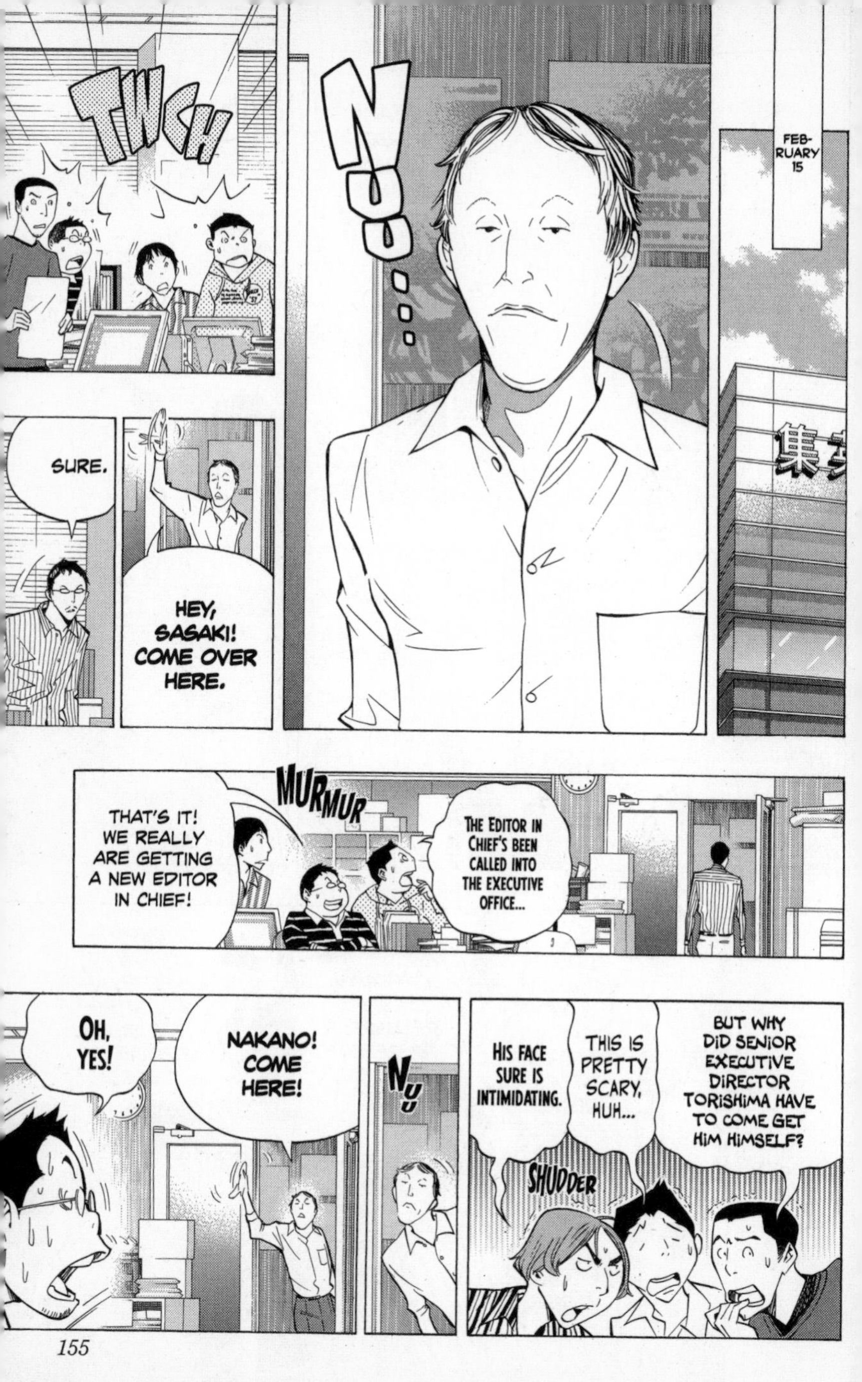
FEB-
RUARY
15
NUU...
TWCH
HEY, SASAKI! COME OVER HERE.
SURE.
THE EDITOR IN CHIEF'S BEEN CALLED INTO THE EXECUTIVE OFFICE...
MURMUR
THAT'S IT! WE REALLY ARE GETTING A NEW EDITOR IN CHIEF!
BUT WHY DID SENIOR EXECUTIVE DIRECTOR TORISHIMA HAVE TO COME GET HIM HIMSELF?
THIS IS PRETTY SCARY, HUH...
HIS FACE SURE IS INTIMIDATING.
SHUDDER
NUU
NAKANO! COME HERE!
OH, YES!

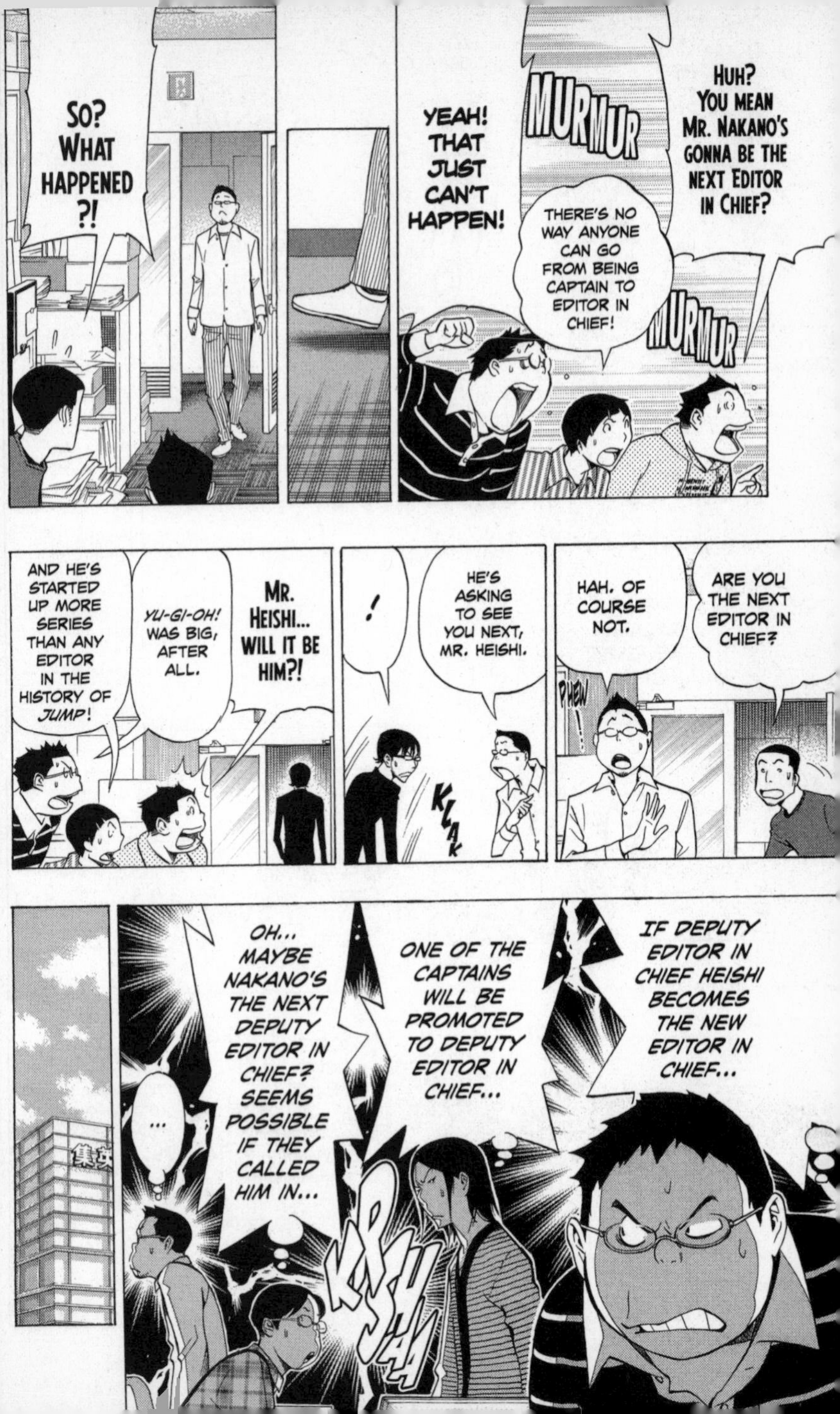
HUH? YOU MEAN MR. NAKANO'S GONNA BE THE NEXT EDITOR IN CHIEF?
MURMUR
YEAH! THAT JUST CAN'T HAPPEN!
THERE'S NO WAY ANYONE CAN GO FROM BEING CAPTAIN TO EDITOR IN CHIEF!
MURMUR
SO? WHAT HAPPENED ?!
ARE YOU THE NEXT EDITOR IN CHIEF?
HAH. OF COURSE NOT.
PHEW
HE'S ASKING TO SEE YOU NEXT, MR. HEISHI.
!
KLAK
MR. HEISHI... WILL IT BE HIM?!
YU-GI-OH! WAS BIG, AFTER ALL.
AND HE'S STARTED UP MORE SERIES THAN ANY EDITOR IN THE HISTORY OF JUMP!
IF DEPUTY EDITOR IN CHIEF HEISHI BECOMES THE NEW EDITOR IN CHIEF...
ONE OF THE CAPTAINS WILL BE PROMOTED TO DEPUTY EDITOR IN CHIEF...
OH... MAYBE NAKANO'S THE NEXT DEPUTY EDITOR IN CHIEF? SEEMS POSSIBLE IF THEY CALLED HIM IN...
...
KRSHAA

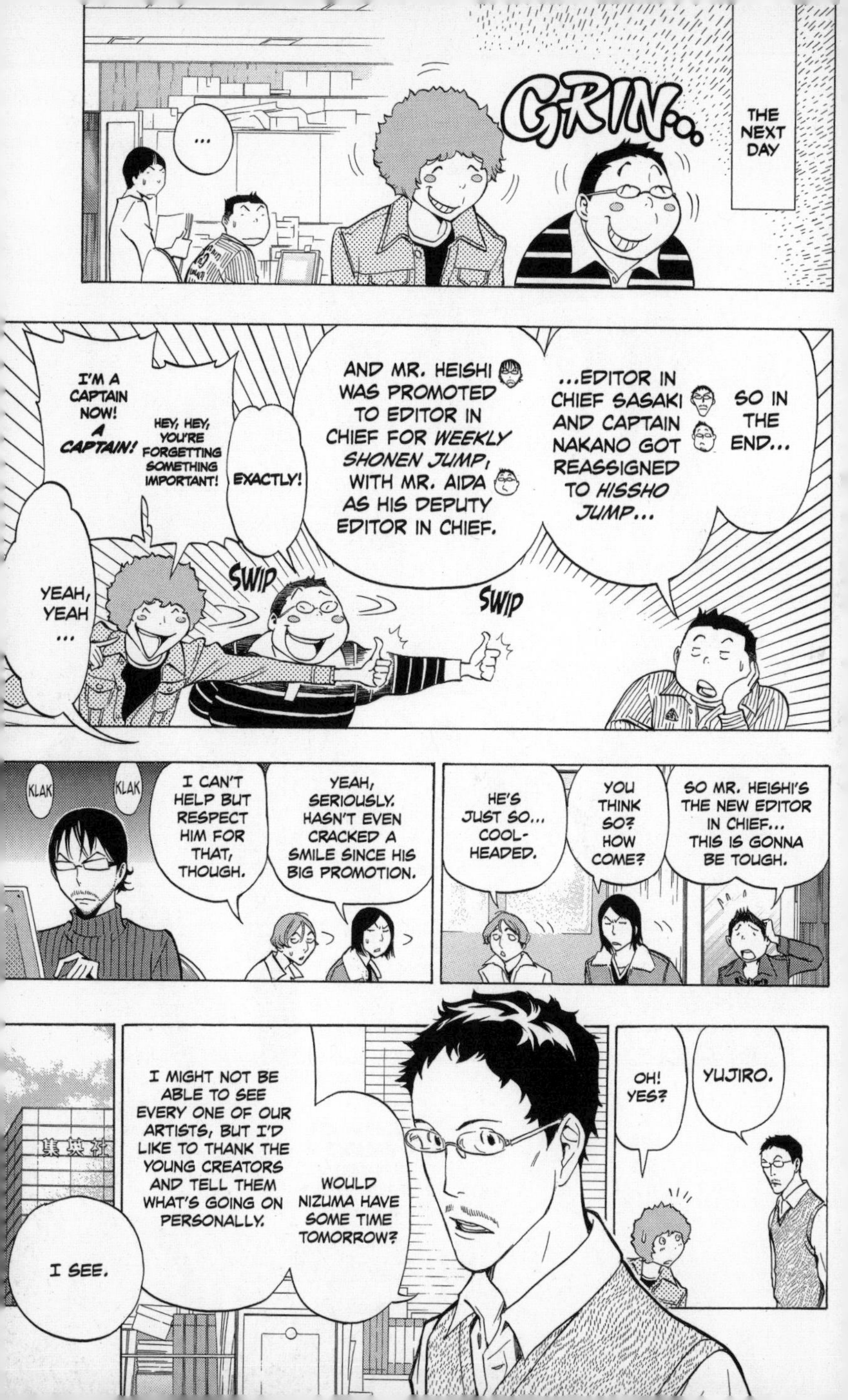
THE NEXT DAY
GRIN...
...
SO IN THE END...
...EDITOR IN CHIEF SASAKI AND CAPTAIN NAKANO GOT REASSIGNED TO *HISSHO JUMP*...
SWIP
AND MR. HEISHI WAS PROMOTED TO EDITOR IN CHIEF FOR *WEEKLY SHONEN JUMP*, WITH MR. AIDA AS HIS DEPUTY EDITOR IN CHIEF.
SWIP
EXACTLY!
HEY, HEY, YOU'RE FORGETTING SOMETHING IMPORTANT!
I'M A CAPTAIN NOW! A *CAPTAIN!*
YEAH, YEAH...
SO MR. HEISHI'S THE NEW EDITOR IN CHIEF... THIS IS GONNA BE TOUGH.
YOU THINK SO? HOW COME?
HE'S JUST SO... COOL-HEADED.
YEAH, SERIOUSLY. HASN'T EVEN CRACKED A SMILE SINCE HIS BIG PROMOTION.
I CAN'T HELP BUT RESPECT HIM FOR THAT, THOUGH.
KLAK
KLAK
YUJIRO.
OH! YES?
WOULD NIZUMA HAVE SOME TIME TOMORROW?
I MIGHT NOT BE ABLE TO SEE EVERY ONE OF OUR ARTISTS, BUT I'D LIKE TO THANK THE YOUNG CREATORS AND TELL THEM WHAT'S GOING ON PERSONALLY.
集英社
I SEE.

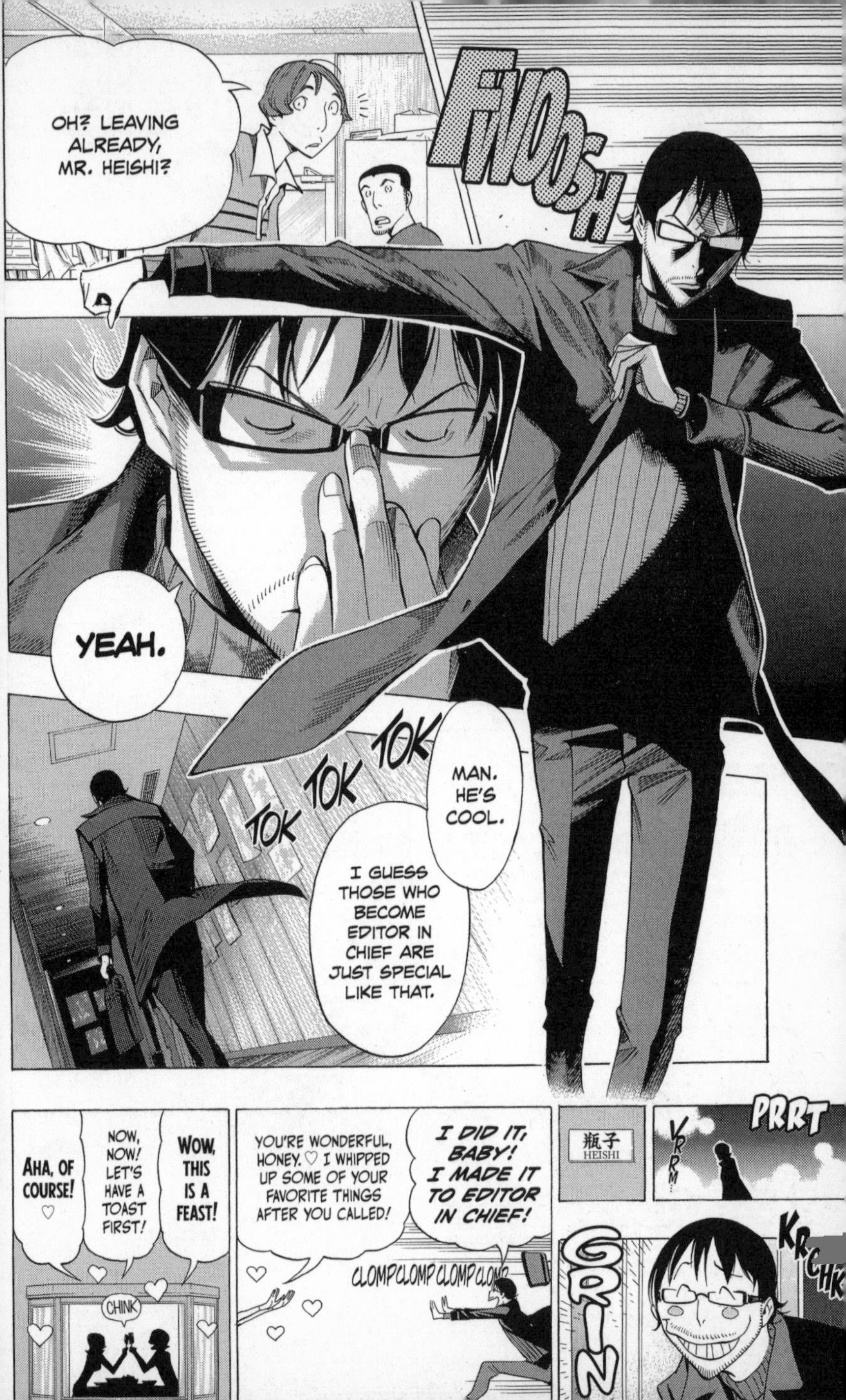
FHOOSH
OH? LEAVING ALREADY, MR. HEISHI?
YEAH.
TOK TOK TOK
MAN. HE'S COOL.
I GUESS THOSE WHO BECOME EDITOR IN CHIEF ARE JUST SPECIAL LIKE THAT.
PRRT
VRRM...
瓶子
HEISHI
KRCHK
GRIN
I DID IT, BABY! I MADE IT TO EDITOR IN CHIEF!
YOU'RE WONDERFUL, HONEY. ♡ I WHIPPED UP SOME OF YOUR FAVORITE THINGS AFTER YOU CALLED!
CLOMP CLOMP CLOMP CLOMP
WOW, THIS IS A FEAST!
NOW, NOW! LET'S HAVE A TOAST FIRST!
AHA, OF COURSE! ♡
CHINK

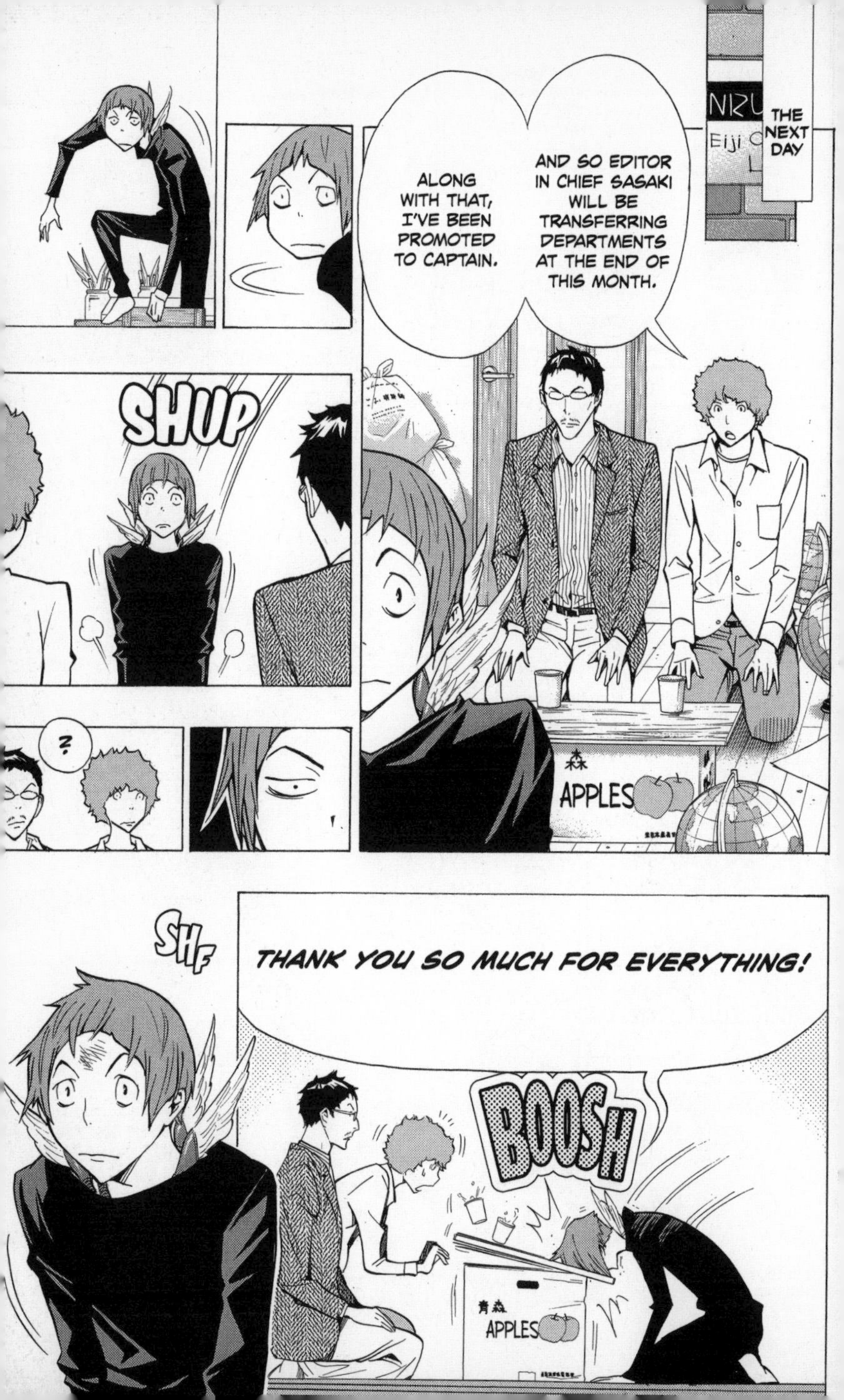
THE NEXT DAY
AND SO EDITOR IN CHIEF SASAKI WILL BE TRANSFERRING DEPARTMENTS AT THE END OF THIS MONTH.
ALONG WITH THAT, I'VE BEEN PROMOTED TO CAPTAIN.
APPLES
SHUP
?
THANK YOU SO MUCH FOR EVERYTHING!
SHF
BOOSH
APPLES

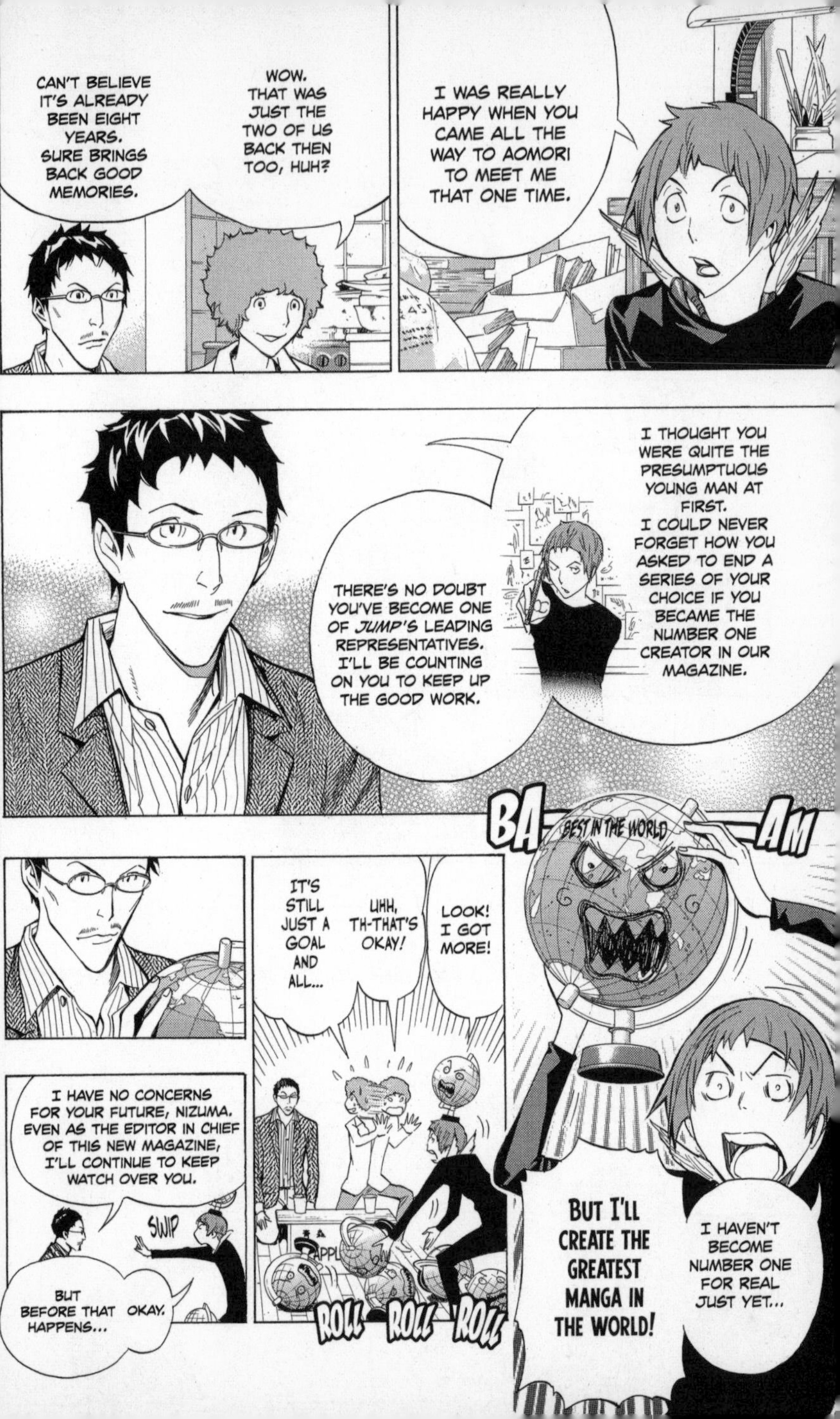
I WAS REALLY HAPPY WHEN YOU CAME ALL THE WAY TO AOMORI TO MEET ME THAT ONE TIME.
WOW. THAT WAS JUST THE TWO OF US BACK THEN TOO, HUH?
CAN'T BELIEVE IT'S ALREADY BEEN EIGHT YEARS. SURE BRINGS BACK GOOD MEMORIES.
I THOUGHT YOU WERE QUITE THE PRESUMPTUOUS YOUNG MAN AT FIRST. I COULD NEVER FORGET HOW YOU ASKED TO END A SERIES OF YOUR CHOICE IF YOU BECAME THE NUMBER ONE CREATOR IN OUR MAGAZINE.
THERE'S NO DOUBT YOU'VE BECOME ONE OF *JUMP*'S LEADING REPRESENTATIVES. I'LL BE COUNTING ON YOU TO KEEP UP THE GOOD WORK.
BA-AM
BEST IN THE WORLD
I HAVEN'T BECOME NUMBER ONE FOR REAL JUST YET...
BUT I'LL CREATE THE GREATEST MANGA IN THE WORLD!
LOOK! I GOT MORE!
UHH, TH-THAT'S OKAY!
IT'S STILL JUST A GOAL AND ALL...
ROLL ROLL ROLL
I HAVE NO CONCERNS FOR YOUR FUTURE, NIZUMA. EVEN AS THE EDITOR IN CHIEF OF THIS NEW MAGAZINE, I'LL CONTINUE TO KEEP WATCH OVER YOU.
SWIP
OKAY.
BUT BEFORE THAT HAPPENS...

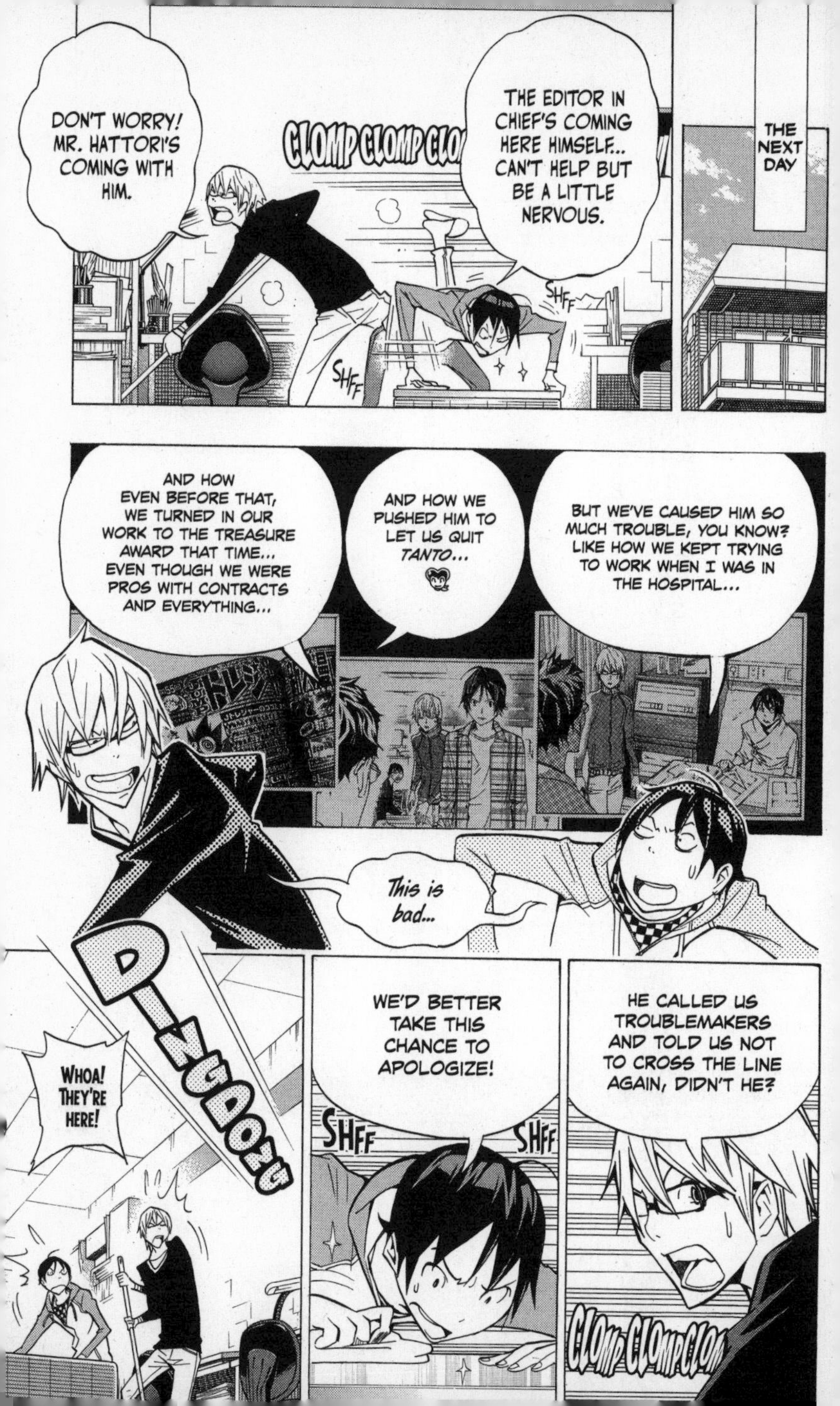
THE NEXT DAY
THE EDITOR IN CHIEF'S COMING HERE HIMSELF... CAN'T HELP BUT BE A LITTLE NERVOUS.
CLOMP CLOMP CLO
DON'T WORRY! MR. HATTORI'S COMING WITH HIM.
SHFF
SHFF
BUT WE'VE CAUSED HIM SO MUCH TROUBLE, YOU KNOW? LIKE HOW WE KEPT TRYING TO WORK WHEN I WAS IN THE HOSPITAL...
AND HOW WE PUSHED HIM TO LET US QUIT *TANTO*...
AND HOW EVEN BEFORE THAT, WE TURNED IN OUR WORK TO THE TREASURE AWARD THAT TIME... EVEN THOUGH WE WERE PROS WITH CONTRACTS AND EVERYTHING...
This is bad...
HE CALLED US TROUBLEMAKERS AND TOLD US NOT TO CROSS THE LINE AGAIN, DIDN'T HE?
CLOMP CLOMP CLOM
WE'D BETTER TAKE THIS CHANCE TO APOLOGIZE!
SHFF
SHFF
DINGDONG
WHOA! THEY'RE HERE!

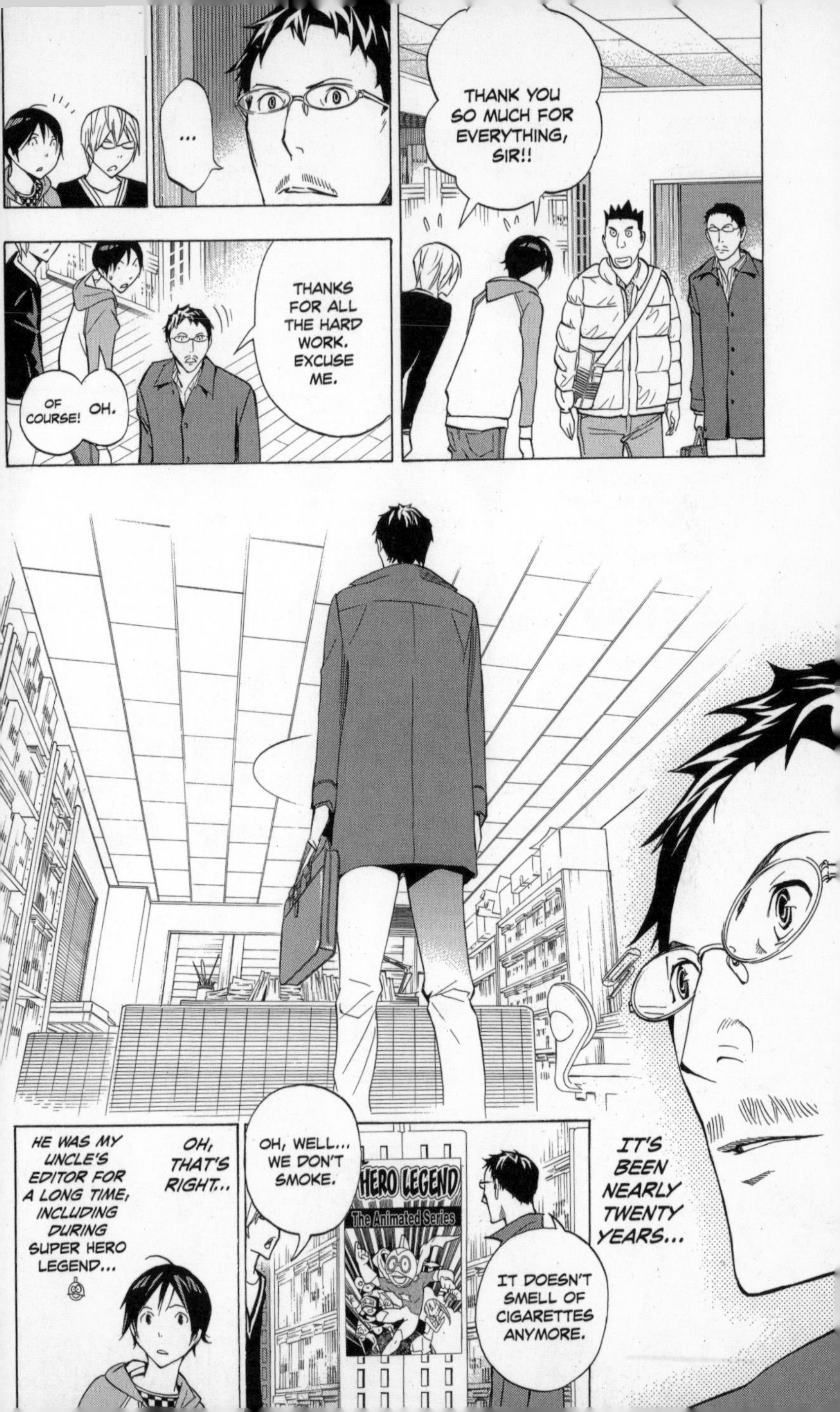
THANK YOU SO MUCH FOR EVERYTHING, SIR!!
...
THANKS FOR ALL THE HARD WORK. EXCUSE ME.
OH.
OF COURSE!
IT'S BEEN NEARLY TWENTY YEARS...
IT DOESN'T SMELL OF CIGARETTES ANYMORE.
HERO LEGEND
The Animated Series
OH, WELL... WE DON'T SMOKE.
OH, THAT'S RIGHT...
HE WAS MY UNCLE'S EDITOR FOR A LONG TIME, INCLUDING DURING SUPER HERO LEGEND...

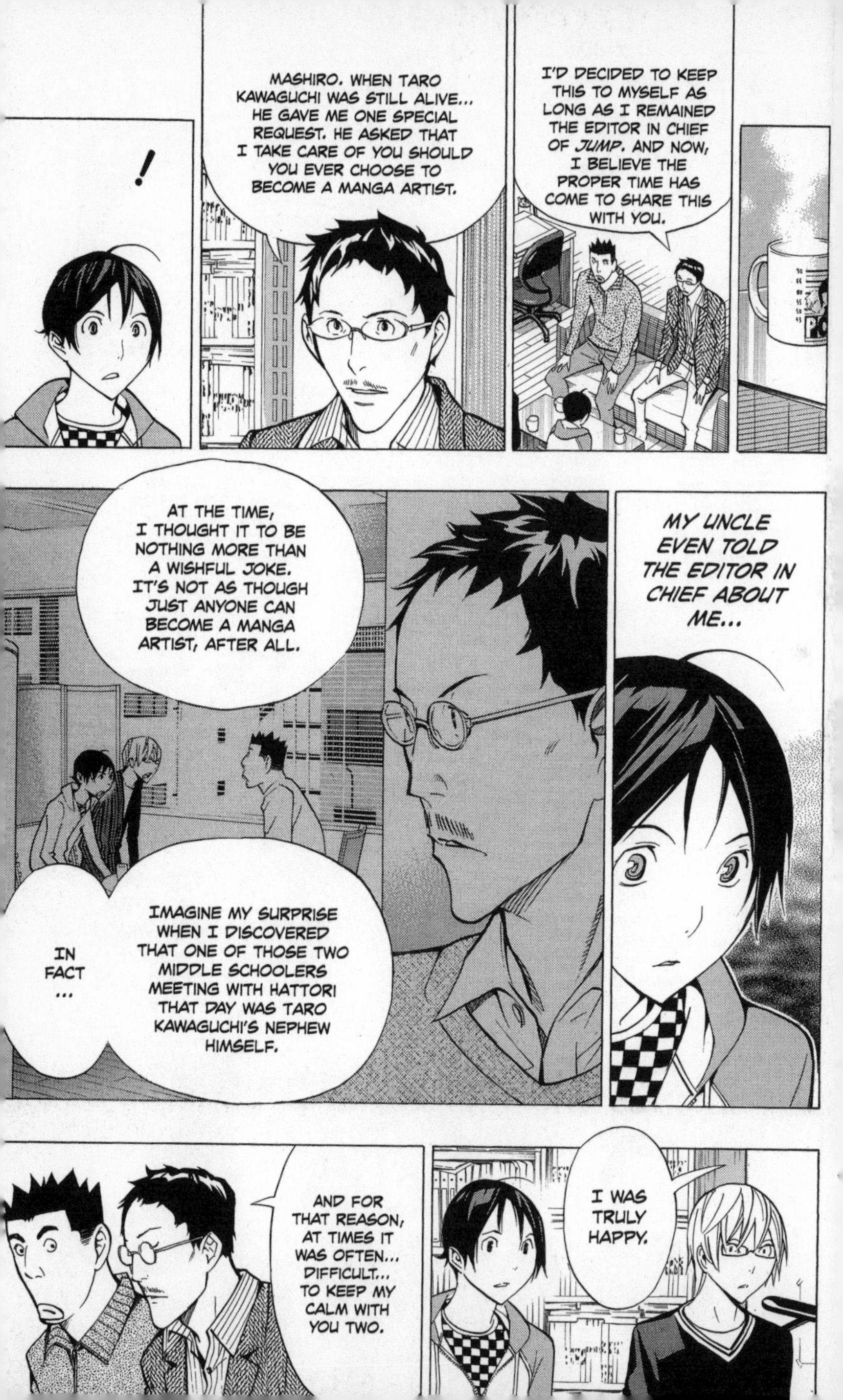
I'D DECIDED TO KEEP THIS TO MYSELF AS LONG AS I REMAINED THE EDITOR IN CHIEF OF JUMP. AND NOW, I BELIEVE THE PROPER TIME HAS COME TO SHARE THIS WITH YOU.
MASHIRO. WHEN TARO KAWAGUCHI WAS STILL ALIVE... HE GAVE ME ONE SPECIAL REQUEST. HE ASKED THAT I TAKE CARE OF YOU SHOULD YOU EVER CHOOSE TO BECOME A MANGA ARTIST.
!
MY UNCLE EVEN TOLD THE EDITOR IN CHIEF ABOUT ME...
AT THE TIME, I THOUGHT IT TO BE NOTHING MORE THAN A WISHFUL JOKE. IT'S NOT AS THOUGH JUST ANYONE CAN BECOME A MANGA ARTIST, AFTER ALL.
IN FACT...
IMAGINE MY SURPRISE WHEN I DISCOVERED THAT ONE OF THOSE TWO MIDDLE SCHOOLERS MEETING WITH HATTORI THAT DAY WAS TARO KAWAGUCHI'S NEPHEW HIMSELF.
I WAS TRULY HAPPY.
AND FOR THAT REASON, AT TIMES IT WAS OFTEN... DIFFICULT... TO KEEP MY CALM WITH YOU TWO.

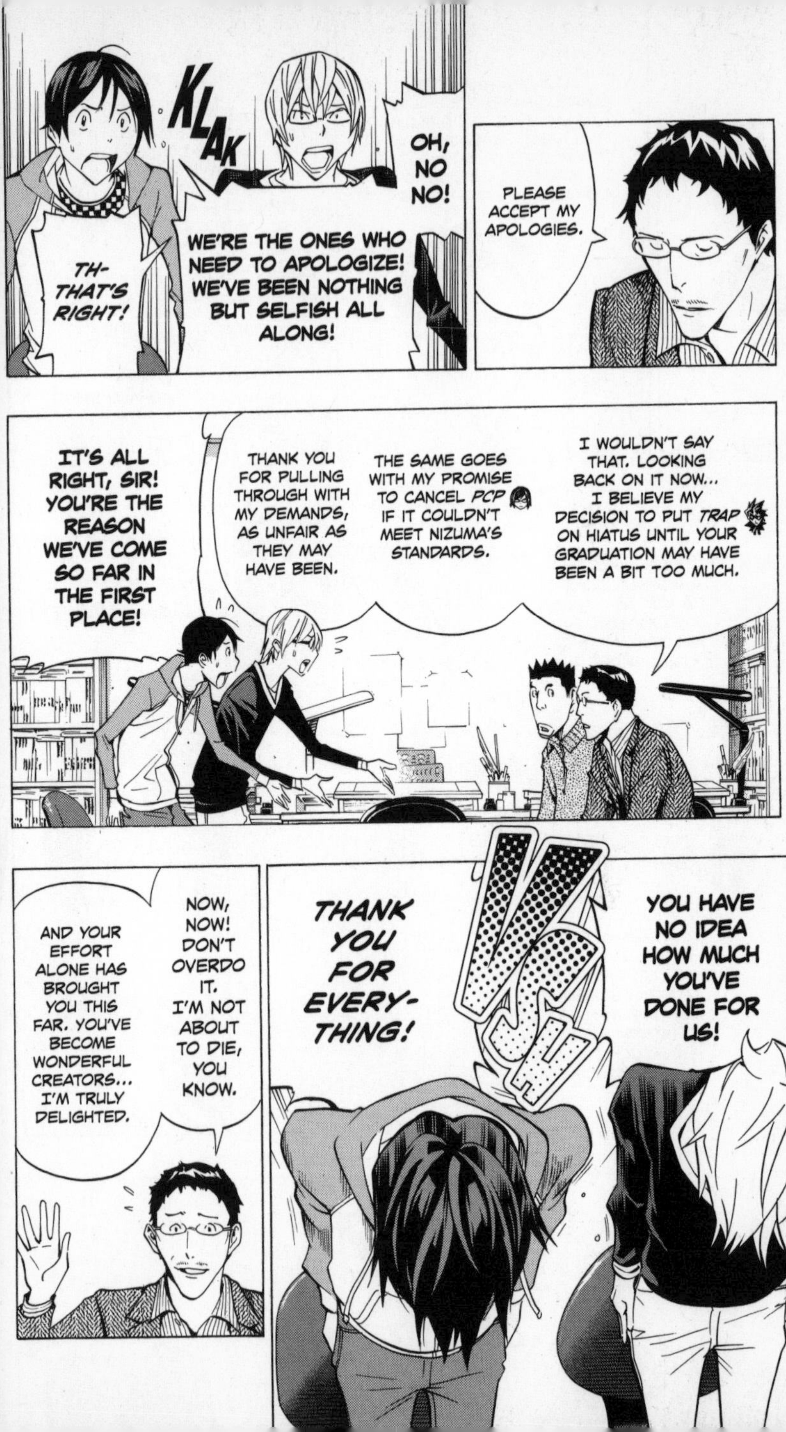
PLEASE ACCEPT MY APOLOGIES.
OH, NO NO!
KLAK
WE'RE THE ONES WHO NEED TO APOLOGIZE! WE'VE BEEN NOTHING BUT SELFISH ALL ALONG!
TH-THAT'S RIGHT!
I WOULDN'T SAY THAT. LOOKING BACK ON IT NOW... I BELIEVE MY DECISION TO PUT *TRAP* ON HIATUS UNTIL YOUR GRADUATION MAY HAVE BEEN A BIT TOO MUCH.
THE SAME GOES WITH MY PROMISE TO CANCEL *PCP* IF IT COULDN'T MEET NIZUMA'S STANDARDS.
THANK YOU FOR PULLING THROUGH WITH MY DEMANDS, AS UNFAIR AS THEY MAY HAVE BEEN.
IT'S ALL RIGHT, SIR! YOU'RE THE REASON WE'VE COME SO FAR IN THE FIRST PLACE!
YOU HAVE NO IDEA HOW MUCH YOU'VE DONE FOR US!
THANK YOU FOR EVERY-THING!
NOW, NOW! DON'T OVERDO IT. I'M NOT ABOUT TO DIE, YOU KNOW.
AND YOUR EFFORT ALONE HAS BROUGHT YOU THIS FAR. YOU'VE BECOME WONDERFUL CREATORS... I'M TRULY DELIGHTED.

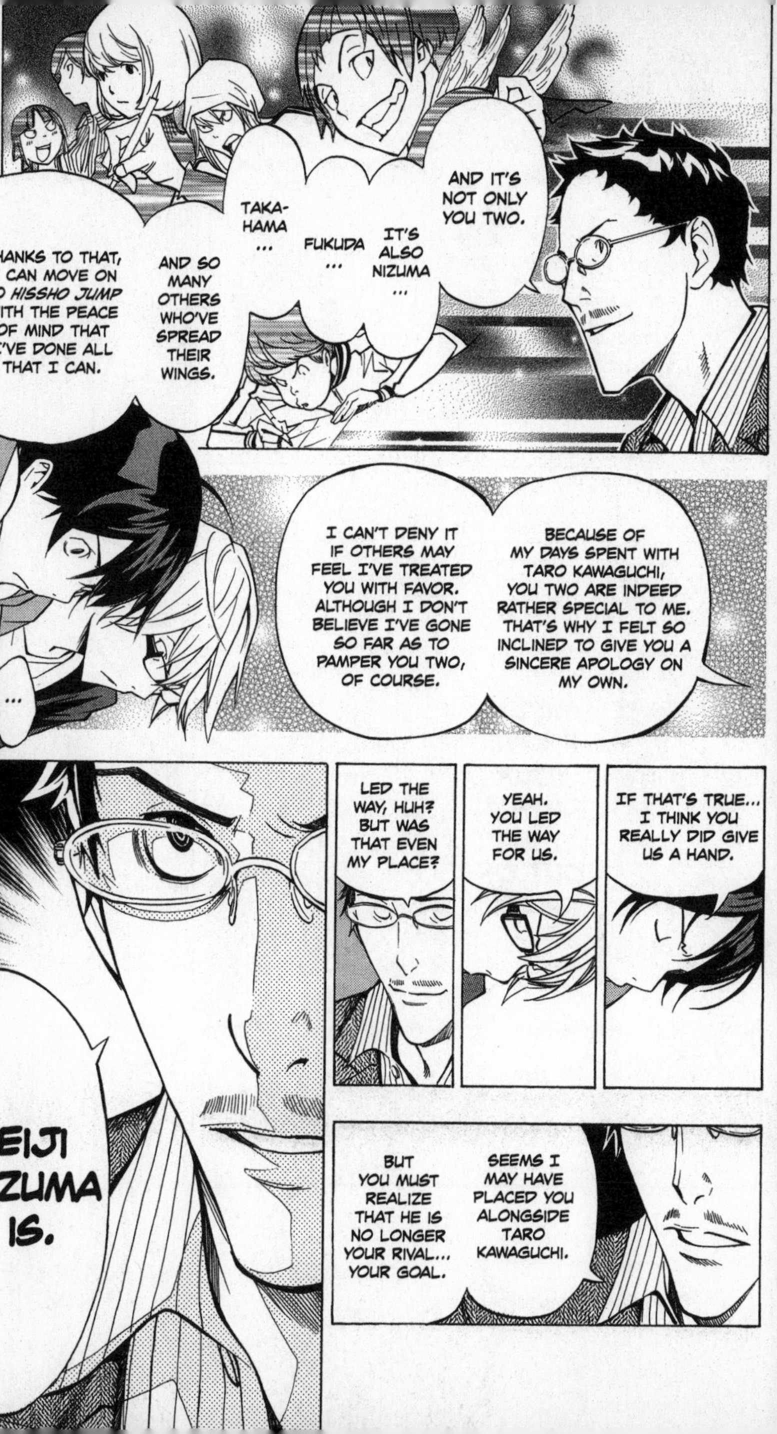
AND IT'S NOT ONLY YOU TWO.
IT'S ALSO NIZUMA...
FUKUDA...
TAKA-HAMA...
AND SO MANY OTHERS WHO'VE SPREAD THEIR WINGS.
THANKS TO THAT, I CAN MOVE ON TO *HISSHO JUMP* WITH THE PEACE OF MIND THAT I'VE DONE ALL THAT I CAN.
BECAUSE OF MY DAYS SPENT WITH TARO KAWAGUCHI, YOU TWO ARE INDEED RATHER SPECIAL TO ME. THAT'S WHY I FELT SO INCLINED TO GIVE YOU A SINCERE APOLOGY ON MY OWN.
I CAN'T DENY IT IF OTHERS MAY FEEL I'VE TREATED YOU WITH FAVOR. ALTHOUGH I DON'T BELIEVE I'VE GONE SO FAR AS TO PAMPER YOU TWO, OF COURSE.
...
IF THAT'S TRUE... I THINK YOU REALLY DID GIVE US A HAND.
YEAH. YOU LED THE WAY FOR US.
LED THE WAY, HUH? BUT WAS THAT EVEN MY PLACE?
SEEMS I MAY HAVE PLACED YOU ALONGSIDE TARO KAWAGUCHI.
BUT YOU MUST REALIZE THAT HE IS NO LONGER YOUR RIVAL... YOUR GOAL.
EIJI NIZUMA IS.

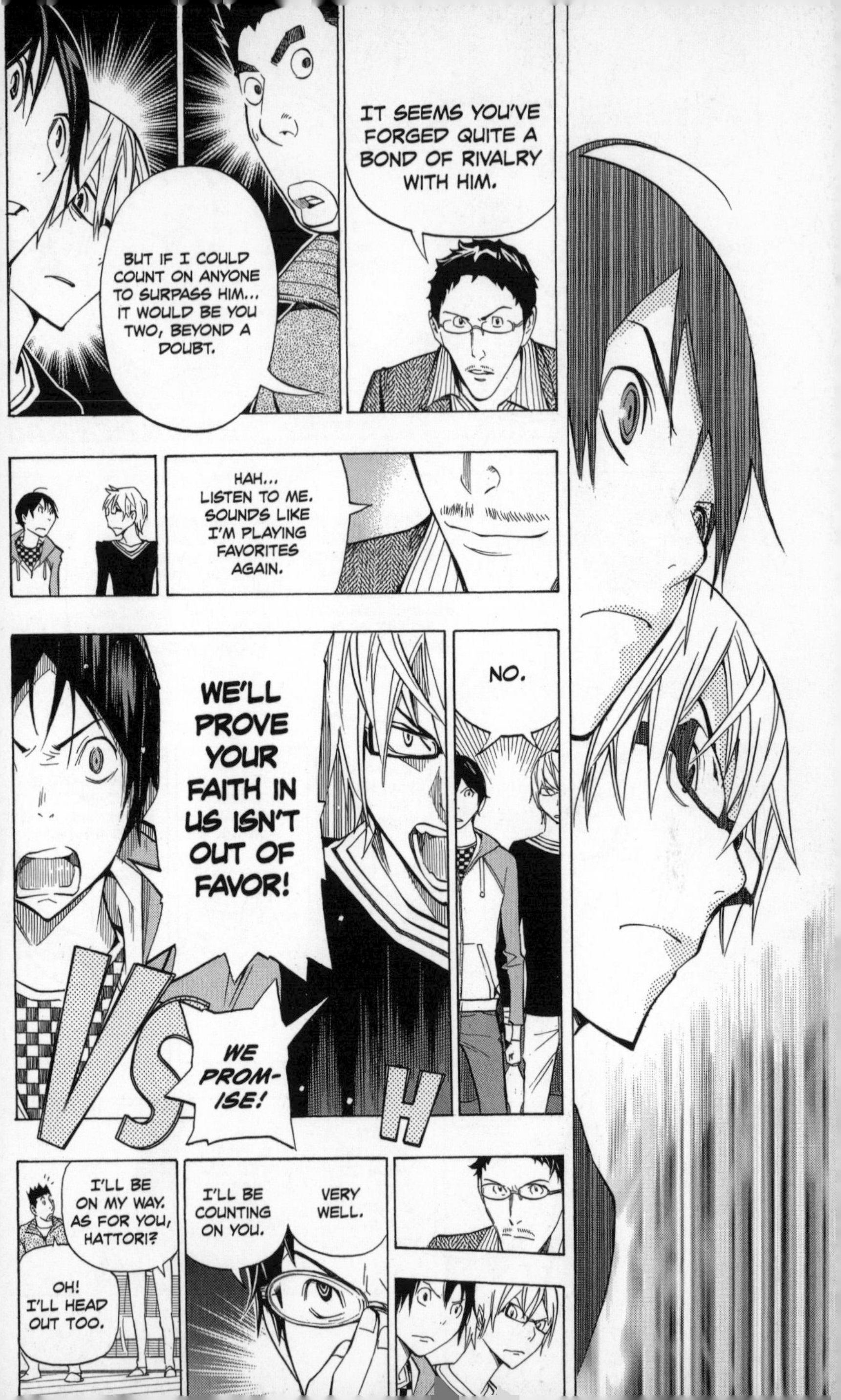
IT SEEMS YOU'VE FORGED QUITE A BOND OF RIVALRY WITH HIM.
BUT IF I COULD COUNT ON ANYONE TO SURPASS HIM... IT WOULD BE YOU TWO, BEYOND A DOUBT.
HAH... LISTEN TO ME. SOUNDS LIKE I'M PLAYING FAVORITES AGAIN.
NO.
WE'LL PROVE YOUR FAITH IN US ISN'T OUT OF FAVOR!
WE PROM-ISE!
VSH
VERY WELL.
I'LL BE COUNTING ON YOU.
I'LL BE ON MY WAY. AS FOR YOU, HATTORI?
OH! I'LL HEAD OUT TOO.

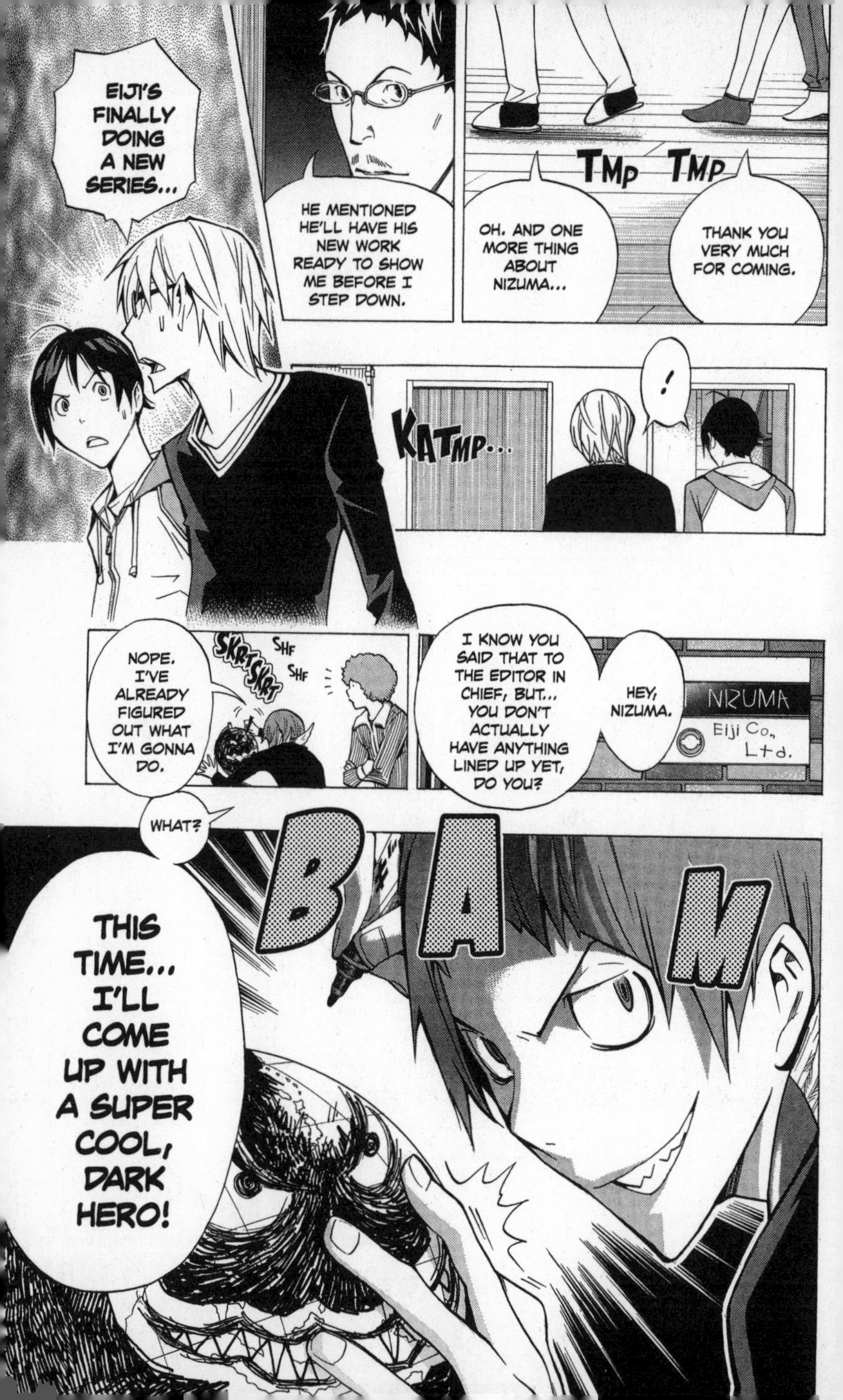

THANK YOU VERY MUCH FOR COMING.
TMP TMP
OH. AND ONE MORE THING ABOUT NIZUMA...
HE MENTIONED HE'LL HAVE HIS NEW WORK READY TO SHOW ME BEFORE I STEP DOWN.
!
KATMP...
EIJI'S FINALLY DOING A NEW SERIES...
NIZUMA
Eiji Co., Ltd.
HEY, NIZUMA.
I KNOW YOU SAID THAT TO THE EDITOR IN CHIEF, BUT... YOU DON'T ACTUALLY HAVE ANYTHING LINED UP YET, DO YOU?
SHF SHF
SKRT SKRT
NOPE. I'VE ALREADY FIGURED OUT WHAT I'M GONNA DO.
WHAT?
BAM
THIS TIME... I'LL COME UP WITH A SUPER COOL, DARK HERO!

OHBA'S STORYBOARD

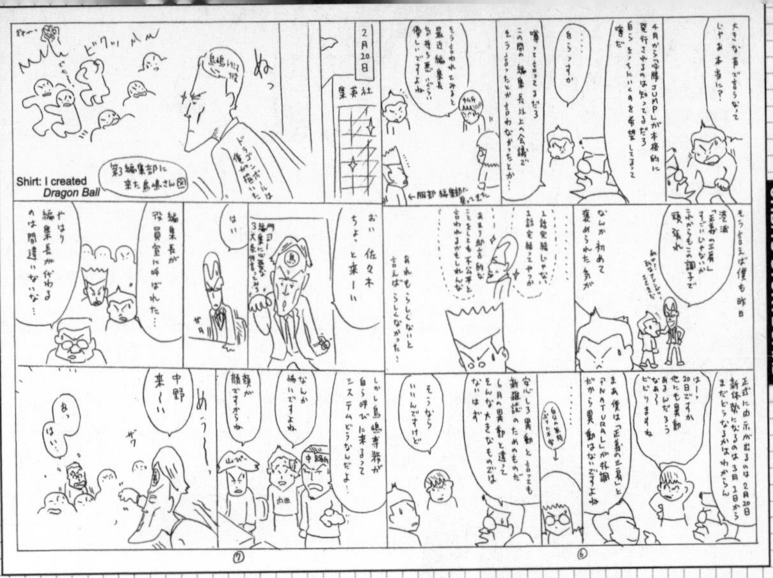
Shirt: I created
Dragon Ball

OBATA'S STORYBOARD

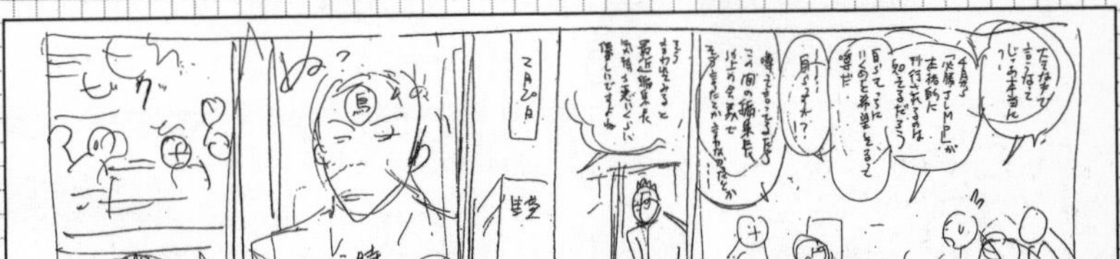

COMPLETE!

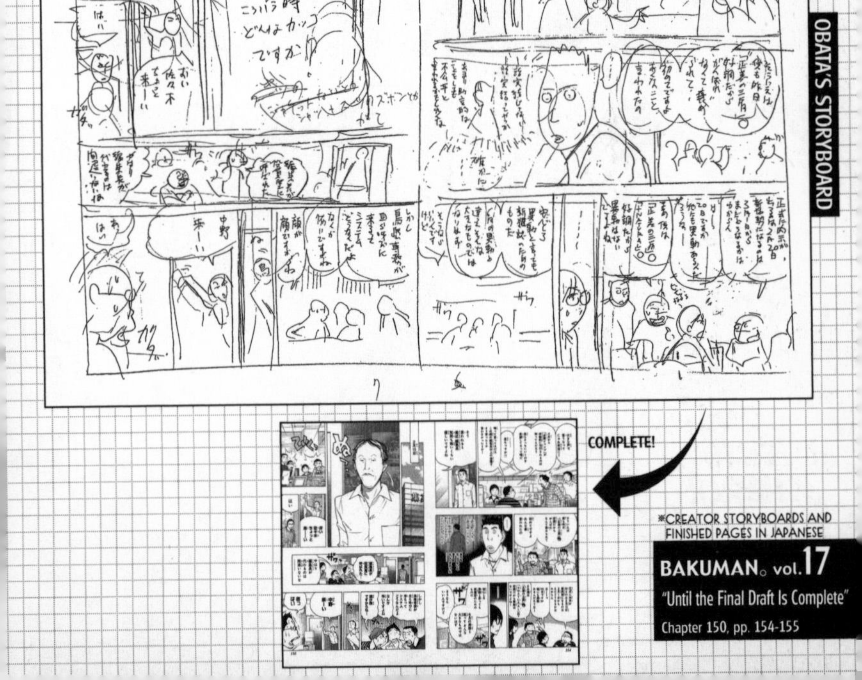

※CREATOR STORYBOARDS AND FINISHED PAGES IN JAPANESE

BAKUMAN。 vol.17

"Until the Final Draft Is Complete"

Chapter 150, pp. 154-155

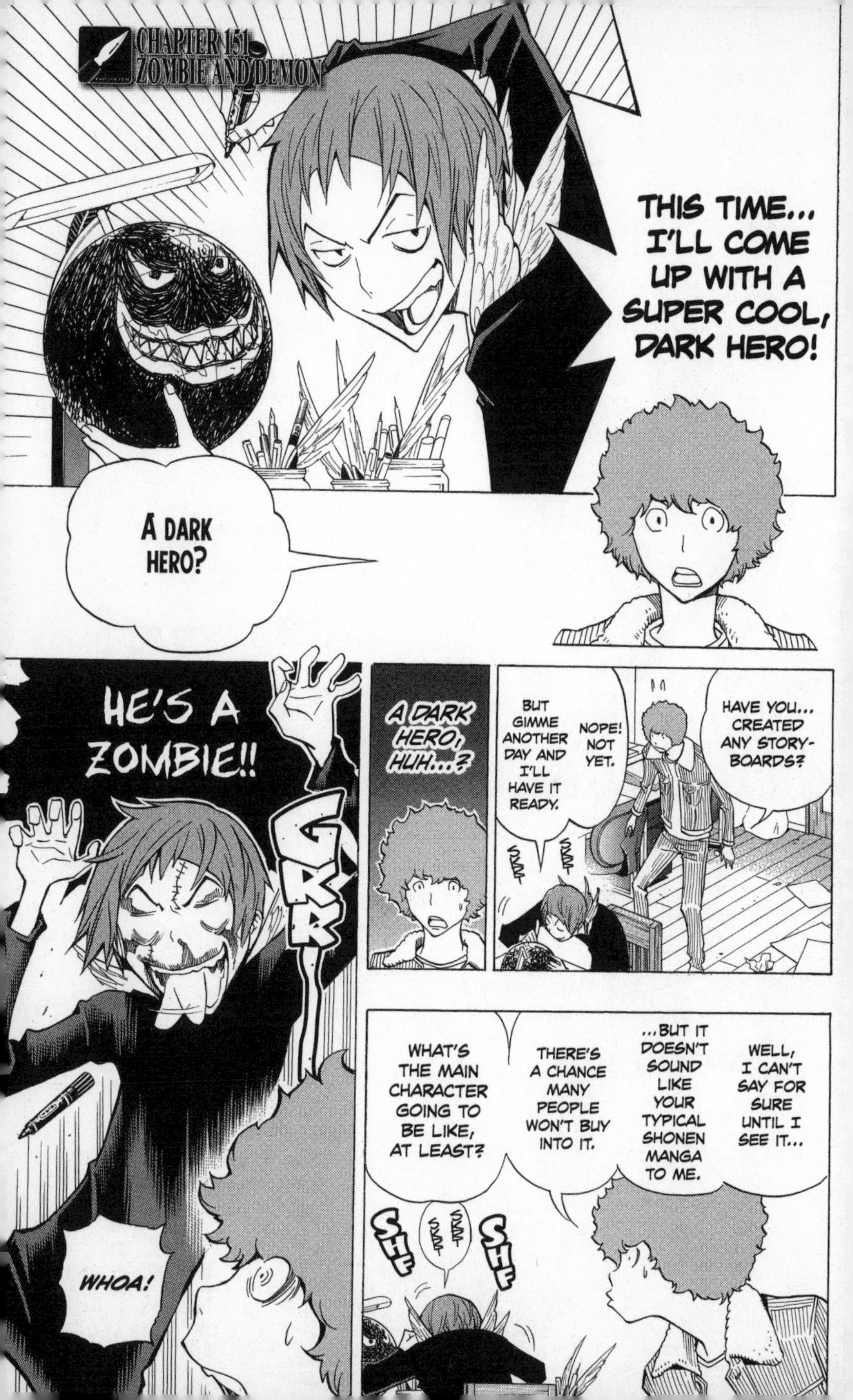
CHAPTER 151: ZOMBIE AND DEMON
THIS TIME... I'LL COME UP WITH A SUPER COOL, DARK HERO!
A DARK HERO?
HAVE YOU... CREATED ANY STORY-BOARDS?
NOPE! NOT YET.
BUT GIMME ANOTHER DAY AND I'LL HAVE IT READY.
SKRT
SKRT
A DARK HERO, HUH...?
WELL, I CAN'T SAY FOR SURE UNTIL I SEE IT...
...BUT IT DOESN'T SOUND LIKE YOUR TYPICAL SHONEN MANGA TO ME.
THERE'S A CHANCE MANY PEOPLE WON'T BUY INTO IT.
WHAT'S THE MAIN CHARACTER GOING TO BE LIKE, AT LEAST?
SHF
SKRT SKRT
SHF
HE'S A ZOMBIE!!
GRR
WHOA!

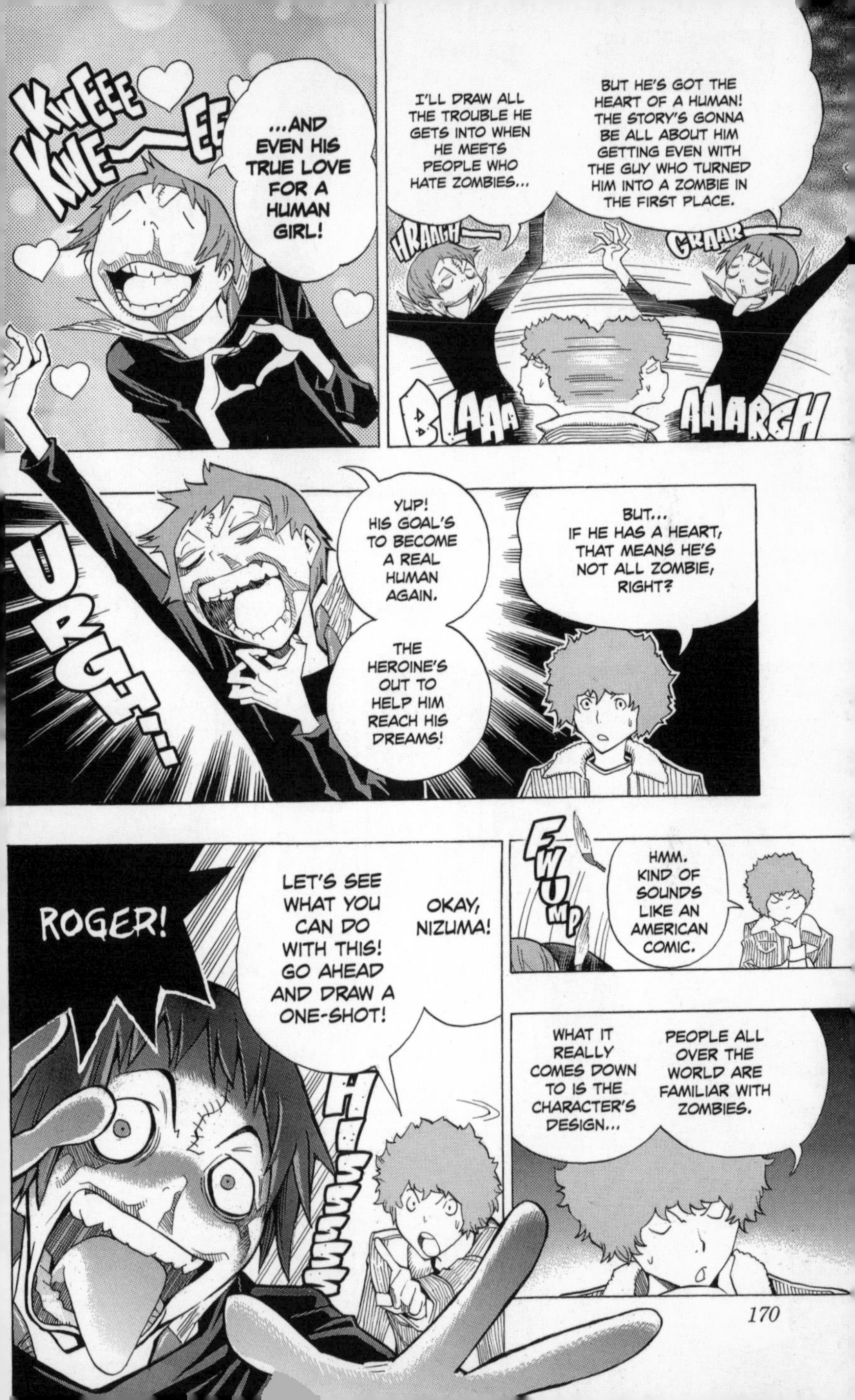
I'LL DRAW ALL THE TROUBLE HE GETS INTO WHEN HE MEETS PEOPLE WHO HATE ZOMBIES... BUT HE'S GOT THE HEART OF A HUMAN! THE STORY'S GONNA BE ALL ABOUT HIM GETTING EVEN WITH THE GUY WHO TURNED HIM INTO A ZOMBIE IN THE FIRST PLACE.
GRAAR
HRAAGH
AAARGH
BLAAA
KWEEE KWE—EE
...AND EVEN HIS TRUE LOVE FOR A HUMAN GIRL!
BUT... IF HE HAS A HEART, THAT MEANS HE'S NOT ALL ZOMBIE, RIGHT?
YUP! HIS GOAL'S TO BECOME A REAL HUMAN AGAIN.
THE HEROINE'S OUT TO HELP HIM REACH HIS DREAMS!
URGH...
HMM. KIND OF SOUNDS LIKE AN AMERICAN COMIC.
FWUMP
PEOPLE ALL OVER THE WORLD ARE FAMILIAR WITH ZOMBIES.
WHAT IT REALLY COMES DOWN TO IS THE CHARACTER'S DESIGN...
OKAY, NIZUMA!
LET'S SEE WHAT YOU CAN DO WITH THIS! GO AHEAD AND DRAW A ONE-SHOT!
HISSSS
ROGER!

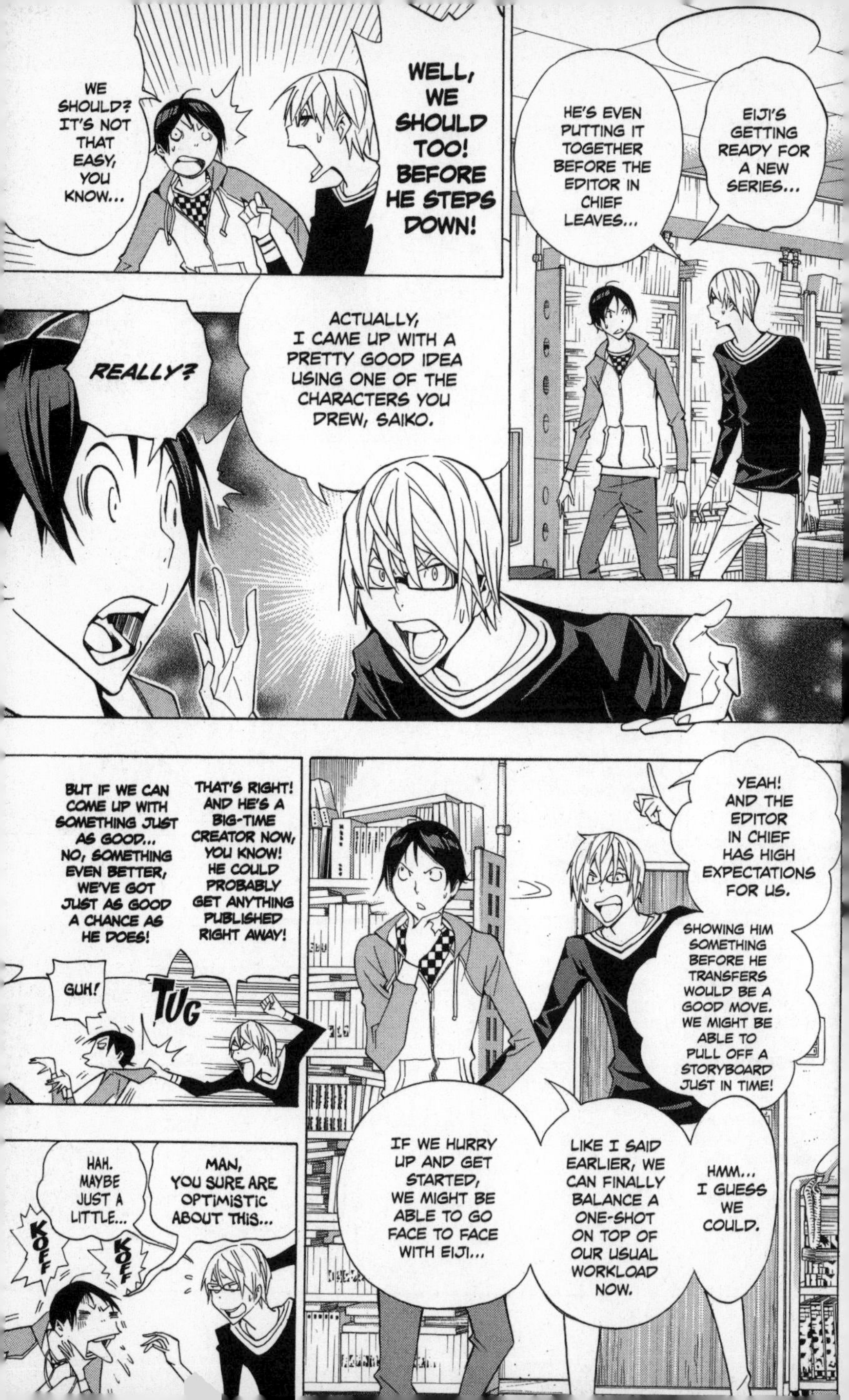
EIJI'S GETTING READY FOR A NEW SERIES...
HE'S EVEN PUTTING IT TOGETHER BEFORE THE EDITOR IN CHIEF LEAVES...
WELL, WE SHOULD TOO! BEFORE HE STEPS DOWN!
WE SHOULD? IT'S NOT THAT EASY, YOU KNOW...
ACTUALLY, I CAME UP WITH A PRETTY GOOD IDEA USING ONE OF THE CHARACTERS YOU DREW, SAIKO.
REALLY?
YEAH! AND THE EDITOR IN CHIEF HAS HIGH EXPECTATIONS FOR US.
SHOWING HIM SOMETHING BEFORE HE TRANSFERS WOULD BE A GOOD MOVE. WE MIGHT BE ABLE TO PULL OFF A STORYBOARD JUST IN TIME!
HMM... I GUESS WE COULD.
LIKE I SAID EARLIER, WE CAN FINALLY BALANCE A ONE-SHOT ON TOP OF OUR USUAL WORKLOAD NOW.
IF WE HURRY UP AND GET STARTED, WE MIGHT BE ABLE TO GO FACE TO FACE WITH EIJI...
THAT'S RIGHT! AND HE'S A BIG-TIME CREATOR NOW, YOU KNOW! HE COULD PROBABLY GET ANYTHING PUBLISHED RIGHT AWAY!
BUT IF WE CAN COME UP WITH SOMETHING JUST AS GOOD... NO, SOMETHING EVEN BETTER, WE'VE GOT JUST AS GOOD A CHANCE AS HE DOES!
TUG
GUH!
MAN, YOU SURE ARE OPTIMISTIC ABOUT THIS...
HAH. MAYBE JUST A LITTLE...
KOFF
KOFF

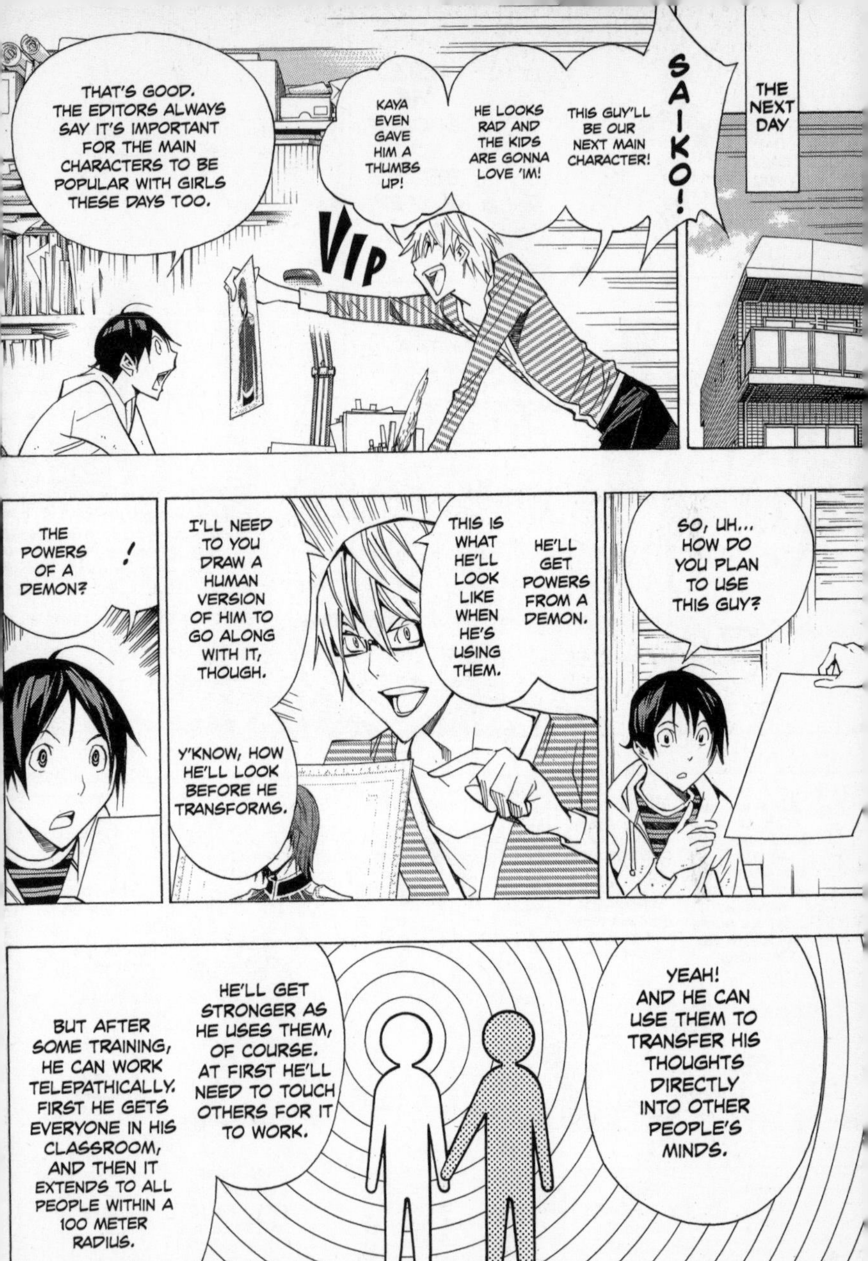
THE NEXT DAY
SAIKO!
THIS GUY'LL BE OUR NEXT MAIN CHARACTER!
HE LOOKS RAD AND THE KIDS ARE GONNA LOVE 'IM!
KAYA EVEN GAVE HIM A THUMBS UP!
VIP
THAT'S GOOD. THE EDITORS ALWAYS SAY IT'S IMPORTANT FOR THE MAIN CHARACTERS TO BE POPULAR WITH GIRLS THESE DAYS TOO.
SO, UH... HOW DO YOU PLAN TO USE THIS GUY?
HE'LL GET POWERS FROM A DEMON.
THIS IS WHAT HE'LL LOOK LIKE WHEN HE'S USING THEM.
I'LL NEED TO YOU DRAW A HUMAN VERSION OF HIM TO GO ALONG WITH IT, THOUGH.
Y'KNOW, HOW HE'LL LOOK BEFORE HE TRANSFORMS.
!
THE POWERS OF A DEMON?
YEAH! AND HE CAN USE THEM TO TRANSFER HIS THOUGHTS DIRECTLY INTO OTHER PEOPLE'S MINDS.
HE'LL GET STRONGER AS HE USES THEM, OF COURSE. AT FIRST HE'LL NEED TO TOUCH OTHERS FOR IT TO WORK.
BUT AFTER SOME TRAINING, HE CAN WORK TELEPATHICALLY. FIRST HE GETS EVERYONE IN HIS CLASSROOM, AND THEN IT EXTENDS TO ALL PEOPLE WITHIN A 100 METER RADIUS.

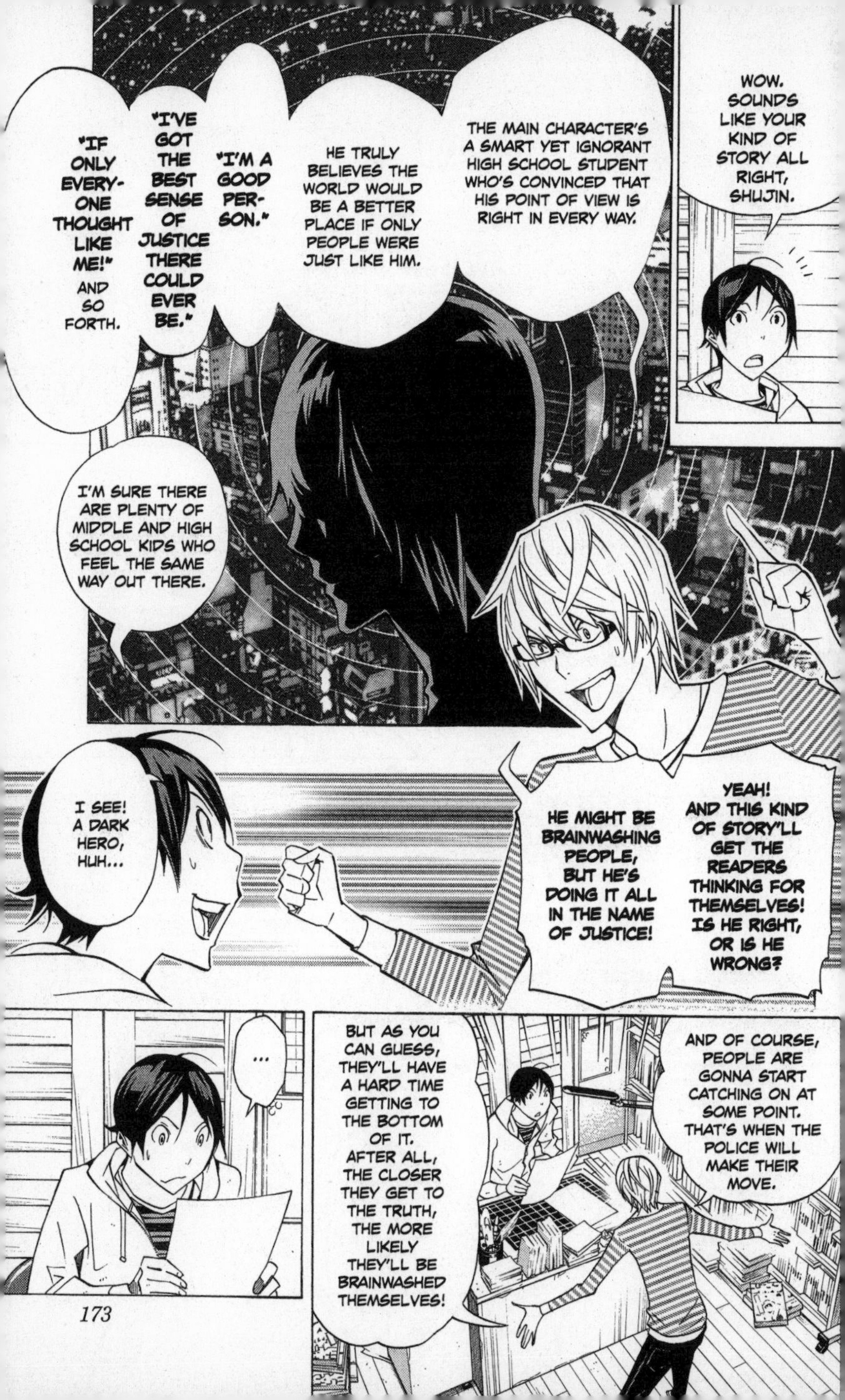
WOW. SOUNDS LIKE YOUR KIND OF STORY ALL RIGHT, SHUJIN.
THE MAIN CHARACTER'S A SMART YET IGNORANT HIGH SCHOOL STUDENT WHO'S CONVINCED THAT HIS POINT OF VIEW IS RIGHT IN EVERY WAY.
HE TRULY BELIEVES THE WORLD WOULD BE A BETTER PLACE IF ONLY PEOPLE WERE JUST LIKE HIM.
"I'M A GOOD PERSON."
"I'VE GOT THE BEST SENSE OF JUSTICE THERE COULD EVER BE."
"IF ONLY EVERYONE THOUGHT LIKE ME!" AND SO FORTH.
I'M SURE THERE ARE PLENTY OF MIDDLE AND HIGH SCHOOL KIDS WHO FEEL THE SAME WAY OUT THERE.
YEAH! AND THIS KIND OF STORY'LL GET THE READERS THINKING FOR THEMSELVES! IS HE RIGHT, OR IS HE WRONG?
HE MIGHT BE BRAINWASHING PEOPLE, BUT HE'S DOING IT ALL IN THE NAME OF JUSTICE!
I SEE! A DARK HERO, HUH...
AND OF COURSE, PEOPLE ARE GONNA START CATCHING ON AT SOME POINT. THAT'S WHEN THE POLICE WILL MAKE THEIR MOVE.
BUT AS YOU CAN GUESS, THEY'LL HAVE A HARD TIME GETTING TO THE BOTTOM OF IT. AFTER ALL, THE CLOSER THEY GET TO THE TRUTH, THE MORE LIKELY THEY'LL BE BRAINWASHED THEMSELVES!
...

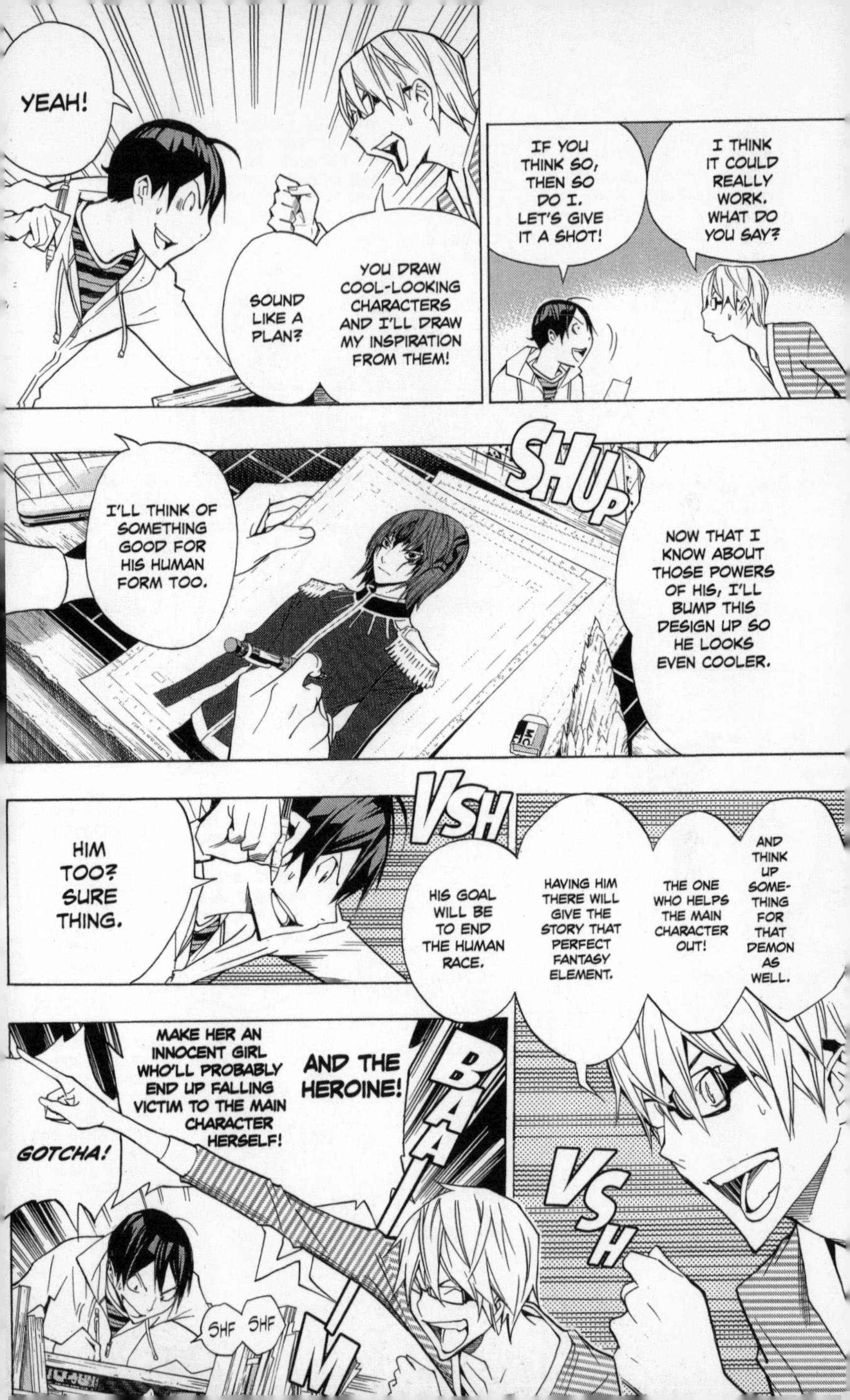
I THINK IT COULD REALLY WORK. WHAT DO YOU SAY?
IF YOU THINK SO, THEN SO DO I. LET'S GIVE IT A SHOT!
YOU DRAW COOL-LOOKING CHARACTERS AND I'LL DRAW MY INSPIRATION FROM THEM!
SOUND LIKE A PLAN?
YEAH!
SHUP
NOW THAT I KNOW ABOUT THOSE POWERS OF HIS, I'LL BUMP THIS DESIGN UP SO HE LOOKS EVEN COOLER.
I'LL THINK OF SOMETHING GOOD FOR HIS HUMAN FORM TOO.
VSH
AND THINK UP SOME-THING FOR THAT DEMON AS WELL.
THE ONE WHO HELPS THE MAIN CHARACTER OUT!
HAVING HIM THERE WILL GIVE THE STORY THAT PERFECT FANTASY ELEMENT.
HIS GOAL WILL BE TO END THE HUMAN RACE.
HIM TOO? SURE THING.
VSH
BAAAM
AND THE HEROINE!
MAKE HER AN INNOCENT GIRL WHO'LL PROBABLY END UP FALLING VICTIM TO THE MAIN CHARACTER HERSELF!
GOTCHA!
SHF SHF

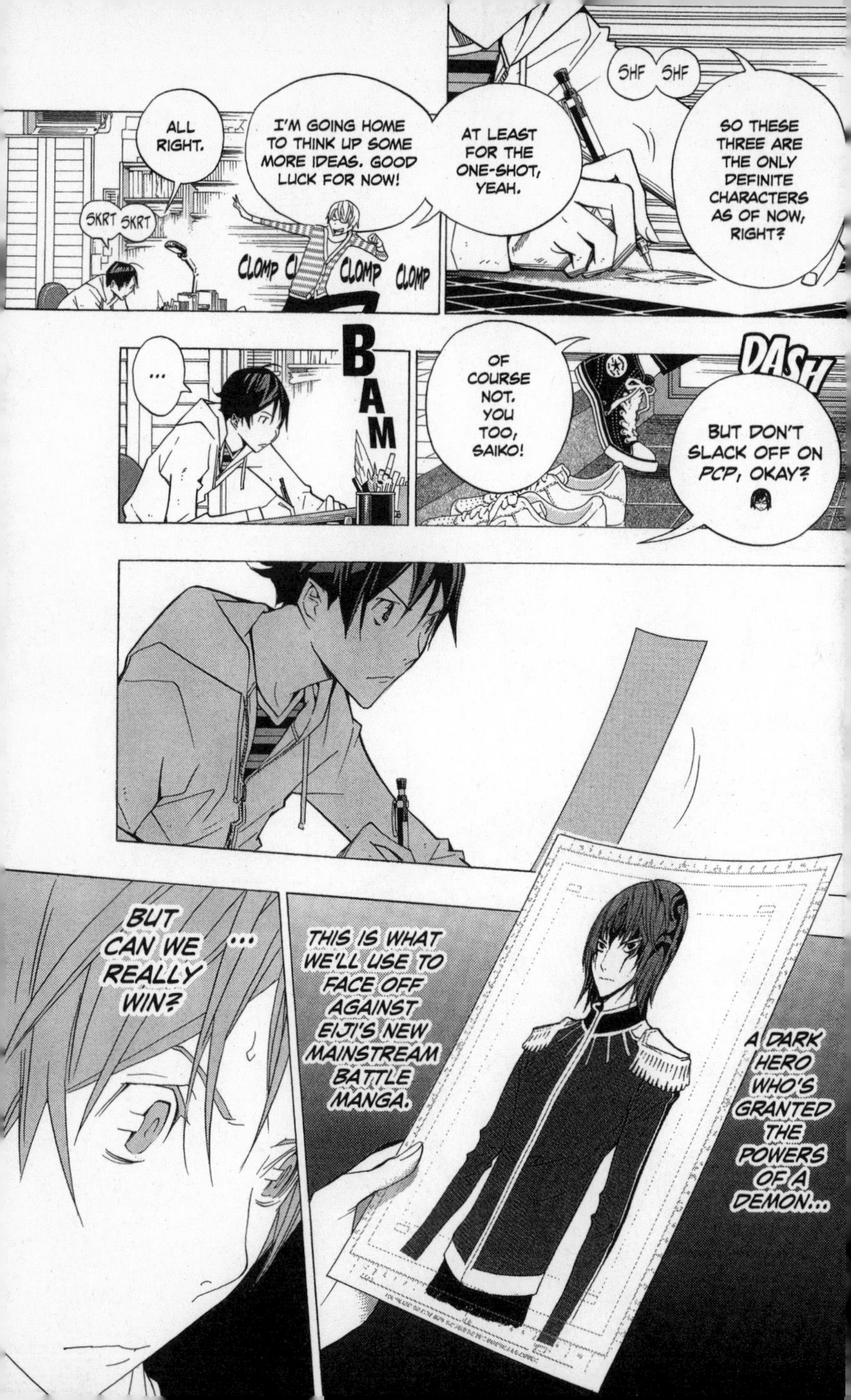
SHF SHF
SO THESE THREE ARE THE ONLY DEFINITE CHARACTERS AS OF NOW, RIGHT?
AT LEAST FOR THE ONE-SHOT, YEAH.
I'M GOING HOME TO THINK UP SOME MORE IDEAS. GOOD LUCK FOR NOW!
CLOMP CL CLOMP CLOMP
ALL RIGHT.
SKRT SKRT
DASH
BUT DON'T SLACK OFF ON PCP, OKAY?
OF COURSE NOT. YOU TOO, SAIKO!
BAM
...
A DARK HERO WHO'S GRANTED THE POWERS OF A DEMON...
THIS IS WHAT WE'LL USE TO FACE OFF AGAINST EIJI'S NEW MAINSTREAM BATTLE MANGA.
...
BUT CAN WE REALLY WIN?

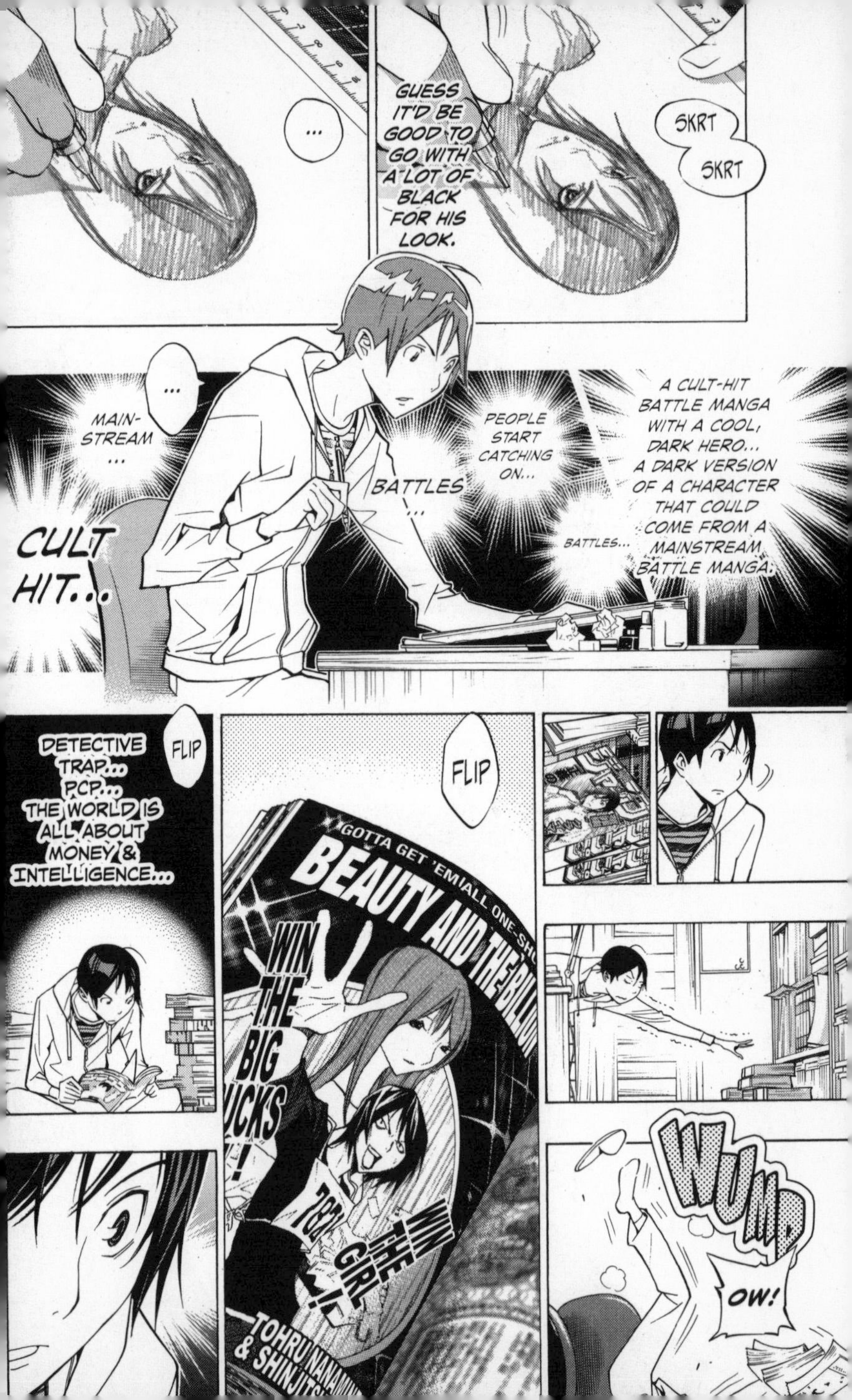
GUESS IT'D BE GOOD TO GO WITH A LOT OF BLACK FOR HIS LOOK.
SKRT
SKRT
...
A CULT-HIT BATTLE MANGA WITH A COOL, DARK HERO... A DARK VERSION OF A CHARACTER THAT COULD COME FROM A MAINSTREAM BATTLE MANGA.
BATTLES...
PEOPLE START CATCHING ON...
BATTLES ...
...
MAIN-STREAM ...
CULT HIT...
WUMP
OW!
FLIP
GOTTA GET 'EM ALL
BEAUTY AND THE
WIN THE BIG BUCKS!
WIN THE GIRL!
FLIP
DETECTIVE TRAP... PCP... THE WORLD IS ALL ABOUT MONEY & INTELLIGENCE...

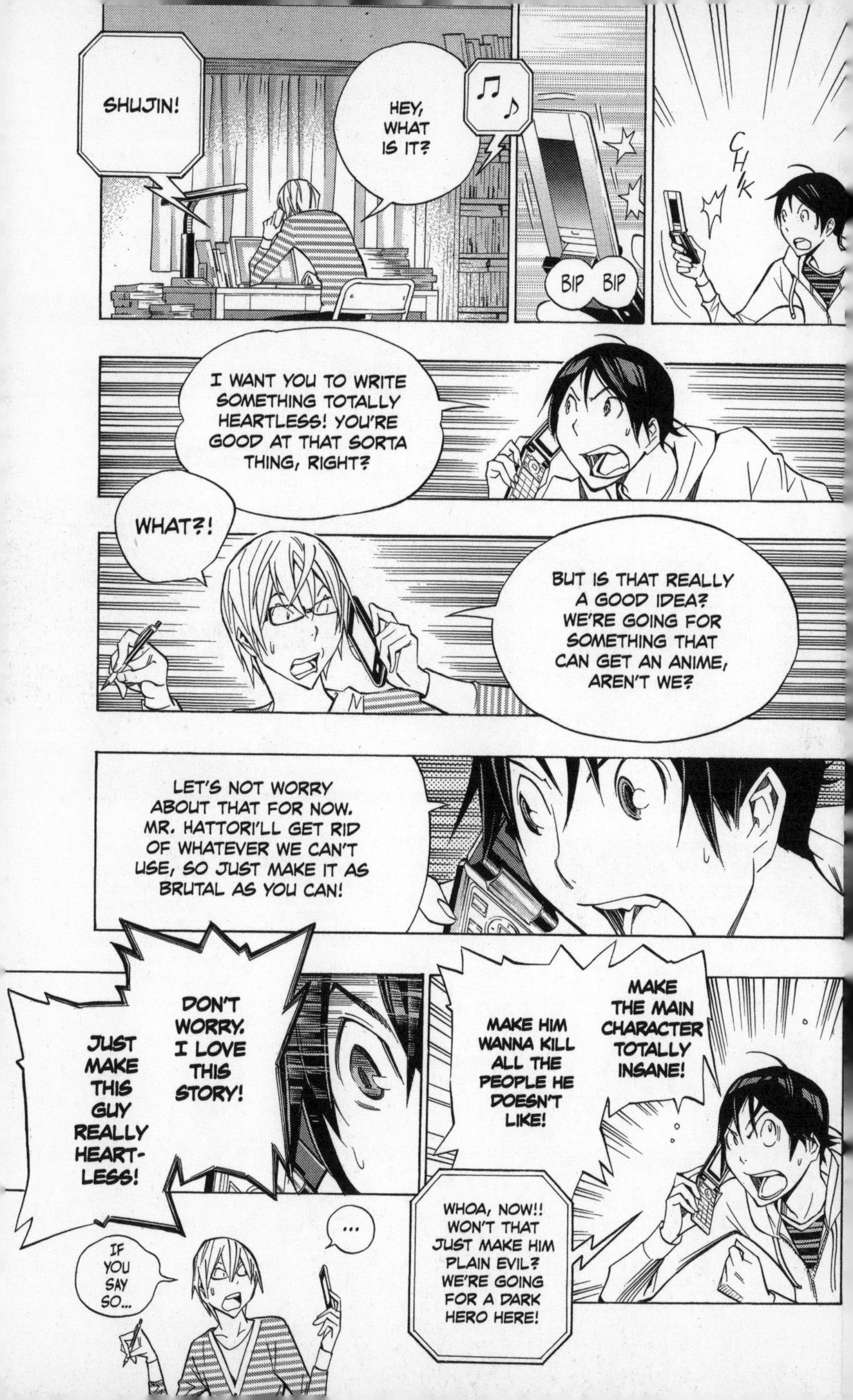
CHIK
♫ ♪
BIP BIP
SHUJIN!
HEY, WHAT IS IT?
I WANT YOU TO WRITE SOMETHING TOTALLY HEARTLESS! YOU'RE GOOD AT THAT SORTA THING, RIGHT?
WHAT?!
BUT IS THAT REALLY A GOOD IDEA? WE'RE GOING FOR SOMETHING THAT CAN GET AN ANIME, AREN'T WE?
LET'S NOT WORRY ABOUT THAT FOR NOW. MR. HATTORI'LL GET RID OF WHATEVER WE CAN'T USE, SO JUST MAKE IT AS BRUTAL AS YOU CAN!
MAKE THE MAIN CHARACTER TOTALLY INSANE!
MAKE HIM WANNA KILL ALL THE PEOPLE HE DOESN'T LIKE!
WHOA, NOW!! WON'T THAT JUST MAKE HIM PLAIN EVIL? WE'RE GOING FOR A DARK HERO HERE!
DON'T WORRY. I LOVE THIS STORY!
JUST MAKE THIS GUY REALLY HEART-LESS!
...
IF YOU SAY SO...

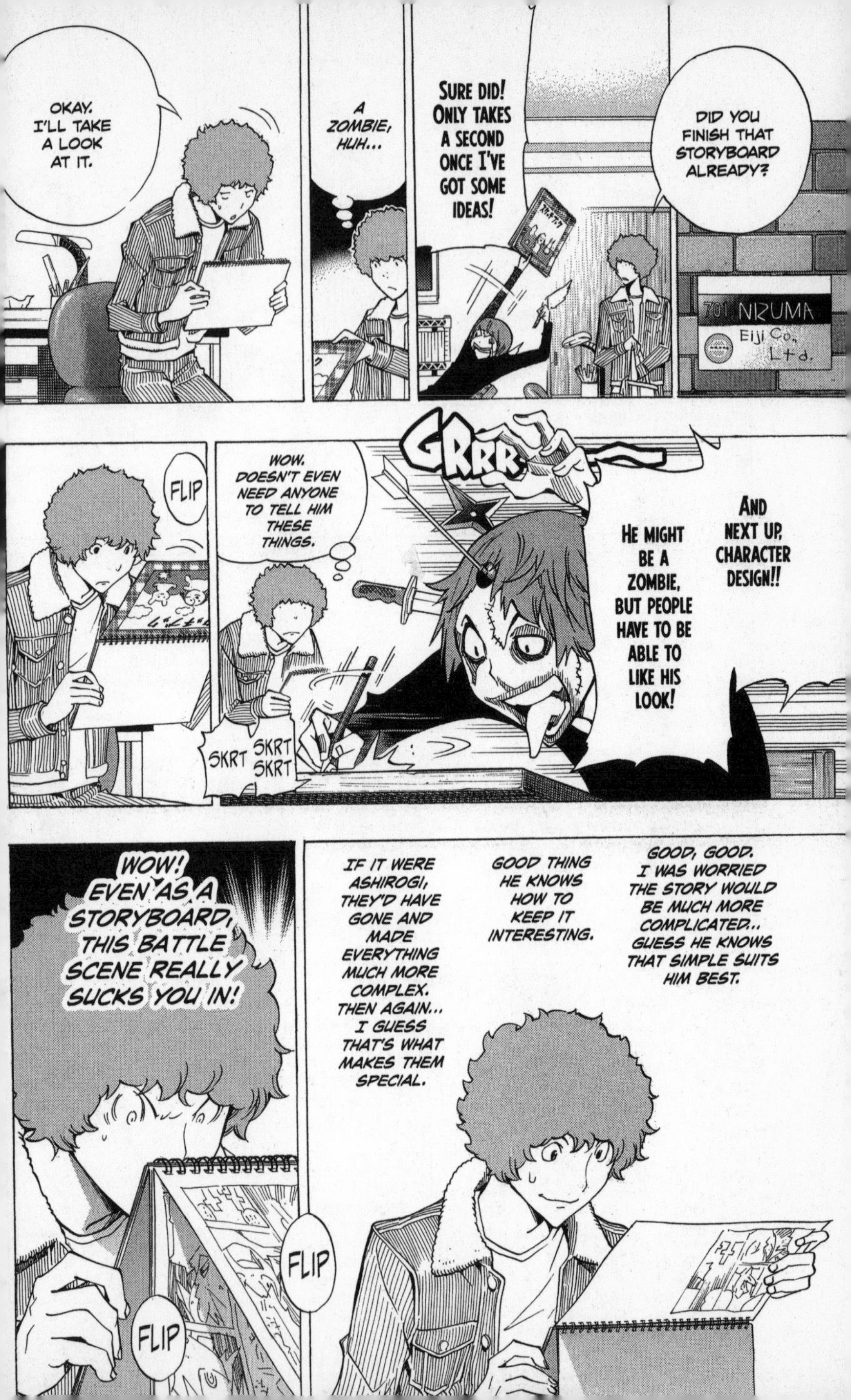
DID YOU FINISH THAT STORYBOARD ALREADY?
701 NIZUMA
Eiji Co., Ltd.
SURE DID! ONLY TAKES A SECOND ONCE I'VE GOT SOME IDEAS!
A ZOMBIE, HUH...
OKAY. I'LL TAKE A LOOK AT IT.
GRRR
AND NEXT UP, CHARACTER DESIGN!!
HE MIGHT BE A ZOMBIE, BUT PEOPLE HAVE TO BE ABLE TO LIKE HIS LOOK!
WOW. DOESN'T EVEN NEED ANYONE TO TELL HIM THESE THINGS.
SKRT SKRT
SKRT
FLIP
GOOD, GOOD. I WAS WORRIED THE STORY WOULD BE MUCH MORE COMPLICATED... GUESS HE KNOWS THAT SIMPLE SUITS HIM BEST.
GOOD THING HE KNOWS HOW TO KEEP IT INTERESTING.
IF IT WERE ASHIROGI, THEY'D HAVE GONE AND MADE EVERYTHING MUCH MORE COMPLEX. THEN AGAIN... I GUESS THAT'S WHAT MAKES THEM SPECIAL.
FLIP
WOW! EVEN AS A STORYBOARD, THIS BATTLE SCENE REALLY SUCKS YOU IN!
FLIP

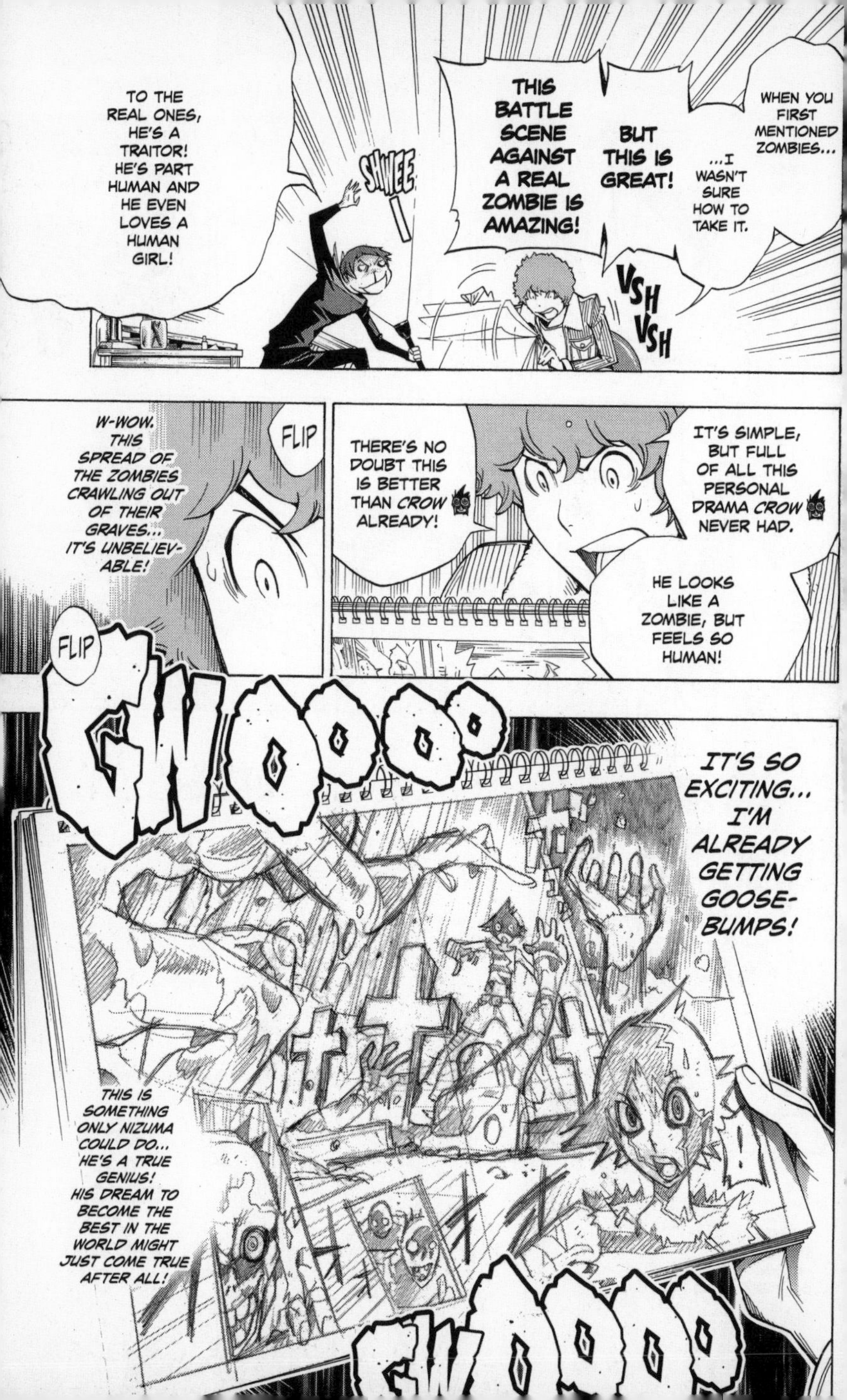
WHEN YOU FIRST MENTIONED ZOMBIES...
...I WASN'T SURE HOW TO TAKE IT.
VSH VSH
BUT THIS IS GREAT!
THIS BATTLE SCENE AGAINST A REAL ZOMBIE IS AMAZING!
SHWEE
TO THE REAL ONES, HE'S A TRAITOR! HE'S PART HUMAN AND HE EVEN LOVES A HUMAN GIRL!
IT'S SIMPLE, BUT FULL OF ALL THIS PERSONAL DRAMA *CROW* NEVER HAD.
HE LOOKS LIKE A ZOMBIE, BUT FEELS SO HUMAN!
THERE'S NO DOUBT THIS IS BETTER THAN *CROW* ALREADY!
FLIP
W-WOW. THIS SPREAD OF THE ZOMBIES CRAWLING OUT OF THEIR GRAVES... IT'S UNBELIEVABLE!
FLIP
GWOOOO
IT'S SO EXCITING... I'M ALREADY GETTING GOOSEBUMPS!
THIS IS SOMETHING ONLY NIZUMA COULD DO... HE'S A TRUE GENIUS! HIS DREAM TO BECOME THE BEST IN THE WORLD MIGHT JUST COME TRUE AFTER ALL!
GWOOOOO

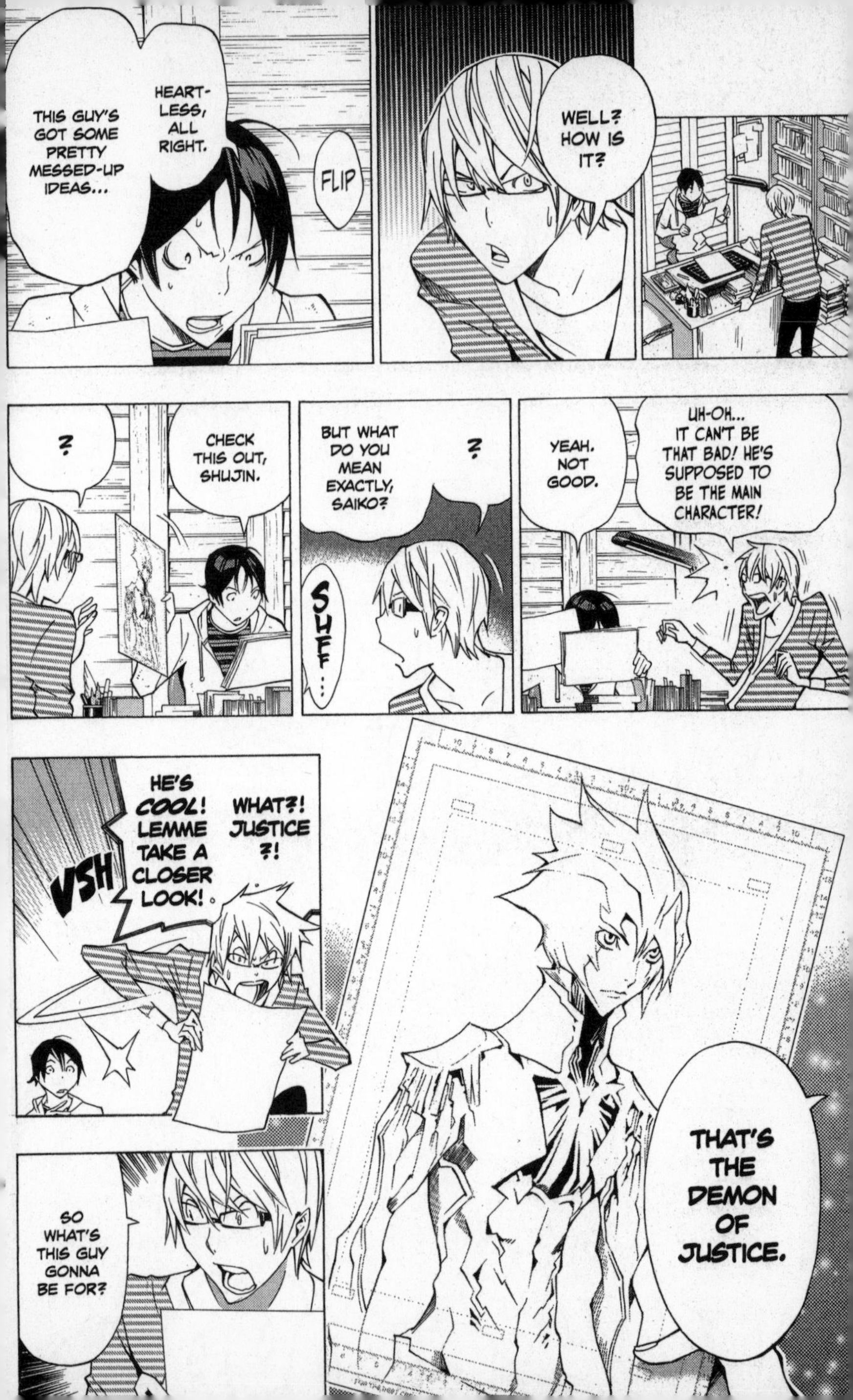
WELL? HOW IS IT?
FLIP
HEART-LESS, ALL RIGHT.
THIS GUY'S GOT SOME PRETTY MESSED-UP IDEAS...
UH-OH... IT CAN'T BE THAT BAD! HE'S SUPPOSED TO BE THE MAIN CHARACTER!
YEAH. NOT GOOD.
?
BUT WHAT DO YOU MEAN EXACTLY, SAIKO?
SHUFF...
CHECK THIS OUT, SHUJIN.
?
THAT'S THE DEMON OF JUSTICE.
WHAT?! JUSTICE?!
HE'S COOL! LEMME TAKE A CLOSER LOOK!
VSH
SO WHAT'S THIS GUY GONNA BE FOR?

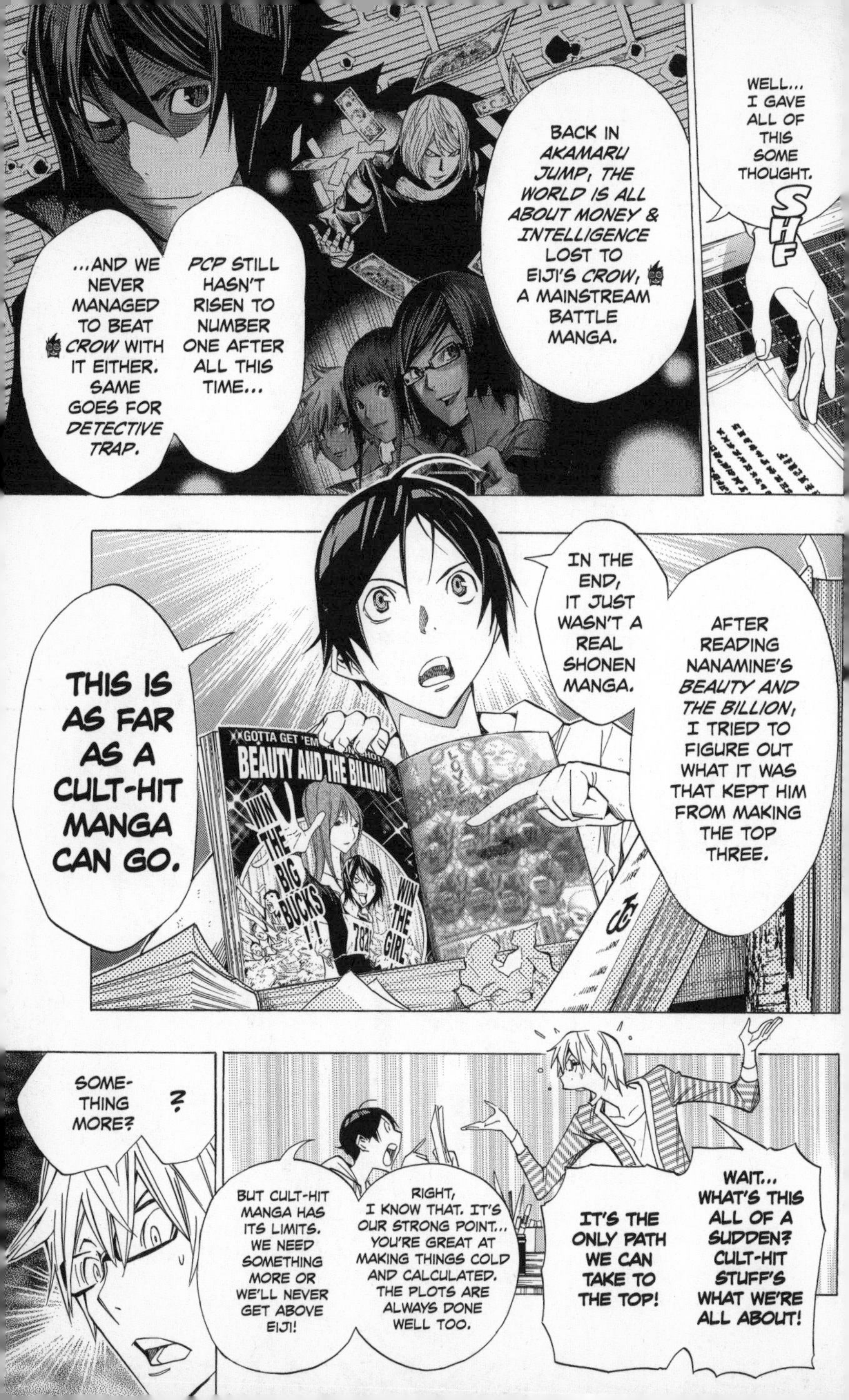
WELL... I GAVE ALL OF THIS SOME THOUGHT.
SHF
BACK IN AKAMARU JUMP, THE WORLD IS ALL ABOUT MONEY & INTELLIGENCE LOST TO EIJI'S CROW, A MAINSTREAM BATTLE MANGA.
PCP STILL HASN'T RISEN TO NUMBER ONE AFTER ALL THIS TIME...
...AND WE NEVER MANAGED TO BEAT CROW WITH IT EITHER. SAME GOES FOR DETECTIVE TRAP.
AFTER READING NANAMINE'S BEAUTY AND THE BILLION, I TRIED TO FIGURE OUT WHAT IT WAS THAT KEPT HIM FROM MAKING THE TOP THREE.
IN THE END, IT JUST WASN'T A REAL SHONEN MANGA.
BEAUTY AND THE BILLION
WIN THE BIG BUCKS!!
WIN THE GIRL
THIS IS AS FAR AS A CULT-HIT MANGA CAN GO.
WAIT... WHAT'S THIS ALL OF A SUDDEN? CULT-HIT STUFF'S WHAT WE'RE ALL ABOUT!
IT'S THE ONLY PATH WE CAN TAKE TO THE TOP!
RIGHT, I KNOW THAT. IT'S OUR STRONG POINT... YOU'RE GREAT AT MAKING THINGS COLD AND CALCULATED. THE PLOTS ARE ALWAYS DONE WELL TOO.
BUT CULT-HIT MANGA HAS ITS LIMITS. WE NEED SOMETHING MORE OR WE'LL NEVER GET ABOVE EIJI!
SOME-THING MORE?
?

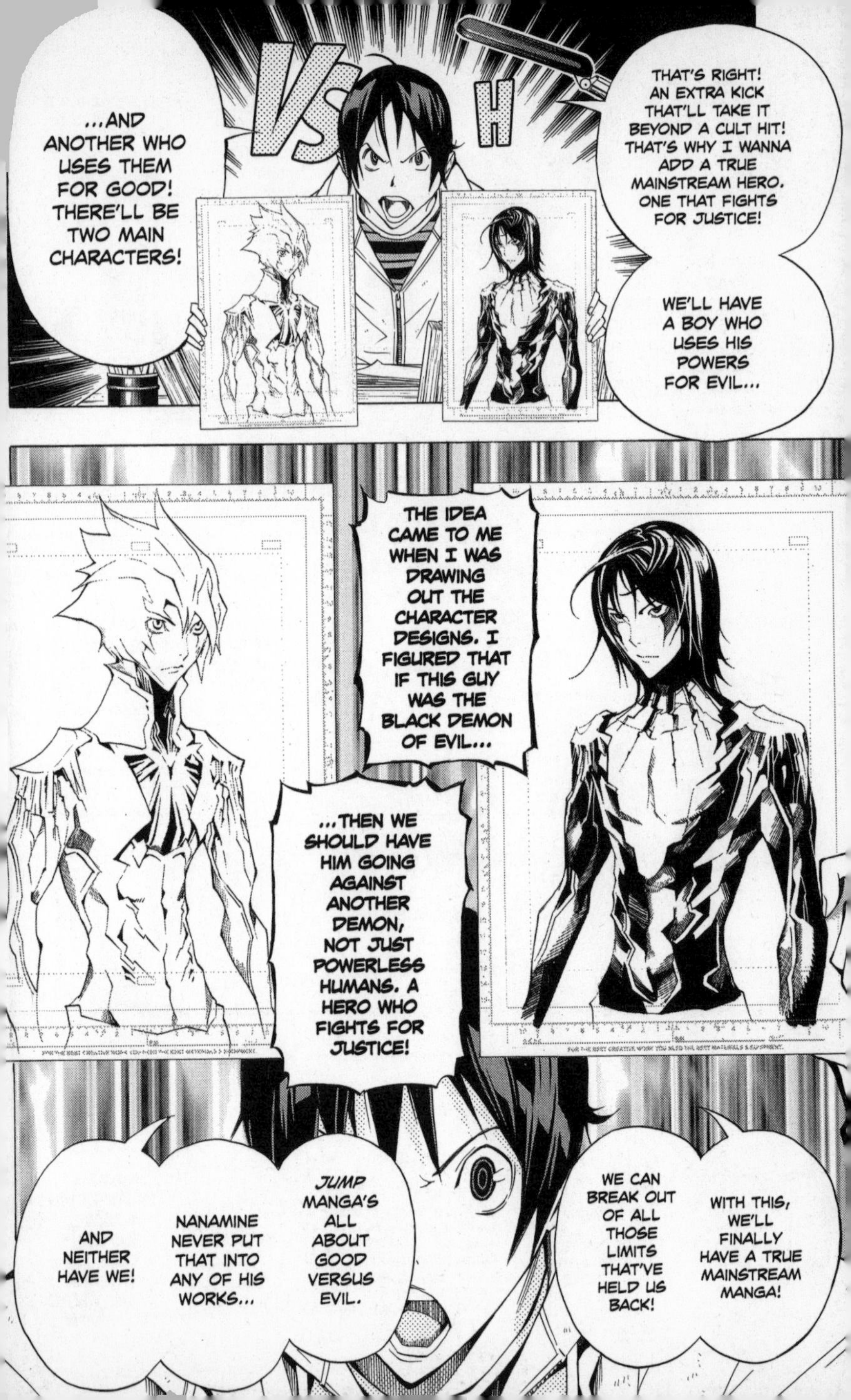
THAT'S RIGHT! AN EXTRA KICK THAT'LL TAKE IT BEYOND A CULT HIT! THAT'S WHY I WANNA ADD A TRUE MAINSTREAM HERO. ONE THAT FIGHTS FOR JUSTICE!
WE'LL HAVE A BOY WHO USES HIS POWERS FOR EVIL...
...AND ANOTHER WHO USES THEM FOR GOOD! THERE'LL BE TWO MAIN CHARACTERS!
THE IDEA CAME TO ME WHEN I WAS DRAWING OUT THE CHARACTER DESIGNS. I FIGURED THAT IF THIS GUY WAS THE BLACK DEMON OF EVIL...
...THEN WE SHOULD HAVE HIM GOING AGAINST ANOTHER DEMON, NOT JUST POWERLESS HUMANS. A HERO WHO FIGHTS FOR JUSTICE!
WITH THIS, WE'LL FINALLY HAVE A TRUE MAINSTREAM MANGA!
WE CAN BREAK OUT OF ALL THOSE LIMITS THAT'VE HELD US BACK!
JUMP MANGA'S ALL ABOUT GOOD VERSUS EVIL.
NANAMINE NEVER PUT THAT INTO ANY OF HIS WORKS...
AND NEITHER HAVE WE!

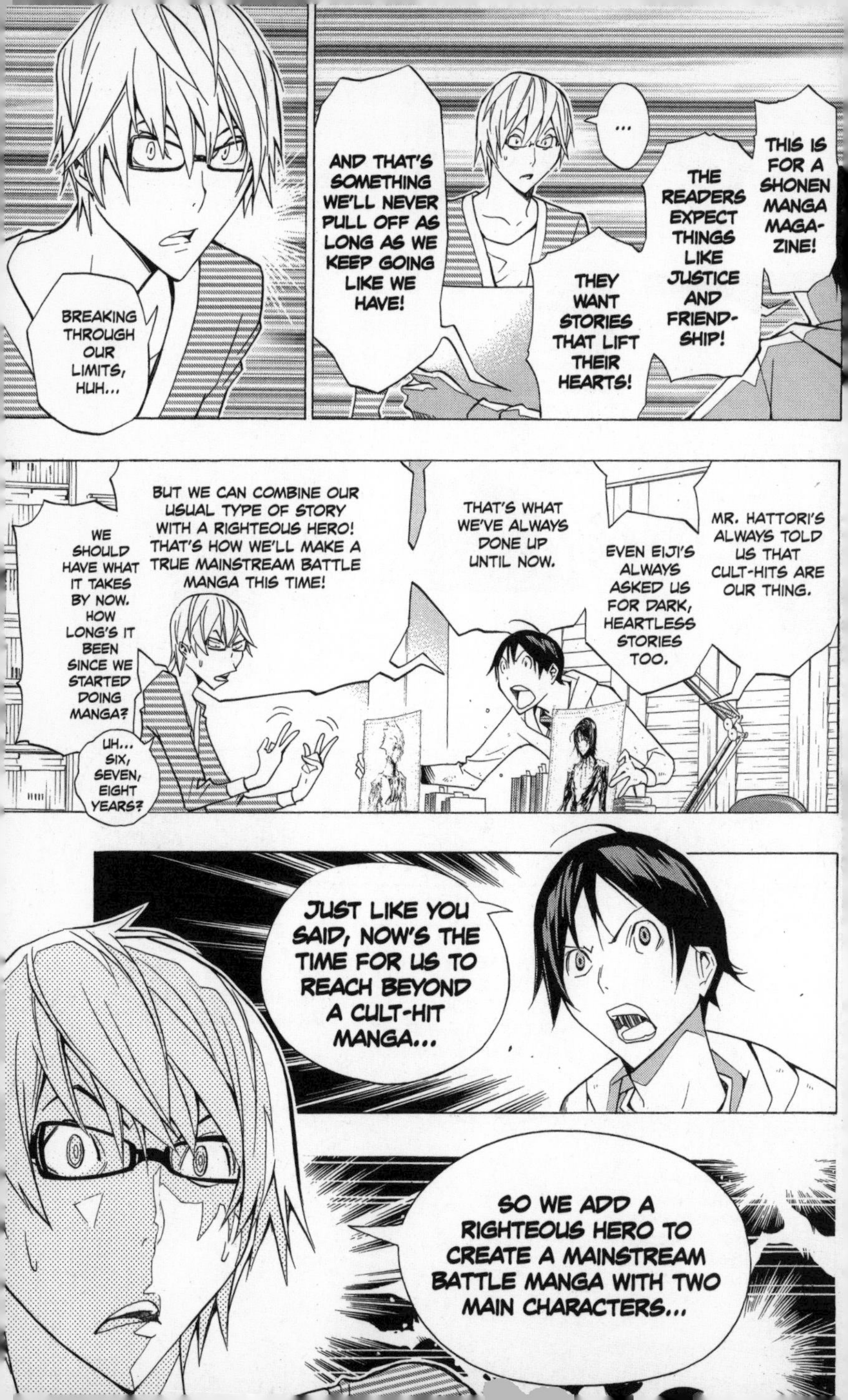
THIS IS FOR A SHONEN MANGA MAGAZINE!
THE READERS EXPECT THINGS LIKE JUSTICE AND FRIENDSHIP!
THEY WANT STORIES THAT LIFT THEIR HEARTS!
...
AND THAT'S SOMETHING WE'LL NEVER PULL OFF AS LONG AS WE KEEP GOING LIKE WE HAVE!
BREAKING THROUGH OUR LIMITS, HUH...
MR. HATTORI'S ALWAYS TOLD US THAT CULT-HITS ARE OUR THING.
EVEN EIJI'S ALWAYS ASKED US FOR DARK, HEARTLESS STORIES TOO.
THAT'S WHAT WE'VE ALWAYS DONE UP UNTIL NOW.
BUT WE CAN COMBINE OUR USUAL TYPE OF STORY WITH A RIGHTEOUS HERO! THAT'S HOW WE'LL MAKE A TRUE MAINSTREAM BATTLE MANGA THIS TIME!
WE SHOULD HAVE WHAT IT TAKES BY NOW. HOW LONG'S IT BEEN SINCE WE STARTED DOING MANGA?
UH... SIX, SEVEN, EIGHT YEARS?
JUST LIKE YOU SAID, NOW'S THE TIME FOR US TO REACH BEYOND A CULT-HIT MANGA...
SO WE ADD A RIGHTEOUS HERO TO CREATE A MAINSTREAM BATTLE MANGA WITH TWO MAIN CHARACTERS...

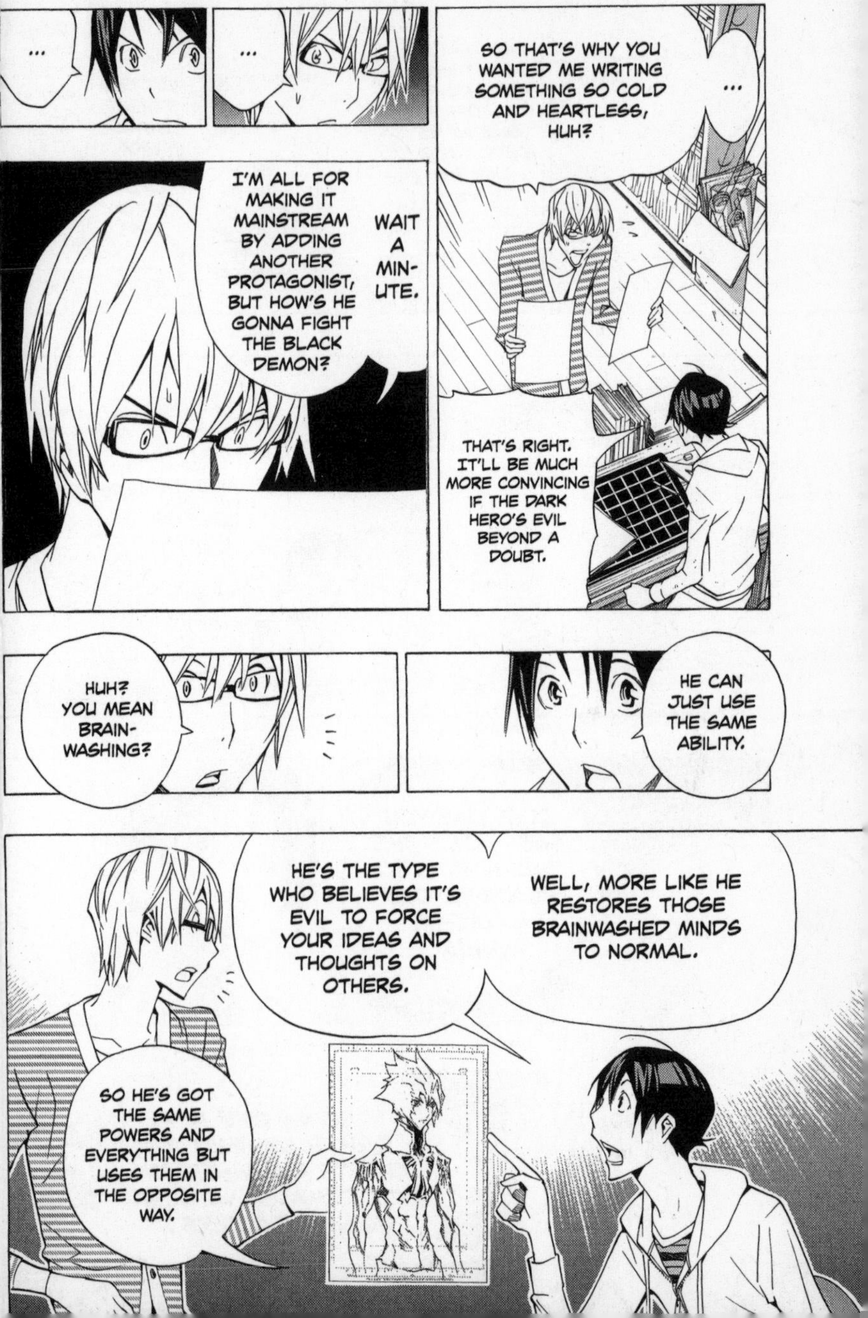
...
SO THAT'S WHY YOU WANTED ME WRITING SOMETHING SO COLD AND HEARTLESS, HUH?
THAT'S RIGHT. IT'LL BE MUCH MORE CONVINCING IF THE DARK HERO'S EVIL BEYOND A DOUBT.
...
...
WAIT A MIN-UTE.
I'M ALL FOR MAKING IT MAINSTREAM BY ADDING ANOTHER PROTAGONIST, BUT HOW'S HE GONNA FIGHT THE BLACK DEMON?
HE CAN JUST USE THE SAME ABILITY.
HUH? YOU MEAN BRAIN-WASHING?
WELL, MORE LIKE HE RESTORES THOSE BRAINWASHED MINDS TO NORMAL.
HE'S THE TYPE WHO BELIEVES IT'S EVIL TO FORCE YOUR IDEAS AND THOUGHTS ON OTHERS.
SO HE'S GOT THE SAME POWERS AND EVERYTHING BUT USES THEM IN THE OPPOSITE WAY.

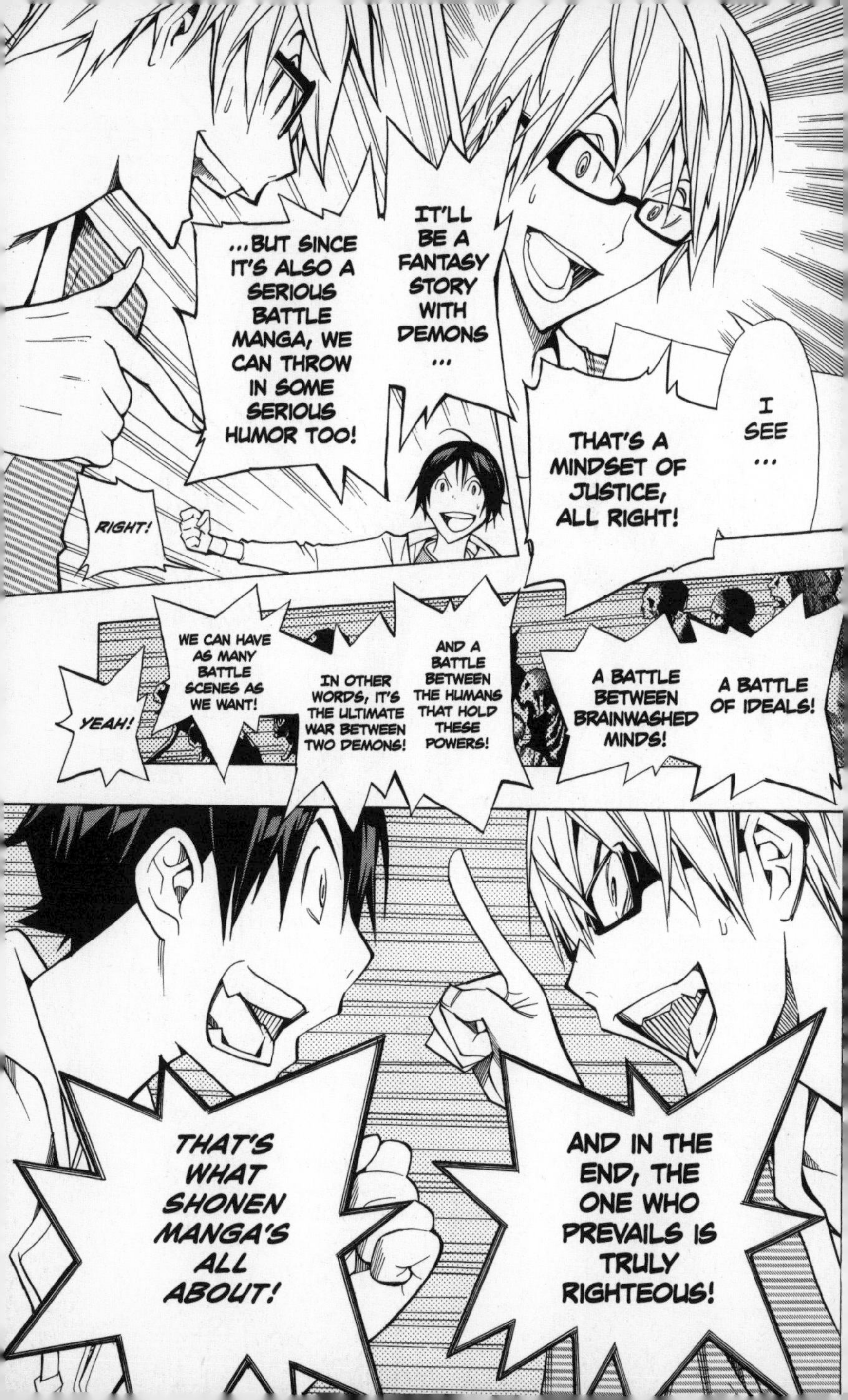
IT'LL BE A FANTASY STORY WITH DEMONS...
...BUT SINCE IT'S ALSO A SERIOUS BATTLE MANGA, WE CAN THROW IN SOME SERIOUS HUMOR TOO!
I SEE...
THAT'S A MINDSET OF JUSTICE, ALL RIGHT!
RIGHT!
A BATTLE OF IDEALS!
A BATTLE BETWEEN BRAINWASHED MINDS!
AND A BATTLE BETWEEN THE HUMANS THAT HOLD THESE POWERS!
IN OTHER WORDS, IT'S THE ULTIMATE WAR BETWEEN TWO DEMONS!
WE CAN HAVE AS MANY BATTLE SCENES AS WE WANT!
YEAH!
AND IN THE END, THE ONE WHO PREVAILS IS TRULY RIGHTEOUS!
THAT'S WHAT SHONEN MANGA'S ALL ABOUT!

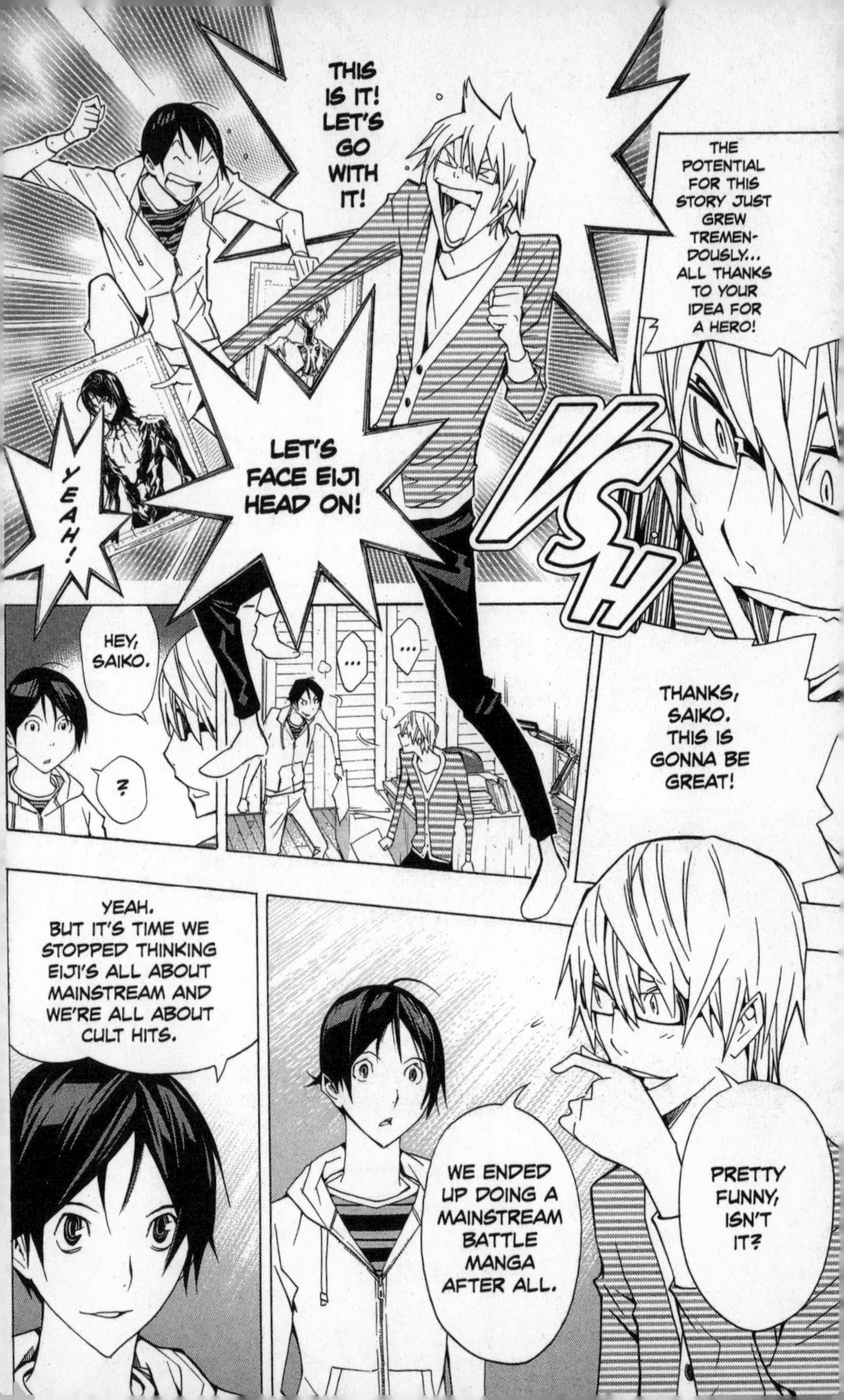
THE POTENTIAL FOR THIS STORY JUST GREW TREMEN-DOUSLY... ALL THANKS TO YOUR IDEA FOR A HERO!
VSH
THANKS, SAIKO. THIS IS GONNA BE GREAT!
THIS IS IT! LET'S GO WITH IT!
LET'S FACE EIJI HEAD ON!
YEAH!
...
...
...
HEY, SAIKO.
?
PRETTY FUNNY, ISN'T IT?
WE ENDED UP DOING A MAINSTREAM BATTLE MANGA AFTER ALL.
YEAH. BUT IT'S TIME WE STOPPED THINKING EIJI'S ALL ABOUT MAINSTREAM AND WE'RE ALL ABOUT CULT HITS.

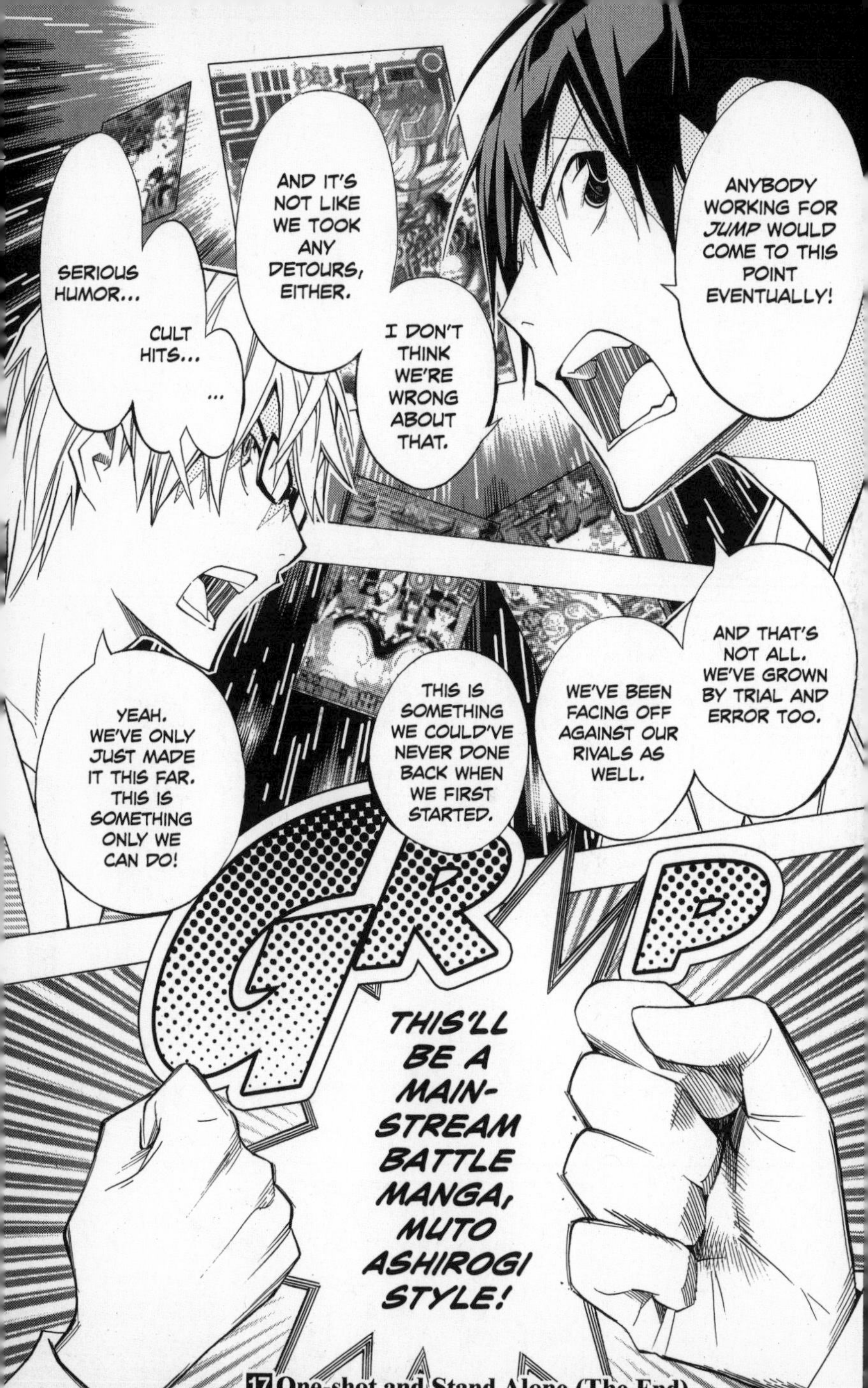

ANYBODY WORKING FOR *JUMP* WOULD COME TO THIS POINT EVENTUALLY!
AND IT'S NOT LIKE WE TOOK ANY DETOURS, EITHER.
I DON'T THINK WE'RE WRONG ABOUT THAT.
SERIOUS HUMOR...
CULT HITS...
...
AND THAT'S NOT ALL. WE'VE GROWN BY TRIAL AND ERROR TOO.
WE'VE BEEN FACING OFF AGAINST OUR RIVALS AS WELL.
THIS IS SOMETHING WE COULD'VE NEVER DONE BACK WHEN WE FIRST STARTED.
YEAH. WE'VE ONLY JUST MADE IT THIS FAR. THIS IS SOMETHING ONLY WE CAN DO!
GRIP
THIS'LL BE A MAIN-STREAM BATTLE MANGA, MUTO ASHIROGI STYLE!

17 One-shot and Stand Alone (The End)

OHBA'S STORYBOARD

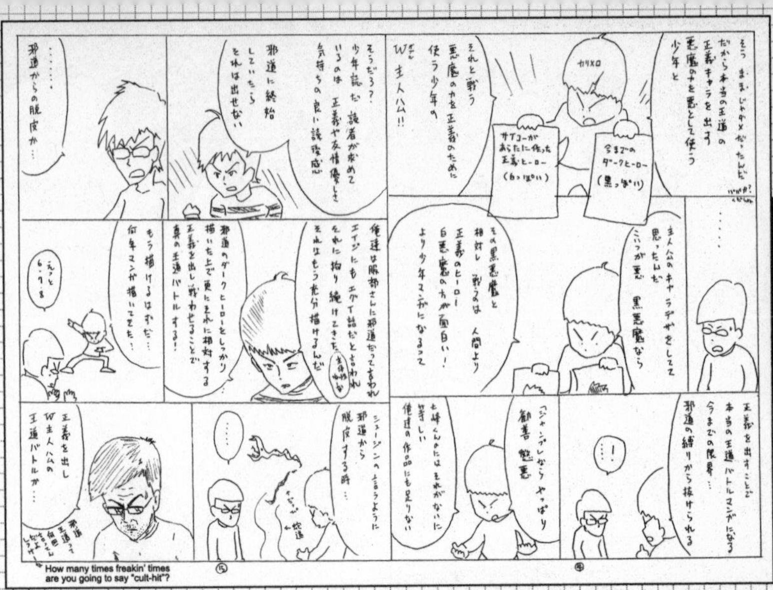

そう ままじゃダメだったんだ だから本当の王道の正義キャラを出す 悪魔の力を悪として使う少年と
カリメロ
今までのダークヒーロー (黒っぽい)
サイコーがあらたに作った正義ヒーロー (白っぽい)
それと戦う悪魔の力を正義のために使う少年のW主人公!!
……
主人公のキャラデザをしてて思ったんだ こいつが悪 黒悪魔なら
その黒悪魔と相対し 戦うのは人間より正義のヒーロー 白悪魔の方が面白い! より少年マンガになるって
正義を出すことで本当の王道バトルマンガになる 今までの限界… 邪道の縛りから抜けられる
…!
「ジャンプ」ならやっぱり勧善懲悪
七峰くんのにはそれがないに等しい 俺達の作品にも足りない
そうだろ? 少年誌だ 読者が求めているのは 正義や友情優しさ 気持ちの良い読後感
邪道に終始していたらそれは出せない
……邪道からの脱皮か…
俺達は服部さんに邪道だって言われ エイジにもエグイ話だと言われ それに拘り続けてきた それはもう充分描けるんだ
邪道のダークヒーローをしっかり描いた上で更にそれに相対する正義を出し戦わせることで真の王道バトルにする!
もう描けるはずだ… 何年マンガ描いてきた…
えっと 6・7・8
シュージンの言うように邪道から脱皮する時…
……
正義を出し W主人公の王道バトルか…
How many times freakin' times are you going to say "cult-hit"?

OBATA'S STORYBOARD

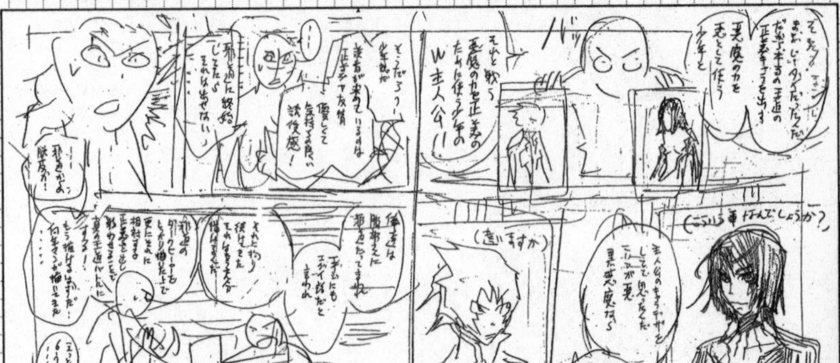

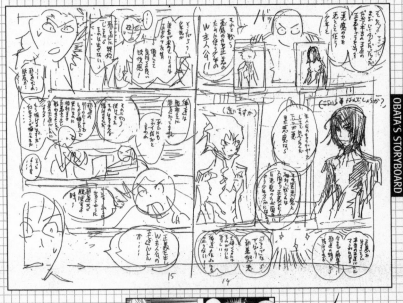

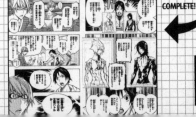

COMPLETE!

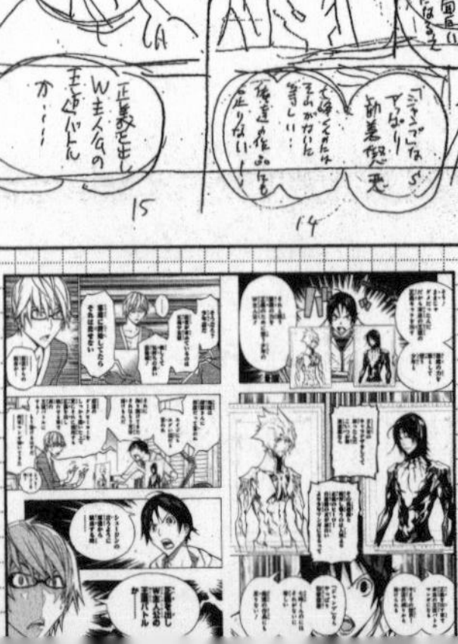

※CREATOR STORYBOARDS AND FINISHED PAGES IN JAPANESE

BAKUMAN。vol.17

"Until the Final Draft Is Complete"

Chapter 151, pp 182-183

BAKUMAN。

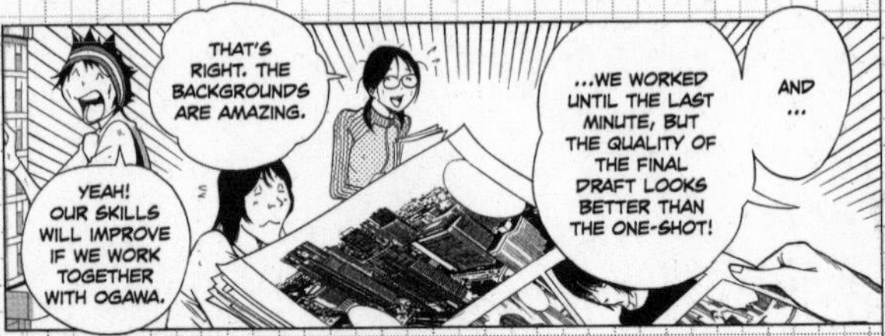
AND ...
...WE WORKED UNTIL THE LAST MINUTE, BUT THE QUALITY OF THE FINAL DRAFT LOOKS BETTER THAN THE ONE-SHOT!
THAT'S RIGHT. THE BACKGROUNDS ARE AMAZING.
YEAH! OUR SKILLS WILL IMPROVE IF WE WORK TOGETHER WITH OGAWA.

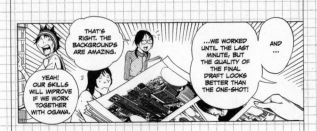

In the NEXT VOLUME

It's zombie vs. demon as Akito and Moritaka challenge Eiji with their brand-new series! Their entire career has been building up to this point, but can they really pull it off? First things first—survive the crazy deadlines!

Available March 2013!

THIS is the LAST PAGE.

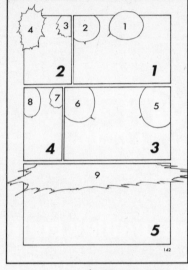

← Follow the action this way.

*BAKUMAN*₀ has been printed in the original Japanese format in order to preserve the orientation of the original artwork.

Please turn it around and begin reading from right to left. Unlike English, Japanese is read right to left, so Japanese comics are read in reverse order from the way English comics are typically read. Have fun with it!